CUBA

A New History

CUBA
A New History

Richard Gott

YALE UNIVERSITY PRESS
New Haven and London

First published by Yale University Press in 2004

Copyright © 2004 by Richard Gott

Designed by Sandy Chapman

Printed in the United States of America

Library of Congress Cataloging-in-Publication Data

Gott, Richard, 1938-
  Cuba : a new history / Richard Gott.— 1st ed.
     p. cm.
  Includes bibliographical references and index.
  ISBN 0-300-10411-1 (cl : alk. paper)
  1. Cuba—History. I. Title.
  F1776.G68 2004
  972.91—dc22

                                                          2004007556

A catalogue record for this book is available from the British Library

ISBN 978-0-300-11114-9 (pbk)

10 9 8 7 6 5 4

Contents

Acknowledgements

Work on this book in Cuba itself would not have been possible without the generous support of José Fernández de Cossio Rodríguez, Cuba's ambassador in London, and of Rene Monzote, the press attaché, who took a friendly interest in the project and opened many doors, as well as securing interviews with prominent members of the government. I first arrived in Havana in 1963 carrying letters of introduction from Hugh Thomas, and I returned years later with a similar but different list from his daughter Bella. My thanks to all of them for their comradely assistance.

In Cuba, I am indebted to my old friend Pablo Armando Fernández and his wife, Maruja, for many conversations and much conviviality over the years; and to Phil Agee, 'CIA agent turned travel agent', indefatigable optimist and promoter of US–Cuban exchanges. No researcher into the Cuban past can remain unaffected by the dedicated investigations of the wonderful community of Cuban historians, often working away in the conditions of medieval monasticism, and I was sent off in different directions by Jorge Ibarra, Fé Iglesias, Guillermo Jiménez, Fernando Martínez, Olga Portuondo and Eduardo Torres-Cuevas.

In London I have been helped by Mary Turner, who made always useful suggestions; by Emily Morris, who guided me through the pitfalls of the Cuban economy; by Victoria Brittain, who provided African expertise; and by Robin Blackburn, with whom I have had a lifetime of Cuban conversations. Many others, including Alistair Hennessy, Fred Halliday, Tony Kapcia, Hal Klepak and Jean Stubbs, have wittingly or unwittingly provided illumination and encouragement, while Maximilien Arvelaiz bears a heavy responsibility for re-awakening my interest in the contemporary history of Latin America.

Adam Freudenheim of Yale University Press (now of Penguin) dreamt up the idea for this book in the first place and was an exceptionally positive editor. I was fortunate to have the support and eagle-eyed talents of Sandy Chapman as my editor on the final lap. James Dunkerley, benign boss of the

Institute of Latin American Studies of the University of London, made thoughtful comments on an early draft for which I am more than grateful.

My wife, Vivien Ashley, has been an endlessly stimulating companion on expeditions to Cuba and I owe particular thanks to her, as well as to Jeremy Thompson and the staff of the endoscopy unit of Chelsea & Westminster hospital, for keeping me going over a long and difficult period.

Richard Gott
London and Havana, 2004

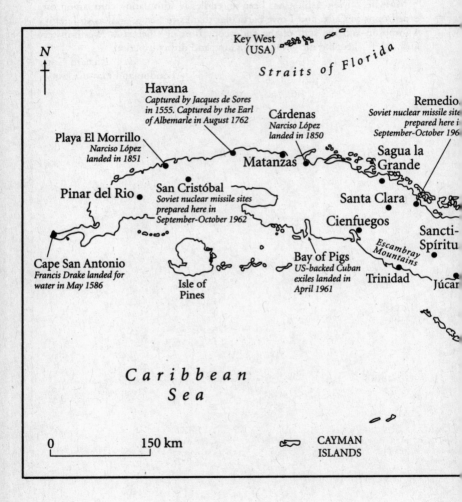

N

Key West (USA)

Straits of Florida

Havana
Captured by Jacques de Sores in 1555. Captured by the Earl of Albemarle in August 1762

Cárdenas
Narciso López landed in 1850

Remedio
Soviet nuclear missile site prepared here i September-October 196

Playa El Morrillo
Narciso López landed in 1851

Matanzas

Sagua la Grande

Pinar del Rio

San Cristóbal
Soviet nuclear missile sites prepared here in September-October 1962

Santa Clara

Cienfuegos

Sancti-Spíritu

Escambray Mountains

Cape San Antonio
Francis Drake landed for water in May 1586

Isle of Pines

Bay of Pigs
US-backed Cuban exiles landed in April 1961

Trinidad

Júcar

C a r i b b e a n   S e a

0   150 km

CAYMAN ISLANDS

BAHAMAS

*Atlantic
Ocean*

Morón

Camagüey
(Puerto Príncipe)

Holguín

Bayamo

Manzanillo

Sierra Maestra

Santiago

Baracoa
*Diego Velásquez landed
in 1511. Antonio Maceo
landed in April 1895*

Playitas
*José Martí and Máximo
Gómez landed in April 1895*

HAITI

Playa Las Coloradas
*Fidel Castro and Che Guevara
landed from the Granma in
December 1956*

Daiquirí
*US General William
Shafter landed in
June 1898*

Guantánamo
*Christopher Columbus landed in
April 1494. Admiral Edward Vernon
landed in July 1741*

Prologue

I first travelled to Cuba in October 1963, at a time when one of the great hurricanes that periodically flagellate the Caribbean cut a swathe through the centre and east of the island. Hurricane Flora wiped out the coffee crop, destroyed homes and farmland and took many lives. Roads, railways and bridges were swept away. Fidel Castro, like a true revolutionary leader but also like a typical captain-general of the Spanish colonial era, took personal charge of the relief efforts. On television each night battling tirelessly against the floodwaters, he encouraged his afflicted people with the thought that 'a Revolution is a force more powerful than Nature'. Another unhappy event recorded that month was the funeral in Santa Isabel de las Lajas of Beny Moré, 'el Bárbaro del Ritmo', a singer still universally acknowledged as one of Cuba's greatest performers. His coffin was carried by a platoon of soldiers, with thousands of mourners thronging the village street.

Havana in those days was still a wealthy and prosperous capital. Its colonial buildings were already crumbling, but its immense suburbs – with small palaces filled with scholarship children from the countryside – were not so different from the flamboyant cities of the American South. The colourful and imaginative political posters for which the Revolution was already famous were allegedly produced by graphic designers from the US advertising firm of J. Walter Thompson, whose Havana branch had gone over in its entirety to the Revolution. To a visitor from decadent and still war-ravaged Europe, the attraction of 'Communist' Cuba had much to do with its surviving capitalist veneer. I recorded my first guarded impressions for *Tribune*, a London leftist weekly:

> Amazing self-confidence is reflected in every facet of the Revolution, now about to enter its sixth year. Many things make one unhappy about Cuba, but one can never get away from the central fact of the Revolution, that it is still wildly popular. Five years of centralised government, more enthusiastic than competent; five years of self-acknowledged mistakes; five years of

growing hostility from the United States, culminating in the present blockade; five years of increasing scarcity; none of these apparently have dampened the ardour or spoilt the charm of the Cuban Revolution.

The flight from Europe to Cuba took 24 hours in those days, the turbo-prop British-built Viscount of the Spanish airline Iberia touching down at most of the islands in the mid Atlantic on the way. With me, I had two volumes of the collected works of Thomas Balogh, the Hungarian-born British economist, required reading for all progressive Latin American econo-mists at the time, as well as a small Stilton cheese in a china jar.

The cheese, purchased at Paxton and Whitfield, the famous London cheese shop in Jermyn Street, had been given to me by Claudio Véliz, my Chilean colleague at the Royal Institute of International Affairs, where he ran the Latin American programme. Having himself just returned from a visit to Havana, Claudio thought that a ripe Stilton would be a suitable present for Carlos Rafael Rodríguez, the brains behind the Cuban Communist Party. Latin American Communists of that generation (Rodríguez had joined Batista's cabinet in 1942) shared the tastes of the bourgeoisie, as I discovered later with Pablo Neruda, the Chilean poet, who enjoyed receiving homage from his admirers in the shape of crates of whisky and tins of caviar.

The officials at Havana airport paid nervous attention to the Stilton, prodding it with knitting needles lest it should turn out to be a bomb. 'Operation Mongoose', the US campaign to destabilise Cuba in the wake of the abortive Bay of Pigs invasion, had recently been abandoned, but terrorist attacks against the island from exile groups in Miami were still frequent. In November, the month after my visit, according to a CIA report later made public, an agent gave a pen-syringe to a Cuban contact in Paris to be used to assassinate Castro – on the day that President Kennedy was shot. The Cubans were understandably careful with unannounced visitors bearing gifts.

When in Havana, Véliz had commissioned Che Guevara, then the Cuban minister of industries, to write an article for *International Affairs*, the quarterly magazine of Chatham House, and one of my tasks was to collect his manuscript. I had introductions to several Latin Americans working in Guevara's economic ministry, and soon, with their help, I was able to travel around the island and to observe the Revolution at first hand, while waiting for an opportunity to meet Guevara.

I drove to Pinar del Rio, I flew to Santiago and I journeyed into the hills of the Sierra Maestra to inspect Castro's former guerrilla encampment. The road from Havana to Santiago was blocked by the flood damage, and it was only possible to travel outside the city in a four-wheel-drive jeep, a present from the Soviet Union. Returning to Havana, I saw Castro climbing out of his car at my hotel, and I spent an evening listening to him speak at a meeting in the Plaza de la Revolución. I interviewed Antonio Nuñez Jiménez, the guerrilla professor who had introduced Guevara to the problems of Cuba's peculiar geography. I met Nicolas Guillén, the Afro-Cuban poet from a radical family, and I was eventually able to present Carlos Rafael with the now rather sweaty Stilton cheese, before we went on to discuss the latest agrarian reform – the vibrant topic of the hour. I even gave a lecture on the European Common Market to bemused officials at Guevara's ministry.

Not until the last evening was there any sign of the man I had come to see. I was taken to a reception in the gardens of the Soviet Embassy, one of those routine diplomatic occasions that were held each year to celebrate the anniversary of the October Revolution, exciting in its novelty to the Cubans invited. Guevara strode in after midnight, accompanied by a small coterie of friends, bodyguards and hangers-on, wearing his trademark black beret, and with his shirt open to the waist. He was unbelievably beautiful. Before the era of the obsessive adulation accorded to musicians, he had the unmistakable aura of a rock star. People stopped whatever they were doing, and just stared at the Revolution made flesh. 'If he entered a room, everything began revolving around him . . . ' Julia Costenla, an Argentine journalist who had had a similar experience, told Jon Lee Anderson when he was researching his biography of Guevara. 'He was blessed with a unique appeal . . . He had an incalculable enchantment that came completely naturally.' That was how he was.

Guevara had a charismatic attraction in real life, long before he became a Mantegna icon in death and a hypnotic image on a pop art poster in the age of Andy Warhol. Like Helen of Troy, he had an allure that people would die for. In Havana, on that warm autumn night, he was found a seat in a corner of the embassy garden and everyone gathered round. Introductions were made, and the conversation flowed. I have not much memory of what was discussed. I was merely a youthful neophyte with little knowledge and less Spanish, attracted moth-like to Cuba in those years – like hundreds of other rebels and adventurers from Europe and the Americas – by the incandescent flame of Revolution. Guevara told me, somewhat roughly, that he had not finished the article I had come to collect. The text would arrive in the post in London a few weeks later.

The Revolution was not having an easy time. The *fidelistas* had been in power for five years, but many of the people I met, working in the economic ministries and at the University of Havana, were in a state of despair. The old order was visibly crumbling, but the new era was still failing to be born. In Santiago, I talked to a young professor from the East German city of Leipzig who gave a course of lectures on Marxist philosophy at seven o'clock in the morning. He was depressed to find no Cuban student awake at that hour. Yet to a revolutionary tourist, the country's state of flux was itself both attractive and hopeful. The Cubans wore their new Marxist–Leninist clothing with unseemly abandon. A Cuban acquaintance visiting Prague, I noted, had been shocked to find that Kafka was not a national hero. Revolutionary free-thinking was still permitted in Cuba. 'Abstract art flourishes in a way that would give Khrushchev cause to wince,' I wrote, 'and *La Dolce Vita* plays to full houses in Havana.' After five years of dramatic upheaval, the Revolution's future course still seemed largely unmapped. Blank pages were there to be written on.

Che Guevara I was never to meet again – though on another October day just four years later I had an almost accidental rendezvous with his dead body. At five o'clock on a Monday afternoon in October 1967, I was present at the airstrip of the Bolivian hill town of Vallegrande when a helicopter landed with a stretcher strapped to its landing rails. Guevara had been shot a few hours earlier, on the orders of the Bolivian army's high command. Tipped off about his capture the previous evening, by an American officer at a military training mission near Santa Cruz, I had driven for many hours in the darkness to Vallegrande, the forward base of the Bolivian army. There I was told by a jittery commander that I would not be allowed to travel on to La Higuera, the village further on where Guevara was being held. Without a military permit, it was impossible to move outside the towns that year in Bolivia.

By late afternoon, the entire population of Vallegrande was assembled at the airfield, and when the helicopter arrived, the dead guerrilla's body was transferred to a small Chevrolet van. Driven off into the village, the van turned into the grounds of the tiny local hospital and the body was laid out on the flat basins of a laundry hut open to the elements. The operation was under the control of a Cuban–American agent of the CIA, known to us then as 'Eduardo González', one of two such agents operating in the guerrilla zone at the time. When I asked where he came from, his enigmatic reply was 'From nowhere'. He and I were the only two people present who had seen Che Guevara alive, and could testify that this was indeed him.

Crowds of villagers pushed into the laundry yard to get a glimpse of yet another dead guerrilla, and for half an hour or so I joined them, captivated by his haunted open eyes. Later I made the long, eight-hour journey back through the night by jeep to Santa Cruz, seeking a means of communicating the news to the outside world.

The death of Guevara in 1967 ended many people's romantic association with the Cuban Revolution, a development accentuated the following year when Castro spoke out against the Prague Spring of Alexander Dubček and formally enlisted the Revolution in the ranks of the supporters of the Soviet Union. As a journalist, I continued to visit Havana during the 1960s, pursuing my own researches into the history and struggles of Latin America's guerrilla movements. Like many others, I retained the memory of my early enthusiasm for the Revolution as well as an abiding affection for Cuba's people and their unequal struggle, and a continuing interest in their island's long history. I returned to Havana thirty years later to write it down,

Introduction: the Cuban people

The attractive terrace café of the Casa Granda hotel, open to the street, looks over the leafy colonial square at the centre of Santiago de Cuba. On the far side stands an antique wooden house with arabesque decoration, built in the early sixteenth century (some believe) for Diego de Velásquez, the island's Spanish conqueror. To the left is a modest, modern twentieth-century cathedral, and to the right is the balcony of the offices of the town council where Fidel Castro addressed the crowds on 2 January 1959, the first day of the Revolution.

On Saturdays the terrace is crowded with the fond friends and parents of a succession of *quinceañeras*, pretty fifteen-year-old girls dressed in flowing white crinoline dresses, who have shyly come to celebrate their birthdays – and their rite of passage into the adult world. The girls and their families come in all shapes and sizes and colours – black, white and mulatto. The scene appears to be the re-enactment of a ritual with a long tradition, yet like many things in Cuba it could not have happened a hundred years ago. Social mixing of the races, flaunted in the heart of town, would not have been possible.

The Cubans of today are a people of recent creation. Not until after Castro's Revolution did their society begin to come together as a unified and homogenous nation. Under Spanish imperial rule over several centuries, until 1898, Cuba's population was divided by race and class and ethnic origin, and the country's history was characterised by endemic violence and ingrained racism, white against black and all the shades in between. People in towns and in much of the countryside lived out their lives in considerable fear and uncertainty. Conquest, resistance, piracy, slave rebellions, freebooting invasions and frustrated wars of independence and abortive revolutions succeeded each other with scant breathing space in between. Up until 1959, Cuban politics were decided by the gun. Visiting travellers in the nineteenth century often noted that women were nowhere to be seen. They remained at home with good reason.[1]

Cubans today appear to be largely white or mulatto, yet for much of the island's history more than half the population was black, and the great majority of the blacks were slaves. The black/white ratio did not change much until the middle of the nineteenth century, when the efforts of the Spanish colonial authorities to 'whiten' the population by encouraging white immigration, coupled with the difficulty of importing slaves during the decades when slavery was permitted but the trade was illegal, tipped the balance in favour of the whites. Slavery was not formally abolished until October 1886.[2]

Cuba's blacks were not themselves a homogenous group. They came from many tribes and nations along the length of the West African coastline, from Senegal in the north to Angola in the south – and even from Mozambique on Africa's south-east coast. They brought with them different languages, different beliefs, different customs, and different music, and through much of the nineteenth century they preserved these differences in the new Cuban home to which they had been transported. The black clubs and aid societies formed for their mutual benefit maintained these particularities.

The first generation of black slaves were brought with the original waves of Spanish conquerors at the beginning of the sixteenth century, and were set to work in the gold and copper mines, and later on the tobacco farms. In the eighteenth and nineteenth centuries, most of them lived and worked on the sugar plantations, while others were kept as domestic slaves. Yet a large number of blacks – varying over the centuries but always more than elsewhere in the Caribbean – were not slaves at all. Described as 'free coloureds' or 'free men of colour', they were usually urban workers, employed as labourers and artisans, or sometimes existing as independent small traders. The twentieth century was to see fresh black immigration, from Jamaica and Haiti. They came as contract labourers, with tickets home, but many stayed behind. These free blacks were not alone in the Cuban underclass. Much intermarriage at the lower end of the social scale created a mulatto element in the population, often seen by outsiders, not altogether accurately, as the country's predominant characteristic. In practice, Cuba's racial mix has remained notably stratified and divided.

The white section of Cuba's population was also separated into different groups over the centuries. While most came from mainland Spain, many sailed from the Canary Islands. Others came from the rest of Europe, indeed from all the countries of the former Habsburg empire – from Spain, Italy, France, Austria, Poland, Holland – as well as from Scandinavia. In the twentieth century, a small stream of North American settlers followed in the wake of the US occupation of 1898–1902.

Like the Afro-Cubans, the migrants from Spain retained a fierce sense of regional difference, proudly claiming their origins in Galicia or Asturias, Andalusia or León, Catalonia or the Basque Country. During the nineteenth century, and well into the early decades of the twentieth-century Republic, they too kept their traditions alive in clubs and 'casinos' and in mutual aid societies – ensuring that their children got a good education and their daughters married within their own specific communities.

Many of Cuba's whites came as settlers and farmers, but most soon branched off into urban pursuits, dominating the country's bureaucracy as well as its commerce, trade and industry. As the principal element in the country's politics, both in colonial government and in the opposition movements and in the leadership of the insurrectionary wars, the Spanish settlers and their descendants have always had the largest share in the island's history books, until more recent scholarship began to redress the balance by examining the story of other, less favoured groups.

Always troubled by the presence of the country's black majority, the white settlers sought to maintain their dominant position by endlessly calling for immigration from Europe. This was often purposely encouraged by the racist ruling elites, both before and after liberation from Spain in 1898. Their avowed aim of 'whitening' the population, and keeping the white settlers numerically on top, was largely successful. Waves of immigrants continued to arrive in Cuba from Spain until the early 1930s (including Angel Castro, Fidel's father). By the middle of the twentieth century, the black element in the population had declined – according to the official statistics – from over 50 per cent to less than 30 per cent.

A third element in Cuba's ethnic mix, the trace of indigenous blood that runs through most of its people except for the most recent immigrants, has usually been ignored or denied. It is vigorously downplayed by most Cuban historians in Havana today, although those in Santiago are more free-thinking. The official line, doggedly maintained over the years in spite of increasing evidence to the contrary, is that the Tainos, the indigenous peoples who occupied the island for many centuries before the arrival of Columbus, were destroyed during the early years of conquest.

This is clearly not so. Many of the island's original peoples survived, in official reserves and in mountain settlements, at least until the nineteeenth century, and they also cohabited with more recent arrivals, particularly with blacks. Their place-names are still in evidence, and many of the words in their vocabulary pepper the Spanish language spoken in Cuba today. 'Cuba' itself is an Indian word. Columbus heard the native inhabitants of the Bahamas refer to 'Cuba' and 'Cubanacán' as a great island to the south. The airy *bohíos* of the Indians – huts built from palm fronds – were adapted by the Spanish settlers and can still be seen in forgotten areas of the countryside, or resurrected in the architectural vernacular of tourist hotels on the beach.

Another minority group in the population, the Chinese, were brought in as indentured workers to replace the African slaves in the middle of the nineteenth century. When the international campaign against the slave trade was finally successful, plantation owners were obliged to find a fresh source of labour.

Cuba's disparate peoples – Indians, Spanish, African and Chinese – have had a long and always-violent history, largely dominated by two ever-present themes: the search for internal security and the threat of external attack. As a large island set in a hostile sea, off the coasts of two great continents, it could hardly have been otherwise. Cuba's violent history long pre-dated colonial rule. In the centuries before the Spaniards made a permanent settlement, the indigenous island inhabitants had themselves been displaced and moved on by successive generations of Latin America's forest peoples, pouring out from the Orinoco delta and travelling by log canoe up the chain of Caribbean islands to Cuba. The continuing sense of external danger and internal uncertainty that the pre-Conquest peoples experienced was compounded by the arrival of Diego de Velásquez and his Spanish conquistadors in 1511.

Not least among the problems faced by Cuba's first peoples, as by later migrants, was the violence of their physical environment. The frequency of tropical storms, hurricanes and tornadoes has been a phenomenon at work throughout history, as it still is today. The historical impact of the annual hurricane season, bringing death and destruction in its wake, has been highlighted in an arresting study by Louis Pérez of the natural forces affecting Cuba's development. He tells of how the word *huracán* passed into the Spanish vernacular from indigenous usage. 'The Taíno Indians used "*huracán*" to mean malignant forces that took the form of winds of awesome proportions and destructive power, winds that blew from all four corners of the earth.'[3]

Into this perennially violent and hostile environment came the first Christian adventurers in the sixteenth century, bringing with them soldiers and seamen, settlers and traders, artisans and priests – and black slaves in ever-increasing numbers. The first generation of newcomers soon abandoned the island, sailing off to conquer Mexico and Peru in the 1520s and Florida in the 1530s. They left a pathetic remnant of permanent settlers behind, men and women as frightened and uncertain of their position as were the indigenous peoples with whom they were now at war.

The settlers constructed a handful of small towns for themselves in the early years of conquest, at different points through the island, but for many years their writ did not run far beyond their peripheral defences. The surviving elements of the indigenous population, often intermarried with Spaniards and with black slaves, held out for centuries in the mountains, a permanent brooding presence sparked at regular intervals into resistance or rebellion. Much of the island, for much of its history, was virgin territory, untouched by law or government or property rights. In this land, literally off the map, forgotten groups of Indians and fugitive black slaves lived in *palenques*, stockaded villages wholly independent of the state. From this tradition grew the banditry that plagued the countryside from the mid-eighteenth century on, and produced much of the rough rebel soldiery of the independence wars of the nineteenth century, and indeed of the rebellions of the twentieth century as well.

Sporadic conflicts between settlers and Indians continued throughout the first century of conquest, and this ever-present internal danger was soon complemented by violence from abroad – another abiding characteristic of Cuba's history. The Spaniards were followed into the Caribbean by the seamen and settlers of other European nations – the French, the British and the Dutch. These newcomers carried the internecine wars of Europe into this fresh, tropical setting, fighting there at intervals for more than two centuries. They occupied the islands adjacent to Cuba and, in the shape of corsairs and pirates and freebooters, hovered permanently off the coast, darting in whenever they saw an opportunity to trade, to make money or to cause havoc among those who refused to collaborate.

If life was brutal and short for the white settlers during the early centuries, it was even less rewarding for the black slaves. Those who survived the harsh conditions of the Atlantic passage were marked with a red-hot iron brand, sent off to work on plantations and beaten or mutilated if they showed signs of rebellion or reluctance to work. Men hugely outnumbered women, and some religious foundations, to save money, employed only male slaves, creating a well-spring of resentment and sexual frustration.[4]

By the nineteenth century, the European vulture states that had extended their frontiers to the Caribbean and to Central America had been joined by the United States as a potential predator. While elsewhere in Latin America, the vice-royalties of the Spanish empire fell to the forces of local settler armies, Cuba remained loyal to the Crown. Paradoxically, it was the intensity of the rivalry between Europe and the United States that helped to keep Cuba in Spanish hands until the end of the century. The life of the Spanish empire in the Caribbean was prolonged beyond its natural span, rather as, in another part of the world, the Turkish empire was kept alive into the twentieth century by Europe's great powers, lest worse befall.

Spain was finally forced out of Cuba in 1898, three years after the outbreak of the final independence war in 1895. Even then, in spite of the efforts of Cuban forces, the *coup de grâce* was provided by the United States, which invaded and occupied the island in 1898 and obliged the Spanish empire to capitulate. US troops, led among others by Theodore Roosevelt, landed near Guantánamo Bay, while US ships destroyed the Spanish fleet off Santiago.

Spain's final exit from Cuba that year, and the United States' subsequent withdrawal in 1902, created no relief from violence for the island's inhabitants. Internal rebellion and external intervention continued to characterise the country's history for the first six decades of the twentieth century, until after Castro's Revolution in 1959. The glorified yet baneful tradition established during the wars of independence, of taking up arms and departing with a handful of men to the *manigua* (Cuba's rural hinterland), was constantly revived when elections, correct or corrupt, produced a contested result. After Batista's *coup d'état* of 1952, young men (and women) considered it perfectly normal and acceptable to take up arms and head for the hills, wreaking havoc in the countryside, while their accomplices in the cities stockpiled weapons from abroad, deployed explosives and engaged in what a later age would describe as 'terrorism'.

The Revolution's one undeniable achievement was to bring internal security and tranquillity to the island for the first time in its history, although it came at a high price. External dangers did not disappear; indeed they remained much the same. The Americans threatened to restore their hegemony over Cuba, and dispatched an invasion force in 1961. In 1962, another great European empire, the Soviet Union, briefly entered the history of Cuba, rather late in the day, and gave the world a collective heart attack by its intemperate decision to station nuclear missiles on the islands.[5] Just as Europe's other empires had once done, the Soviet Union extended its frontiers to the Caribbean, and sought to make its imprint on the island. The Russians claimed that they had done so to help Castro's struggling Revolution against its enemies, but like all great empires they had their own agenda.

In response to this outside intervention, and following a well-established pattern from the days of the Monroe Doctrine in the 1820s, the United States decreed an economic embargo on the island's external commerce, and sponsored piratical attacks reminiscent of the seventeenth century. Later, towards the end of the twentieth century, with the Cubans trying desperately to keep aloof, the seas around the island were once again filled with illegal traders. Many pirate ships that would once have been laden with tobacco and snuff, sugar and rum, now carried marijuana and cocaine.

Among these small ships were the frail craft that brought illegal migrants to Florida from Cuba, as well as from the other islands of the Caribbean. Unregulated migration, except at occasional moments in 1980 and 1994, was not permitted, either by Cuba or by the United States. Yet as the wealth of the United States grew ever larger, at the same time as the poverty of the Caribbean islands and the small countries of Central America increased, so the powerful economic magnet of North America became well-nigh irresistible.

The Cuban people, as this book seeks to illustrate, have had a conflictive and violent past, and this entrenched tradition has not altogether disappeared in the twenty-first century. The Revolution may have brought social peace to the island after 500 years, but it has not come without cost. When Castro invokes the Garibaldian choice of 'Patria o Muerte' – Fatherland or Death – at the end of his speeches, he is not using the words as romantic rhetoric. For him, and his people, they have a deeply felt relevance that echoes across the centuries.

I

Insecure settlement:
slaughter, slavery and piracy, 1511–1740

Hatuey and Diego Velásquez: Indian cacique *versus Spanish* conquistador*, 1511*

Hot and damp in all seasons, the small port of Baracoa on Cuba's north-east coast reflects little of the historical aura that might be considered its due. Rickety wooden houses line a handful of streets crushed between the mountains and the ocean, together with a couple of ancient stone forts, remnants of Spanish imperial power, and a more modern, Soviet-style hotel beside the airstrip, a rain-stained concrete memento of another vanished empire. In the gardens of the small museum within one of the forts stands a bust of Hatuey, leader of the indigenous resistance forces in Baracoa at the time of the first Spanish landings in 1511, and himself, like so many in Cuban history before and since, a refugee from the country to the east that is now called Haiti. Cuba is an island, but it is also an integral part of the immense archipelago of the Caribbean, and its history reflects this immutable geographical reality.

Accessible by land today along a dramatic switchback road cut across the mountains, Baracoa has been cut off and isolated from the rest of the island through the centuries. Its external contacts have been across the sea, to Haiti to the east across the Windward Channel, and northwards to the United States – to which, in the 1930s, it used to ship out coconuts and bananas from its tiny harbour.

Castro's Revolution built the access road in the 1960s when there was still money to spend on gargantuan projects. Promised by the old dictator Batista in the 1950s but never finished, the road also provided a brief moment of economic opportunity when two of the Revolution's heroes, Che Guevara and Raúl Castro, came here in 1963 to open a cocoa factory, funded by the benevolent state. Bars of chocolate are still for sale at places where cars have to slow down on the sharp curves of the mountain road, an example of individual desperation rather than steady commerce.

Another sign of difficult times is the fact that more than half of the local population have turned away from the Catholic Church and are now enrolled in Protestant evangelical chapels, the great systemic change in today's Latin America from which Cuba is by no means immune. It is a nice irony that Baracoa was the site of the first landing in Cuba of Catholic warriors from Spain, soldiers from a European empire soon to be engaged in a life-or-death struggle with the supporters of the Protestant doctrines of Martin Luther.

Baracoa was a foolish place for the first conquistadores to have chosen, but maybe they were unfamiliar with the terrain and did not have much choice, or maybe they took advice from Columbus who glimpsed and glowingly reported on it during his first voyage to the Caribbean in 1492. Baracoa is the nearest harbour to Haiti, and it was from there that Diego de Velásquez launched his expedition to conquer Cuba in 1511.[1]

The inhabitants of Baracoa at that time, as of most of Cuba, called themselves Tainos, and were perceived as a simple people by the first Spanish visitors. One eyewitness described them as 'meek, humble, obedient, and very hospitable, little given to sexual pleasures or other exerting physical activities'.[2] The Tainos cultivated the yucca root, harvested it and baked it to produce cassava bread. They also grew cotton and tobacco, and ate maize and potatoes. 'They had food in abundance,' wrote Bartolomé de las Casas, the Dominican priest who came with the conquerors, 'and they had everything they needed for living: they had many crops, well arranged, of which – their abundance of everything and the quenching of our hunger with it – we were ourselves witness.'[3]

The Tainos were not the original inhabitants of Cuba. A more ancient people on the island were the Guanahatabeyes, themselves migrants from the forests of the South American countries that are today Venezuela and Colombia. Their artefacts are still to be found at the opposite end of the island from Baracoa, principally on the western Peninsula of Guanahacabibes which commemorates their name. They lived 'like savages, without houses or towns,' recorded Velásquez the conqueror, 'eating only the meat they are able to find in the forests, as well as turtles and fish'.

Archaeological evidence suggests that the Guanahatabeyes had been driven to the west as a result of the arrival of two subsequent waves of migrants, the Tainos and the Siboneys, who had also travelled northwards from the mainland, moving out of the Orinoco delta and up the West Indies' island chain. Both belonged to the group known in South America as Arawaks and they lived together in a master–slave relationship. The Siboneys were 'a most simple and gentle kind of people', according to Las Casas, living alongside the Tainos, but acting towards them in the manner of a servant class.

The pre-Columbian history of Cuba, with the exception of a few pioneering works of ethnology and archaeology, still exists chiefly in the realm of conjecture and the creative imagination, and its early colonial history is also an unfamiliar narrative, largely neglected even by the island's own historians.

Yet during the first two centuries of colonial rule a series of events took place, on and around the island, that left a permanent mark on its people, and on its society and economy. The fusion between indigenous Indians and Spanish settlers; the arrival of an immense black population from the coast of Africa; the establishment and construction of one of the great Spanish cities of Latin America; and the formation of an agricultural, cattle-raising economy – eventually to blossom, with slavery, into the sugar-exporting, wealth-creating machine of the nineteenth century – all these were important developments in the early history of the colony.

Also significant was Cuba's integration into the quarrels of continental Europe soon after the conquest. As a colony of the Spanish empire, Cuba found itself in the frontline of Europe's wars, as the frontiers of the old continent extended themselves across the Atlantic and into the Caribbean. The imperial authorities tried to keep Cuba isolated from the global economy of the time, and to make the island solely dependent on Spain, but the task was beyond them. Long before the arrival of the Russians in the late twentieth century, the settlements of Cuba were regarded as legitimate prey by the official fleets (and the unofficial pirates) of the French, the English and the Dutch – as well as, later, of the North Americans. Cuba also developed a close trading relationship with its near neighbours, as it had done in pre-Columbian times – with Haiti, with Jamaica, with Florida and with Central America and Mexico. Indeed the island's wealth, during its first three centuries under Spanish rule, was built as much on illicit trading and contraband as on legitimate trade with the mother country and her colonies.[4]

The Tainos had first spotted Columbus sailing off their northern coast on 28 October, 1492, probably at Baracoa, and he had passed along the south coast during a second voyage from Europe in 1494, landing at various inlets – including what was later to become the great US naval base at Guantánamo. Columbus gave a friendly account of Cuba in his journal, describing villages of large houses 'looking like tents in a camp, without regular streets but one here and another there. Within they were clean and well-swept, with well-made furniture. All were of palm branches, beautifully constructed.'[5]

The first permanent Spanish settlement in the Caribbean was established to the east of Cuba, at the port of Santo Domingo, on the island they called Hispaniola. Nicolás de Ovando was the first ruler there, in 1498, and he enrolled the local Indians into a forced-labour system that would become the model for Cuba. He also encouraged the new settlers, arriving from Spain in regular shiploads, to raise cattle and grow sugar.

Not until 1511 was an expedition sent out from Hispaniola to Cuba. Velásquez had orders to conquer and settle the island, but his men were greeted with stiff Indian resistance that was to last for several decades. The first leader of the indigenous forces of whom the chroniclers speak was Hatuey, a Taino cacique, or chieftain, originally from Hispaniola. Over the centuries,

Hatuey became the iconic representative of the aboriginal Indian population of Cuba, evoked at regular intervals by all those who sought to give an alternative twist to the island's history, and ending up – ultimate insult – as the name of a popular brand of beer, a name that survived the nationalisation of its parent company during the Revolution.

Hatuey had been a witness to a great massacre of Indians at Xaraguá in Hispaniola, organised by Ovando in 1503, and, seeing no future on that island, he crossed the water to Cuba with many of his followers. They established themselves in the mountains above Baracoa, and, when the Spaniards followed their canoes to Cuba in 1511, Hatuey was in charge of mobilising the local resistance. He knew from his own experience what was in store.

Velásquez, Hatuey's opponent, had first sailed to the Indies in Columbus's second expedition of 1494, at the age of 29. Velásquez has been rather under-celebrated by historians, yet he was one of the great early conquerors of Latin America, the governor of Hispaniola and Cuba, and the ruler of the Yucatán. He might well have conquered Mexico had he not been thwarted in this ambition by Hernán Cortés.

The first of a long line of autocratic and charismatic figures who have put their mark on Cuban history over the centuries, Velásquez was born near the Spanish city of Valladolid in 1465. He is described as 'a man of high ability, of singularly handsome person, of engaging manners, of much popularity, and of abundant force of character for successful leadership and command of men'.[6] Regarded by his contemporaries as an efficient administrator, he was perceived as the richest man in the Americas of his time. What is claimed to be his original home and office still stands on the corner of the main square of Santiago de Cuba, a wonderful, well-proportioned Moorish building with lattice-work windows and cool courtyards, reminiscent of Arab buildings from Damascus to Seville, and a reminder of how closely the conquest of the Americas followed on the Spanish *Reconquista* of Arab Spain.

In the genocidal campaigns against the Indians of Hispaniola Velásquez had been an effective military commander. He had been present at the massacre at Xaraguá in 1503 that had prompted Hatuey's flight to Cuba. Made from a different mould than Ovando, Velásquez planned to treat the Cuban Indians in a less brutal manner. He understood from his early experience in Hispaniola that it was an error to slaughter the local population since the settlers needed the Indians, not just to hand over their land, but to supply them with food and labour.

Velásquez set off for Cuba in the final days of 1510, sailing from the north-west coast of Hispaniola with three ships and an army of 300 men. Crossing the 60 miles of the Windward Passage, he established himself at Baracoa, baptising it Nuestra Señora de la Asunción. Greeted from the first day with hostility by the Indians, he searched for their leader in the mountains above Baracoa. Hatuey was hunted down, captured and burnt alive.

A famous story recalls the particular nature of Hatuey's anger at the attempt by the Christian invaders to convert him to their faith. Hatuey's death scene is recorded in *A Short History of the Destruction of the Indies*, the influential book written at the time by Las Casas, the priest and landowner who had accompanied Velásquez's invasion force. Hatuey, when tied to the stake, was given a brief outline of the Christian myths by a Franciscan friar:

> The friar told him that, if he would only believe what he was now hearing, he would go to Heaven there to enjoy glory and eternal rest, but that, if he would not, he would be consigned to Hell, where he would endure everlasting pain and torment.
>
> Hatuey thought for a short while and then asked the friar whether Christians went to Heaven. When the reply came that good ones do, he retorted, without need for further reflection, that, if that was the case, then he chose to go to Hell, to ensure that he would never again have to clap eyes on those cruel brutes.[7]

Their leader had been killed, but the Indians kept up their attacks on the Spanish newcomers. Resistance was now in the hands of Caguax, an ally of Hatuey's and himself another refugee from Hispaniola. Velásquez called for assistance, and Pánfilo de Narváez arrived from Jamaica, the island directly to the south of Cuba that had been seized and occupied by the Spaniards two years earlier, in 1509. Pánfilo, an adventurer in his late 30s, was another conquistador from Valladolid, and became the real conqueror of Cuba. He was soon to make his brutal mark on the island, and later led expeditions to Mexico and to Florida. Arriving from Jamaica with a troop of 30 men with cross-bows, Pánfilo was put in charge of an invasion force that fanned out into the interior, moving by land and sea. Near Bayamo, an Indian settlement on the lower slopes of the Sierra Maestra that has played a significant role throughout Cuba's history, he defeated the Indian forces, and killed Caguax.

Within three years, Pánfilo's military columns – now swollen to 500 men with a score of horses – had moved through the entire island. On their way to the west, they massacred the inhabitants of Caonao, near Manzanillo, another shocking event faithfully observed and recorded by Las Casas:

> When the locals had come some ten leagues out from a large settlement in order to receive us, and regale us with victuals and other gifts – and had given us loaves and fishes and any other foodstuffs they could provide – the Christians were suddenly inspired by the Devil and, without the slightest provocation, butchered, before my eyes, some three thousand souls – men, women, and children – as they sat there in front of us. I saw that day atrocities more terrible than any living man has ever seen, nor ever thought to see.[8]

As the Spaniards advanced through the island, the surviving Indians fled to the mountains or crossed to the small islands, or keys, that lie off the coast. From these relatively safe vantage-points, which in the twenty-first century have been developed as tourist resorts, they would launch attacks on the new Spanish settlements, abandoning their early attempts to be friendly. Their violent eruptions became so alarming to the settlers that an expedition was sent out in 1523 to crush the 'Key Indians', but the resistance continued for several more years. Settlers were killed by Indians in Bayamo in 1527 and outside Santiago in 1529.

Mountain Indians, called Cimarrones, also attacked outlying settlements in the 1520s. Guama, their leader, was based for years above Baracoa where, after a struggle lasting for more than a decade, he was defeated and killed in 1532. Sporadic outbreaks of resistance continued throughout the sixteenth century, but the Indians were certainly cowed by the dogs and the massacres, and undermined by European disease.

Within a few years of the initial conquest, several strategic points across the island had been brought under the effective control of the conquerors. Velásquez presided over the formation of half a dozen small Spanish settlements, their names expressing the avowedly Christian sentiments of the invading force: San Salvador de Bayamo, La Santísima Trinidad, San Cristóbal de La Habana, Sancti Spíritus, Santa María del Puerto del Príncipe (Camagüey) and Santiago de Cuba. The settlements were established in areas where a large Indian population already existed – in the best places for recruiting local labour.[9]

The Spaniards had come in hope of finding gold, and they were pleased to find it in the rivers and the hills of the Oriente. Yet supplies were small and the deposits were soon exhausted, lasting for little more than 25 years. Cuba sent 84,000 ounces of gold to Spain in the first 30 years, but production had declined steeply by 1539 to only 650 ounces.[10] Copper was also found in the island, exploited at the mine of El Cobre in the hills near Santiago, and although production has proceeded intermittently there from that day to this, it did not have the immediate appeal and value of gold.

The Spanish rulers soon realised that settler life on Cuba could not depend solely on the exploitation of the island's mineral wealth. The perspicacious Velásquez saw clearly that its future development would lie with agriculture, and he called for horses and cattle to be brought over from Hispaniola in 1514, as well as seeds and agricultural implements. The serious task of proper settlement was about to begin. Moving away from Baracoa, Velásquez made his permanent headquarters on the south coast, on the shores of the excellent harbour at Santiago.

Conquest and settlement went hand in hand for the Spanish. The pattern for Cuba had been established in Spain itself in earlier centuries, when the Christians of Castile had slowly pushed the Muslim Arab population out of the countryside, and eventually from the Spanish mainland itself. There, the land recovered from the Muslims was known as *realenga*, royal land, to be recognised as the property of the king. This was distributed to Christian soldiers and farmers, who were charged with its development and with defending it against Muslim counter-attack.

This original land settlement system, typical of reconquered Spain, was seamlessly transferred to the Americas, first to Hispaniola and then to Cuba. The island's land was declared to be the property of the king of Spain, and, in 1513, Ferdinand of Aragón issued a decree to establish the rights and duties of his prospective settlers:

> So that our subjects may be encouraged to go forth and settle in the Indies, and so that they may live with all the comfort that we wish for them . . . it is our will that there be distributed houses, lots, and lands to all those who go to colonise new regions in those places . . . and, having laboured and built dwellings on those lands, and having resided four years in those places, we grant them the right, from that moment on, to sell and to do with that property as they please, freely and independently.[11]

Vecinos, meaning 'neighbours', but referring in the colonial context to local representatives of the king, were appointed to be responsible for dividing up the *realenga*. The *vecinos* would farm it out in smaller portions, *encomienda*, to the men who would organise the actual work, known as *encomenderos*. This was the theory behind the *encomienda* system, and doubtless it worked well enough in the Spanish lands of the Reconquista, with a superabundance of impoverished subjects locally available to take over abandoned Arab farms. In Cuba, Ferdinand's decree was virtually meaningless, since there was a serious shortage of white settler labour. The *encomenderos* had not crossed the Atlantic with the intention of working themselves. They wanted 'to live with all the comfort that we wish for them', as their monarch had so graphically phrased it. The actual work of tilling and harvesting would have to be done by the Indians, the only labour available.

'You have arrived at a good moment,' Las Casas was told when he first landed at Santo Domingo in 1502. 'There is to be a war against the Indians and we will be able to take many slaves.' The news, he reported, 'produced a great joy in the ship'. Similar scenes were soon to unfold in Cuba. Since all land on the island was deemed to belong to the king, all Indians on it were perceived as serfs. They were to be the workforce of the settlers.

Velásquez also had the title of '*repartidor* of Indians', a job that licensed him to share out the Indian population among the settlers, providing each *vecino* with a group of Indians to be used as slaves, a system known as *repartimiento*. Each *vecino* was granted a group of local Indians, ranging from 40 to 300, who would then be directly employed by the *encomenderos*.

Velásquez has acquired a benign reputation from the chroniclers, and in spite of the inherent injustice of the system, he tried to ensure that the Indians were treated well. Under his edicts, they were supposed to be chiefly engaged in agriculture, and to work for their *encomendero* for only one month in the year. In practice the system did not work and was to prove disastrous for the Indians.

Velásquez's apparently beneficial schemes were eventually abandoned. In the history of all empires, it has proved difficult to enslave the local population for the benefit of foreign invaders. The indigenous inhabitants refuse to work, die off or leave to go elsewhere. Slaves have to be brought in from outside. The Indians of Cuba proved no exception to this. Many had been massacred during the punitive expeditions of Pánfilo, but many simply withdrew their labour and disappeared into the hills.

Soon it was necessary to find workers from outside Cuba. The settlers embarked on slave-hunting expeditions in the Caribbean, seizing Indians from nearby islands. Desperate for labour, they sailed ever further afield, securing fresh supplies from the South and Central American mainland, and even as far as North America. Accounts of the treatment of these captured Indians parallel those written later about the Atlantic slave trade. An Italian traveller described what he had seen off the coast of Venezuela in the middle of the sixteenth century:

> The [Indian] slaves are all marked in the face and on the arms by a hot iron with the mark of a C [for Charles V]; then the governors and captains do what they like with them; some are given to the soldiers, so that the soldiers afterwards sell them, or gamble them away among each other. When ships arrive from Spain, they barter these Indians for wine, flour, biscuit, and other requisite things. And even when some of the Indian women are pregnant by these same Spaniards, they sell them without any conscience.
>
> Then the merchants carry them elsewhere and sell them again. Others are sent to the island of Spagnuola [Hispaniola], filling with them some large vessels built like caravels. They carry them under the deck, and being nearly all people captured inland, they suffer severely the sea horrors, and not being allowed to move out of those sinks, what with their sickness and their other wants, they have to stand in the filth like animals; and the sea often being calm, water and other provisions fail them, so that the poor wretches, oppressed by the heat, the stench, the thirst, and the crowding, miserably expire there below.[12]

With such treatment, the Indian slaves brought to Cuba soon followed the island's indigenous population into oblivion, or, making their labour unavailable, they joined the bands of earlier refugees living in the island's inaccessible swamps and hills. When imported Indians could no longer be coerced into slavery, the settlers had yet again to look elsewhere. They turned, in desperation, to the purchase of black slaves from Africa.

The settlers had not been helped by the lobbying activity of Las Casas, a man so distressed by the massacre of Indians that he resolved to bring their sufferings to the attention of the Spanish monarch. He abandoned the lands he had been given on the island, and devoted the last 50 years of his life to the Indian cause. He campaigned in Mexico and Madrid, crossed and re-crossed the Atlantic, and kept up a barrage of letter-writing over the years. The Spanish monarch and his advisers must have dreaded his onslaughts. Las Casas's history of the conquest, and his account of the early treatment of the Indians, became one of the most famous texts that illuminate the history of the sixteenth century. He was almost single-handedly responsible for the initial construction of the 'black legend' of Spanish atrocities, later peddled by the English and the Dutch, that was to acquire almost biblical status in Protestant Europe over the centuries. His statistics may have been exaggerated, but it is difficult to ignore his first-hand account.[13]

His lobbying in Spain was effective in causing the Crown to realise that the Indians could not be left indefinitely to the mercies of the colonists. In 1529, some 20 years into the conquest, and after the death of Velásquez in 1524, the Crown created the position of 'Protector of the Indians', and gave the task to two Catholic priests. Yet this admirable royal gesture met with little success. As so often in colonial societies, those sent out to represent the reforming instincts of the home government soon succumb to the social pressures exerted by the local settlers. In the Cuban case, both clerics took the side of the colonists, and soon began repressing the Indians on their own account.

Ten years later, in 1542, the Crown abolished the *encomienda* system altogether, issuing new laws that recognised the Indian as a vassal rather than a slave. To no avail. Most of the Indians had already dwindled away. So too, to the alarm of the authorities, had the settlers. Many of the first Spanish immigrants – sailors, traders, artisans and farmers – had left the insecure and uncertain prospects of southern Spain to look for a new life. Yet some who arrived in Cuba with the intention of establishing themselves as farmers and small-holders never received secure title to land, or were not granted a sufficient number of Indians with which to work it. Favouritism and bureaucratic ineptitude were not absent from the medieval world.

Others had not come to farm at all. Their ambition was to find gold. When they found it to be in short supply, hundreds headed off to help in the search for the rich deposits being found on the South American mainland. By moving from Baracoa to Santiago, Velásquez had laid the foundations for Cuba's role as a jumping-off ground for further Spanish conquests to the south and the west – to Jamaica, to Darien, to Mexico and to Peru.

Many of the first generation of Spanish adventurers, men like Pánfilo, used Cuba as a stepping-stone to the mainland. Fresh exploring expeditions were fitted out each year. The first, led by Francisco Hernández de Córdoba, set off from Havana to the Yucatán in 1517. The adventurers told Velásquez on their return of the existence of territories infinitely more attractive than Cuba. They spoke in lyrical tones of discovering 'thickly peopled countries, with masonry houses, and people who covered their persons and went about clothed in cotton garments, and who possessed gold and who cultivated maize fields . . .'[14]

These regions appeared as a more enticing prospect than Cuba, and the travellers' tales whetted the appetite of Velásquez himself, and of several others. One was Hernán Cortés, the mayor of the cheerless settlement at Baracoa, and later of Santiago. 'I came here to get rich,' he is supposed to have said, 'not to till the soil like a peasant.' Cortés, born in 1485, came from the town of Medellín in Estremadura and had sailed to Santo Domingo in 1504, joining Velásquez's expedition to Cuba in 1511. Eight years later, in February 1519, he prepared a large expeditionary force and sailed out from La Santíssima Trinidad to launch what was to become the conquest of Mexico. 'I and my companions suffer from a disease of the heart,' recorded a contemporary chronicler, 'that can be cured only with gold.' With Cortés sailed a force of 380 young men, Cuba's finest, settlers who had come from Castile, Andalusia and Extremadura.

The departure of Cortés, and subsequent expeditions from Cuba to Mexico and Florida (one of them led by Pánfilo), marked the start of a new chapter in the history of the Spanish empire of the Americas, moving away from the Caribbean to the vast territories of the Aztecs and the Incas. Cuba was the launching pad for this new development, but not the immediate beneficiary. The discovery of new civilisations on the mainland, and the subsequent expeditions organised to reinforce the initial bridgehead established by Cortés, would have a major impact on the society being established in Cuba. Not only was the island denuded of some of its brightest new talents, but the way was paved for Cuba's essentially insignificant and peripheral role – as a mere staging post on the way to (and the way back from) the American mainland.

The gold-inspired enthusiasm for exploration and settlement elsewhere left the bleak Spanish settlements in Cuba depleted and diminished over many decades. The population of the island in 1544, according to one contemporary estimate, was less than 7,000, made up of 5,000 Indians, 800 black slaves, and only 660 Spanish settlers.[15] After 30 years of settlement, the settlers had barely a toehold. Not until much later in the sixteenth century, when the treasure fleets bringing silver from Peru and Mexico were obliged to assemble in Havana, before risking the dangers of the Atlantic, did Cuba begin to flourish economically – and to re-establish itself as an important link in the Spanish empire's golden chain.

What happened to Cuba's Indians?

In most versions of Cuba's early history, the Indians depart swiftly from the scene. Although Ferdinand of Aragón gave strict orders for the Indians to be protected, and Velásquez was anxious not to allow them to be wiped out, the reality of conquest led to the rapid disappearance of the majority of the Indian population. They died from wanton slaughter of the kind perpetrated by Pánfilo, and from the European diseases brought by the conquerors. Increasingly, too, they died at their own hands. The cultural shock to their society was immeasurable. Fernando Ortíz, the twentieth-century Cuban anthropologist, wrote of the baleful impact on the local people of a foreign and entirely different civilisation:

> There arrived together, and in great quantities, iron, gunpowder, the horse, the wheel, the sail, the compass, money, wages, writing, the printing-press, books, the master, the King, the Church, the banker . . . A revolutionary upheaval shook the Indian peoples of Cuba, tearing up their institutions by the roots and destroying their lives.[16]

The violent repression inflicted by the conquerors was both reprehensible and counter-productive. For while there was certainly Indian resistance, notably from those like Hatuey and Caguax who had had experience of the Spaniards in Hispaniola, many accounts survive of the local Indians welcoming the invaders in a friendly fashion. Their well-meant gestures of friendship were often misinterpreted, or simply ignored. In the history of all empires, the settlers in the front line of conquest are invariably the most brutal, and the Spanish in Cuba were no exception. No Spanish commander was able to control the excesses of his troops. He could certainly do little about their dogs.

Hunting-dogs were among the most fearsome weapons used by the Spaniards in the early days. Irish greyhounds were introduced onto the island, and bred to search out and slaughter the Indians, 'tearing them to pieces . . . and burying them alive', according to Las Casas's report.[17] The dogs were used in later centuries to pursue escaped black slaves, and news of their infamous purpose spread to the rest of the Caribbean and to North America.[18] In this context, many Indians chose to commit suicide, often immolating their families as well. 'Some began to flee into the hills,' wrote Las Casas, 'while others were in such despair that they took their own lives. Men and women hanged themselves and even strung up their own children.'[19]

Traditional histories of Cuba have ignored or downplayed the role of the Indians in the development of the island in later centuries, and it is usually argued that they had disappeared by the end of the sixteenth century, through slaughter, disease and suicide. 'It does not seem at all likely to me,' wrote the distinguished American historian Irene Wright in 1910, 'that the present-day Cuban retains even a corpuscle of aboriginal red.'[20]

This rubbing-out of the Indians from the story of the Cuban past has a long history, yet it seems probable that the Indians remained a significant and continuing presence in Cuba over many centuries. Although the Spanish settlers created solid establishments for themselves in half a dozen small towns, the great expanse of the island remained effectively beyond their control. In vast swathes of swamp and mountain, and on islands off the coast, thousands of Indians must have survived unscathed for many decades, and perhaps for centuries. In the sixteenth and seventeenth centuries, these forgotten Indian survivors were joined by runaway black slaves, to form *palenques*, the independent towns and villages that provided succour to the more general resistance movements of the nineteenth and twentieth centuries. The *palenques* – similar to the Maroon settlements that developed in other Caribbean islands – are often perceived by historians as centres of black resistance, but in origin they were a mixture of Indians and Blacks.

The first 50 years of the sixteenth century also saw the creation of a large mestizo population, with the Spanish male settlers satisfying themselves with Indian women. This occurred elsewhere on the Latin American continent well on into the seventeenth century. The soldiers and settlers who arrived during the first generation of conquest and settlement had sailed across the Atlantic with few women. A census in 1514 in Hispaniola showed that 40 per cent of the officially recognised wives of Spanish men were Indian. One authority concludes that 'a large proportion of the modern population of the Dominican Republic, Puerto Rico and Cuba is able to claim partial descent from the Tainos'.[21]

In most cases, succeeding generations of mestizos claimed the name and language of their Spanish fathers, yet they indubitably carried the culture and genes of their Indian mothers as well. The Indian element in the Cuban population, engendered in the first century of conquest, was certainly diluted over the years, by fresh waves of settlers and slaves, but it has never entirely disappeared. The American reporter Grover Flint, in Cuba during the independence war of 1895–8, described meeting 'Major Miguelín, known as the *"Indio Bravo"*, a veteran of the Ten Year War . . . He was a bronzed sharp-eyed man, who boasted Indian blood . . .'[22]

Informed of the presence of 'a tribe of wild Indians' in the mountains of eastern Cuba in 1901, Stewart Culin, an anthropologist from the University of Pennsylvania, travelled to Baracoa and found villages with Indians and mestizos, whom he was able to photograph.[23] Later in the twentieth century, Antonio Nuñez Jiménez, the Cuban geographer and revolutionary, encountered pure Indians in the foothills of the Sierra Maestra in 1945. He, too, published a photograph of one of them.[24]

Although the Indian population was clearly destroyed as a continuing civilisation and culture, the record suggests that individual groups of surviving

Indians may have 'disappeared' because it suited Cuban authorities, at certain moments in the island's history, to say that they had. Their 'elimination' occurred in the first instance as a result of quarrels over land between the settlers and the Spanish Crown. In the course of the sixteenth century, and largely as a result of the efforts of Las Casas, Indians were placed under the protection of the Spanish Crown. Their lands and persons could not (legally) be touched by the colonists. As a result of this pro-Indian policy, it was in the interests of the settlers, always avaricious for land, to suggest that the Indians had all been killed off. If there were no Indians, if it was accepted that they had all been killed, then those people who lived on the land, and thought of themselves as Indians, could not claim royal protection. Specific areas where Indians had once lived – and might indeed still be living – could be rightfully claimed by the settlers.

Later, in the nineteenth and twentieth centuries, progressive Cubans were happy to downplay the survival of the Indians since those who promoted *indigenismo*, and sought to praise and promote Cuba's Indian heritage, were usually conservative racists who wanted to glorify the Indian past and downgrade the contribution of the black African element in the population. Novelists in the nineteenth century, anxious to preserve Hispanic culture, often sought Indian images for their historical fiction as a counterweight to the arguments of those who exalted Cuba's African heritage.[25]

The argument was also championed by musicians. Antonio Bachiller y Morales, a nineteenth-century Cuban musicologist, argued that the unique qualities of Cuban music derived from indigenous rather than Afro-Cuban sources. In his book *Cuba Primitiva*, published in 1880, he discussed the songs and dances of the Siboney Indians, and concluded that 'the music of our Indians has been incorporated into [Cuban folk song] to a greater extent than we had earlier imagined'.[26] The purpose of these and later attempts to privilege Indian traditions over black contributions was to try to free Cuban culture from 'contamination' by 'the African factor'.[27] Most of Cuba's own historians in the period after the Revolution have refused to admit, or even to discuss, the possible survival of the Indians. A similar wall of silence exists in the other countries of the Caribbean.

Importing a black slave population

No such reticence affects contemporary research into Cuba's African population. Black slavery, and the need to keep slaves under tight control, was part of Cuba's heritage from the earliest years of settlement, and has long been recognised as such. The unwillingness of whites to work, the dearth of Indian labour and the failure of the programme to seize Indians from other islands and the mainland obliged the Spanish authorities to seek a fresh solution, one adopted by other empires at other times. Slaves were to be brought in from countries so distant that they would have no hope of escaping, and of a colour so different that they would be instantly recognised should they seek to escape.

The presence in Spain itself of black slaves from Africa had been an established aspect of that society since long before the conquest of the Caribbean. More than 100,000 black slaves were at work there in the fifteenth century, mostly in Andalusia.[28] As a result, slaves were part of the normal complement of a colonising expedition, most of them brought as personal servants, and were present in Cuba after 1511. Requests for slave assistance with state-construction projects were made as early as 1516; Velásquez had asked the Spanish king for 'a dozen Negroes' to be sent over from Santo Domingo to build fortifications to secure Santiago against attack. The wealthier settlers, meanwhile, had already been procuring black slaves on their own account, although the cost of importing slaves was always perceived as a heavy burden. This pattern of legal and illegal trade, established in the early years, was to continue over the centuries.

Not until the 1520s did the authorities in Santiago examine the possibility of importing slaves on a large scale – as workers in the mines and the fields. In 1527, concerned about the depopulation of the island – with the Indians apparently dying off and many of the younger settlers leaving for Mexico – the Crown made a decision that would affect the island's immigration pattern for the next 350 years. Orders were given for 'a thousand Negro slaves' to be taken to Cuba, 'to lessen the labours of the Indians' – although in this particular incident, the record suggests that the requested Blacks never arrived; the dwindling group of settlers had insufficient funds to purchase them.[29] Indeed after the initial enthusiasm, there was no immediate rush to acquire new slaves. The number of slaves disembarking each year in the 1530s was rarely above double figures, another indication that settlement was proceeding slowly as settlers leached away to Mexico.[30]

Whatever the exact number of slave arrivals in the early decades, the royal decision had been made. Cuba's future as a black and mulatto country was assured. The forced migration of these black slaves from Africa – coupled with the landing and settlement of Spaniards in the sixteenth century, and the subsequent dispossession and gradual elimination of most of the indigenous peoples – was to have a profound and lasting impact on the island's history. Cuba's society, its culture and its economy, as well as the physical make-up of its people, were to be irreversibly affected by this historic population transfer.

The slave trade to Cuba was to last for another three centuries, a period in which just under a million Africans were forcibly transferred to the island. The great majority (perhaps 85 per cent of the total) arrived in the nineteenth century to work on the sugar plantations, then the source of the island's prosperity. Slave landings, although contested and illegal in the final years of the trade, did not finally stop until slavery was formally abolished in 1886. Other countries in the Americas had long abandoned the practice, but Cuba (together with Brazil and the United States) was among the last to retain it. The astonishing wealth of the sugar planters depended on its continuation.

In the 1520s and again in the 1540s, largely through the writings and political activity of radical critics like Bartolomé de las Casas, the attention of the Spanish monarch was drawn to the conditions of the Indians in the mines. The Crown was under pressure to prohibit their employment, yet it could not avoid hearing the desperate cries of the settlers for labour. The settlers wanted black slaves, and they wanted them to be imported free from tax. They told the bishop in Bayamo that the island was being ruined 'by lack of Indians and Negroes', and in 1542 they obliged the authorities in Santiago, Puerto Príncipe and Sancti Spíritus to send out an urgent appeal for more slaves: 'Here the chief urgency is Negroes . . . We pray licence for each citizen to bring four Negroes and Negresses, free of all duty.'[31]

To allow the settlers to avoid import taxes, the Cuban authorities had sanctioned (or turned a blind eye to) the unauthorised arrival of cheap slaves from the Barbary Coast of Morocco, as well as from the Mediterranean islands of Sardinia, Mallorca and Menorca. These posed a threat to the royal ambition to convert the population of the Americas to Catholicism, for they were not only cheap but Muslim. A royal decree of 1543 ordered the expulsion from Cuba of all slaves from North Africa, 'because the Negroes who live in that part of the Levant say that they belong to the Moorish or Mahometan caste, and, as others would associate with them in a new land where the Catholic faith is now being implanted, it is against our interest to introduce such people'.[32]

After the 1540s most blacks arrived directly from the West African coast. A small number, as a result of upheavals in Spain's colonies, came later with their owners from the New World: from Jamaica in 1655, from Saint-Domingue in the years after 1791, from Louisiana in 1808 and later in the nineteenth century from Florida, from Mexico and from the independent republics of South America.

In the early period the plantation slaves were mostly male and since the population failed to reproduce itself the slave trade continued without let or hindrance, although 'enlightened' planters began to import larger numbers of female slaves at the end of the eighteenth century. The continuing gender imbalance was used as an argument by some planters in the nineteenth century to justify the trade.

Black landings increased throughout the sixteenth century, and at its end some 12,000 black slaves were present on the island, forming probably the largest single group in the immigrant population.[33] More regular transports began to arrive after the crowns of Spain and Portugal were linked together in 1581. Cuba now had access to Portugal's existing slave trade with Africa, and slaves continued to arrive both legally and illegally. Some were transported on

Portuguese ships arriving at Havana, others came via the contraband trade, sailing into small ports along the coast. The large and forbidden local trade was one in which merchants and traders all happily took part, as did state officials and the clergy.

Initially this African influx occurred on a relatively small scale, yet by the start of the seventeenth century the Africans had come to form half the population, causing regular spasms of alarm among the white settlers. Their condition of slavery was never accepted by the African migrants. The first and subsequent generations of black slaves were just as prone to rebellion as their Indian predecessors. A government report of 1532, which refers to a total of 500 black slaves on the island (and an Indian population of between 4,500 and 5,000), also gave news of the first black slave revolt – at a gold mine in Jobabó, near Bayamo. The rising was soon crushed, and the heads of the leaders were stuck on poles outside the town.[34] A further black rebellion, in league with local Indians, occurred in 1538, and the authorities sent out *rancheadores* to crush it. 'Se ha hecho justicia, y ya está la isla segura', the governor reported subsequently. Justice has been done, and the island is secure.[35]

Settler fears of being outnumbered by blacks were aroused in the early years, and both blacks and Indians were kept under fierce control. Freed blacks could neither travel nor earn their living independently without fear of punishment, an extension of the laws that had first been applied to the Indians. It was illegal for blacks to be itinerant sellers of meat or fruit, noted a report from the 1550s. Those caught would be punished with 300 lashes (while Indians found in canoes or on horseback would receive 200 lashes, and 300 lashes after a second offence, with an ear cut off).[36]

In 1606, the white citizens of Havana presented a memorial to the governor, alerting him to their estimate of some 20,000 blacks in the colony. If these were to rebel and join forces with the pirates hovering offshore, wrote these alarmed citizens, the island itself might easily be lost to Spain.[37] This early fear of slave rebellion coinciding with outside intervention was to permeate the consciousness of the white settlers over the next three centuries

The beat of Drake's drum, 1586

Some way into Havana's narrow harbour entrance stands the ancient Castillo de la Real Fuerza, a miniature Spanish hill fortress of the sixteenth century parked on the shore of the Caribbean. Constructed as a two-storey central square with four corner circles, its grey stone walls are now surrounded by the barrels of old cannons of a later era. Backing on to the Plaza de Armas, it is often filled with visitors, and a roof-top bar gives a fine view over the city and the harbour. This delightful urban castle, constructed in the 1560s, was more of a symbol of Spanish power than a defensive tool, being too far inland to be a direct threat to the probing pirate ships that arrived offshore in the sixteenth century. For two hundred years it was the office and residence of the Spanish governor.

The Castillo was built on the orders of Philip II of Spain to combat the threat of European piracy. For already within the first generation of Spanish settlement in Cuba, the island had become a focus of attack from European nations that challenged Spain's claim to possession of the New World. The Caribbean in the sixteenth century became one of several arenas where the Catholic empires of southern Europe clashed with the Protestant powers of the north. Primarily a military and naval struggle, it was characterised by powerful religious fanaticism and ideological conflict, and fuelled by the intransigent demands of trade.[38]

First off the shores of Cuba in the 1520s were ships from France, Spain's principal enemy in Europe. A French ship seized a rich cargo sent by Cortés from Mexico to Spain, as early as 1523. The French were followed in quick succession by the Portuguese, the English and the Dutch, their pirate ships hovering endlessly off the Cuban coast. Foreign vessels were to remain offshore for more than two hundred years, preying on the Spanish treasure ships emerging from Havana, carrying valuable cargo from Mexico and Peru, and presenting a permanent threat to the island's production and commerce.

With the Spanish newcomers barely settled in Cuba, the impact on the tiny European population of the young colony was considerable. In 1550, the settlers on the island numbered only 322 households, and Havana itself boasted only 60 in 1570.[39] Few soldiers guarded the island and many young men had gone to make their fortunes on the mainland. Little resistance was made to attacks from the sea, and foreign ships were able to come and go much as they pleased.

The first pirate raids on Cuba were fuelled by the rivalry in Europe between France and Spain. In 1519, the Spanish kingdom of Ferdinand II had translated itself into the Holy Roman Empire of Charles V. This vast imperial state, incorporating much of Europe, was to be almost continuously at war with France for over 40 years, until 1559. The conflict between Charles V and Francis, the French monarch, soon extended to the waters of the Caribbean, and French privateers caused increasing havoc there from the 1520s onwards, plundering ships and ports.[40]

The ports of Baracoa, Santiago and Havana were sacked regularly by French ships. A French fleet occupied Havana in 1537, on the eve of Hernando de Soto's expedition to Florida. French corsairs blockaded Santiago between 1538 and 1540. Baracoa was plundered in 1546, and Santiago again in 1554 and 1558. The French campaign against the Spanish in the Caribbean culminated in the sack of Havana in 1555 by Jacques de Sores, described in contemporary documents both as 'a Lutheran' and as 'one of the best corsairs in France or England'.[41]

The attack by Jacques de Sores was an important landmark in Cuban history, being greeted – unusually – with a degree of resistance, showing the first signs of embryonic nationalism. Free Indians and black slaves joined forces with the settlers (the *vecinos*) to fight against a foreign invader, derided as a shipload of French 'heretics'. A group of surviving Indians, established in a reservation at Guanabacoa on the eastern side of the harbour, eagerly made common cause with their new rulers.

The resistance was ineffective, largely owing to the lack of leadership provided by the Spanish governor, and Jacques de Sores won the day. Havana was captured and burnt to the ground.[42] The French victory had no wider repercussions, for it was not within the capacity of the French corsair to seize the entire island. He was content to sack the town and sail away. A European peace settlement was in any case already at hand, and events in the Caribbean, as usual, depended on decisions taken far away. Four years later, in 1559, France and Spain were no longer at war, signing a peace treaty at Cateau-Cambresis, south of Calais.

Peace in Europe was a significant achievement, yet halting the semi-independent operations of pirates and corsairs in the Americas was not so easy. Another French captain, Jean Ribault, established a colony of Huguenot soldiers on the coast of Florida at Fort Caroline in 1562, posing a threat to Catholic control over the Florida Strait, the strategic waterway north of Havana. Pedro Menéndez de Avíles, the Spanish captain usually in charge of the treasure fleet, was detailed off to destroy this colony of heretics, slaughtering the French colonists in 1565 'not as Frenchmen but as Lutherans'. According to his own account, 'we cut the throats of a hundred and thirty-two', and his ferocity – well reported in Europe – was to deter other Europeans from attempting to settle in the Spanish New World for years.[43]

Menéndez's reward was to be made governor of Cuba, but like so many later Cubans he was more attracted by the possibilities of Florida, and he built a fortress at Saint Augustine on the Atlantic coast, just south of Jacksonville. This small settlement, corralled against the sea by hostile Indians, never flourished, and the new king in Spain refused to allow Menéndez to wage 'a war of fire and blood' against his adversaries. Two hundred years later, Florida was still little more than an outpost of Havana.

A new and dynamic monarch ruled in Spain in the 1560s, a ruler who intended to bring order to Spain's American empire – and to its Cuban gateway. Philip II was to rule for 40 years, from 1556 to 1598, and he left an indelible mark on the city of Havana. Son of the German-oriented Emperor Charles V, Philip had been brought up as a prince in Castile with Hispanic perspectives, and he had little concern with the wider Habsburg empire. The traditional Austrian territories of the Habsburgs had been bequeathed by Charles V to his brother Ferdinand, who became the new Holy Roman Emperor. Philip had the more interesting part of the legacy, inheriting Spain and the Americas – including Cuba – as well as Spanish Italy and the Nether-lands. Twenty years later, in 1581, as some kind of compensation for the loss of Austria, he was able to add Portugal and its empire to his global interests.[44] The link with Portugal brought the profitable territories of Brazil and Angola – and the African slave trade – into the Spanish portfolio, as well as the services of the Portuguese navy.

Philip II's first task in the Caribbean, after de Sores's capture of Havana, was to meet the threat of European attack. He was to construct great fortifi-cations in all the principal harbours, and to organise the proper defence of the treasure fleet that brought silver to Seville from Mexico and Peru and stopped at Havana on the way.

Cuba had lost its imperial importance in the early years, when much of its embryonic Spanish population abandoned the island for greater wealth and glory on the mainland. Now it was to acquire fresh significance as geographers and navigators began to understand its specific peculiarities. Ships that were swept westward across the Atlantic from the North African coast by the force of the prevailing wind arrived opportunely at Santiago on Cuba's southern coast. Ships that left from the northern shore at Havana were swept back eastward with equal facility through the Bahamas, driven by the westerly winds that predominated in the northern Atlantic. Havana became the fulcrum around which Spanish commerce with the Americas was to revolve over the next three centuries. Its future position as a vital Spanish redoubt was now assured, but first it was necessary to secure its defence against European predators.

In 1561, six years after the French raid on Havana, Philip ordered great forti-fications to be erected at the harbour there. The Castillo de la Real Fuerza was the first great symbolic construction that projected Spanish power into the Caribbean. Similar, and rather more substantial fortresses were eventually built at San Juan in Puerto Rico, and at Cartagena on the Colombian coast. Philip also devised a new convoy system whereby all treasure ships sailing from Havana to Seville were to be provided with an armed escort.

The Spanish fleet, bearing goods for the colonies, had been accustomed to leave from Seville (and later from Cadiz), and to sail down the coast of Africa to the Canary Islands, and sometimes to Cape Verde. From there it would sail west with the prevailing wind until it came to Havana. Here it would divide into two separate fleets, the *Nueva España* fleet, which sailed to the Mexican port of Vera Cruz, and the *Tierra Firme* fleet, which sailed to the South American mainland, stopping at Cartagena, in Colombia, and to Nombre de Dios (and later Porto Bello) in Panama.

On their return journey, carrying silver, gold and emeralds, the two fleets would meet in Havana, before starting the journey across the Atlantic. This haphazard method of transferring treasure from the Americas to Spain had proved highly vulnerable to pirates. An irregular and informal convoy, accompanying ships that came and went from Seville, had been in operation since the 1520s. Philip now provided the wherewithal to increase protection.

Under the new system, the ships making up the treasure fleet would first sail to Havana from the Latin American mainland. There they would assemble in the harbour, often more than a hundred at a time at the end of the sixteenth century, and their crews would wait, possibly for several months, before the transatlantic naval convoy was ready. They would then sail for Spain, closely guarded by naval ships, crossing the Atlantic to Seville. The treasure fleet usually sailed once a year, in the autumn before the hurricane season.

The presence in Havana of so many foreign sailors – for the crews of Spanish ships came from all over Habsburg Europe and beyond – gave the town of Havana the cosmopolitan flavour that it has retained over the centuries. To service this transient population, Havana became a city of carpenters and builders, of shopkeepers and prostitutes, of bankers and businessmen. Ship-repair became a central activity, and later became an important industry, supplying ships for the Spanish navy, using the hard tropical wood available locally.

Impoverished and underpopulated, yet rich at Havana when the treasure fleets called by, Cuba remained prey to outside intervention in the final decades of the sixteenth century. Peace having been made with the French state in 1559, and their settlements destroyed in Florida, the principal threat to the Spanish Caribbean now came from independent piratical operators, and would last for the next two hundred years. The pirates might threaten Cuban towns, or simply operate as independent traders along the coast, bringing goods from Europe and collecting beef and cow hides from the cattle ranches of the settlers. Most of these independent operators, in the early years, were French or Portuguese. Later they were to be English and Dutch.

Much of Cuba was covered with cattle ranches during the first two centuries of Spanish occupation. Sugar and tobacco were to come later. The Cuban people in those years were mainly poor and rough, living in isolation from the outside world.[45] Because of strict laws forbidding trade or commerce with foreigners, most of them raised livestock and cultivated small subsistence plots, sometimes trading hides or salted beef. This might be done officially in Havana, or illegally – and more lucratively – in the provinces, with smugglers and pirates.

The new generation of European pirates in the Caribbean came in many disguises and under different names: buccaneers, corsairs, privateers. Sometimes, from the Dutch word, they were called free-booters or filibusterers. The 'buccaneers' came ashore in search of bacon. The Cuban Indians had learnt (from the natives of Haiti) a process of preserving meat by drying it and then smoking it over a fire of green leaves and branches. The Indians called the rack on which the meat was laid out a *boucan* or *buccan* [bacon], while those who prepared and sold the meat were referred to as *boucaniers* or buccaneers.[46]

Pigs had been brought to Cuba from Europe by the first Spanish settlers. The early litters had been allowed to roam freely over the island, becoming a vital source of food, not just for the settlers but also for the pirates who arrived in forgotten coves to replenish their water and their stores. They learnt to appreciate the pig meat dried on the *boucan*, and the word became associated with the pirates themselves, the men who brought home the bacon.

The 'privateers' were different from buccaneers in that their operations were officially licensed by the state from which they came. These were privately owned ships, granted the right by the French or English monarch (and later the Dutch) to operate against enemy shipping in time of war.[47] All such operators were engaged in contraband along the coast, for which the Spanish word was *rescates*, a term used to refer to barter or ransom, a transaction usually considered to involve deceit or deception.[48] The pirates brought slaves and luxury goods from Europe, the settlers provided them with meat and hides. The early settlers had brought cattle with them as well as pigs, and the great cattle ranches of Cuba, run by the increasingly rich and privileged descendants of the first settlers, serviced the inexhaustible demand of Europe for cheap leather. Twenty thousand hides a year were (legally) exported in the 1570s, the production of leather far exceeding the local demand for meat.

European pirates and illegal traders came ashore at many points along Cuba's undefended coast. Since they were essentially traders, the opportunities for barter and exchange were not unwelcome to wealthy Cuban ranchers. Philip II, in his anxiety to defend Havana and the treasure fleet, had neglected the rest of the island. Building fortifications at Havana afforded little protection against pirates, since they could come ashore at whichever one of Cuba's myriad small inlets they might choose. The eastern end of the island had been left largely defenceless, permanently exposed to infiltration and attack. The treasurer of neighbouring Santo Domingo reported in October 1595 that corsairs had been active in local harbours in the previous four years,

> as numerous and as assiduous as though they were ports of their own countries . . . They make their incursions safely and find persons with whom to barter, for the land is sparsely settled and full of horned cattle, so that anywhere they put in they find opportunity awaiting in the presence of negroes and other wretched delinquents who live outside the law in the bush . . .[49]

These piratical actions along the shores of the Caribbean islands were a particular stock-in-trade of the English privateers who predominated throughout the Caribbean in the last two decades of the sixteenth century. England had now replaced France as Spain's principal enemy, and the two countries were to be at war for eighteen years, from 1585 until the death of Queen Elizabeth in 1603. The war had a considerable impact on Cuba outside Havana, and the privateers were soon attacking cattle farms and sugar mills, landing at unprotected settlements along the coast. The isolated Cuban settlers were only too happy to barter with the English pirates.[50]

Philip II realised in 1586 that his Caribbean empire, gateway to South America, was under serious threat. The 40-year-old Francis Drake, the most famous English privateer of his age, had come cruising along the shores of Cuba that year. A piratical operator typical of his time, Drake was already familiar with the West Indies, and was himself a well-known figure there. He had received a 'regular privateering commission' from Queen Elizabeth some 15 years earlier and made a preliminary voyage to the Caribbean in 1572. He had plundered the town of Nombre de Dios, the Panamanian collection point where the treasure fleet loaded silver from Peru (to be replaced in the 1590s by Porto Bello).

With the outbreak of war between Spain and England in 1585, Drake was again sent out to the West Indies. This was no piratical operation, for he sailed at the head of a huge English fleet – 22 ships with 2,000 men and 12 companies of soldiers. He had orders to attack Spain's principal towns in the Caribbean, and he sacked the great city of Santo Domingo in January 1586.

The Cuban authorities believed that Cuba must now be in his sights, and they prepared for an imminent attack by the legendary English pirate. Levies were ordered up from every small town, 300 soldiers were sent from Mexico, with six months' supply of food, and Havana eventually assembled a force of nearly 1,000 armed men, ready to repel the English enemy. Guns were prepared at La Fuerza, and at the forts of Punta and Morro at the entrance to the harbour. An iron chain, buoyed up by logs, was placed across the water.

It was a false alarm. Drake sailed south from Santo Domingo to the South American mainland and seized Cartagena instead. The authorities in Havana were obliged to gear themselves up a second time when they heard that he had left Cartagena and turned north towards Cuba. News came that Drake's fleet had touched the island at its western extremity, landing briefly for water at Cape San Antonio, and his entire fleet was glimpsed from the shore at Havana at the end of May. Yet the attack never came. Maybe the great English captain had second thoughts, maybe his troops were too ill, maybe he was deterred by the Spanish preparations to receive him. He sailed away northwards to the coast of Florida and attacked the more vulnerable settlement at St Augustine instead.

Drake had refrained from attacking Cuba, but the fright he had given Philip II would have a significant effect on Spanish policy towards the island. His voyage in 1586 is often held to mark the end of the first era of Cuba's colonial history. Everthing the islanders had requested – ships, guns, fortifi- cation, soldiers – was suddenly forthcoming when, as Irene Wright put it so graphically, 'Philip heard among his islands, along his own coasts, the beat of Drake's drum and the roll of the guns of the Tudor navy. They ushered in other times.'[51]

Spain had relied on its own naval strength to protect its possessions in the Caribbean for nearly a century. Drake had underlined the vulnerability of these distant settlements. Although Havana had successfully deterred his attacks, Cuba's other ports, notably Santiago, had been left undefended. With the island's tiny defence force concentrated in the capital, Santiago was an easy target, and was captured and sacked by freelance French operatives, it was never to be the island's capital again.

The lessons of Drake's voyage were soon learnt by the authorities. Spanish protection was insufficient, the colonies would have to be properly fortified and organised to protect themselves.[52] A great military engineer from Rome, Gian Battista Antonelli, was sent out to Havana in 1586, to report on the island's defences. He began work on the two embryonic forts at the entrance to the harbour – the fort of San Salvador de la Punta on the western side, and the Morro castle on the eastern promontory. Built by slaves with the help of soldiers and prisoners, the works were not finished for another 40 years, in 1630. Antonelli was to spend many years in the Caribbean, designing forts for San Juan and Santo Domingo, and constructing roads for Cuba as well as an aqueduct for Havana, providing the city with a permanent supply of fresh water.

The measures taken were sufficient. Nearly two centuries passed before the English were able to prevail against Spain in the Caribbean. Drake had made a dramatic impact, but the English did not have the organisation or the economic strength at the end of the sixteenth century to operate permanently on a global scale. They were, after all, a small country, operating far from home.[53] Drake himself returned to England after his great expedition of 1586, to take a prominent part in the defeat of the Spanish Armada, sent to capture England in 1588. When he returned to the West Indies, to make further attacks against Spanish settlements, he found that their defences had grown stronger. His final years of piracy illustrated England's relative weakness, and they ended in failure. He died off the coast near Nombre de Dios in January 1595.

The amount of Spanish loot that the English captured was insignificant compared with the Latin American treasure that arrived in Spain. The campaigns of the English, both before and after the death of Drake, had some minor effect on the sailings of the *flota* from Havana, and on at least three occasions, in 1590–91, in 1594–5 and in 1601–2, the fleet was held up for six months in Havana harbour before it was safe to sail.[54] The postponement of the Havana sailings may well have had a dismaying impact on the Spanish treasury, and probably impeded the operation of the Spanish war machine, but the balance of power in the Caribbean had swung back towards Spain.

The English kept out of Cuba for more than half a century, while other European nations became the principal threat to Spanish power in the region. In spite of the efforts made to protect the island through the construction of great fortifications, Cuba continued to come under attack from ships of the European powers, affecting its trade, its economic development and the general well-being of its inhabitants. The external threat remained as real as in the days of Drake, the by-product of distant but continuing quarrels in Europe. The French, the Portuguese and the English had been seen off – for a while – but the fiercely Protestant Dutch soon took their place, becoming the dominant power in the Caribbean in the first decades of the seventeenth century.

Spain was at war with the Dutch in Europe, and the conflict soon became global. In 1624, a Dutch fleet seized Bahia, the chief town of Brazil, and in 1628 its target was Havana, or more specifically the silver fleet. Admiral Piet Heyn of the Dutch West India Company, the most famous Dutch privateer, was in charge on both occasions. With a fleet of 32 ships, 700 cannon and 3,500 soldiers, he lay off Havana, waiting for the fleet's arrival from Mexico. At dawn on 8 September, the 15 ships of the Spanish *flota* sailed straight into the middle of his armada, then lying off the bay of Matanzas. Piet Heyn shepherded the silver fleet into the bay and captured eight ships, sinking a ninth. 'Fabulous indeed were the captured treasures of silver, gold, pearls, indigo, sugar, Campeachy wood [mahogany], and costly furs, which sold in the Netherlands for no less than fifteen million guilders.'[55] Dutch school-children sang a song for ever after to celebrate the deeds of the famous corsair: 'Piet Hein's name is small, but his deeds are great; he has captured the silver fleet.'

Other Dutch pirates were less fortunate. A few years later, Cornelius Jols sailed from Curaçao in 1635 and attacked and looted Santiago. He was successful on that occasion, but when he tried to repeat his triumph the following year, he was captured and executed. Santiago was repeatedly under attack, both from the Dutch and the French. Their pirates and corsairs preyed on the copper mines at El Cobre, and on the sugar cane grown in the eastern province. The Santiaguinos soon became excellent *corsarios* in their own right. When a new governor, Francisco Riana de Gamboa, arrived in Cuba in 1634, he gave instructions for the island's defences to be further strengthened, and small *guarda-costas* were built in the Havana boatyards to patrol the coastal waters. A flotilla of Cuban *corsarios* was available for the first time to attack the shipping of enemy nations with footholds in the Caribbean islands. Cuban sailors, among them Thomé Rodríguez, Felipe Giraldino and Francisco Miguel Vázquez, began to harass the British in Jamaica and Florida, as well as the French and the Dutch elsewhere in the Caribbean.[56]

The foreigners were not the only threat. The Spanish were also at the mercy of the weather. Sailing across the Atlantic in flimsy craft was always a risk, and the silver fleet was peculiarly vulnerable to the elements. Ships usually gathered at Havana in June or July, before setting off with their escort for Spain, and a notable disaster occurred in 1622. The ships had assembled rather late that year, and not until September was the fleet ready to sail – some 27 ships under the Marqués de Cadereyta. The delay had a tragic outcome, for the fleet ran into the teeth of an autumn hurricane just one day out of Havana. Eight ships were lost, including three treasure galleons, and 500 people were drowned.[57] The armada was late again the following year, and although two cautious attempts were made to leave the harbour, the main fleet decided to spend the winter months in Havana. The result was unfortunate for Spain, since the Spanish treasury, effectively deprived of two years' income, grew severely short of funds.

Cuba's population remained static during these years of isolation, and totalled little more than 30,000 in the middle of the seventeenth century. Slaves continued to arrive, but few white settlers made the journey. A disastrous epidemic of 1649 killed perhaps a third of the island's people. Not until 1655 did the figures improve, when a sudden influx of 10,000 prosperous Spanish settlers arrived from Jamaica, anticipating the move made by French settlers in Haiti 150 years later.[58] The settlers had been forced out of Jamaica by the British, after Oliver Cromwell had sent a fleet to attack Spain's possessions in the Caribbean. Cromwell had originally hoped to capture Cuba and Santo Domingo, and he despatched an English squadron of 55 ships to do just that, accompanied by transport vessels with 9,000 soldiers on board. Spanish resistance at Santo Domingo proved too strong and the English fleet abandoned their plans to seize Cuba, turning their attention instead to Jamaica, a weaker and poorly defended target. The depleted Spanish force on Jamaica was easily overawed by the English armada and the island's defenders were obliged to surrender. Thousands of Spanish settlers, unwilling to accept English rule, sailed north to Cuba, hoping – vainly – that one day they would be able to return.

With the English occupying the neighbouring island, and Cuba itself now vulnerable to attack by Spain's European enemy, Spain made efforts to recover English Jamaica in 1657, and again in 1658. Another, smaller English fleet, captained by Christopher Myngs, was sent out in 1662 to frighten the Spanish. With a fleet of just 12 ships and 2,000 men, he landed at Aguadores and captured Santiago with ease.[59] Pedro de Morales, the town's Spanish governor, had not dared to call out the local *criollo* militia, and his regular Spanish force was inadequate to deal with the English threat. He retreated to Bayamo, while much of the civilian population of Santiago withdrew to the Indian town of El Caney, a few miles inland.

Myngs sacked the town and destroyed the Morro fortress at the entrance to the harbour, blowing up its powder magazine. Since there were no long-term plans to secure a Cuban foothold, he withdrew after a few days. His more limited and successful aim was to open up trade between Santiago and Jamaica, and to emphasise to the Spanish that Jamaica would never again be theirs. Soon a thriving trade in copper, sugar and slaves opened up between the two islands, a mutually convenient arrangement that was beyond the capacity of Spain to prevent.[60]

A few years later, Henry Morgan, the famous Welsh buccaneer, was ordered by Sir Thomas Modyford, Jamaica's governor, to sail to Cuba in 1688 to verify the details of a threatened Spanish attack. Morgan landed on Cuba's south coast, with 10 ships and 300 men, and advanced some 50 miles inland to Puerto Príncipe (Camagüey):

> As soon as the pirates had possessed themselves of the town, they closed all the Spaniards – men, women, and children – and slaves in their several churches, and pillaged all the goods they could set their hands on. Then they searched through the country, daily bringing in many goods and prisoners with much provision. With this in hand, they set to making great cheer after their custom, without remembering their poor prisoners, whom they left to starve in the churches.[61]

The continuing danger to Cuban settlements from piratical attacks from Jamaica was reduced after Spain signed a treaty with England two years later, in 1670, that officially recognised the existence of England's colonies in the Caribbean. A comparable treaty was signed with France at Ryswick in 1697: in exchange for recognition of its authority over Saint-Domingue, the western end of Hispaniola, France agreed to end the raids of its buccaneers. For Cubans, these treaties at the end of the seventeenth century evoked the hope that their long period of insecurity was over, and that the island might now be able to develop in peace.

Sugar and tobacco: the seventeenth-century development of the island's wealth

The seventeenth century was Cuba's second century of colonial rule, yet it was only during this period that the settlers were able to establish the foundations of an economy that was eventually to bring prosperity. The heirs to the first generation of conquerors had settled themselves in large cattle ranches across the island in the sixteenth century, and sat back to allow nature to do its work, albeit with the assistance of black and Indian labour. Beef and leather, sold officially or via smugglers, provided a useful income, as did pigs and bacon, but this established little more than a subsistence economy. The settler towns, notably Havana and Santiago, performed rather better, gradually assuming an essential role as the Spanish gateway to the Americas, servicing the passing trade, repairing ships, storing victuals and entertaining the crews of warships, commercial vessels and the silver fleet.

In the seventeenth century, however, the island's economic rhythm began to change, with the harvesting and commercial production of sugar and tobacco. These two crops began to draw level with cattle as the principal source of agricultural income and by the eighteenth century began to make substantial contributions to the island's wealth.

Sugar was not indigenous to the Caribbean; it came originally from the Pacific. Cultivated in Spain by the Arabs for many centuries, it was brought across the Atlantic by the Spanish on their early voyages, and grown commercially in Hispaniola soon after. The first boxes of sugar produced there were presented by Nicholás de Ovando to King Ferdinand on his deathbed in 1516.[62] The Emperor Charles V, Ferdinand's successor, encouraged production in Cuba in 1523, authorising 4,000 gold pesos to be granted to 'responsible' settlers in Cuba for the construction of sugar mills. State support for the sugar industry was made available to private enterpreneurs from the start, the finance being provided by the *Casa de Contratación* in Seville, the trade promotion finance house founded two decades earlier in 1503.

The first large-scale sugar plantations – with three sugar mills under construction in the area around Matanzas – were established in Cuba in 1576. These primitive mills, with wooden rollers, were powered by mules or oxen, and the juice was caught in earthenware trays. After boiling in open pans the end result was a coarse brown sugar, sufficient for consumption on the island but hardly an export luxury.[63] These simple methods of production continued throughout the seventeenth century.

Cuba with Hispaniola and Puerto Rico were the first Spanish colonies in the Americas to plant sugarcane, and the first to employ slaves. They were also the first to embark on plantation agriculture. Yet none made much progress in the first two centuries of settlement, and the other European colonies in the Caribbean were left to race ahead.

While sugar came from the Pacific, tobacco – the second product for ever associated with Cuba – was indigenous to South America and the Caribbean. The Tainos grew and smoked tobacco, but it was some years after the conquest before Spanish settlers appreciated its delights. Blacks from Africa were the first outsiders to take to it with enthusiasm, growing it, smoking it and selling it to the crews of the treasure fleets at Havana. 'Negro stuff', the Spaniards called it, disparagingly, until they perceived a commercial opportunity at the beginning of the seventeenth century. Blacks were soon forbidden from trading the home-grown tobacco harvested on their *vegas*, or tobacco fields, although in later centuries they became involved in its production. 'It is true that whites alone cultivate some tobacco farms [*vegas*],' wrote the creole oligarch Francisco Arango in 1826, 'but most *vegas* are cultivated by blacks under the command of a white.'[64]

Serious tobacco production began in the seventeenth century in the rich lands between Havana and Trinidad and in the west towards Pinar del Rio. The Spanish state soon perceived in it a source of revenue that might help to offset the cost of garrisoning the island against predatory attacks from the ships of its European enemies, and an official monopoly on the sale of tobacco was introduced in 1717. Local producers were obliged to sell their tobacco to agents of the Crown. Riots by the producers led to a relaxation of the monopoly, but it was to be another hundred years before the industry took off, sparked by the arrival in eastern Cuba of French traders from Saint-Domingue who perceived its market potential.[65] The foundations of a new economy had been laid, but progress remained slow.

The Spanish empire under challenge, 1741–1868

Guantánamo falls to Admiral Vernon, 1741

The American military call it Gitmo, the Cubans call it Caimanera, the British once called it Cumberland Bay. Christopher Columbus, arriving here in 1494, called it *Puerto Grande*, or Great Port. Guantánamo Bay is the largest harbour on the south side of Cuba, larger even than the splendid inlet at Cienfuegos or the handsome stretch of water at Santiago de Cuba. A bone of contention between Cuba and the United States throughout the twentieth century, it achieved wider notoriety in the early twenty-first century when a US camp on its shores was used to house prisoners flown in from distant Afghanistan.

Almost entirely surrounded by high hills, the vast bay of Guantánamo is an enclave cut off from its immediate hinterland. Spanish settlers avoided it, finding the climate unhealthy and overly hot. The area is mosquito-ridden at all times. Columbus's seamen found Indians barbecuing fish on the shore when they landed, and the Great Navigator gave them permission to help themselves. The locals said they were preparing a feast for their chief, and had been roasting the fish on the beach lest it spoil in the fierce heat of the day. Admitting philosophically that they could catch more the following night, they shared their catch with their unexpected visitors.

Guantánamo became a favoured spot for outside intervention. Spanish settlers arrived in force some years after Columbus's preliminary inspection, and American soldiers landed four hundred years later – and have remained ever since. The British came ashore more than a century before the Americans, although the armada captained by Admiral Edward Vernon that sailed into the harbour in 1741 included a contingent of 600 potential settlers from the Thirteen Colonies.[1]

Ships from England had been cruising past Cuba since the days of Drake, often engaging in piratical trading. In the eighteenth century, as their embryonic empire grew stronger and the Spanish grew weaker, the British became more aggressive, seizing Guantánamo in 1741 and Havana 20 years later. Their imperial interest in the island was limited, but their commercial ambition was boundless. Naval attacks were the prelude to the British financial invasion of the nineteenth century. Admiral Vernon's landing paved the way to a new era in Cuba's history in which hegemony over the island was disputed, first by Britain and Spain, and later by Britain and the United States.

Vernon was sent out to the Caribbean in 1739, with orders to cause havoc in the Spanish empire, much as Drake had done 150 years earlier. War with Spain had broken out again that year, provoked by the success of the Cuban *guarda-costas*, the small vessels built and manned locally that harassed British commercial shipping. Captain Robert Jenkins, an apparent victim of their attacks, had had an ear cut off as a punishment, and his case, when brought before parliament in London, aroused popular enthusiasm for war. 'Something must be obtained to prevent the Spaniards from insulting us again . . . ,' Sir William Pulteney, the opposition leader, wrote to Vernon in August 1740. '"Take and hold" is the cry. This plainly points to Cuba, and if the people of England were to give you instructions, I may venture to say ninety-nine in a hundred would be for attacking that island.'[2]

Vernon, like Drake before him, would have preferred to seize Havana, but in 1741 as in 1586 it was thought to be too well defended. Santiago, with its great fortifications at the harbour mouth, was difficult to attack directly, and Vernon initially looked elsewhere, sailing south towards Panama in 1740. He hoped to seize the isthmus, and to cut Spain's commercial lifeline to its Pacific territories. The two Spanish forts at Porto Bello were destroyed, and the victory made his name famous in England, but with too few soldiers available to establish a permanent base, he retreated to Jamaica.[3]

With his forces greatly reduced, Vernon turned his attention to Cuba, advancing on Guantánamo in July 1741, with a force of 8 warships and 40 transports, 4,000 soldiers, a troop of 1,000 blacks from Jamaica and 600 prospective settlers from the North American colonies.[4] His immediate plan was to land in the bay, and to advance to Santiago by land. Later he hoped to drive on to Havana – to capture the entire island and prepare it for British settlement, as had happened with Jamaica a century earlier.

Landing at Guantánamo, he re-named it Cumberland Bay, after the second son of the British king. 'I think this spot the best chosen for a British settlement of any in this island,' he wrote, 'and am glad to find the Americans begin to look on it as the Land of Promise already.'[5] On paper, Vernon's strategic plan looked promising, but General Thomas Wentworth, the commander of the British land army, was reluctant to advance – and the Spaniards were more than prepared for him. Wentworth had the larger force, but the Spaniards were more familiar with the terrain. A small Cuban guerrilla group, made up of whites and blacks, Indians and mulattoes, prevented the British from advancing along the track to Santiago.

Cooped up in the unfriendly bay, unable to forage for food, and with his men falling sick from yellow fever, Vernon was obliged to withdraw at the end of the year, and he sailed back to Jamaica. Later, in 1748, the British tried a frontal assault on Santiago's harbour fortifications, with a comparable lack of success. The European quarrel between Britain, Spain and France was patched up that year, and for a brief moment Cuba appeared safe from further British attack.

Havana falls to the Earl of Albemarle, 1762

Peace in Europe lasted for less than a decade. France and Britain were again at war in 1754. The conflict in the years between 1754 and 1763, familiar to Americans as 'the French and Indian War' and to Europeans as 'the Seven Years' War', was the first 'world war' of modern times, spreading out from Europe to the Caribbean and embracing both India and North America. Cuba was inevitably affected, although the island itself was not touched in the early years of the war. Spain initially remained neutral, allowing France and Britain to settle their quarrels in distant continents on their own.

When war came to the Spanish Caribbean, the result was disastrous for Cuba, which suffered its most humiliating defeat since the sack of Havana by Jacques de Sores two centuries earlier. Spain mistakenly joined forces with the French in 1761, after France had already lost its possessions in Canada and India. Pitching Spain into the balance against Britain was a last desperate, and unsuccessful, throw by the French. Cuba was dragged into a European conflict in which it had little interest. The British had coveted the island since Vernon's expedition, and a fresh British armada was sent to Havana under Admiral Sir George Pocock. The overall commander was George Keppel, the third Earl of Albemarle. Some 50 ships with 4,000 soldiers sailed from Portsmouth in 1762, picking up supplies in Barbados and major reinforcements in Jamaica.

Havana was well defended against attack from the sea. Philip II's engineers and their successors had done their job well. Albemarle took a leaf from Vernon's book and decided to attack by land. Some of Pocock's ships were left to hover off Havana, to give the impression of an imminent attack, while Albemarle put a substantial force ashore in early June at Cojímar, to the east of Havana.[6] His small army advanced on Havana by land, brushing aside the resistance of blacks and Indians led by the local cacique of Guanabacoa. In mid-August, after a 40-day siege, Havana surrendered. The Spanish captain-general sailed away, and Albemarle assumed his role. The British attack, the largest military operation ever launched against Cuba by a foreign power, involved some 14,000 British troops, nearly 300 of whom were killed.[7]

The British occupation of Havana, and a small slice of Cuba's northern coastline from Mariel to Matanzas, lasted for just ten months. The Treaty of Paris, signed in February 1763, marked the formal end to the Seven Years' War, and recognised the French and Spanish defeat. New dispositions were made in the New World. The British agreed to withdraw from Cuba, securing Spain's North American territory of Florida instead, thus enabling them to consolidate their existing empire on the mainland. The Earl of Albemarle handed Havana back to a new captain-general from Spain.

The brief British occupation is often perceived by historians as the moment when Cuba entered the modern age, opening the port of Havana to foreign commerce in a spectacular and unprecedented fashion – a thousand ships unloaded their cargo that year, cargo that included 10,000 slaves. More significant than Britain's brief rule was the opening of Cuba to its possessions in North America. American merchants now established themselves legally in Havana, and Cuban traders headed off to North American ports. These contacts survived the British departure and were revived and strengthened when the American Revolution exploded in 1776. Havana became an important meeting-place for war fleets sailing to the mainland.

Yet nothing stable emerged from this opportunistic relationship between the island and North America. When the Thirteen Colonies were finally free of British rule in the 1780s, Spain reimposed many of its earlier controls over Cuba's foreign trade. The nascent United States turned its attention away from Cuba to begin trading with the wealthy French colony of Saint-Domingue. The sugar, molasses, cocoa and coffee that the Americans had once briefly bought from Cuba were now purchased from the French. Only when revolution broke out in Saint-Domingue in 1791 did Cuba again become a favoured trading partner of the United States.

Spain's fresh interest in Cuba, 1763–1791

While the British occupation of Havana may have provided a kick-start to Cuba's economic development, the real change occurred after the island's return to Spain. Cuba began to benefit from the 'enlightened despotism' of Charles III, ruler in Madrid from 1759 to 1788. The brief loss of Cuba, and the potential threat to other Spanish holdings in the Americas, brought a new earnestness to Spanish politics. Under Charles III, and his capable minister the Conde de Campomanes, reform became the order of the day – reforms that affected the Church, education, taxation and the land tenure system. New maps were drawn, new roads constructed and agricultural improvement encouraged. Local initiatives were applauded – to be described centuries later as 'decentralisation'. In different towns throughout Spain more than 70 Sociedades de Amigos del País (friends of the country) were founded, government-supported institutions of local notables who met together to promote economic and social research, local educational initiatives and technological innovation.

News of these metropolitan reforms spread to Spain's colonies and, for the first time in centuries, Madrid began to take a fresh and intelligent interest in its colonial empire. Scientific expeditions were sent out to explore its obscurer regions, and to make a note of future economic possibilities. These Spanish winds of change soon blew over Cuba, and a new generation of enlightened landowners, planters and entrepreneurs came together in Havana to discuss economic development and to promote the new ideas coming from Europe.

The conduit for this debate was Luís de las Casas y Aragorri, the captain-general throughout the 1790s. With close connections to the island's sugar barons, he gathered a group of reformist landlords and lawyers around him, of whom the most prominent was Francisco de Arango y Parreño. A Sociedad Económica de Amigos del País was formed in Havana in 1793, on the Spanish model, its membership including the 27 most powerful sugar magnates. The word 'económica' was added to disavow any political purpose. It soon spawned a Consulado Real de Agricultura, Industria y Comercio in 1794, and a daily newspaper, the *Papel Periódico*. In the absence of anything resembling a colonial parliament, these institutions allowed the Cuban elite to feel that they had some input into the way the country was run, and gave the captain-general some useful insights into what was an embryonic public opinion (albeit formed only by the white elite).

Cuba's Sociedad Económica was chiefly concerned with stockraising, sugar and tobacco, the principal preoccupations of its members, but it also gathered existing research on mining, commerce and industry and brought it to the attention of interested parties. It took a particular interest in technological advances in sugar and tobacco production, but it also promoted research into chemistry, botany and mathematics (and translated books dealing with these topics into Spanish). Its wider interests included education and inland transport.[8] For a small Caribbean island, this extensive intellectual activity was no mean achievement. The Sociedad was, in effect, the vehicle that brought the European Enlightenment to Cuba.

Arango, a rich young Cuban planter, was the leading figure in these initiatives. He applied new scientific techniques to the sugar industry, and brought steam power from England. He also set up the Junta de Fomento, a branch of the Sociedad Económica that acted effectively as a ministry of development, a forerunner of the state-sponsored planning institutions popular in Latin America in the twentieth century. Arango befriended Baron Alexander von Humboldt, the German economist and naturalist, who visited Cuba in 1800 and 1804, and wrote a seminal text on the island's economy that reintroduced the Europeans (and later the Americans) to its economic potential. Much of his work derived from discussions with Arango.[9]

Arango was a champion of free trade and played an important role over a long life in persuading the Spanish monarch of its benefits to the island. A proto-nationalist with modernist enthusiasms, balanced by a strong sense of conservatism and hierarchy, Arango was a precursor of later prominent Cubans, men with similar interests and preoccupations for whom the island must always have seemed too small.

The slave rebellion in Saint-Domingue, 1791

The alarms and excursions caused by the extension of European wars to the Caribbean in the eighteenth century had their familiar impact on Cuba, but the island's history was to be more profoundly affected by a slave rebellion in its nearest neighbour. A successful slave revolt in August 1791 in Saint-Domingue (later to be renamed Haiti), the richest European colony in the Caribbean at that time, led to the arrival in Cuba of thousands of entrepreneurial French refugees. Their settlement gave added impetus to the agricultural revolution that was to provide the island with a century of ever-expanding wealth.

The western half of Saint-Domingue (originally known to the Spanish as Hispaniola) lay just 60 miles from Cuba. The peoples of the two islands were linked closely by their common Indian and Spanish ancestry, and while the eastern portion of Hispaniola (and the city of Santo Domingo) had remained in Spanish hands since the time of Columbus, the western section had been seized from the Spanish by French buccaneers in the middle of the seventeenth century. French ownership was formally recognised by the Treaty of Ryswick in 1697. Confusingly, the French called their end of the island 'Saint-Domingue'.

The rebellion of 1791, in which 500,000 black slaves took up arms against their white owners, brought the threat of 'Revolution' – the subversive message from Paris after 1789 – to Cuba's doorstep. Saint-Domingue had been transformed in the course of the eighteenth century into a treasure island for the French settlers, who imported slaves to work on their plantations of sugar and coffee, cotton and indigo. Immense wealth was generated, both for France and for the estate owners. Some 800 plantations produced an average of 71,000 tons of sugar a year, and nearly 3,000 coffee farms produced more than 30,000 tons of coffee, more than 60 per cent of the world's supply at that time.[10] The eastern, Spanish half of the island remained virtually undeveloped in this period, with a population of barely 125,000.

Yet the economy and society of Saint-Domingue was seriously flawed. The French colony had a population of more than half a million in the 1780s, of which 90 per cent were slaves. There were just 40,000 whites and 20,000 free mulattoes. Since the balance of forces was tipped so dramatically in favour of the blacks, a successful slave revolt had long been a possibility and it was further encouraged by the revolution in France of 1789. The slave uprising was brief and brutal. Stories of rape and massacre lost nothing in the telling, reverberating around the Caribbean for more than a century. It was followed by revolution and civil war, and by foreign intervention – bringing yet more death and destruction. Yet by later standards, the death toll was not especially high – perhaps 10,000 black slaves killed and 2,000 whites. Slave deaths would usually pass unnoticed, but the unexpected massacre of the whites appeared notably shocking at the time. The cause of the rebellion's success was held to be the gross disproportion of the races in Saint-Domingue, and this simple belief created an immediate and widespread fear among whites in Cuba and elsewhere in the Caribbean that something similar might happen to them and to the tiny white populations of other islands.

The first refugees arrived in Cuba in 1793, congregating chiefly in Havana with the expectation that they would soon return home. When the entire island of Hispaniola fell to the black rebels in 1795, including the Spanish end and the city of Santo Domingo, the migration of settlers accelerated. In 1798, when a British intervention force that had tried to crush the black revolution was obliged to withdraw, the tide of refugees became a flood. Many settled in Santiago and in the surrounding countryside of eastern Cuba. A larger migration came in 1803, when Europe was again at war, and when Napoleon's attempt to re-establish French (and white) rule in Saint-Domingue ended in disaster for France. All told, some 30,000 French refugees came to Cuba in the decade after 1791. These were the 'boat people' of their time, a foretaste of the mass migrations that would take place in later centuries.

Glad to be alive, the French migrants gave a lead to the lethargic Spanish settlers, and French-style coffee plantations sprang up in the foothills of the Sierra Maestra and around Guantánamo. They came with their capital and labour, their agricultural expertise, their familiarity with foreign trade and external markets and their capacity for hard work. One French visitor described how the new settlers brought 'the remnants of their wealth, some slaves, but especially their knowledge, their experience, and their activity. From that moment the two great Antilles changed roles: San Domingo lapsed into barbarism, Cuba placed her foot in the chariot of fortune.'[11] Other newcomers arrived at the start of the nineteenth century. Thousands of impoverished Spanish settlers came from the eastern end of Hispaniola, and from the vast (formerly Spanish) territory of Louisiana that Napoleon sold to the Americans.[12]

With this injection of migrant energy, Cuba changed from an under-developed settlement of small towns, cattle ranches and tobacco farms, into what would later be described as 'agribusiness' – large, semi-industrial plantations of sugar and coffee, characterised by the use of slave labour on a hitherto unimaginable scale. The new settlers helped to drag 'Cuban agriculture out of the sixteenth century and into the nineteenth century', in the words of one historian, and they did so in just a few decades.[13]

This was to be the most prosperous century in the island's history. Cuba was still a land of cattle and tobacco in the 1820s, but sugar and coffee were becoming a substantial – and soon to be dominant – sector of the economy. Three thousand cattle ranches and 5,000 tobacco farms were still flourishing in 1827, but they had been joined by 1,000 sugar mills and 2,000 coffee haciendas. Cotton (76 farms) and cocoa (66 plantations) were further down the list. Yet something of old Cuba still survived. While workers engaged in these new agricultural developments were producing for the market, at home and abroad, a substantial proportion of the rural population remained as simple subsistence farmers, a way of life unchanged since the days of Diego Velásquez.[14]

The development of the sugar industry was to have a significant impact on the politics and culture of the island, since it led to a huge increase in Cuba's slave population. This in turn helped to fuel the growth of the island's white racism, reinforced by the migrants from Santo Domingo and Louisiana. The image of the Haitian revolution, and the inflated memory of its excesses – echoed not just in Cuba, but in the United States and Latin America as well – was to hover over Cuba throughout the nineteenth century and beyond, a permanent intimation of what might happen to the white population if faulty political or administrative decisions were made. Many whites in Cuba felt that they lived permanently in the shadow of a slave rebellion on the Haitian model. They were not altogether wrong, for many Cuban blacks found inspiration in the Haitian example.

The sharp increase in the slave population, 1763–1841

Cuba's blacks were quite capable of waving the Haitian banner, and the prospect of establishing a black republic was attractive to many of them. The arithmetic was going their way.[15] Almost 100,000 African slaves arrived in the colony in the 30 years after 1762, more than in the whole of the previous three centuries. In the 250 years between 1511 and 1762 some 60,000 African slaves had been landed, at an average rate of only 240 a year. With the expansion of the sugar industry in the late eighteenth century the figures jumped dramatically, with slave landings averaging 3,300 a year.

The slave population reached 85,000 in 1791, and it doubled over the next 25 years, to 199,000 in 1817. Ten years later, in 1827, it had increased by almost half, to 287,000. There were more slave imports in the 1830s than in any earlier decade, and by 1841, 436,000 slaves lived on the island – nearly 45 per cent of the one million population.

The total number of blacks, of course, was much larger, for not all blacks on the island were slaves. In Spain itself the authorities had allowed slave-

owners to grant freedom to their slaves, and this policy had been extended to
Cuba. Compared with other islands of the Caribbean (and the states of North
America), Cuba had far more free blacks. In the first part of the nineteenth
century the number of former slaves and their progeny – the 'free people of
colour' – had almost trebled (from 54,000 in 1792 to 153,000 in 1841). The
census of 1841 would reveal what had long been suspected – that the slaves and
the 'free people of colour' formed a substantial and verifiable majority (58 per
cent). [16]

The white settler population did not hide its alarm at the news. Yet in
reality the blacks had probably outnumbered the whites since the start of the
seventeenth century, and perhaps even earlier, and the predominance of blacks
was to continue until well into the middle of the nineteenth century. The 1841
census merely gave an official stamp to the figures. What frightened the whites
was the existing capacity of the blacks to organise themselves.

Although the treatment of recalcitrant black slaves had always been harsh,
the Spanish (and Portuguese) colonial system had certain peculiarities, in both
Cuba and Brazil, that were unusual in the Americas. These were in some sense
beneficial to black people, since blacks were not categorised simply as 'blacks'
or 'Africans', but were allowed to take pride in their particular ancestry. They
always knew from which part of Africa they had come. The white settlers,
adopting a Spanish tradition, belonged to *cabildos* (later referred to as
'fraternal societies') that were organised on the basis of their place of origin in
Spain. The blacks, certainly since the late sixteenth century, were allowed to
do the same, grouping themselves together, both slave and free, in *cabildos*
modelled on the societies of the whites.

The Spanish considered this to be a benevolent form of social organisation
that would help the different tribes of Africans to adjust to the special circumstances of Cuba, while retaining something of their local customs. Bishop
Pedro Agustín Morell de Santa Cruz, bishop of Havana in the middle of the
eighteenth century, was so impressed by the attachment of the blacks to their
African *cabildos* that he granted them the Church's official recognition in 1755,
hoping in this way to facilitate and speed up their religious instruction. [17]

The black *cabildos* of slaves and 'free coloureds' were formed along tribal or
ethnic lines. Slaves were differentiated by their white owners according to
their place of origin, with a variety of different names that identified distinct
ethnicities from along the African coast – Mandinga, Gangá, Mina, Lucumí,
Carabalí, Congo, Macua and several others. These were usually corruptions of
the original African tribal names devised by the slave-owners, but they were
soon used by the slaves themselves. [18]

The Mandingas and Gangás came from the region of Sierra Leone, known
there as the Malinkes; the Minas came from the Gold Coast (now Ghana),
where they were called the Akans. Two groups came from what is today
Nigeria: the Lucumís were the Yoruban-speaking peoples from Benin, while

the Carabalís were people from Biafra, otherwise known as the Ibos and the Efiks. The Macuas came from the eastern side of Africa, and were kin to the Makwas of Mozambique.[19] Slaves from Angola who arrived at the end of the sixteenth century were called 'Congos', after the river running through the territory where they had once been collected by Portuguese slavers. Nearly four hundred years later, some of their descendants were to fight in defence of their former homeland in Castro's armies.

The white settlers labelled each ethnic group with certain temperaments, often inconsistently, according to Robert Paquette.

> The prevailing prejudices around 1840 seemed to be that the Mandingas and Gangas were the 'most tractable and trustworthy'; the Lucumís were 'quick-tempered, warlike, cunning,' but 'hard-working'; the Minas and Carabalís resembled the Lucumís; the Congos were 'stupid, great drunkards, and sensualists'; and the Macuas were 'brutal as the Congos.'[20]

Although the blacks were tightly controlled by the state, their lives in the early years of colonial rule were not affected by the kind of social discrimination that became common in later centuries. There was little personal or social prejudice against them and free blacks went to church or walked through the town on equal terms with whites. They were also allowed to carry arms and were enrolled in the Batallón de Pardos y Morenos, Havana's black militia.[21] It was not until the nineteenth century that treatment of them became less friendly, notably after the whites grew fearful of a repeat of Saint-Domingue.

The first zephyrs of independence, 1795–1824

The new Cuban society emerging at the start of the nineteenth century was not immune to the ideas spreading from the European Enlightenment nor to the notions of independence from Spanish rule that were soon to be successful on the Latin American mainland. Cuba experienced several early anti-Spanish rebellions. Black rebels from among the 'free people of colour', rather than from the white aristocratic elite that would spearhead the liberation struggle on the mainland, were the first to organise in Cuba, in conscious imitation of the example of Haiti.

Nicolás Morales, a 56-year-old free man from Bayamo, described as 'pitch black in colour', began organising as early as 1795. His group sought to unite black and white, and his supporters included a handful of whites. His programme was to abolish taxes 'that oppressed the poor'; to distribute land to the poor 'since the rich had all of it'; and to send priests 'back to their convents'. Betrayed before time, and posing no serious threat to the state, Morales and his fellow rebels were imprisoned. The mulatto militiaman who had betrayed them was rewarded with 200 acres of land.[22]

A more serious attempt at independence was pioneered in 1810, at a time when the Spanish state was weakened by Napoleon's invasion of Spain. A number of 'free people of colour' enrolled in the black militia joined a white independence movement led by two conservative aristocrats and a wealthy white officer, all of them masons.[23] They sought independence but had no plans to change the island's social structure. According to their proposed constitution, the slaves would remain as slaves, and whites would continue to rule. The first political movement in Cuba to evoke the Indian past, they devised a flag with the figure of an Indian woman, entwined with a tobacco leaf. They called themselves *indios* or *yukuinos*, perceiving Cuba as an extension of the Yucatán. The figure of Hatuey, the sixteenth-century cacique, was recovered from oral memory and exalted as 'the first victim of the Spaniards'.[24]

The involvement in the rebellion of members of the black militia served to mobilise Havana's white population against it, creating for the first time a phenomenon that would reappear throughout the century and become a key element in Spanish control of the island. A white volunteer militia manned by young men from the families of recent immigrants was created to assist the colonial authorities. A French visitor described the militia simply as 'honest men of Havana' who had come together in battalions 'from the same Spanish province'.[25] Loyalty to the specific regions of Spain from which the settlers came had been encouraged by the white *cabildos* from the earliest century of settlement, and the emotional pull thus fostered inspired the *voluntarios* and reinforced their passionate support for the motherland. Conservative in their political attitudes, and racist in tone, they became an essential bulwark of the Spanish state.

The rebellion of 1810 was crushed by these 'empire loyalists' – assisted by some of the new French migrants from Saint-Domingue and with the active leadership of the captain-general, Salvador José de Muro Salazar, the Marqués de Someruelos. An effective ruler, described as 'a good politician and a good organiser', Someruelos came out onto the streets of Havana in person to defeat the rebels. The white leaders were sentenced to ten years in prison, with subsequent banishment outside the Americas, while two black slaves involved received 200 lashes and a prison sentence of eight years, chained with shackles.

A fresh rebellion in 1812 again evoked the example of Haiti. This was not a slave revolt but the island's first country-wide black revolt aimed at independence, a political movement organised by 'free people of colour'. José Antonio Aponte, its leader, was a skilled black woodworker in Havana, by ethnic origin a Lucumí, a Yoruba-speaker from the Bight of Benin.[26] A former commander of the Havana black militia, and a man of some stature in his community, he was the head of his local Yoruba *cabildo*. He made his living through the production of religious imagery, carving sculptures incorporating Christian and African elements.

Like many of Cuba's free blacks, Aponte was well informed about the politics of the outside world, notably about events in Saint-Domingue. His personal heroes – to judge from the pictures found on the walls of his house – were the Haitian leaders Toussaint l'Ouverture and Henri Christophe. (He also possessed a portrait of George Washington.) Copies of the Haitian declaration of independence of 1804 were found in his home, as well as letters written by Christophe.[27]

Oppressed peoples have always had their own intelligence and communication networks, suggests Robert Paquette, and blacks in nineteenth-century Cuba were no exception.

Slaves and free coloureds walked the docks of Cuba's port towns; they hawked news and goods with peddlers and foreign smugglers; they picked up white table talk and passed it to more worldly comrades on Sundays, festival days, and in the Afro-Cuban *cabildos*; they overheard conversations among the whites; they mixed with the thousands of slaves who had emigrated with their French masters from Saint-Domingue; and they heard the messages from the drums.[28]

Aponte was just such a recipient of foreign intelligence. Cuba's blacks had been alerted to news of the meeting of the Spanish Cortes assembled in Cadiz in 1812, a near-revolutionary assembly with representatives from the colonies present. An end to the slave trade was under discussion, and even the abolition of slavery itself. News of these debates soon reached Havana, and some slaves were led to believe that the Spanish authorities had decreed an end to slavery.[29]

The moment seemed right for an anti-Spanish insurrection of the kind taking place elsewhere in Latin America. If Cuba's slaves were to join in, Aponte's rebellion would surely have a good chance of success. Several black *cabildos* were mobilised and secret meetings were held in Havana and some provincial towns. The rebellion's stated purpose was 'to abolish slavery and the slave trade, and to overthrow colonial tyranny, and to substitute the corrupt and feudal regime with another, Cuban in nature, and without odious discriminations'.[30] There was an international dimension, too. Friendly groups of abolitionists in the United States and Brazil were informed of the impending rebellion, as well as those in Haiti.[31]

In Puerto Príncipe (Camagüey) and in Oriente, the rebels were poised for action – free people of colour as well as slaves and whites. The conspiracy was supported by men in many different trades – shoe-makers and carpenters, saddle makers and charcoal burners, bellringers and ox-cart drivers.[32] Aponte's plan was to seize power in Havana when Spanish troops had been drained off from the capital to deal with these local revolts.

Liberal historians have tended to portray Aponte as a forerunner of the independence struggle later in the century, yet he was more probably a black nationalist in the Haitian mould. Hilario Herrera, Aponte's principal lieutenant in Oriente, was a veteran of the revolution in Saint-Domingue, and another of that gallery of Cuban heroes – from Hatuey and Caguax to Máximo Gómez – who came from the nearby island.

As usual, it was difficult to keep plans secret. The conspiracy in Puerto Príncipe was betrayed to the authorities, and, although slave revolts went ahead on a handful of sugar estates around Havana, the security services of the Marqués de Someruelos were soon in action throughout the island. Herrera escaped to Haiti, but Aponte was detained in Havana. With five other 'free men of colour', and three slaves, he was sentenced to hang. Someruelos gave orders for their severed heads to be exhibited 'in the most convenient public places as a warning to others', and Aponte's was displayed in an iron cage at the entrance to the city. The fierce repression effectively put a stop to further rebellions for more than a decade, but the memory of Aponte's conspiracy was celebrated within the black community for many years.

The independence struggle was resumed in the 1820s by dissident whites who were influenced by the success on the mainland of Simón Bolívar. The great Venezuelan liberator had advanced through Colombia, Ecuador, Peru and Bolivia, and forced Spain's armies to withdraw. José Francisco Lemus, once an officer in Bolívar's army in Colombia, led the Cuban section of Bolívar's movement, called the Soles y Rayos de Bolívar.[33] Like the earlier conspiracy of 1810, the supporters of the Soles y Rayos de Bolívar also invoked Cuba's pre-Columbian past, calling for the creation of a new and independent state to be known as Cubanacán – one of the Indian names for Cuba. Their conspiracy was given added impetus by events in Spain, where a successful counter-revolution in April 1823 was expected to lead to a clampdown in Cuba. The conspirators planned for an invasion by a 'Bolivarian' force of 3,000 men, ready and waiting in Puerto Cabello in Venezuela, that would coincide with an uprising in Cuba itself.[34] The Spanish authorities were too quick for the conspirators, and the plot was uncovered before they were ready. The invasion from Venezuela never materialised.[35] Lemus and his colleagues were arrested and sent into exile.

Among those caught up in the repression that followed was Felix Varela, a professor of philosophy at the San Carlos seminary. An influential cleric and a man ahead of his time, Varela was both a supporter of Latin American independence and an advocate of the abolition of slavery. He had already taken this then unpopular position when a member of the Cuban delegation to the Cortes in Madrid in 1820. He was obliged to go into exile after the Soles y Rayos conspiracy, first to Spain and then to the United States, where he was a frequent contributor to exile journals. From there, he helped to educate the next generation of Cuban intellectuals, not all as illuminated as he. His memory has often been evoked across Cuba's political spectrum as the model of an admirable and progressive citizen.

So what made Cuba so different from the rest of Spanish America? Signs of political discontent were not lacking. The ideas of the Enlightenment, the spread of freemasonry, the memory of the American Revolution, the impact of the French Revolution and the wars of Napoleon and the shock of the black revolution in Saint-Domingue – all had a notable impact on Cuba. Many educated Cubans, both white and black, felt themselves to be part of a wider world in a state of flux, and began charting new paths for the island's future, yet their efforts were in vain. There were occasional slave rebellions and revolts by 'free men of colour', but none achieved the critical mass secured by the black rebels in Haiti.

Support for Cuban independence might in theory have come from the small settler armies proclaiming independence on the Latin American mainland. Yet Bolívar himself expressed little interest in extending his military campaigns northwards to Cuba. Only after the final defeat of Spain's continental armies, at Ayacucho in Peru in December 1824, did he make tentative plans to send troops to Havana. He often reflected on his reluctance to extend the struggle to the Caribbean, and wrote in one of his many letters that it was 'more important to have peace than to liberate these islands. An independent Cuba would take us a great deal of work.' Even Bolívar was not immune to the belief that a liberated Cuba might become 'another Republic of Haiti'.[36]

The ubiquity of the security services was also a factor, ensuring that most conspiracies were uncovered within weeks, and often crushed before they could get off the ground. Failing to mobilise any substantial or influential portion of the population, none of them posed a serious threat to continuing Spanish control.

Although a handful of progressive individuals favoured independence from Spain, Cuba's economic elite was conservative, fearful of the economic and social consequences of a break with the colonial motherland. Without Spanish support, the planters would not be able to sustain the slave system on which their economic power was based, nor would they be strong enough to crush slave revolts. Their reluctance to rebel was also the result of fresh economic policies pursued by the Spanish authorities. Spain finally liberated the island's trade, abolished the controversial tobacco monopoly and allowed prominent Cubans to hold positions of influence in the direction of the island's economic affairs. This, coupled with the wealth generated in the wake of the Haitian collapse, ensured that few were tempted to take the South American route to liberation.

Powerful voices advocate white immigration

The Spanish authorities believed their secret weapon in curbing the separatist ambitions of the white settlers was the existing preponderance of blacks. 'The fear of the Negroes,' said a Spanish minister in the 1830s, 'is worth an army of 100,000 men.' This was the Spanish trump card that would 'prevent the whites from making any attempts at revolution'.[37] This was an accurate assessment, for even the white, independence-minded intellectuals emerging in the 1830s were not immune to the racist virus.

Central to Cuban history during the nineteenth century was the debate about race. Cuba's blacks were perceived as a threat to the white elite and to its imagined notion of the island's future community. Yet Cuba's future prosperity depended on the constant supply of black labour to work in the sugar plantations. How could the island continue to sustain this profitable industry and ensure the security of the whites at the same time? This was the obsessive concern of the elite over many decades, and numerous possibilities were under continuous review. Maybe the slave trade should be halted. Maybe the slaves should be better treated. Maybe more female slaves should be imported. Maybe policing should be improved. Maybe the free blacks should be expelled to prevent them making common cause with the slaves. Maybe white immigration should be encouraged, to make the black–white ratio more favourable to the whites.

The blacks themselves never had much of a public voice, although men like Aponte were inspired by the Haitian revolution. The vision of a black republic became less compelling in later years, when most blacks were content to envisage a society in which they would simply have equal rights with whites. They did not seek an exclusively black government, nor would this have been possible any longer, since by the 1860s the racial balance had swung towards the whites. Slave landings were less frequent, while white immigration proceeded apace.

The development of Saint-Domingue had once appeared exemplary, both to Madrid and Havana. Its slave economy was seen as the key to its economic success, and was noted as such by Cuba's Sociedad Económica in 1794:

Before the calamitous ruin of the Colony of Saint-Domingue, and before the horrible destruction and unheard-of crimes committed there by the Negroes were known, the first thing that came to mind when the development of our Island was discussed was the free and unlimited introduction of Negroes. This was the conclusion reached from the great prosperity enjoyed by that unfortunate Colony – prosperity which was due entirely to the multitude of slaves that cultivated its soil.[38]

Faced with the rebellion of 1791, the dream of slave-driven prosperity appeared more like a nightmare. Madrid believed that it would be only a matter of time before Cuba's slave population would explode in a similar way, and its initial reaction was to halt the slave trade to all its Caribbean islands. Yet the Cuban elite in the Sociedad Económica had other ideas. The powerful planters, desperate for labour, were just getting into their stride. Their visions of wealth from sugar, and the chance to seize the world markets of Saint-Domingue, depended on the unimpeded flow of African slaves.

Francisco Arango, their articulate spokesman, argued forcefully in favour of their unlimited import. Cuba was not like Saint-Domingue, he wrote. The whites in Cuba were not in a tiny minority; the island had almost as many whites as blacks. There was no immediate cause for alarm. If the state would encourage white immigration, the blacks could be kept under control. Arango produced an immigration scheme designed to break up the large concentrations of blacks in the countryside through the construction of villages for white immigrants. These, he wrote, 'if located in convenient places, would be a powerful check on the seditious ideas of rural slaves'.[39]

Arango looked for allies within the Sociedad Económica to further his proposals. The society emphasised the importance of continuing the slave trade. Control rather than abolition was its slogan: 'It is necessary to proceed carefully – with the census figures in hand – in order that the number of Negroes may not only be prevented from exceeding that of the whites, but that it may not be permitted to equal that number.'[40] This was the racist arithmetic that would dominate the island over the next century and beyond.

Arango's idea for rural villages replete with white settlers was well-received by Luis de las Casas, the captain-general in the 1790s. Slave imports and white immigration would go together, and Las Casas made plans to establish new towns in unpopulated regions.[41]

Little progress was made during the chaotic period of the Napoleonic wars, and the cause of white immigration was not taken up again until 1815. A new captain-general, José Cienfuegos, and his enthusiastic treasurer, Alejandro Ramírez, established a fresh organisation in 1817, the Junta de Población Blanca. The Madrid government assisted white immigration with land grants and tax relief, and the programme was made financially possible by a special tax of six pesos on the import of all male slaves, payable to the Junta de Población Blanca.[42] Since some 56,000 slaves were landed at Havana between 1818 and 1821, the money to finance white immigration was not lacking.

Arango's dream of encouraging white immigration was soon under way. A new settlement was located at Cienfuegos, at the head of the great bay of Jaragua, named in honour of the captain-general.[43] A contract for recruiting settlers was granted to Colonel Louis de Clouet, a monarchist refugee from Louisiana, and by 1823, 845 settlers had arrived at Cienfuegos, from Philadelphia, Baltimore and New Orleans. Other white colonies, with varying fortunes, were established at Santo Domingo, to the west of Santa Clara; at Mariel, west of Havana; at Guantánamo; and at Nuevitas in Camagüey. Although these colonisation projects were designed to combat the population's ethnic imbalance, the government had additional motives in uncertain times. Colonisation in hitherto desolate areas, planting Spanish migrants of unquestioned loyalty, would help to ward off subversive independence movements.[44]

The work of those who hoped to see a 'white Cuba' was carried on in the 1830s by a group of intellectuals associated with José Antonio Saco, a prolific journalist, debater and agitator. Saco was the editor of the *Revista Bimestre*, an offshoot of the Sociedad Económica.[45] His contributors were an elite group that followed in Arango's footsteps – interested in education, political autonomy and the ideas of the French Physiocrats. They had moved a step beyond Arango, holding no brief for the government in Spain, but they did not advocate independence. They were the first generation of Cuban intellectuals with a utopian and romantic vision of 'Cuba' as an entity separate from Spain. As such, they were permanently in conflict with the *peninsulares*, the more recent immigrants from Spain and the Canary Islands (and from continental Latin America), who gave thanks for Cuba's Hispanic heritage.

Saco wrote extensively on different aspects of Cuban society, and was a severe critic of the idiocies and stupidities of colonial government. The flaw in his vision and that of his friends was a virulent dislike of the fact that Cuba was largely peopled by blacks. One member of his group, Gaspar Betancourt Cisneros, a planter from Puerto Príncipe who wrote under the name El Lugareño, argued in favour of peopling Cuba with 'superior beings'. These he defined as Germans and Saxons.[46]

Saco had racist views powerfully expressed. His proto-nationalism saw no future for the blacks on the island. 'The Cuban nationality of which I have spoken, and the only one that should concern all sensible men, is that formed by the white race.'[47] He took up Arango's campaign, arguing that 'upon white immigration depend agricultural improvement, the perfection of the arts, in one word, the prosperity of Cuba in every sphere; and the steadfast hope that the crumbling edifice which now threatens us, will be restored confidently on a solid and indestructible base.'

Saco warned of a new threat when slaves gained their freedom in the British Caribbean in the 1830s. If more white settlers did not arrive soon, the blacks of Jamaica and Haiti might make common cause with the blacks in Cuba:

> The colonisation of Cuba is necessary and urgently required to give to the white population of Cuba a moral and necessary preponderance over its black inhabitants . . . It is necessary to counter the ambitions of 1,200,000 Haitians and Jamaicans who seek her lovely beaches and unused lands; it is necessary to neutralise as far as possible the terrible influence of the three million blacks who surround us – the millions to come by natural increase – and who will drag us down in the near future in a bitter, bloody holocaust.[48]

Two solutions were on offer to deal with the perceived threat from the black population. One, advocated by successive captain-generals, was repression. The other, favoured by Saco and his friends, was annexation by the neighbouring slave-owning republic of the United States.

A new era of repression had already been inaugurated on the island in the wake of the Soles y Rayos conspiracy. Francisco Dionisio Vives was sent out to Havana as the captain-general, with orders to hold onto the island whatever the cost. He stayed for nearly ten years, establishing one of the longest and most repressive regimes of any Spanish ruler. In the crisis atmosphere brought about by the collapse of the Spanish empire in Latin America, a special military tribunal was created in Cuba in 1824 that aimed to crush those 'who promote disturbances that alter public tranquillity'. The Comisión Militar Executiva y Permanente placed the island under martial law for the next 50 years. It was designed to curb the political activity of whites, and to tightly control the free black population as well. Their social and recreational activities – often used to camouflage subversive movements – were kept under permanent surveillance. Festivals and dancing, as well as social and religious gatherings, now had to be registered and were often forbidden altogether.

Vives was particularly concerned by the possibility of the free blacks making common cause with the slaves, and he outlined his misgivings at the end of his long reign in 1832:

> The existence of free blacks and mulattoes in the middle of the enslavement of their comrades is an example that will be very prejudicial some day, if effective measures are not taken in order to prevent their [the slaves] constant and natural tendency toward emancipation, in which case they may attempt by themselves or with outside help to prevail over the white population.

His suggested solution was to expel the entire coloured population from the island, an idea often re-examined by later captain-generals.[49]

Vives's successor, General Miguel Tacón Rosique, had been a soldier in Spain's struggle to retain its colonies in Latin America, and he kept up the tradition of repression, ruling the island with little reference to the government in Spain. When Madrid ordered the abolition of the Comisión Militar, Tacón kept it going. When Madrid decreed that elections should be held in Spain in 1836, Tacón refused to allow them to take place in Cuba. When General Manuel Lorenzo, governor of Oriente, supported the progressive Spanish decrees, and proclaimed the radical constitution of 1812 – an attempt to set up a pro-slavery but 'democratic' government under Spanish control – Tacón sent troops to Santiago to crush him. Tacón kept the island under lock and key.

This repression turned Cuba's intellectuals against Spain, and many began to think seriously about alternatives: independence or annexation to the United States. One of the first to suffer under Tacón was Saco, sentenced to internal exile in 1834 on the grounds of the 'great influence that he had on the youth of Havana'. He lived in Paris for many years, writing a history of slavery.

Always fearful that an independent Cuba would be dominated by blacks, he became an early advocate of US annexation.

Much political debate in Cuba during the nineteenth century was to centre on this possible relationship. Saco was a regretful supporter, writing in January 1837 that his 'chief desire' had always been 'for Cuba to exist for the Cubans', but he felt that 'this perhaps cannot be so, for this government is pushing us towards a revolution'. There would, he thought, 'be no other solution than to throw ourselves into the arms of the United States. This is the idea that we must now propagate and sow in the minds of all.'[50] If Cuba were to fall into foreign arms, he wrote, 'in none could she fall with more honour or glory than in those of the great North American Confederation. In them, she would find peace and consolation, strength and protection, justice and liberty.'[51] The eloquently expressed vision of Saco, stronger in the United States than in Cuba, has never quite disappeared from Cuba's political debate.

The seeds of US intervention, 1823–1851

The notion that Cuba might be taken over by the United States did not emerge from thin air. The possibility of annexing the island had been long discussed in the United States itself. Successive US administrations were alarmed at the thought that a black republic might emerge in Cuba, and were concerned by the possible repercussions on the slave-owning states of the American South. 'Other considerations connected with a certain class of our population', warned President Martin Van Buren in 1829, 'make it the interest of the Southern section of the Union that no attempt should be made in the island to throw off the yoke of Spanish dependence, the first effect of which would be the sudden emancipation of a numerous slave population, the result of which could not but be very sensibly felt upon the adjacent shores of the United States.'[52]

During the 1820s, as Spain was driven from the Latin American mainland, the United States moved purposefully to become an actor on the Cuban stage. The Americans had been interested in Cuba since 1776, and had occasionally discussed its future with other interested parties. Yet they had firmly remained as an observer of the Latin American independence wars. Then, rather suddenly, after their formal acquisition of Spanish Florida in 1821, they realised that Cuba had drawn ever closer to their frontiers. The earlier desultory discussions about the island's future became more serious.[53]

The question of who owned Cuba was now perceived as a matter of US national security. American vessels engaged in the coastal trade, sailing out of the Mississippi, inevitably passed through a channel between American Miami and Spanish Havana. With continuing Spanish control of Latin America now fading, Cuba was potentially under threat from the forces of

Bolívar – as well as from those of the ever-predatory British, the successors to Drake, Vernon and Albemarle.

American concerns were first articulated by John Quincy Adams, the secretary of state, who wished to ensure that Cuba (and Puerto Rico) did not fall under the control of any country other than Spain. He drafted the outline of a new American strategy in a letter of 23 April 1823 written to Hugh Nelson, the American minister in Madrid (see Appendix A):

These islands are natural appendages of the North American continent, and one of them – almost in sight of our shores – from a multitude of considerations has become an object of transcendent importance to the commercial and political interests of our Union.

Adams spelt out his personal belief that, if Spanish rule in Cuba were to come to an end, it must inevitably be replaced by that of the United States – a prophecy that would be fulfilled at the end of the century:

There are laws of political as well as of physical gravitation. And if an apple, severed by the tempest from its native tree, cannot choose but to fall to the ground, Cuba, forcibly disjoined from its own unnatural connection with Spain, and incapable of self-support, can gravitate only towards the North American Union, which, by the same law of nature, cannot cast her off from her bosom.[54]

Later that year, Thomas Jefferson, still an influential voice in American affairs, wrote to President James Monroe to discuss the possible acquisition of 'any one or more of the Spanish provinces'. His letter of October 1823 reflects the long-running ambiguity of the United States about whether Cuba should be annexed and taken over, or allowed to be independent:

I candidly confess, that I have ever looked on Cuba as the most interesting addition which could ever be made to our system of States. The control which, with Florida Point, this island would give us over the Gulf of Mexico, and the countries and isthmus bordering on it – as well as all those whose waters flow into it – would fill up the measure of our political well-being. Yet, as I am sensible that this can never be obtained, even with her own consent, but by war; and its independence, which is our second interest (and especially its independence of England), can be secured without it, I have no hesitation in abandoning my first wish to future chances, and accepting its independence – with peace and the friendship of England – rather than its association, at the expense of war and her enmity.

This attitude became enshrined in the so-called Monroe Doctrine, announced by President Monroe in a message to Congress on 2 December 1823. The Doctrine arose as a by-product of US negotiations with the Russian government in St Petersburg about the northwest coast of the American continent. The Americans had told the Russians, Monroe declared, that the European powers should keep out of the Americas. 'The occasion has been judged proper for asserting, as a principle in which the rights and interests of the United States are involved, that the American continents, by the free and independent condition which they have assumed and maintain, are hence-forth not to be considered as subjects for future colonisation by any European powers.' Monroe warned these powers that the US would consider 'any attempt on their part to extend their system to any portion of this hemisphere as dangerous to our peace and safety'.

The United States had put down markers in the 1820s regarding its interest in the future of Cuba, but the subject did not return to the surface until 20 years later. The American invasion of Mexico in the 1840s, and the annexation of half its territory in 1847, was to spark an unprecedented enthusiasm for imperial expansion. Thwarting this possibility in the Caribbean were the British, now furiously engaged in a campaign, not just against the slave trade, but against slavery itself. Cuba was one of the principal British targets.

Cuban slavery comes under British attack, 1817–1842

For much of the nineteenth century, the Cuban authorities – government, merchants and planters alike – were reluctant to abandon the slave trade. Slavery itself was also sacrosanct, a belief shared by planters in both the United States and Brazil. Slave-owners convinced themselves that Cuba's livelihood depended on the trade, and that their high standard of living could not long survive an end to the cheap labour provided by slaves, endlessly replenished by the Atlantic trade. Cuba had become the greatest slave-importing colony in the history of the Spanish empire, and more than 780,000 slaves were brought there between 1790 and 1867. With the British withdrawal from the trade after 1807, Cuba became the principal centre in the Caribbean of this 'odious commerce'.[55]

As the century progressed, Cuba became increasingly isolated in its support for the trade. The British had closed it down in their colonial empire in 1807 (although not the institution), and embarked on a crusade to halt it every-where. The United States stopped the trade in 1808, while the Spanish government, under pressure from London, was persuaded in 1817 to abolish its own colonial trade by 1820. There was now a Spanish signature on a treaty, but the Spaniards were in no condition to carry out what they were asked to do – even if they had wanted to (which they did not). Cuba's long coastline was never effectively controlled by the Spanish navy until after 1868, the famous *guarda-costas* of earlier centuries being just a memory. African slaves continued to pour into Cuba on an ever-increasing scale, to the dismay and irritation of the moralising British.

The Anglo-Spanish treaty of Madrid of 1817 created an early example of a regime of international inspection. The British navy, under its clauses, was granted the right to search Spanish ships suspected of slaving. If slaves were found on board, they (and the vessel) could be seized. Their fate was then decided by Anglo-Spanish tribunals set up on either side of the Atlantic, in Havana and in Freetown, the capital of Britain's African colony of Sierra Leone.

The slaves freed by the British navy would, if the tribunals so decreed, be handed over to the authorities in either of these two towns. In Cuba, the freed slaves, known as *emancipados*, would be 'prepared' for freedom, a process that might take up to five years – or in most cases for ever. In the meantime, they would notionally receive both wages and religious instruction. Few were actually set free. Of the 9,000 *emancipados* captured at sea between 1824 and 1836 and officially reckoned to be living in Cuba in 1841, only two per cent had obtained their freedom.[56]

The 1817 treaty was easy for the slavers to evade, notably by changing the flag under which they sailed, for the British navy was allowed to board only Spanish-registered ships. Most slavers trading to Havana in the 1820s were registered as Portuguese. It was also easy for Cuba's slave importers to bribe Spanish officials to turn a blind eye. Tacón was alleged to have retired in 1838 with 450,000 dollars of 'head-money', much of it secured in cahoots with the US consul in Havana.[57] Cuba's innumerable small ports and inlets welcomed the slavers, as once in earlier centuries they had provided shelter to pirates and buccaneers. An estimated 11,000 slaves (not to be confused with *emancipados*) arrived in Cuba each year between 1821 and 1836.[58]

The African trade continued regardless. Ships registered in the United States, which was also not party to the search agreements, continued to make the slave run to Cuba. The famous mutiny on board the Baltimore schooner *Amistad* in 1839, in which 53 newly imported slaves seized the ship while sailing along the coast from Havana, drew attention to this loophole.[59] The trade conducted by US-registered ships was not abandoned until two decades later, after Captain Nathaniel Gordon of the slave ship *Erie* had been publicly hanged in New York in February 1862 – the only North American to be executed for slave trading. Charged with shipping slaves to Cuba, he had been seized by a US naval ship off the African coast of Cabinda in August 1860, after collecting a cargo of 900 slaves from the Congo river.[60]

Eventually more threatening to Cuba's prosperity was the international campaign, led by the British, to end slavery itself. In the 1830s it was abolished in the British territories of the Caribbean, and Cuba came under pressure to follow suit. Britain's blockade against slave traders was tightened in 1835, after mutual search agreements had been made with other maritime powers (except the United States). A fresh Anglo-Spanish treaty, the Clarendon Convention, signed that year, allowed British rather than Cuban officials to take control of the *emancipados*, and gave Britain the right to transfer them to neighbouring British colonies. Dr Richard Madden, an ardent abolitionist, was sent out as the British consul in Havana with the title of 'Superintendent of Liberated Africans'. One of his tasks was to look into the fate of the *emancipados* held on the island since the treaty of 1817. Madden was an Irish doctor who had been working as a magistrate in Jamaica, where his pronounced anti-racist views, as slavery was phased out there after 1834, had not been appreciated by the local whites. His reputation had preceded him to Havana, and Tacón wrote in alarm to Madrid, describing him as a dangerous man. 'Living in this island he will have far too many opportunities to disseminate seditious ideas directly or indirectly, which not even my constant vigilance can prevent.'[61]

Madden was entitled under the treaty to receive the *emancipados* that were landed at Havana, and to send them on to the slave-free British territories of Jamaica, Trinidad or Belize. When Tacón refused to allow the trans-shipment, Madden chartered a British ship, the *Romney*, to provide the slaves with shelter. The *Romney* remained at anchor off the harbour, causing considerable anxiety in 1838 to Tacón's successor, Joaquín de Ezpeleta, since it was manned and officered by blacks from Britain's West Indies regiment. The proximity of free British blacks would obviously stir up Cuba's slave population, the new captain-general explained to Madrid. 'Just by their words and dress' Britain's black soldiers would 'arouse in those of their race [in Cuba] a strong desire for freedom at any cost and in defiance of all danger.'[62]

The firm British position, coupled with the brief emergence of a progressive government in Spain, and an outspoken statement from Pope Gregory XVI, had some initial effect on the Cuban attitude. The Pope issued a bull in 1839 condemning slave traders for treating slaves 'as if they were impure animals', and forbidding Catholics to engage in the trade. Those who did so would be excommunicated.[63] The captain-general refused to allow the bull to be published in Cuba, but the mood was already beginning to change. Gerónimo Valdés, captain-general from 1841 to 1843 (and another veteran of the Peruvian campaign of 1824), struck out vigorously against the trade and closed the Havana slave market to new arrivals.[64] In 1841, he ordered more than a thousand *emancipados* to be freed.[65] Yet in spite of an apparently firm hand at the top, slaves continued to arrive on a grand scale over the next 20 years. As many as 200,000 slaves may have been brought to Cuba between 1840 and 1860.[66]

Madden was replaced in 1840 by David Turnbull, another ardent campaigner against the slave trade. A prototype of the 'human rights journalist' of a later era, Turnbull had worked previously as a correspondent for *The Times* of London in Paris and Spain and had published an influential book, *Travels in the West*, describing a journey through the slave plantations of Cuba.[67] He told the World Anti-Slavery Convention in London in 1840, that the slave trade was 'the greatest practical evil that ever afflicted mankind'. His instructions from the British foreign secretary were to persuade the Cuban authorities to obey the treaties of 1817 and 1835 and to investigate the conditions of the *emancipados*.

Turnbull met many friends of Saco, who, although now in exile, still wielded considerable influence. He travelled through the island to check on the fate of the *emancipados* working on distant plantations. When he sought the freedom of an *emancipado* held in slave conditions for sixteen years, he aroused the anger of the captain-general. He was told that his intervention would have 'a very serious bearing on the political administration of the affairs of this island, because it supposes that you are qualified to listen to complaints and to offer protection to the people of colour, and to support their pretensions'. The captain-general feared that 'such a state of things might loosen the ties of subordination and obedience'.[68]

Turnbull also met many free men of colour, some of them community leaders who sought news about post-slavery developments in Jamaica. It was not part of his brief to engage in conspiracies with Afro-Cubans and white groups to secure an end to slavery, nor to promote the cause of independence, but the captain-general was right to be suspicious of his activities.[69] Turnbull was joined in his subversive conversations by Francis Ross Cocking, his assistant at the consulate and the Havana correspondent of *The Anti-Slavery Reporter*, the journal of the British and Foreign Anti-Slavery Society. An English accountant by training, Cocking had first arrived in Havana in 1839 and worked there as a merchant's bookkeeper. He spoke fluent Spanish, having previously lived for ten years in Venezuela where he had met his wife. According to his later account, he joined up in 1841 with a group of 'wealthy, talented and influential Cubans' to discuss independence and the end of slavery.[70] The group, which included both whites and free blacks, worked on a six-point manifesto, drafted by Pedro María Morilla. A version of it appeared in the *Anti-Slavery Reporter*.

1. Whites and free coloureds would cooperate to promote an independence movement.
2. A declaration of independence would be drafted to publicise and justify their movement.
3. Slaves who fought for independence would receive their freedom, and their owners would be compensated after independence.
4. Slaves who engaged in freelance rebellion against their owners would be considered guilty of treason.
5. Plans for slave freedom would be drafted in such a way as to ensure the safety of their owners.
6. An envoy would be sent to the British government to seek assistance in the establishment of a new society for 'all classes and colours of men'.

Turnbull was declared *persona non grata* by the captain-general before the ink was dry on the manifesto, and retreated to Jamaica, while Cocking was left in charge of the consulate for a few months.[71] He remained in Havana until Turnbull's replacement arrived in August 1842. His activities generated the belief among many Cubans that the British might well invade the island if the slave trade continued.[72] 'At this particular period,' he wrote in his 1846 account,

> if I had had a ten gun brig under my command, a few thousand stand of arms, and a mere handful of men to effect a landing, with those arms, at such a place as I could have pointed out, I should have been enabled to establish the independence of the island, and the consequent freedom of the slaves; for there were thousands and tens of thousands ready and prepared to flock, armed, to the place of disembarkation.[73]

Turnbull's replacement as consul, Joseph Crawford, was appointed by a new government in Britain that was less concerned with the anti-slavery campaign, and Cocking's employment was terminated. Turnbull, in Jamaica, encouraged him to join him there in, ostensibly to get a job in the new task of seeking migrant workers to replace the slaves on the Jamaican plantations – including people of colour from Cuba. In practice, Turnbull needed Cocking to help with the embryonic Cuban rebel movement he had been fostering. Cocking returned to Cuba in September, putting in to the south coast ports of Santiago, Manzanillo, Trinidad and Cienfuegos, to check on the state of revolutionary preparedness.

The spirit was higher there than in Havana, but Cocking was disappointed to find that most whites were still concerned about the impact on the island's prosperity of an end to slavery. He discovered that the United States, Britain's rival in the Caribbean, had also sent agents to the island to promote the idea of Cuban independence, but without giving freedom to the slaves. The idea had been making inroads among some of the whites with whom he had once had dealings.

The blacks were in a more positive mood, and he was pleased to discover that some members of his old Havana group had 'agents travelling all over the island'. They had 'raised a spirit of revolt which it was not easy to prevent from breaking out'.[74] Realising that a black uprising would be doomed to disaster without white support, Cocking did 'everything a man could do' to persuade the blacks that an uprising, 'unsupported as they then were by the wealth and power of the white natives', would be premature.

He left Cuba in May 1843 and sailed for England, where he attended the second World Anti-Slavery Convention in London as the Cuban expert of the Anti-Slavery Society, before retreating to Caracas to live with his wife's relations. It was there that he wrote his account of his part in the Cuban conspiracy. Some doubt has always existed about the veracity of Cocking's account, but as Robert Paquette points out, the later dispatches to London of Joseph Crawford 'prove beyond a shade of doubt that Creoles and Afro-Cubans were mulling schemes to overthrow the Spanish government and that Cocking had entangled himself in them'.[75] Crawford had told London in August 1842 of the existence of 'several' revolutionary cabals in Havana, 'all the particulars of which, I am told, have long been known to Mr Turnbull'. He wrote of his fears that Cocking too had been 'up to his neck in the revolutionary schemes of the Creoles'.

A variety of conspiracies were on offer to dissatisfied Cuban whites in the early 1840s. They could vote for emancipation and hope for British assistance, or they could choose to keep their slaves and join a US conspiracy, as some did ten years later with the expeditions from New Orleans of Narciso López. Before that could happen, the island was overwhelmed by a black explosion – and its subsequent fierce repression.

Black rebellion: the conspiracy of La Escalera, 1843–1844

Early one March morning in 1843, as watchmen were changing shifts at a sugar mill near Cárdenas, drums began beating out the rhythms of rebellion. Slaves at the sugar plantation attached to the Ingenio Alcancía embarked on a well-planned revolt, killing the mill's engineer and two other employees, and destroying many of its ancillary buildings. Later they moved on to neighbouring estates to recruit other slaves, and to enlist the support of workers on the newly built railway line, marching according to a contemporary account 'in military order, clad in their holiday clothes, with colours flying, and holding leathern shields'.[76]

This was the start of a rebellion, 'the conspiracy of La Escalera', that involved both slaves and 'free people of colour'. Cocking claimed in his own report, written in Caracas in 1846, that the Cárdenas revolt was the work of one 'head-strong' coloured chieftain.[77] While no direct connection has been found between this rebellion and the subversive activities of the British consulate, Turnbull's and Cocking's journeys through the island had served to encourage the black belief that Britain would not stand aloof.

This was the most significant insurrection between Aponte's rebellion in 1812 and the outbreak of the first independence war in 1868, and is remembered more for the ferocity with which it was suppressed than for the revolt itself. The *escalera*, which gave its name to the incidence of rebellion and repression, was a simple wooden ladder to which detainees were tied and then lashed or tortured.[78] The ladder was one of several punishments used on sugar estates to break the spirit of potentially rebellious slaves.

At the Ingenio Alcancía the authorities took no chances, summoning troops as well as the local *rancheadores*, men with bloodhounds, and *monteros*, or poor whites. The rebels were driven into the hills above Jovellanos, doing considerable damage as they fled. Four whites were killed and two severely wounded, but the slaves bore the brunt of subsequent repression. 'Many blacks have been shot,' wrote the governor of Matanzas, 'and as many more hung by the white inhabitants and the soldiery.'[79]

The rebellion exploded across western Cuba like a fire-cracker, springing up in different and unexpected places. Rumours of an uprising planned for Christmas Day swept the island. A revolt at the Triunvirato sugar plantation in Matanzas in November was (legend has it) spearheaded by a black slave known as 'La Negra Carlota', who died with machete in hand. Her name was later given to 'Operation Carlota', the Cuban military intervention in Angola a century later.

Leopoldo O'Donnell, captain-general in 1843, ordered the arrest of thousands of blacks in the sugar heartland around Matanzas, both slaves and free men of colour. His aim, he declared in February 1844, was 'to return the slaves to their habitual state of discipline and servitude without grave damage to the proprietors, and at the same time to punish in a severe and exemplary manner the chiefs [of the slaves] and the white and free people of colour who have introduced this germ of unrest and insubordination'.[80]

From January to the end of March 1844, O'Donnell and the Comisión Militar unleashed a reign of terror on the coloured population around Matanzas, an 'intense period of search, seizure, torture, confession, trial, and punishment'.[81] Richard Burleigh Kimball, a New York lawyer visiting Cuba in 1844, described the agents of the Comisión Militar as 'sordid, brutal and sanguinary'. Their interrogations were 'accompanied by the most violent chastisement, often inflicted in such a manner as sooner or later to produce death'.[82]

Another American visitor, Dr John Wurdemann, described the 'slaughter-houses' established in Matanzas and Cárdenas, and reported how accused men 'were subjected to the lash to extort confessions . . . A thousand lashes were in many cases inflicted on a single Negro; a great number died under this continued torture, and still more from spasms, and gangrene of the wounds.'[83] A British correspondent noted in August 1844 that 'all is apparently tranquil here, but it is the tranquillity of terror.'[84]

Historians have agreed on the scale and extent of government repression, but for many years no one could decide whether a conspiracy to stage a rebellion had actually existed. The Comisión Militar described these events as the *Conspiración de la gente de color contra los blancos* (the conspiracy of coloured people against the whites), but most Cuban historians have been reluctant to accept that the rebellions were directed by blacks against whites. Recent research suggests that the Spanish authorities were probably right. Several conspiracies were being organised – by slaves seeking freedom and by men of colour seeking advancement, and with whites dithering on the sidelines. The freelance activities of the British consulate in Havana must surely have contributed to the atmosphere in which such rebellions became imaginable. Yet no single over-arching conspiracy existed sufficient to have justified the severity of the government's repression.

La Escalera was just the kind of rebellion whose possibility had held Cuba's tiny white population in a state of permanent tension for more than half a century. Their fears had been further exacerbated by the results of the census of 1841, which showed that slaves outnumbered whites for the first time in Cuban history. Cuba's total population of just over one million included 418,000 whites, 436,000 slaves and 153,000 free people of colour.[85]

Dr Wurdemann noted the very explicit fears of Cuba's white settlers at the time of La Escalera: 'All the horrors of the San Domingo massacres were to have been repeated. Many of the whites were to have been flayed and broiled while alive, and with the exception of young women, reserved for a worse fate, all, without discrimination of age or sex, were to have been massacred.'[86]

The Spanish authorities had long been concerned by Cuba's free black population, a considerably larger proportion than that in other Caribbean islands or the United States (but similar to that of Brazil). O'Donnell could not get rid of them, as Vives had wished to do, but he used the excuse of the Escalera conspiracy to exile free blacks who had not been born in Cuba. All such male adults were given two weeks to leave the island in March 1844. From then until June 1845, according to Pedro Deschamps Chapeaux, 'at least 739 free people of colour fled; 416 of them to Mexico; 92 to Africa, 40 to the United States, and the rest to Jamaica, Brazil, and Europe. Surveillance by Spanish agents continued in Mexico and elsewhere to prevent their return to Cuba. Eventually a royal order prohibited any free person of colour, or *emancipado*, from entering Cuba.'[87]

O'Donnell's ferocity was much appreciated by Cuba's white elite. When it was finished, and some people began to question its wisdom, a number of sugar barons and merchants assembled in the Junta de Fomento to send a sycophantic message of support for their captain-general to Queen Isabella in Madrid. The slaves in the countryside, it said, had been stirred up by 'the free and emancipated in the cities' who had plotted 'an extensive, vast and horrible uprising'. Their conspiracy had ramifications in 'foreign countries' and had 'counted on outside auxiliaries of the same colour'. The 'lives and fortunes' of Cuba's inhabitants would not have been saved had not 'the finger of Providence . . . inspired your Majesty with the happy thought of putting the command of this island in the expert and diligent hands of the distinguished individual who governs today'.[88]

The drama of the early 1840s revealed an important truth about Cuban opinion. It was possible to mobilise the whites for independence, and the blacks for an end to slavery, but it was not possible to get them to work together. The whites were frightened of ending slavery, and the blacks were not overly concerned about independence. The blacks had looked to the British, who had liberated the slaves of neighbouring Jamaica in 1834. The whites now looked in the opposite direction, to the United States, whose slave-holders still ruled in the South.

Narciso López and the threat of US annexation, 1850 and 1851

The frightening events of 1843–4, terrifying to the black population and alarming to the ever-fearful whites, led to increasingly vocal demands in Cuba for the island to be taken over by the United States. Sentiment in favour of annexation had grown within wealthy sectors of society in the 1840s, and remained an important element in Cuban politics over the next century. One influential advocate was Cristóbal Madán, a wealthy Cuban planter in exile in New York. He was the brother-in-law of John O'Sullivan, an American journalist who had coined the expression 'Manifest Destiny' in 1845, a notion justifying US expansion that became a dominant political slogan. America's destiny, wrote O'Sullivan, was 'to overspread the continent allotted by Providence for the free development of our yearly multiplying millions'. Cuba was not explicitly mentioned, but for many US politicians and soldiers inspired by the slogan, it was next on the list – after Louisiana, Florida and the formerly Mexican territory of Texas. Politicians thought in terms of purchasing the island from Spain, soldiers envisaged a 'filibustering' expedition that would repeat their successful conquest of much of Mexico.

Both O'Sullivan and Madán were supporters of Cuban annexation, and argued that the growing trade relationship between the island and the mainland should be complemented by a political connection. The United States had become Cuba's largest trading partner by the middle of the century; it bought the bulk of the island's sugar and supplied it with manufactured goods. Spain and Britain were left far behind. North American ships sailed to Havana from all the ports of the east coast – from Boston and New York, and from Philadelphia and New Orleans – to provide Cubans with the necessities of modern life:'box shooks, staves, caskets, barrels, hoops, nails, tar, textiles, salt fish, corn, lard, flour and rice.'[89] The ships returned to the US ports with sugar, cocoa, tobacco and coffee. Anthony Trollope, the British novelist who toured the Caribbean in 1859, described how Cuba's trade was falling into the hands of the Americans, and he envisaged Havana becoming 'as much American as New Orleans'.[90]

Increased trade went hand in hand with settlement. The presence of North American settlers to the east of Havana had been noted by Richard Madden in the 1830s. He wrote how 'some districts on the northern shores of the island, in the vicinity especially of Cárdenas and Matanzas, have more the character of American than Spanish settlements'.[91] Richard Davey, a visitor in

1898, noted how the country had been overrun by Americans 'during the last seventy years'. They had introduced 'every form of Protestantism', including Episcopalians and Quakers, and even Shakers.[92]

The Cubans themselves had become more interested in the United States than in Europe, exemplified by the final destination of an exile like Madán. Where once such exiles would have chosen to live in Madrid or Paris, increasing numbers now rooted themselves in North American cities. In this changing climate, the annexation of Cuba became a natural subject for discussion, both in Havana and Washington, clouded only by the thought that a US takeover might involve a war with Britain, still the major contender in the Caribbean.

Yet the balance of power was shifting by mid-century. The United States was asserting its commercial and political influence with greater vigour, less fearful of European intervention.[93] Offers to purchase Cuba were made to Spain by successive US governments, although invariably rejected by Madrid. President James Polk offered $100 million in 1848, and President Franklin Pierce increased the offer to $130 million in 1854. Pierce was advised by his ambassadors in Europe that if Madrid refused to sell, 'then, by every law, human and divine, we shall be justified in wresting it from Spain if we possess the power'.[94]

Happy to propose purchase, the US government considered military action to be more problematic; it had little stomach for a fight. Freelance adventures were another matter. Advocates of annexation, both Cuban and American, soon took matters into their own hands, organising 'filibustering' expeditions to the coast of Cuba. These small-scale landings, involving a few hundred US adventurers, planned to link up with what they hoped would be Cuban resistance on the island. Prominent among the adventurers was Narciso López, a former Spanish officer who led two expeditions to Cuba. One landed at Cárdenas in 1849, a second at Playa El Morrillo, west of Havana, in 1851.

Born in Venezuela in 1797, López had fought in the independence wars as a young man on the Spanish side. Retreating to Spain in the 1820s, he had had a successful military-administrative career in the service of the Spanish state, successively the governor of Cuenca, Valencia and Madrid. Emigrating to Cuba and establishing himself in commerce, he became governor of the province of Trinidad. He was well connected to one of the wealthy Cuban families that supported US annexation, being the brother-in-law of the US-educated reformer Francisco de Frías, the Count of Pozos Dulces.[95]

Falling out with the Spanish authorities, López became enamoured of the idea of Cuban independence, claiming inspiration from the Soles y Rayos de Bolívar conspiracy of his youth. His professed aim was to recreate Bolívar's plan to liberate the island. His first expedition, sailing from New Orleans in May 1850, briefly captured Cárdenas, but when his reluctant companions heard rumours of an advancing Spanish army, they swiftly retreated to their ship.

A second expedition, landing at Playa El Morrillo in 1851, also ended in disaster, and López was captured. On 1 September, in the plaza beneath the Punta fortress at the entrance to Havana harbour, he was executed by the *garote vil,* the screw-induced strangulation long favoured by the Spanish state. 'It was not my wish to injure anyone,' he told the great crowd that had assembled to watch the event, 'my object was your freedom and happiness.'[96]

The end of slavery in the United States in 1863 and political changes in Spain itself caused a reformist wind to blow over Cuba, encouraged by two relatively progressive officers who ruled in Havana from 1859 to 1866 – Francisco Serrano y Domínguez and Domingo Dulce. Serrano conceded some political space to the Creole elite, permitting cultural societies and magazines to flourish and even allowing a degree of political debate. The Casino Español was established in this period, a Spanish club and recreational institution that brought together state bureaucrats, military officers and rich planters.[97] Replicated in towns throughout the island, these settler clubs remained powerful until the end of the century, providing a solid organisational base for those who supported the link with Spain.

Under continuing pressure from the British abolitionists, and now from the United States, Spain finally agreed to suppress the slave trade in 1867, a promise it had first made half a century earlier. Fearful lest the measure should encourage the ambitions of the black population, it was accompanied by the intensification of racial segregation. Local governors were instructed 'to tighten the bonds of obedience and respect that the coloured race owes to the white race, because emancipation of the slaves in the United States might cause the spread of news and doctrines inciting that race to become unruly'.[98] Yet the whites were now beginning to breathe more easily. A census in 1860–61 indicated for the first time that the island now had a white majority. An increase in white immigration during the 1850s had quietly expanded the white labour force and the whites now numbered 716,000 against 643,000 blacks.

The chief concern of the planters, now that the slave trade had ended, was the search for fresh sources of labour. They looked first to the Yucatán, following in the tracks of the early Spanish colonists in the sixteenth century. Thousands of Yucatecas, most of them pure blood Mayan Indians, were brought to Cuba between 1848 and 1861 and worked under contract on the sugar estates.[99] Next they turned to China, and 'the coolie trade' brought nearly 130,000 Chinese labourers to the island between 1853 and 1874. Some 95,000 of them came from the Chinese mainland, loaded onto ships at the Portuguese colony of Macao.[100] Others came from elsewhere in Asia, from the Spanish colony of the Philippines, from the British colony of Hong Kong, from the French colony of Indochina.[101] They travelled in appalling conditions, similar to those suffered by the Africans, and many died on the voyage.

The old slaving firms arranged their transport, and wrote out their work contracts. By the end of the century, the Chinese numbered 14,863, or about one per cent of the Cuban population.[102] The Chinese empire cancelled the traffic in coolies in 1873, leaving the Cuban estate owners with neither slaves nor coolies.[103]

The 'coolies' worked in the cane plantations, in the sugar mills and on railroad construction connected to the sugar industry. Many remained behind after their contracts had finished and would make their way to the towns, to work as domestics or in trade, and to open restaurants and laundries. They had all come as single men, without women, and many were soon married to Cubans, both white and black.

The Chinese immigrants integrated into Cuban society in other ways as well. When the cry for Cuban independence was raised in 1868, many of them joined the struggle, making common cause with the black rebels rather than with the wealthy Spanish whites who had sought to use them as an alternative to slave labour.[104] Together with other members of the despised underclass, they threw themselves into the fiery cauldron that would help to forge the Cuban nation, through the 30 years of rebellion and civil war that was about to engulf the island.

3
Wars of independence and occupation, 1868–1902

The Grito de Yara and the outbreak of the Ten Year War, 1868

The delightful and prosperous town of Bayamo lies under the shadow of the Sierra Maestra at the entrance to Oriente Province. A colonial town of single-storied houses and rectangular streets, sometimes curved round the gorge of the river that bears its name, it has at its centre a leafy square where children are paraded in the evening in gaudily painted goat carts. Municipal events here are presided over by a large bronze statue of Carlos Manuel de Céspedes, a local lawyer and landowner who seized the town in October 1868 in the name of a movement claiming Cuba's independence from Spain. He announced that the town was now the provisional capital of the island, and that he was independent Cuba's 'captain-general', with the legal authority of a colonial governor. His declarations were later recalled by rivals within the independence movement as evidence that he harboured dictatorial ambitions – as he quite possibly did.

Earlier in the month, Céspedes had assembled his friends and slaves at his small estate of La Demajagua, near Manzanillo, to make a formal declaration of an event recorded as the Grito de Yara. The *grito* was the cry or shout that had traditionally launched the earlier independence movements in Latin America half a century earlier; Yara was the name of a nearby inland town. Later referred to as 'the father of the nation', the 49-year-old Céspedes had acquired a measure of revolutionary experience during travels in Europe and was a member of a wider political conspiracy seeking independence.

In November, the revolt spread to the west, to Puerto Príncipe (Camagüey), where the chief organisers were Salvador Cisneros Betancourt and Ignacio Agramonte, both from families of wealthy planters. They were joined by an experienced soldier, Manuel de Quesada, who had fought in the US–Mexican war. The Spanish authorities in Cuba now faced a war designed to break the chains of their colonial domination. They fought back in a long-drawn-out conflict, piling horror on horror, that was ultimately lost by the advocates of independence who had started it.

Ever since the slave rebellion in Saint-Domingue in 1791, Spain had crushed all opposition to its continuing rule in Cuba. Martial law kept the slaves in their barracks, fierce repression decimated the free blacks and the threat of exile hung over wealthy white dissidents from the middle and upper class. The possibility of black majority rule, were the island to become independent, coupled with the enchantments of unprecedented prosperity for the island's elite created by the sugar industry, kept most white settlers in firm support of their Spanish motherland. Only at society's intellectual margins (and often by those in exile) was the possibility of a Cuba free from Spain under discussion, and then usually in the context of a union with the United States.

Suddenly in 1868 a few determined men seized Bayamo and Camagüey and raised the flag of rebellion. They did so at a moment when Spain itself was engaged in a civil war at home – with its monarchy overthrown and its prime minister assassinated. Yet whatever its own troubles, Spain never relaxed its imperial grip on its wealthy Caribbean island. Successive captains-general waged war in Cuba with singular ferocity. While the independence war in its first phase lasted for 10 years, the wider battle continued, off and on, for 30, until US intervention meant the Spaniards were finally forced to withdraw from the island in 1898. In some eyes, the struggle went on for over 90 years – until the revolution in 1959.

The Ten Year War was both a civil war and a race war. On one side was a handful of determined white landowners, joined by their black slaves and by free blacks. On the other were Spanish armies joined by groups of racist white settlers, many of them recent immigrants from Spain whose children banded together in killer battalions of *voluntarios* or 'volunteers'. The tradition of violent resistance to established authority that took root during the independence war was to be endlessly reasserted in almost every subsequent decade – reappearing in one form or another in 1878, 1879, 1895, 1906, 1912, 1933 and 1956.

Céspedes's timing appeared propitious, for the integrity of Spain itself was under threat. Madrid exploded in the month before the Cuban rebellion with the 'Glorious Revolution' of 18 September 1868 which sent the Spanish monarch, Queen Isabella, into exile. In the wake of several humiliating defeats in Spain's former empire during the 1860s, two senior generals – Juan Prim and Francisco Serrano, a former captain-general in Cuba – launched an insurrection to overthrow the Queen's long-established and immobile regime. The impact of this metropolitan upheaval on Cuba was not dissimilar to the effect that the French Revolution of 1789 had on Saint-Domingue. Both revolutions served to weaken the links between motherland and colony, and caused uncertainty about the motives and programme of the new revolutionary authorities. In both cases, metropolitan revolution led to colonial rebellion.

Spain had long been on the verge of an internal breakdown, for a series of external disasters had left it leaderless and exhausted. Spanish forces were defeated in Santo Domingo in 1865 and a second fleet was defeated off the coast of Peru the following year.[1] Cubans who witnessed the Spanish ships limping back to Santiago received the distinct impression that Spain was a weak and demobilised power, deprived of its imperial lustre. The dismal performance of the French army of Napoleon III in Mexico in 1867 (and the subsequent execution of Maximilian I) added fuel to the belief that the decadent European powers were not able to control or influence events in the Americas. In October 1865 the Morant Bay rebellion had exploded in British Jamaica. In September 1868 Puerto Rico erupted in an anti-Spanish independence rebellion (the Grito de Lares). Rarely had Spain's empire been at such a low ebb.

The Spanish defeat in Santo Domingo was of particular significance since many Dominicans with military experience came over to live, and eventually to fight, in Cuba. Among them was Máximo Gómez, the most accomplished rebel general of the independence wars. Several hundred former soldiers, many of them black, sought work in Cuba's Oriente, and some obeyed Céspedes's call in 1868. These were the original *mambí*, the pejorative word given by white Spanish troops to the black rebels in Santo Domingo. Derived from *mbi*, a reference to their African origin, it was used to suggest that they were all bandits and criminals. The word *mambí* was used again by the Spanish in the Cuban war, where it gained greater currency and was soon assumed by the blacks themselves as a badge of honour.[2]

Céspedes's insurrection of October 1868 did not spring out of thin air. The intellectual ground had been well prepared. Political movements and masonic conspiracies had been active in the country, notably in Oriente, over several years. Cuban landowners were unusually restive, hostile to the Spanish tax burden they had been obliged to assume. The Mexican silver subsidies that had funded Cuban economic development in the eighteenth century had long since disappeared. Sugar-rich Cuba had replaced Mexico as Spain's milch cow and was expected to pay for an empire that Spain itself now found difficult to finance. Cuban taxpayers contributed towards the Spanish expeditions to Mexico in 1862 and to Santo Domingo between 1863 and 1865, as well as to the naval war against Peru and Chile in 1866 and to a series of ongoing military campaigns in Africa. To cap it all, the Cubans had to pay the salaries of the Spanish diplomatic corps in Latin America.[3]

Humiliated by defeat in foreign wars, a liberal government in Madrid had collapsed in 1867, to be replaced by an ultra-conservative regime. A high tide of reaction soon reached Cuba and martial law was reaffirmed, the press was silenced and political gatherings banned. With all reformist options exhausted, many Cubans were ready to rebel. When Spain shook off its reactionary government, and proclaimed its own revolution in September

1868, it must have seemed a golden and unrepeatable moment to those seeking independence.

Céspedes's troops had captured Bayamo, and secured the surrender of the Spanish garrison, ten days after the Grito de Yara. One of Céspedes's officers, Pedro Figueredo, wrote the triumphant verses that became Cuba's national anthem:

> Al combate corred Bayameses
> Que la patria os contempla orgullosa,
> No temáis una muerte gloriosa
> Que morir por la patria es vivir.
>
> [To the battle, Bayameses,
> Let the fatherland proudly observe you.
> Do not fear a glorious death,
> To die for the fatherland is to live.]

Radical liberals, who had long promoted the cause of independence, now turned to violence to secure their political ends. 'To die for the fatherland' became a tradition that would trouble the country for nearly a century. The rebels understood what they were doing, though they had little inkling of the sharp divisions within their ranks. Maybe, too, they did not realise that their struggle would last so long, nor that it would be so fierce and ruthless. Spain was prepared to pay any price to keep its hold on Cuba.

General Lersundi and the volunteers seize Havana, 1868–1869

General Francisco Lersundi, the captain-general in Havana at the time of Céspedes's rebellion, was a conservative and fiercely pro-settler figure who organised immediate action against the rebels. Appointed after the rightist turn in Spain in 1867, he was just as hostile to the revolution in Madrid as to the rebellion in Cuba, and he was quite prepared to take on the rebels on his own. 'La isla de Cuba es de España, mande quien mande en la Peninsula,' he declared in a famous telegram to Madrid, 'y para España es preciso defenderla y conservarla, cueste lo que cueste.' (Cuba belongs to Spain, whoever rules in the Peninsula, and Spain's task is to defend and keep it, whatever the cost.)

Lersundi's first act was as bold as that of Céspedes. He declared his own independence from Spain and refused to recognise the new regime in Madrid. Receiving a telegram from the exiled Queen Isabella asking him not to surrender to the Madrid government, he celebrated her birthday with a traditional reception in her honour. Fearing that the new government might seek to negotiate with the rebels, and perceiving that Spanish rule in the Caribbean was under real threat, he sent his second-in-command, General Blas de Villate, the Count of Valmaseda, to recover Bayamo by force.

Some Cuban liberals hoped that the revolution in Spain would re-ignite a reformist colonial programme. Lersundi was not their man. When a group of leading reformist planters from the Matanzas sugar zone, including Julián Zulueta and Miguel Aldama, requested a meeting, hoping to avoid a damaging war, Lersundi dismissed them with contempt. Reform was off the agenda. Zulueta remained loyal to Spain and stayed in Cuba to defend his plantations, but Aldama fled with his family to New York and became a spokesman for the rebels. His many sugar mills were confiscated by the state.[4]

In the early months, Lersundi was hard-pressed to meet the rebel threat. Only 22,000 regular Spanish soldiers were stationed on the island and many were permanently off-duty, engaged in work on their own account to reinforce their meagre pay.[5] Antonio Gallenga, a correspondent of *The Times*, noted that Lersundi could not rely on his Spanish troops, since most were 'consumed and devoured by various diseases inherent to the climate'.[6] Nor was revolutionary Spain in a position to send reinforcements. Troops were needed at home to deal with the threat to the Madrid government from its internal enemies.[7]

Lersundi looked for local forces in the autumn of 1868, to confront both Madrid and Céspedes, and there was no shortage of volunteers. Most Spaniards on the island backed the Spanish cause. Recent immigrants and their children, the *peninsulares*, were happy to fight, to reassert Spanish sovereignty in a Cuba they perceived as an integral part of metropolitan Spain.[8] Many immigrants succumbed to the prevailing sentiments of white racism voiced by the island's elite, and shared the generalised fear that independence would turn Cuba into 'another Haiti', a black-ruled dictatorship. Even autonomy and free trade, the programme of Aldama's reformists, was considered a threat to their privileged position as Spaniards.

The *peninsulares* had the typical characteristics of European white settlers, exhibited in other places and at other times. Like French settlers in Algeria, and British settlers in southern Africa, these Spanish settlers in Cuba combined a fierce loyalty to their place of origin with a deep hostility to the black and native population with whom they were obliged to co-exist. Gallenga described 'the lower classes' of immigrants from the Spanish peninsula as 'prejudiced and bigoted'.[9]

Lersundi mobilised this white racist faction in Havana, and used it to re-form and rearm the old volunteer militia. The *voluntarios* had existed in earlier centuries, but had been established more formally as an auxiliary to the armed forces in 1825, at the time when martial law was permanently imposed. Revived during the troubles of the 1840s, and re-formed in 1855, the *voluntarios* came into their own in 1868 and throughout the Ten Year War. Lersundi paid them with money levied from Spanish merchants, landowners and slave traders, the powerful group that had long dominated the island's institutions. The *voluntarios* soon spread to towns throughout the country, expanding from 10,000 to 35,000 men. Gallenga estimated that there were about 11,000 in Havana and perhaps 60,000 in the rest of the island. They had become a law unto themselves, he wrote. 'They became the only masters, if not of the country, at least of all the chief cities, and especially of Havana. They reorganised and armed themselves at their own pleasure.'[10]

Gallenga noted that they were used as much for internal repression as for fighting the rebels. Known anti-Spanish dissidents in Santiago and Havana were rounded up, and executed without trial:

> Their object is not to go out and fight the insurgents in the disaffected districts – for that is the task they leave to the regular troops – but to overawe the sympathisers and supporters of the Rebel party, to ferret out their accomplices, and to do duty as a police force, terrorising the cities. These battalions, and the Council of their Colonels, together with the *Casino Español* or Spanish Club – a Havana institution which has been copied in all other cities – constitute a State within the State.

Gallenga was later to compare the situation in Havana with that of Paris during the Commune.

General Serrano, the prime minister in Madrid, was aware of Lersundi's activities and ordered his dismissal, appointing the benign General Domingo Dulce in his place. Dulce had had an earlier stint in Havana in 1866, and was sent out with a mandate to offer an amnesty to the rebels and to take up the cause of reform – just as Lersundi had feared. Lersundi withdrew reluctantly from the island at the end of 1868, voicing special words of praise for the *voluntarios*, who remained behind as armed advocates of his 'no surrender' position. They were to dictate the future of the island in the years ahead and made short work of Lersundi's replacement.

Dulce arrived in Havana in January 1869 as the representative of the self-styled revolutionary government in Madrid, and he came with a programme of moderate reform. He promised a pardon to the rebels, as well as freedom of the press and of assembly. He had even brought a plan for elections with him, and held out the possibility of Cuba being represented in the Cortes in Madrid. Peace envoys were sent out to Céspedes, to discuss peace terms and to offer an amnesty to any rebel prepared to surrender within 40 days.

Dulce soon found that he was faced with war on two fronts. On one side, in the provinces, stood the republican advocates of independence. On the other, in the cities, was the pro-Spanish party, still passionately defending the cause of the overthrown Queen. Madrid preferred a negotiated settlement, and, with few troops at his command, Dulce had no immediate possibility of launching an offensive against the rebels. Yet reform was made impossible by the activities of the *voluntarios* who controlled Havana. They 'garrisoned the forts which command the cities,' wrote Gallenga, 'and banished the regular troops from their walls'. They 'had the Captain-General and all the authorities, military, naval, and civil, under their thumb'.[11] Soon they were preparing a *coup d'état* of their own.

Dulce tried to curb their power, but without success. In the very month of his arrival, the *voluntarios* attacked the Villanueva theatre in Havana and the Café Louvre, two centres where reformist Cubans had been accustomed to assemble. Several people were killed. In March, when a group of 250 political prisoners were assembled at the Havana jetty, for embarkation to prison in Spain's African colony of Fernando Po, the *voluntarios* organised hostile demonstrations in the Plaza de Armas. Exile for the prisoners was perceived as an act of leniency by Dulce; the *voluntarios* would have preferred them to be executed. Dulce went out in person to calm the passions of the crowd, and the prisoners were allowed to leave, but there was a price to be paid. Dulce was obliged to make a statement giving full support to the *voluntarios*.

It was not enough. On the night of 1 June, a large crowd assembled outside his palace shouting 'Muere Dulce!', Death to Dulce! The *coup d'état* was in full swing. The commanders of the various battalions of *voluntarios* came to tell him that he would have to resign. Detained and transferred to a warship, Dulce sailed for Spain on 5 June – a humiliating and ignoble end to his brief service in Havana. He was replaced by General Caballero de Rodas, who willingly accepted the demands of the *voluntarios*. From their base at the Casino Español these settler troops and the peninsula elite were to remain as the de facto colonial government for much of the rest of the war, with a minor hiccup when a Spanish Republic was briefly proclaimed in February 1873.[12]

Rebel arguments over slavery and annexation

The initial success of Céspedes's rebel forces, which had seized Bayamo and Holguín, was short-lived. They suffered a serious defeat in January 1869 at the hands of the Count of Valmaseda, whose troops were able to re-enter Bayamo, the Spanish triumph rather mitigated by the town's patriotic citizens preferring to burn it down rather than surrender. The initiative now swung back to Agramonte's rebel group in Camagüey, their support for the rebellion reinforced by an incident in which their negotiator, summoned to meet Dulce's envoy, was assassinated by the Volunteers. Yet serious differences had already emerged in the rebel camp between Céspedes and Agramonte, and a rebel convention was held in April 1869 to discuss them, under the cover of hammering out a new constitution. The meeting was held at Guáimaro, on the road between Camagüey and Las Tunas.

The immediate question of leadership was settled swiftly. Céspedes was chosen as President, with Manuel de Quesada appointed as military commander. More serious was the question of slavery. Céspedes had released his own slaves at the start of the war, as had the local landowners who joined him, and their freed slaves formed an important nucleus of the rebel army. Yet no call was made for the abolition of slavery altogether. The ambivalence that lay at the heart of all Cuban reformist movements had not disappeared. Céspedes's first manifesto, issued in December 1868, outlined a programme for the country's future, but referred only to 'gradual' abolition and called for slave-owners to be compensated. The sugar plantations were to remain free from attack, and those who made such attacks would be subject to the death penalty. Although the manifesto echoed the American Declaration of Independence ('We believe that all men were created free and equal'), it quickly qualified its application where slaves were concerned ('We desire the gradual, indemnified emancipation of slaves').

The rebels associated with Agramonte in Camagüey were more radical. Coming from cattle country, with fewer slaves, they had less to lose, and they abolished slavery throughout the area they controlled. Céspedes was more cautious. Although himself an abolitionist – and the demand to end slavery had few opponents in Oriente – he feared the political impact of abolition on the plantation owners in the rich areas of Matanzas and regions further west. The meeting at Guámairo reached an unhappy compromise. The new constitution declared that 'all inhabitants of the Republic' were absolutely free, but it also established that freed slaves should remain as paid workers of their masters. This programme was welcomed neither by the slave-owners, nor by slaves and free blacks.

Paradoxically, the Spanish government in Madrid was soon to undercut the rebel programme. In May 1870 it decided to take the matter of Cuban slavery out of the hands of the captain-general in Havana and to make concessions to the rebels. Segismundo Moret, Spain's minister of the colonies, decreed a conditional end to slavery, and under the so-called 'Free Womb Act', freedom was granted to all children born to slave parents as well as to slaves over 60 and those who assisted Spanish troops in their defence of the island.

The compromise reached at Guáimaro was vehemently opposed by Antonio Maceo, the 20-year-old mulatto captain who had emerged as the leader of the black rebels supporting Céspedes. Maceo and Máximo Gómez, who both emerged as outstanding military leaders, had a simple strategy: to organise a slave rebellion on a grand scale, to set fire to sugar plantations and to free the slaves working on them. This would bring in recruits and destroy the economic base of the Spanish state at the same time.

In a war in which the rebels had more machetes than rifles, the strategy had much in its favour. Although the racial balance was swinging towards the whites, the blacks in Oriente still formed a large majority, almost 80 per cent. Their support for the rebellion was essential. The free blacks who had survived the Escalera repression recognised that their interest lay with the rebels, but the slaves, initially promised nothing, were understandably slow to move. Maceo's strategy helped to bring them over to the rebel side.

Many plantations were soon on fire. An offensive by the *mambí* in the valleys north of Santiago in 1869 destroyed 23 sugar mills and 15 coffee plantations, while out of 100 sugar mills operating in the Camagüey area in 1868, only one remained functioning ten years later.[13] Céspedes was soon converted to the strategy, recording that it would be better for Cuba to be free, 'even if we have to burn every vestige of civilisation', but the planters of Camagüey were horrified. Maceo and Gómez knew that the success of their strategy depended on taking the war out of Oriente and into the rich lands of western Cuba, and they planned to do so with fire and the machete. Yet they were never able to secure the support of the entire movement.

Gómez was not as radical as Maceo and usually threw his weight behind the moderates in all rebel councils. A soldier with considerable organisational and political skills, he came from a prosperous family in Santo Domingo where he had been a commander in the Spanish army. When the country disintegrated into civil war in 1865, Gómez lost his lands and property and fled to Cuba, establishing himself as a farmer near Bayamo. In 1868, at the age of 32, he enrolled as a sergeant in Céspedes's army. Often considered to be a caudillo in the making, Gómez never put himself forward to be President, either during the rebel wars or in the subsequent peace, and he died at the age of 69 in 1905.

Slavery was not the only subject that divided the rebels at the meeting at Guáimaro. Céspedes had started the rebellion with a call for independence, but the sentiment in favour of annexation by the United States was still strong within the rebel camp. The Guáimaro convention voted in favour of such an outcome. The US government was preoccupied by the Cuban rebellion and continued to take an interest in the island's future, but when General Ulysses Grant was informed of the rebel request for annexation, he decided to bide his time. Cuba was still a slave state, and the rebels' commitment to ending slavery was still far from clear. Some US officials were still in favour of purchasing the island from Spain, an echo of earlier proposals.

The desire for annexation was strong in several sectors of Cuban society, and many thousands of Cubans voted with their feet. Escaping from the horrors and privations of the war, they set up home in the United States. One oft-quoted figure by a Spanish historian of the time suggests that 100,000 Cubans migrated in the first year alone.[14] Like most such global figures from that era, it is based on unverifiable evidence. Yet even if the figure were halved, it would represent an impressive five per cent of the population.

After the first pitched battle outside Bayamo in 1869, the rebel force avoided frontal engagements with the Spanish army. It operated as a guerrilla force, with small groups living in makeshift camps in the mountains, ready to descend on outlying Spanish forts or to burn sugar plantations and release their slaves. The depredations of the rebels were matched by the scorched earth policy of the Spaniards. The Spanish detained and executed young men found away from home and herded families into the towns from the rural areas – a foretaste of the 'concentration camp' policy that was to characterise a later Spanish war.

Gallenga described how in the towns of central Cuba – Santa Clara, Sagua La Grande, Remedios and Cienfuegos – 'the most terrific executions' were the rule. The Spanish forces

> took the disaffection for granted, and determined that it should never ripen into open rebellion. Not only did they shoot all the Insurgents whom they caught with arms in their hands, but they slew without mercy many of the unarmed fugitives whom terror of their approach had driven into the woods, and they doomed to the same fate others who had remained quietly at home, but who were suspected of sympathy with the rebel cause.[15]

The war continued year after year with neither side able to secure much of an advantage. The Spanish army kept the rebels cooped up in the east and centre of the island. No insurrectionary flame was ever lit in the west, and the plantations of Matanzas kept working. A defensive line, the *trocha*, was constructed 50-kilometre across the middle of the island, a ditch and wooden palisade stretching from Morón in the north to Júcaro in the south, punctuated by 43 small forts. For several years this was an effective barrier that kept the rebels on the eastern side, although this was partly owing to the reluctance of the rebel leadership to advance into western Cuba. When Gómez was finally (and briefly) permitted by the rebel council to break out on a march to the west, in January 1875, the *trocha* proved ineffective in preventing him.

The rebels were weakened by their own internal divisions. These affected not just their capacity to fight, but their relations with their supporters in the United States, the people responsible for sending arms and money to sustain their campaigns. As the vision of the fighters became ever more radical and millenarian, so the exiles in New York and Washington became increasingly disenchanted with the excesses of the war and less willing to finance it.

With no end to the war and no diplomatic denouement in sight, latent disagreements within the rebel ranks came to the surface in 1873. The rebel assembly removed Céspedes from the presidency, and replaced him with Cisneros Betancourt, who later gave way to Tomás Estrada Palma, a school-teacher from Bayamo. Céspedes was killed in a skirmish in 1874. The rebels were now divided on both racial and national lines. Many were opposed to Gómez because he was a Dominican and to Maceo because he was black. Both withdrew from their commands in high dudgeon. Maceo wrote to Estrada to complain about 'a small circle' that did not wish to serve under his orders 'because I belong to the coloured race'.[16]

The fear of 'another Haiti' was still strong, even within the rebel ranks. But Maceo was outraged. 'Since I form a not unappreciable part of this democratic republic, which has for its basis the fundamental principles of liberty, equality and fraternity, I must protest energetically with all my strength that neither now nor at any time am I to be regarded as an advocate of a Negro Republic or anything of that sort . . .' The rebels could ill afford to lose the services of their most charismatic commander.

The Pact of Zanjón, and the Protest of Baraguá, 1878

The Ten Year War unfolded against the backdrop of revolution and civil war in Spain itself. General Prim was assassinated in 1870, his candidate to replace Queen Isabella as the monarch was obliged to abdicate in 1873 and the brief Spanish Republic was overthrown by a military *coup d'état* in 1874. In time-honoured words, Captain Manuel Pavía y Rodríguez, the captain-general of Madrid, declared that it was the duty of his officers 'as soldiers and citizens to save society and the country'.[17] His coup was followed by a wave of repression in both Spain and Cuba that ended the current revolutionary period.

The monarchy was restored at the end of the year, in the person of Alfonso XII, a consumptive 17–year-old cadet being educated at the time at the British military academy at Sandhurst. The agent of the new king's arrival was Brigadier Arsenio Martínez Campos, a young officer who had fought with General Valmaseda in Cuba, as had Antonio Cánovas del Castillo, the new Spanish prime minister. Both Martínez Campos and Cánovas were to play influential roles in Cuban and Spanish affairs until the end of the century.[18]

Martínez Campos was appointed to be captain-general in Cuba and he arrived in Havana early in 1877 with a strategy for peace. He brought reinforcements and promises of reform. The counter-insurgency effort was revitalised, while negotiations began with the exhausted rebels. Gómez, now the only senior figure left in the field, called for a cease-fire in December. Negotiations took place in February 1878, at the *quinta* of Zanjón, near Sibanicú to the east of Puerto Príncipe (Camagüey).[19] If the rebels would lay down their arms, Martínez Campos offered an amnesty, the promise of political reform and freedom for slaves who had fought on the rebel side. Although no mention was made of independence nor of an end to slavery itself, the rebel leadership accepted what was on offer.

Not everything that had been fought for was abandoned. All slaves who had fought with the *mambí* army were freed, as were Chinese workers under contract. A 'patronage law' of 1880 granted eventual freedom to slaves, though it obliged them to work under the 'patronage' of their former owners for a period of eight years (subsequently shortened to six). The government made efforts to promote racial integration after Zanjón, forbidding discrimination against blacks in theatres, cafés and bars and ordering state schools to admit black children on the same basis as white. No one could be excluded from public employment on grounds of ethnic origin.[20] Slavery was finally abolished in October 1886.

Yet many rebels were unhappy with the Pact of Zanjón. Maceo continued to argue that there could be no peace without independence and the complete abolition of slavery. He had always distrusted the wealthy planters of Camagüey who had run the political side of the independence war, and now felt they had abandoned the struggle, securing little of significance in return for peace.

With more than a thousand men under his command in Oriente, many of them black, Maceo requested an interview with Martínez Campos. The encounter between the Spanish general and the black leader took place in March 1878, in a mango grove at Baragua, to the north of Santiago, where both men sat in hammocks under the trees. After greeting Maceo warmly, Martínez Campos told him of his pride 'in meeting personally one of the most celebrated warriors of the Cuban forces'. Flattery got him nowhere, and Maceo outlined his objections: no peace was possible without independence and an end to slavery. The two demands were inseparable.

'No more sacrifice and blood,' said Martínez Campos. 'The time has now come for Cuba to join in the life of advanced peoples. Cuba should march along the channels of civilisation and progress, in the enjoyment of all its rights, and united to Spain.' He explained that he was personally in favour of an end to slavery, but the decision lay with the Cortes in Madrid. As for independence, that was not possible. He would not have come to the meeting if he had known it would be on the agenda.

Maceo made clear that the war would continue, and when Martínez Campos asked how much time he required for resuming hostilities his reply was 'Eight days'. He remained as commander of the rebel forces in Oriente, and his rebel soldiers reaffirmed their commitment to the war. They established a new provisional government and approved a new constitution for an independent Cuba.

The 'Protest of Baragua', symbolising Cuba's continuing desire to resist, was to enter Cuban history and legend, and was much evoked in subsequent years. It took on a new life more than a century later, when Fidel Castro embraced it as an evergreen revolutionary slogan in the 1990s to confront the post-Soviet reality of a country on its knees. Maceo's gesture was a brave one in 1878, supported by his men. Yet most of them were exhausted and had no appetite for further war. Martínez Campos wisely refrained from attacking them and the new provisional government soon prevailed on Maceo to call it a day and to prepare for resistance at some future date. The war came to an end on all fronts in May 1878, and Maceo sailed off into exile, departing from Santiago on a Spanish cruiser. But while the retreat was necessary and inevitable, Maceo had no plans to abandon the struggle and preparations for another war continued, both inside Cuba and without.

A fresh rebellion, remembered as the Guerra Chiquita, or small war, broke out in August 1879, with uprisings in the east – in Gibara, Holguín and

Santiago – as well as in several places in central Cuba. The conspiracy was uncovered before time, with the principal leaders still outside the country, and the Spanish authorities were well prepared. Attempts to send in men and weapons from outside – from Santo Domingo and Haiti – were thwarted. The rebels were as ever divided on the question of race. A white leader, General Calixto García, prevented the black Maceo from taking part, fearing that the rebellion would be categorised by the Spanish authorities as a 'race war'. Not without reason. The governor in Oriente, General Camilo Polavieja, was soon to raise the familiar threat of 'another Haiti'.

With Maceo deprived of command, and García, the rebellion's prime mover, out of the country, the Guerra Chiquita was stillborn. When García eventually landed, he travelled through the county for weeks looking for rebels who could not be found. The rebellion fizzled out after nine months, and the survivors surrendered. With none of the magnanimity that had characterised Martínez Campos, Polavieja organised a fierce repression throughout Oriente that fell most severely on the black population. He ordered the arrest of 265 'conspirators' at the end of 1880, most of them black, and banished them to the prison on Fernando Po, in the Gulf of Guinea.[21]

The Guerra Chiquita never posed a serious military threat to Spanish rule. Polavieja's repression was effective in curbing the blacks, while the position of the rebel whites was undermined by the growing strength of a home rule movement that took advantage of the relatively relaxed political atmosphere in the wake of Zanjón. Now permitted legal identity, the Liberal Party was able to hold meetings, put forward candidates for election, print its own newspaper and send delegates to the Cortes in Madrid.[22] The party took the wind out of the sails of the independence movement, yet it made little headway itself. A much larger vote always went to the Partido Constitucional Unido, a conservative pro-Spanish party that rejected home rule.

Polavieja, meanwhile, made captain-general of the island in 1890, continued with his racist propaganda, seeking to persuade the white population, with some success, that the rebels planned to establish a black republic. He claimed that Maceo aimed to impose 'a government of his race and the creation of a republic similar to that of Haiti'. Such an outcome, he warned, would bring a Yankee invasion.

Among white Cubans, alarmed by the freedom of the slaves, these slanders fell on fertile ground, and the leaders of the independence struggle, now mostly in exile, were obliged to address the issue, ensuring that blacks and whites in their own ranks presented a united front. Racial prejudice in Cuban society was now the chief obstacle to securing independence. Maceo, perceived by his people as 'a new messiah', was obliged to take a back seat. The figure on whom the burden of proving that an independent Cuba would be a black and white nation, at ease with itself, was José Martí, a hero of both Cuban and Latin American history.

José Martí and the fresh dreams of independence

A small, blue-painted building in the unfashionable part of Old Havana, close to the harbour, houses a museum to the memory of José Martí. This was his birthplace, but his memory is evoked throughout the island. A museum exists in every town, and a white plaster bust outside every schoolroom. Surviving photographs reveal a diminutive figure with a large moustache and a noble brow, dressed invariably in a black frockcoat and a white tie. He was just over five feet in height. Much of his life was devoted to Cuba's independence struggle, and he was killed in Cuba in May 1895, aged 42. For all Latin Americans, though particularly for Cubans, Martí belongs in the pantheon that houses the earlier leaders of Latin America's independence struggle against Spain.

Martí was not a natural warrior, and he lived for much of his life as an exile in the United States, but he was a passionate advocate of independence and a determined opponent of those influential Cubans who advocated separation from Spain and union with the United States. 'The hands of every nation must remain free,' he wrote in 1891, 'for the untrammelled development of the country, in accordance with its distinctive nature and with its individual elements.' Annexation by the United States had to be avoided at all costs.[23] Almost his last words, and the quotation by which he is most often remembered, were directed against the danger posed by the United States: 'I know the Monster, because I have lived in its lair – and my weapon is only the slingshot of David.'

Martí was a revolutionary activist and a dedicated political theorist, but he was also a prolific writer, a poet and journalist, and a convincing orator. He wrote regularly on the events of the time, and held several contradictory views, but he was chiefly concerned with the perennial problems that characterised Latin America then and now: democracy and dictatorship, reform and revolution, and the clash between white settlers and indigenous peoples. A typical nineteenth-century intellectual, he also wrote about the purpose of education, the importance of agriculture as a basis for the development of industry and the application of general economic laws to the special circumstances of the continent. Significantly for Cuba, he was an outspoken supporter of racial equality; his message of independence and freedom was addressed to both whites and blacks.[24]

Born in Havana in 1853, Martí was the child of Spanish immigrants, a product of the programme to 'whiten' the Cuban population through immigration. His father was an artillery sergeant from Valencia who became a policeman in Havana; his mother, Leonor Pérez, came from Tenerife in the Canary Islands. Martí came early to politics, for he was still at school at the outbreak of the first independence war in 1868. In January 1869, while freedom flourished for a few weeks in Havana, he helped publish a newspaper,

Patria Libre, which printed his romantic comments on the rebel cause. Immediately identified as a subversive by the Volunteers, he was arrested on charges of criticising a friend who had joined them. Sentenced to six years in prison, although only 16, he was sent to the stone quarry at St Lázaro in Havana, and transferred after six months to the Isle of Pines. In February 1871, he was exiled to Spain.

Spain was in the throes of its own revolution when Martí arrived, and he was soon caught up in the intellectual ferment of the time. While studying philosophy and law at the University of Madrid (and later at Zaragoza), he came under the influence of Julián Sanz del Rio, whose writings were to have a major impact on Spanish and Latin American thought, notably in the field of education. Sanz del Rio was himself the translator and propagator of the work of Karl Krause, the German humanist and contemporary of Hegel, who was also a friend of the great educationalist Friedrich Froebel. Martí's special concern with education – a lasting legacy to Cuba that has survived into the twenty-first century – stemmed from his early contact with this significant school of thought.[25]

In 1875, his formal schooling finished, Martí travelled through Europe before returning to Latin America and establishing himself in Mexico, where his parents were already living in exile. This was his first experience of continental Latin America, and he was particularly struck, as were most visitors to Mexico, by the inbuilt cultural clash between white settlers and indigenous peoples – a major theme of his writing. In both Mexico and Guatemala, where he worked briefly at the university, he had first-hand experience of the most recent generation of Latin American *caudillos* – Porfirio Díaz in Mexico and Justo Rufino Barrios in Guatemala – and he became an ardent opponent of military rule. Later he was to perceive that Máximo Gómez, the hero of the Ten Year War, had some of the propensities of these mainland dictators, and he put much effort to ensure that the future Cuban revolution would remain in the hands of civilian democrats.

The Pact of Zanjón of 1878 included an amnesty for political exiles, and Martí was able to return to Havana. He became active once again in revolutionary groups, and joined the Cuban Revolutionary Committee, set up by Calixto García and based in New York. He made friends with Juan Gualberto Gómez, a mulatto lawyer who became a close colleague in the planning of the war of 1895. Charged with conspiracy during the preparations for the Guerra Chiquita in 1879, he was again sentenced to exile in Spain, but, with the independence movement now based in New York, he soon made his way back across the Atlantic. He lived in New York for the next 15 years, working closely with other Cuban exiles on plans to relaunch the independence war. He wrote for several Latin American newspapers, to earn money, and became the consular representative of Uruguay, Argentina and Paraguay.

Before settling finally in New York, he spent several months in Venezuela, where he developed some of the Bolivarian ideas that were to become part of his own internationalist philosophy. He came to empathise with the plight of the indigenous peoples, and to disapprove of governments run for the benefit of the white settlers. Echoing the Venezuelan educationalist Simón Rodríguez, he argued that Latin America needed home-grown institutions rather than those imported from outside. He also conjured up Bolívar's internationalist dream, arguing for 'a great confederation of the peoples of Latin America'.[26]

Martí was disillusioned in Venezuela, as he had been in Mexico and Guatemala, by the fruits of independence – the creation of a triple alliance of the military, the landowners and the Catholic Church, exemplified in Venezuela by the despotic rule of Antonio Guzmán Blanco. He was also shocked by the chasm that had developed between the riches of Caracas and the poverty of the rural areas surrounding it. 'In the city, Paris; in the country, Persia,' he wrote disdainfully. The independent Cuba he dreamed of would have to take a different course.

Returning to New York, Martí found the political struggle within the large exile community of Cubans to be ever more divisive, made worse by their exhaustion and depression after the failure of the Ten Year War. Martí was now perceived as a prominent exile leader, and, during the absence in Cuba of Calixto García, he was appointed as the interim president of the Cuban Revolutionary Committee. He began preparing the ground for an eventual renewal of the anti-Spanish war and sent an outline of his political position in July 1882 to Gómez and Maceo, the two surviving military leaders, now exiled in Honduras. Martí had no immediate plans to renew the struggle, but was anxious to unite the exile community around the idea of independence – at a time when many people still favoured US annexation. Martí was adamantly opposed to such plans, as he explained in an acid letter to Gómez:

In Cuba there has always been an important group of cautious men, proud enough to abominate Spanish domination yet timid enough not to put their personal well-being in danger by fighting against it. These kinds of men, helped by those who would like to enjoy the fruits of liberty without paying for them at their bloody price, are vehemently in favour of the annexation of Cuba to the United States. All the timid people, all the ones lacking in decisiveness, all the superficial observers, all those attached to wealth, have marked inclinations to support this solution, which they believe to be cheap and easy. Thus they flatter their patriotic consciences, as well as their fears of being true patriots.[27]

Martí outlined his other central theme – the paramount need for racial harmony – in a letter to Maceo:

I have no time to tell you, General, how in my eyes the Cuban problem needs, rather than a political solution, a social solution, and how the latter cannot be achieved except through mutual love and forgiveness between the two races . . . For me, the person who whips up hatred in Cuba, or takes advantage of those hatreds already present, is a criminal. And the person who tries to put down the lawful aspirations to livelihood of a good and prudent race which has already seen enough misfortune, is another.

Agreement on independence and the need for racial equality were arguments relatively easy to win. More difficult was the old problem of whether military or civilian leaders were to control a future political movement or government. All Martí's political instincts favoured a civilian leadership, while Gómez and Maceo, with their powerful memories of the political disagreements during the earlier war, favoured a governing junta, controlled by the military commanders. This, after all, was the model bequeathed by the Spanish imperial system.

The two soldiers came to New York in 1884 to canvass opinion among the exiles. Martí initially agreed to their proposal, but when he found that he had lost the argument, and was expected to be their subordinate, he withdrew from exile for several years.

'A people is not founded in the same way as one commands a military camp,' he wrote to Gómez. 'What are we, General?' he went on. 'The heroic and modest servants of an idea which warms our hearts, the faithful friends of a people who have fallen on bad times, or the brave and fortunate military leaders who, whip in hand and spurs on their feet, are preparing to lead a people into war, only to lord it over this people in the aftermath?'

Martí now devoted himself to his various jobs, as the consul of Uruguay and as a regular commentator on American affairs for *La Nación*, the daily paper of Buenos Aires. He had always been a sharp and critical observer, with a generally positive attitude towards the development of United States society, but the famous events associated with the Haymarket riots in Chicago of 1886, and the subsequent execution of anarchists, led him to adopt a more critical position. Although fiercely anti-capitalist and attracted to the nascent labour movement, he was sharply critical of Karl Marx and of the anarchist philosophers popular in the United States at the time. The harsh treatment of the Chicago anarchists led him to reject the United States as a model for Cuban society, and reinforced his hostility to annexation.[28] He had no illusions about the professed US interest in Cuba's well-being:

Never, except as an idea hidden away in the depths of some generous souls, was Cuba anything more to the United States than a desirable possession, whose only inconvenience is its population, which it considers to be unruly, lazy, and worthy of scorn.[29]

Late in 1887, at a meeting in New York to celebrate the nineteenth anniversary of the Grito de Yara, Martí returned to Cuban exile politics, when passions – his own and those of others – had subsided. The exile organisations

in New York, Philadelphia and Key West had come round to his view – that
the military should be subordinated to the civilian leaders – and he assumed
his natural position as the most charismatic leader of the exile community.
Encouraged by this support, he wrote again to Máximo Gómez in December
1887, asking him to rejoin the struggle but to accept a subordinate position.
'Cuba is no longer the infant, ignorant people that took to the countryside in
the Yara Revolution [of 1868],' he wrote. The country had changed, and
demanded more of its leaders.

Gómez expressed guarded enthusiasm towards Martí's advances, but
neither he nor Martí believed that a new war was an immediate possibility.
The Cubans were still as divided as they had been during the Ten Year War,
and the preferred policy of the United States towards Cuba was still annexation. Martí had much work to do. In 1890 he started a new organisation of
his own. With his 'Krausista' emphasis on the importance of education, he
established the Liga de Instrucción, a training school for the revolutionary
cadres of the future. Martí himself was one of the teachers, and his pupils were
an entirely new audience of Cubans – the thousands of black exiles now
working in New York. The only future for Cuba, he told them, was complete
independence. The struggle ahead would not be run by the prosperous
planters who had proposed and organised the Ten Year War; it would be in
the hands of the great mass of the people.[30]

Martí moved south in the following year, to work with the Cuban tobacco
workers in Tampa, and in January 1892 he formally established the Cuban
Revolutionary Party, a widely based independence movement to be financed
by its individual supporters, each contributing one-tenth of their earnings.
The old dependence on a small number of wealthy patrons demanding
political influence was diminished. The Party envisaged 'a brief and generous
war', and in August Martí went again in search of Gómez and Maceo to ask
for their support.

Maceo was tracked down to Costa Rica, where he had established himself
as a banana grower, while Gómez was found back in Santo Domingo. Both
agreed to rejoin the independence forces, with Gómez as the overall military
commander. Martí now abandoned his work as a journalist, gave up his
newspaper columns and relinquished his consular posts. He devoted himself
to the full-time organisation of a secret revolutionary war, of which he was
acknowledged to be the leader.

The death of the Apostle, May 1895

The straggling beach village of Playitas lies on the southern coast of Cuba, to
the east of Guantánamo Bay, at the head of the road that leads over the
mountains to Baracoa. Martí and Gómez landed here from a small boat early

in April 1895 and headed up into the hills. Their tiny band of revolutionaries had sailed across the narrow channel from Haiti. 'We strap on our revolvers,' Martí wrote in his diary, 'steer towards clearing. Moon comes up red . . . we land on a rocky beach.'

The black military leaders of the rebellion, Maceo and his brother José, and Flor Crombet, had sailed from Costa Rica at the same time, landing on the north coast of Oriente, close to Baracoa. Two commanders in Oriente, Bartolomé Masó, who had played a role in Céspedes's initial rebellion in 1868, and Guillermón Moncada, a black leader in Santiago, had already raised the flag of rebellion in the province in February. A fresh episode in the long struggle for liberation from colonial rule was under way.[31]

For the Spanish nation, the latest instalment of Cuba's independence war was to end in the unmitigated 'Disaster' of 1898 – with the military intervention of the United States, the defeat of the Spanish navy and army in both the Caribbean and the Pacific, and the final collapse of what remained of the great 400-year-old Spanish Empire: in the Philippines, in Puerto Rico and in Cuba itself. Spain was to take half a century to recover from this humiliating blow.

For the Cuban revolutionaries, the eventual outcome of their war was almost as bad. The country was laid waste, the economy left in ruins and, while the new century would witness the dawn of Cuba's much dreamed-of independence, US intervention and occupation were to place chains on the island's political development that would distort its history for much of the twentieth century.

For an external observer like Winston Churchill, who spent a month in Cuba at the end of 1895 and liked to remember the British intervention of 1762, it was easy to be carried away by the possibilities of what might happen at the end of the war. 'I sympathise with the rebellion – not with the rebels,' he wrote:

> It may be that as the pages of history are turned, brighter futures and better times will come to Cuba. It may be that future years will see the island as it would be now, had England never lost it – a Cuba free and prosperous under just laws and a patriotic administration, throwing open her ports to the commerce of the world, sending her ponies to Hurlingham and her cricketers to Lords, exchanging the cigars of Havana for the cottons of Lancashire and the sugar of Matanzas for the cutlery of Sheffield. At least let us hope so.[32]

The British never made the cultural impact on Cuba that Churchill had romantically envisaged, but British capital was prosaically buying up the Cuban railway system even before the war was over.[33]

Martí was a political organiser and not by nature a guerrilla fighter, yet his early account foreshadows the diary entries of Che Guevara. 'I have quite a load,' he wrote in a cheerful letter to his daughter, 'with my rifle over my shoulder, my *machete* and revolver at my belt; a bag with a hundred cartridges slung over one shoulder and maps of Cuba in a large tube dangling from the other; my knapsack containing fifty pounds of medicine, clothes, my hammock, a blanket and books on my back; and your picture on my chest.'[34]

Martí had sailed from New York in January, joining up with Gómez in the Dominican Republic. The two leaders met at Montecristo, a small northern port close to the Haitian border, and issued their first political manifesto. This envisaged a future Cuban Republic that would be different from 'the feudal and theoretical' republics of Spanish America, since Cuba was marked out by its people and its history to be different. The war of independence would be fought in a civilised fashion, blacks would be invited to participate and private property and non-combatants would be respected. After victory, a new economic system would provide work for everyone. The manifesto concluded with the slogan 'La Victoria o el Sepulcro' – looking back to Garibaldi's cry of 'Roma o Morte' and forward to Castro's invocation of 'Patria o Muerte'.

The second half of the slogan was fulfilled rather earlier than any of the signatories could have anticipated. Within six weeks of landing at Playitas, Martí was dead – aged 42. He and Gómez had joined up with Maceo's group not far from Bayamo, and then, on their way to foregather with a local band commanded by Bartolomé Masó, they fell into a Spanish ambush at Dos Rios on 19 May. The contemporary accounts of Martí's death portray him mounted conspicuously on a white horse, a target hard to miss. Some believe he was anxious to prove his physical bravery, to share the dangers experienced by the ordinary rebel soldiers. Others suggest that he courted martyrdom in the wake of continuing political quarrels with the rebellion's military leaders. Although he had settled his earlier disagreements with Gómez, he knew that Maceo still hankered after military predominance in the councils of the revolution.

No adequate record exists of the political infighting during the early months of 1895 to indicate its effect on Martí's morale. He had no experience as a guerrilla fighter, and was more probably incompetent rather than suicidal. For whatever reason, the early and careless loss of its political leader was a serious misfortune for the rebellion – and for the future of Cuba.

Spain and Cuba again at war, 1895–1896

Much had changed in the politics and economy of the island since the last attempt to promote an independence war, and plans for its further transform-ation were already under discussion in the early 1890s, not just by the rebel exiles in New York but by the colonial government in Madrid. In New York, the political clubs organised by Martí had envisaged 'a brief and generous war' for independence. In Madrid, the government planned reforms designed to avoid such an outcome.

Práxedes Mateo Sagasta y Escolar had taken over as a reformist prime minister in Madrid at the end of 1893.[35] His minister in charge of overseas territories, Antonio Maura y Montaner, proposed autonomy or 'home rule' for all of them. Cuba, as well as Puerto Rico and the Philippines, would be allowed to take control of public works, communications, health and education.[36] For Cuba, Maura proposed a change in the electoral law, doubling the number of voters and putting fresh wind into the sails of the Partido Liberal y Autonomista – much to the irritation of Martí. The home rule party was the chief rival of the revolutionaries seeking independence.

Yet the Spanish were reluctant colonial reformers, and Sagasta failed to give much support to the plan of Maura, who resigned in March 1894. Sagasta's government fell a year later, in March 1895, as news of the Cuban rebellion reached Madrid. The tough and difficult times now looming demanded a hardline government in Spain, and Antonio Cánovas, the wily conservative politician who had saved the Spanish monarchy 20 years earlier, was now brought back, at the age of 67, to save the empire.[37]

Cuba also saw the return of a familiar face: Arsenio Martínez Campos, the author of the Pact of Zanjón, had been victorious in Cuba in 1878. By sending him back to Havana as the captain-general, Cánovas hoped that he would find a political solution to the rebellion, as he had done once before. Martínez Campos sailed into Guantánamo Bay in April 1895 with 7,000 soldiers, to join the 9,000 men rushed out a month earlier. The island's existing garrison was a mere 16,000 men. He had come to inspect the defences in Oriente, and was swiftly made aware of the problems that faced him. Although the rebellion was still confined to the eastern part of the island, the rebels had widespread support. He wrote to Cánovas from Havana in June, describing how 'Passing by *bohíos* in the country . . . there are no men to be seen, and women, on being asked after their husbands and sons, reply with terrible frankness: "in the mountains, with so and so".'

Martínez Campos realised from his previous experience that victory could be achieved only if the civilian population were to be subjected to a degree of compulsion that he himself was not prepared to contemplate. He outlined to Cánovas what might have to happen:

> We could reconcentrate the families of the countryside in the towns, but much force would be needed to compel them, since already there are very few in the interior who want to be [Spanish] volunteers . . . the misery and hunger would be terrible: I would then have to give them rations, which reached 40,000 a day in the last war. It would isolate the country from the towns but it would not prevent espionage, which would be done by women

and children. Perhaps we will come to this, but only in a last resort, and I think I lack the qualities to carry through such a policy.[38]

Martínez Campos believed the war to be unwinnable, and he was right to recognise his limitations. 'Even if we win in the field and suppress the rebels,' he had informed Madrid in his June letter, 'my sincere and loyal opinion is that, with reforms or without reforms, before twelve years we shall have another war.' As it happened, the Spanish empire collapsed within three.

The analysis of Martínez Campos was essentially correct. Under the command of Gómez and Maceo, the rebel army had spread through the mountains of Oriente in the course of 1895. The popular mood had changed since the earlier war and the rebels now received support from almost everyone, most notably from the blacks. White supporters of a continuing link with Spain had long prophesied that independence would mean a black republic. Just as they had feared, the new war took the form of a black rebellion. The shadow of Haiti again hovered over the island. Of the 30,000 rebels mobilised by the end of the first year, some 80 per cent were black. The rebel army, wrote Winston Churchill in an American magazine, is 'an undisciplined rabble' that consists 'to a large extent of coloured men'. If the revolution were to triumph, he added, 'Cuba will be a black republic.' [39] Grover Flint, an American correspondent with Gómez near Matanzas, was also struck by the number of blacks in the rebel army. 'Half of the enlisted men were negroes,' he wrote. He also noted the presence of two 'Chinamen (survivors of the Macao coolie traffic . . .), shifty, sharp-eyed Mongols, with none of the placid laundry look about them'.[40]

While Martí's death was a political blow to the rebels, his absence had no perceptible impact on the development of the war. He was replaced as the provisional president of the nascent Cuban republic by Salvador Cisneros Betancourt, the Marqués de Santa Lucía, the septuagenarian veteran of the rebel group in Camagüey that had joined Céspedes in 1868. Masó was appointed as the vice-president and Gómez and Maceo remained commander-in-chief and deputy. Tomás Estrada Palma, the former rebel 'president' had not taken much part in exile politics in the years since 1878 and had worked for many years as a schoolmaster in the United States. At heart he was a supporter of US annexation. He had been recruited by Martí to work as the revolution's agent in New York and he continued so to do. These were all veterans of the earlier war, men with long service in the cause of independence, but they held very different views about strategy and tactics, as well as about politics, and their movement lacked a charismatic leader who might have obliged them to work together.

Gómez was now the dominant figure, and he was determined not to repeat the experience of the earlier war, when the arguments of the planters had prevented his guerrilla army from moving into the rich sugar lands of central and western Cuba. Together with Maceo, he struck out immediately for Camagüey and in October they crossed the old *trocha* line between Júcaro and Morón and rode with a thousand men on horseback towards Sancti Spíritus and Santa Clara. By the end of the year they were threatening Matanzas. No pitched battles took place, but much deployment of fire and flame. The cane fields were burnt, as were the mills and plantation houses. 'It has been a perfect roaring hell of fires all the way to the hills of Trinidad and the sea,' wrote one estate employee in December, 'and we could see nothing but smoke and smouldering ruins, groups of poor people on foot . . . homes burned and clothing stolen.'[41] The strategy became familiar in Cuba as *la tea*, the torch or firelighter.

Early in January 1896 Gómez arrived at the outskirts of Havana, while Maceo, bypassing the capital, advanced towards Pinar del Rio. Their lightning march along the length of the island, achieving in seven months what had taken seven years in the earlier war, had left the Spanish facing defeat. Only radical repression would serve their purposes, and the emollient and experienced Martínez Campos had already told Madrid that this was not a strategy he was prepared to contemplate. In January 1896, after only nine months in command, he resigned and returned to Madrid.

General Weyler's development of the concentration camp, 1896–1897

The new captain-general sent out to Havana in 1896 was a genuine scorched-earth expert. General Valeriano Weyler (1838–1930), Marqués de Tenerife and former captain-general of Barcelona, was another veteran of the earlier Cuban war, chosen by Cánovas for his martial and ruthless qualities. Puritanical and sentimental, Weyler preferred animals to humans and funded a horses' home in Madrid.[42] Present in Washington as a young man as Spain's military attaché during the American Civil War, he was an admirer of the fiercesome tactics of General Sherman, who had cut a long swathe through Georgia in 1864, leaving a trail of burned-out mansions, devastated fields, wrecked railway lines and despairing civilians.[43] Weyler had something similar in mind for Cuba.

Arriving in Havana, Weyler found the rebels at the gates of the city. 'The day after my arrival,' he told Cánovas, 'they prevented milk coming in.' Gómez was just a few miles outside the city, and food from the countryside could only enter the city after the rebels had been paid the transit tax they demanded. Martínez Campos, as his last act, had prepared Havana for an imminent attack. Weyler was much encouraged by the presence in Havana of 'teams of Volunteers', still active in the Spanish cause, guarding 'the post office and the main public buildings'. He wrote to Madrid describing how 'these admirable corps guarded the external section of the city to avoid attack'.[44]

Weyler revealed the extent of his problems in his first despatch home. 'All respect for authority had vanished. There was public muttering everywhere against Spain, everywhere criticism and complaint.' Even in Havana itself, there were 'germs of separatism', and conspiracies to aid the rebels. The tobacco factories were his particular concern, 'since there readers read separatist books and articles, together with news, false or exaggerated, of the war and the revolution, thus fomenting among the workers hatred of Spain'.

Weyler had been sent out to save Cuba, and his first task was to push Gómez from the vicinity of Havana and to force Maceo out of Pinar del Rio. His plan was to force the rebels back to the east of the old *trocha* from Júcaro to Morón, which he now began to refurbish. He also constructed a new *trocha*, west of Havana, from Mariel to Majana. For the first time, the rebels were obliged to fight in open battle, and the forces of Maceo, returning from their marauding excursion in Pinar del Rio to rejoin Gómez, were caught in February and took many casualties. Weyler put 60,000 troops into the province and built an elaborate network of heliograph towers to note the presence of guerrilla groups and to assist with rapid communications.[45]

These were setbacks to the rebel cause, but the two commanders were able to concentrate their forces outside Matanzas, and to ponder their next move. Maceo returned to the region west of Havana, while Gómez moved east to Santa Clara. Their small armies were reinforced in March by the arrival in Oriente of Calixto García with a large cargo of weapons. García took over as commander of the entire eastern region and remained there until the end of the war.

Weyler now embarked on the counter-guerrilla strategy for which the Cuban–Spanish War has become famous – creating the 'concentration camps' and 'strategic hamlets' that were to characterise the irregular wars of the twentieth century. The possibility of *reconcentration* – moving peasant families into towns – had been discussed by Martínez Campos in 1895, and had in fact been tried on an experimental scale during the Ten Year War by Weyler himself. Now he was to put his earlier notions into ferocious practice. His plan was for the entire population of towns and villages in designated military areas to be 'concentrated' in well-defended centres, depriving the rebels of their natural constituency and support. Food for the *reconcentrados* would, where possible, be provided locally from special zones of cultivation, and where food was not available, Weyler was content for them to starve. The population of the western provinces was required to submit to registration, and those disobeying military orders were found guilty of treason and executed.[46] Weyler issued the first concentration orders in October in Pinar del Rio, where Maceo was still active.

The construction of these Cuban 'concentration camps' was soon to be become widely known in the United States, courtesy of American journalists and Cuban exiles. The phenomenon was denounced in the New York newspapers, notably in the *New York Journal*, acquired by William Randolph Hearst in 1895. In the forefront of the human rights journalism of the time, the *Journal* had already warned its readers about General Weyler, describing him in February 1896, as a 'fiendish despot . . . a brute, the devastator of *haciendas* . . . pitiless, cold, an exterminator of men . . . there is nothing to prevent his carnal, animal brain from running riot with itself in inventing tortures and infamies of bloody debauchery.' Grover Flint, describing the 'concentration' of half a million peasants into crowded and unhealthy camps outside the cities, noted that journalists were calling it 'a policy of extermination'.[47] Weyler's strategy, cruel though it was, had a considerable impact on the course of the war. Anticipating the thoughts of Mao Tse-tung, who envisaged guerilla fighters as fish swimming within the 'sea' of the rural population, Weyler largely succeeded in draining the sea, leaving the rebels with little water within which to swim.

By the end of 1896, Gómez and Maceo were in trouble. Weyler's forces had military supremacy in the west – in Pinar del Rio, Havana and Matanzas. To the east, Gómez was in political difficulties, at loggerheads with the civilian leadership. Gómez was the supreme military commander, but his methods and strategy were increasingly questioned by the civilian leadership, both in Cuba and in New York. The civilians, influenced by the planters, had grown hostile to the *tea*, the strategy of torching the plantations and cutting the commercial communications between the rural areas and the Spanish-held towns. Gómez grew restive at the criticism. When a deputation from a group of foreign coffee growers requested that their property should be respected, he told them to 'take your business to your own country'.[48]

A second dispute concerned military appointments. Gómez promoted people who had distinguished themselves in battle, the normal procedure in guerrilla war. Many came from the lower classes or were black. The civilians sought to promote members of the white professional classes – lawyers and doctors – who had joined the revolutionary movement but lacked military experience.[49] Arguments about decisions in the military sphere inevitably had political overtones.

In October Maceo received an urgent message from Gómez urging him to march east to join him. Gómez needed his political rather than his military support. After quarrelling with the civilian politicians, he was threatening to resign. He needed Maceo at his side. Maceo's group had been reinforced in September by a boatload of men, including Francisco Gómez, the son of Máximo, and a welcome load of weapons and ammunition, despatched from the United States by Estrada Palma.

Maceo now set off to rejoin Gómez, to assist him in his confrontation with the civilian leadership. Avoiding Weyler's new *trocha* from Mariel to Majano, he crossed the bay of Mariel by boat and established his camp outside Havana. There, in December 1896, he was surprised by a Spanish troop rather larger than his own and was killed in an insignificant skirmish, together with the young Gómez. The death of Maceo was a blow to the liberation army. *El Titán de Bronce*, the bronze Titan, their bravest, most adventurous, most charismatic leader was dead. 'Sadness was in everyone,' wrote one officer, while another recalled that he had never seen such deep sorrow in men used to danger and death.[50]

Weyler now turned his attention to the surviving rebel commander. Thousands of fresh troops were deployed in central Cuba with the hope of destroying the rebel leadership at the top. With Maceo gone, Gómez was obliged to withdraw his threat to resign and he fought back with vigour. Yet his guerrillas were still on the defensive in the middle of 1897. The war was going Spain's way. Only Calixto García in Oriente achieved some success, capturing the town of Las Tunas in August.

In Madrid Cánovas decided the time was ripe to wave again the flag of reform. Constitutional changes were introduced in Cuba in February 1897, providing local mayors with stronger powers and giving the country a degree of fiscal independence. The new measures were designed not so much to influence opinion in Cuba as to persuade the United States that efforts were being made to end the war. American public opinion remained concerned by the stories of Weyler's repression, and Washington was an attentive observer of Cuban developments, ever poised for action.

But a dramatic and unscheduled event occurred in the Basque Country that altered the direction of the war and accelerated its course towards an unlooked-for conclusion. Cánovas was assassinated on 21 June 1897, while on holiday outside San Sebastián, by Miguel Angiolillo, an Italian anarchist from Barcelona. Angiolillo had planned to kill a member of the Spanish royal family, in revenge for the recent execution of anarchists in Barcelona. While on a visit to Paris, he had encountered Dr Ramón Emetério Betances, a mulatto Puerto Rican activist long involved with Cuban exiles, who persuaded him that the prime minister would be a more significant target, and gave him 500 francs to help him on his way.

Angiolillo's three bullets did as much for the Cuban independence movement as three years of combat. In New York, the newspapers greeted the assassination with excitement, declaring that the Cubans would now surely receive their freedom. In Madrid, the sudden death of Cánovas brought immediate political change, with the return of Praxedes Sagasta, the old Liberal leader, as prime minister, a man now converted to Cuban home rule. Sagasta appointed Segismundo Moret, who had once helped to bring an end to slavery, to be the new minister for the colonies. Moret advocated dominion status for Cuba, along Canadian lines, a notion long popular with influential Cubans. A new constitution was promised, including universal male suffrage and a two-chamber parliament. The offer was appealing, even if the link with Spain would remain.

Weyler read the writing on the wall and resigned. Perceiving that the general's unpopularity in the United States was helping the cause of the US war party, Sagasta was content to see him go. The cost of the war to Spain had been immense – both in money and in men. Some 200,000 soldiers had been sent out to Cuba since 1895, and none were left to deal with other wars. Cuba was not Spain's only preoccupation. Since August 1896 it had faced another colonial insurrection – in the Philippines. The wars in Cuba and the Philippines had run in parallel, with many of the same characters.[51] General Ramón Blanco, the captain-general in Manila had returned to Madrid in 1896 and was transferred to Havana in November 1897.

In the Philippines, with no extra troops available, Spain had been obliged to negotiate. Ramón Blanco had a similar project for Cuba. There would be self-government and negotiations. Weyler's successes had been achieved at a price that Spain could no longer afford. No further military offensives would take place. An amnesty was decreed for all Cuban political prisoners held in Spanish jails. A 'home rule' government was finally established, led by José María Gálvez, an old Autonomist leader from the 1870s.

Spain had secured peace in the Philippines, the better to concentrate on Cuba, but Sagasta's reformist programme made little impact on Máximo Gómez. With his experience of the Pact of Zanjón he rejected all negotiating offers out of hand. He knew that the Autonomists were isolated; only a tiny group still favoured home rule. As so often in the various histories of colonial disengagement, the imperial power had offered too little too late. Cuba was now irreparably divided between independence rebels and loyalist Spaniards, fighting on.

In Madrid the Queen Mother Regent was not happy, complaining that Sagasta's peace programme was a concession to the United States.[52] She was right, but the concession was insufficient. Six months later the history of both Cuba and the Philippines was altered by an American decision to declare war on the Spanish empire. Spain's Pacific fleet was destroyed in Manila Bay on 1 May 1898, and Manila itself fell to American forces on 13 August.[53] A similar fate lay in store for Cuba.

'Remember the Maine!': The US intervention in Cuba, 1898

In the north-eastern suburb of Santiago de Cuba, a handful of comfortable villas and the wooded grounds of the Hotel San Juan surround a small grassy hill where a few antique cannon and stone memorials are displayed. The hill, which once marked the outer defences of the city, is the Loma San Juan, and here, on 1 July 1898 during their invasion of Cuba, units of the United States army fought the only significant land battle against Spanish forces. The fight was unequal, with less than 1,000 Spanish defenders and more than 3,000

American troops, yet it lasted throughout a long day and the US losses were not small – 223 dead and more than 1,000 wounded. The Spanish lost half that number.

The event is well remembered by Americans on account of the presence at the battle of Theodore Roosevelt, then the US assistant secretary of the navy and soon to be the President. His colourful regiment of 'Rough Riders', officially the First US Volunteer Cavalry (but also referred to as 'Teddy's Terrors'), was given much publicity at the time. Commanded by General Leonard Wood – Roosevelt's close friend, President McKinley's doctor and the officer soon to become the ruler of Cuba – the Rough Riders were a cross-section of the US population, recruited, as Roosevelt wrote in his memoir of the war, from 'the wild riders and riflemen of the Rockies and the Great Plains'.[54] A trooper from Arizona, years later, described the contingent as 'millionaires, paupers, shyster lawyers, cowboys, quack doctors, farmers, college professors, miners, adventurers, preachers, prospectors, socialists, journalists, insurance agents, Jews, politicians, Gentiles, Mexicans, professed Christians, Indians, West Point graduates, Arkansan wild men, baseball players, sheriffs and horse-thieves'.[55] One contingent was made up of America's indigenous peoples – Cherokees and Chickasaws, Choctaws and Creeks. The Rough Riders were just one of many volunteer contingents contributing to the US invasion force, but around such characters, myths were easily created. Much of the romance of the Cuban campaign, indelibly etched in the folk memory of the United States, is associated with the presence of this motley assembly of disparate folk.

Cubans recall the US intervention with less affection. Calixto García, the rebel commander closest to Santiago – operating from the lower slopes of the Sierra Maestra – was invited by the Americans to supply troops to divert Spanish forces during the US advance on the city. He sent 3,000 of his men, but none were asked to the subsequent victory celebrations. Cuba was liberated from Spanish control by the American invasion in barely three weeks, yet the Cubans had been fighting for more than three years. They watched bleakly from the sidelines as their victory was taken from them.

Roosevelt was a prominent figure at the battle at San Juan Hill, and so too was William Randolph Hearst, owner of the jingoistic *New York Journal*.[56] His newspaper, and those of his rivals in a prolonged circulation war, had done their best to stir up the American newspaper-reading public – and by extension the US government – to favour US military intervention against Spain, publishing pro-Cuban propaganda throughout the Cuban–Spanish war. Hearst could not stay away from the war that he had so ardently promoted.

Hearst had prepared the ground for intervention, but the *casus belli*, the event that made war inevitable, was entirely unexpected and could not be laid at his door. It had occurred five months earlier in Havana harbour. On

15 February 1898 the US battleship *Maine* had been lying peacefully at anchor when, without warning, a gigantic explosion swiftly sank it, killing 258 American sailors.

'The *Maine* was sunk by an act of dirty treachery,' Roosevelt recorded in his diary, and the US press blamed a Spanish mine for the disaster, a view shared by a subsequent US official enquiry. The Spanish authorities disagreed, claiming that an internal explosion had occurred on the ship, a view later echoed by Irene Wright in 1910. 'The opinion generally prevailing,' she wrote, 'is that the *Maine* was not wilfully wrecked by either Spaniards or Cubans, but was blown up by an explosion within her own hull.'[57] Rather solid evidence for this view was produced many years later by US Admiral Hyman Rickover, who combed through the evidence in the 1970s. The admiral concluded that an internal coal fire, in a bunker adjacent to the magazine, had indeed caused the explosion. Such fires had occurred on other occasions on other US ships, though without such dire results.[58]

The sinking of the *Maine* was an accident, but no American believed that at the time. The misgivings that had prevented Washington from taking action earlier in the war were swept away. Urged on by the press, the US government had no choice but to take up arms. Negotiations took place between the United States and Spain between February and April, but there was no possible meeting of minds. European countries other than Spain pleaded with both sides to accept a negotiated settlement. Nothing came of this intervention. War was declared on Spain on 25 April 1898 and US officers were told to prepare for an invasion, not just of Cuba, but of Spain's other island possessions in the Caribbean and in the Pacific. Puerto Rico was in the American sights, as well as the Philippines and the Pacific island of Guam. The United States was soon engaged in a far more ambitious project than simply securing the freedom of Cuba. What had once been perceived as 'Cuba's war of national liberation' was to become the 'Spanish–American War', the destruction of the far-flung remains of the 400-year-old empire of Spain.

The American attitude to the *Maine* disaster was a mixture of horror and patriotic pride, coupled with an irresistable desire for revenge. Volunteers flocked to the colours. Scenes of extraordinary public rejoicing at the prospect of war were witnessed by John Black Atkins, a correspondent who arrived in Manhattan in April and described them in the pages of the *Manchester Guardian*.

> The United States flag was everywhere hung across the streets and from the windows. Warlike sentiments and war bulletins were stuck in the shop windows. Men and women and dogs went about the streets wearing American medallions or 'favours'. Bicycles were decorated with the national colours as though for a fancy dress parade. Everywhere one saw the legend 'Remember the *Maine*.'[59]

The *Maine* was the excuse, but had it not occurred some other event would almost certainly have sparked a war. The United States was in a notably expansionist mood. Its internal frontier had been conquered. Centuries of Indian resistance had been brought to an end, symbolised by the massacre at Wounded Knee in December 1890, when the Seventh Cavalry slaughtered the Sioux Indians in South Dakota. The popular mood was changing too, and politicians were not lacking to give it a voice. Roosevelt and his friend Henry Cabot Lodge were only the most prominent of the figures seeking a wider world role for the United States.

This new mood had been reinforced by the timely arrival of the 'yellow press' – combative, competitive and fiercely nationalist newspapers with a mass circulation. These papers both helped to create, and took advantage of, the jingoistic atmosphere, and had followed events in Cuba since 1895 with close attention. The details of a foreign war, so close to home and with such obvious implications for US security, was a useful circulation builder. The Cuban exiles in New York, notably Tomás Estrada Palma and his team, had not been slow to provide the newspapers with a steady supply of information and assistance, emphasising the abuse of human rights. The reported atrocities of Weyler, and the sufferings of the Cuban people, became common currency in the United States.

Urged on by a strident public opinion fuelled by the press, the US government had paid close attention to events in Cuba since 1895. The 60-year history and experience of the Monroe Doctrine was not about to be lightly abandoned. Yet the government was divided in its opinions and reluctant to intervene. President Grover Cleveland had recommended neutrality, and was happy to consider mediation, but was loath to contemplate intervention. The US made an offer of mediation to Cánovas in April 1896, declaring that it was 'concerned in all struggles for freedom', but the Spanish prime minister dismissed the offer. Silent diplomacy continued, but other possibilities were now examined and other US government institutions took an interest. The Office of Naval Intelligence asked for war plans to be drawn up in June 1896, for a possible war against Spain.

A presidential election campaign in the autumn of 1896 had kept Cuba in the public eye. The outgoing Cleveland was accused of 'doing nothing about Cuba'. With the press printing regular atrocity reports from Cuba, the election brought defeat to William Jennings Bryan, a Democrat hostile to expansionism, and victory to William McKinley, the Republican candidate. McKinley became President in March 1897, appointing Roosevelt to be the assistant secretary of the navy. A new ambassador to Madrid was told to warn the Spanish government that if steps were not taken to end the Cuban conflict, the United States would take measures itself.

Gómez's refusal to negotiate meant that time was running out for Spain. The sinking of the *Maine* made intervention inevitable. On 22 April 1898, just three days before the formal American declaration of war, Spain made one last desperate throw of the dice. In a letter to Gómez, Ramón Blanco suggested an alliance between Spain and Cuba against the United States: 'The Cubans will receive arms from the Spanish army and, with the cry "Hurrah for Spain, Hurrah for Cuba", we will repel the invader, and keep free from a foreign yoke the descendants of a single race.'[60]

Such an outcome was not to be. Blanco's belated and humiliating appeal to Hispanic unity, and to the freedom-loving instincts of the white race, evoked no favourable response from the black and mulatto troops in the rebel camp. Gómez sent back a pithy reply, saying that it was 'too late', although his letter to Blanco suggests his apparent trust in the honourable intentions of the United States.

> You represent an old and discredited monarchy, and we fight for the same principles as Bolívar and Washington. You say that we belong to the same race, and invite me to fight against a foreign invader. I know only one race, humanity . . . Spain has done badly here, and the United States are carrying out for Cuba a duty of humanity and civilisation . . . I do not see the danger of our extermination by the US to which you refer . . . If that should come to pass, history will judge.

As indeed it might.

History, as written in Cuba and elsewhere, has not been overly charitable in its consideration of the eventual results of US intervention. Yet most of Cuba's rebel leadership welcomed it at the time. Martí and Maceo might well have objected, but both were dead. The important Cuban decision makers were Gómez, the military commander, and Masó, the president of the 'provisional government'. Gómez, by rejecting Blanco's offer of partnership, had implicitly accepted US intervention, while Masó gave it a warm welcome. The glorious revolution begun by José Martí is about to triumph, Masó declared, 'thanks to the magnanimous assistance of the USA; our arms, which were never conquered by the Spaniards in three years of war, will soon have gained their victory'. Masó supported the invasion, although he lived to regret his decision and later became a vocal opponent of the Platt Amendment that wrote the permanent threat of US intervention into the constitution of independent Cuba.

The position of Calixto García, the commander in Oriente, was ambivalent. Long out of touch and out of sympathy with the Cuban exile leadership in the United States, he was barely aware that the Americans were about to land in his area of operations until an American lieutenant arrived secretly at his mountain base in May 1898. He did not know whether to cooperate or not and was forced to make a pragmatic decision on the spot, agreeing to assist the invasion forces. A large contingent of his men were ferried along the coast by the Americans to land at Daiquirí, to the east of

Santiago. García was visited by William Hearst, and he thanked the editor for his newspaper's support for the Cuban cause, presenting him with a rebel flag. García, like Masó and many others, came to regret the US invasion, but he only lived long enough to see the early months of the occupation, for he died suddenly when visiting Washington in December.

The ambivalence of many Cubans about the US invasion was partly the result of the 'Teller Amendment', a clause added to the April declaration of war and ratified by the US Congress that declared that the occupation of Cuba should not be permanent. The amendment, put forward by Senator Henry Teller under pressure from the lobby of Cuban exiles, was a categoric rejection of any colonialist intent:

> The United States hereby disclaims any disposition or intention to exercise sovereignty, jurisdiction or control over said island except for pacification thereof, and asserts its determination, when that is accomplished, to leave the government and control of the island to its people.

The Teller Amendment persuaded many Cubans to believe that the invasion would come with no strings attached; it also ensured that the intervention was perceived in the United States at the time, and for most of the first half of the twentieth century, as a disinterested gesture, a humanitarian action that liberated the island from a repressive colonial regime. American policy, as it worked out in practice, was never quite so clear-cut or so morally unambiguous.

The first US victory in the Spanish–American war took place at sea on the other side of the world, just five days after the declaration of war. An American fleet commanded by Commodore George Dewey destroyed Spain's Pacific fleet in Manila Bay on 1 May. The way lay open to the American conquest of the Philippines.

Spain's Atlantic fleet, commanded by Admiral Pascual Cervera, was ordered to sail from Cádiz to the Caribbean, and many Americans feared that its destination would be the east coast of the United States. The fleet had come to defend Cuba, not to attack the US mainland, and by the end of May it was safely harboured in Santiago's great bay. It remained there for more than a month, bottled up by a large US fleet, commanded by Admiral William Sampson, that hovered outside.

Sampson's fleet had sailed from Key West after the declaration of war on 25 April, and arrived off Oriente in June. After bombarding the fortifications on the Morro, exploring expeditions were sent out to find a suitable place to land an expeditionary force. A thousand men were landed at Guantánamo Bay, meeting considerable resistance from Spanish forces, but linking up with a rebel Cuban contingent.

The principal US invasion force, with more than 15,000 soldiers commanded by General William Rufus Shafter, did not leave Tampa until 14

June. 'It was a most happy-go-lucky expedition,' wrote Richard Harding Davis, the correspondent for *Harpers*, 'run with real American optimism and readiness to take big chances . . . As one of the generals on board said: "This is God Almighty's war, and we are only His agents".'[61] The general was probably Leonard Wood, the commander of the Rough Riders, who wrote to his wife about what he perceived to be the start of a new policy for the United States: 'Hard it is to realise that this is . . . the first great expedition our country has ever sent oversea and marks the commencement of a new era in our relations with the world.'[62]

General Shafter spent the time reading an account of the disastrous expedition to Guantánamo in 1742 by Admiral Edward Vernon. Recalling the problems of that British episode, he decided to land his force closer to Santiago. The initial assault took place at Daiquirí on 22 June, after heavy bombardment of the Spanish positions from the sea. This was an open beach, apart from the dock and the iron pier used for the loading of ore from the works of the Spanish–American Iron Company, but 6,000 men were brought ashore on the first day.

The Spanish resistance was poor, and the Americans soon foregathered with a local Cuban force of 1,500 men who had arrived from Bayamo. Calixto García's contingent of 3,000 from the Sierra Maestra was ferried in a few days later. 'The insurgents were men incredibly tattered and peaked and forlorn,' wrote John Black Atkins. 'On many of them a few ribbons of clothing suggested the outline of a jacket or trousers. They were lean as men might be who had been living on cocoanuts and mangoes. Whenever one lighted a fire a Cuban presented himself, at the sign of the smoke, quietly and inexplicably like a genie, and asked for food.'[63]

Atkins noticed how rapidly the American soldiers became disenchanted with their Cuban allies, partly because 'the Cuban insurgent regarded every American as a kind of charitable institution, and expected him to disgorge on every occasion. The Cuban was continually pointing to the American's shirt, coat, or trousers, and then pointing to himself, meaning that he desired a transfer of the property.' There was an additional reason for the lack of comradeship between the two armies: the Americans were mostly white, the Cubans were mostly black.

Within a week, the US invasion force had disembarked and was advancing along interior roads towards their rendezvous with the Spanish at the Loma San Juan on 1 July. The American victory sealed the fate of Spanish forces on the island, and two days later the US secured a comparable success at sea. The Spanish admiral had no desire to suffer the fate of the Pacific fleet in Manila Bay, yet with Santiago itself about to fall to US land forces, he was ordered to leave the harbour lest his ships should fall into American hands. It was a suicidal gesture, and on 3 July the entire Spanish fleet sailed out of the harbour to be greeted by the Americans. The Spanish ships were attacked, dispersed and sunk. It was not so much the fleet that committed suicide as the Spanish empire.

The US victory by land and sea was now complete, and surrender terms were agreed two weeks later, on 17 July. Decisions had to be made in Havana, Washington and Madrid, and the subsequent detailed negotiations were difficult and prolonged, but the US flag now flew from the palace in Santiago, and General Leonard Wood was appointed as the city's new governor.

General Wood and the US occupation of Cuba, 1898–1902

The United States ruled Cuba for four years under what was, in effect, a military dictatorship. The Spanish captain-general was replaced by an American general. The nature and duration of the American occupation from 1898 until 1902 was endlessly contested in the US Congress, and much argued over by American officers on the island itself. What changes were needed in Cuba, and how long was the occupation to last?

The Americans had no previous experience of running a foreign country, and the older generation of US officers in Cuba could only look back to their experiences 30 years earlier when they had administered the Southern states at the end of the Civil War. This was the model with which they were familiar, and the one that they were to follow in Cuba.

With the Spanish fleet destroyed, and the island effectively occupied by American troops, the officers of Spain and the United States observed all the civilities of the epoch. General Adolfo Jiménez Castellanos, the very last captain-general, bowed out at a formal ceremony in Havana in December 1898, and handed over the keys of the city to General John Brooke, the third senior general in the US army. General Wood replaced him a year later, but remained in Santiago throughout 1899. The Americans retained the Spanish administration, and Spanish officials and government employees were confirmed in their posts. Many remained far into the independence era.

The Cubans – soldiers, officers and people – were treated less generously, both by the incoming Americans and by the outgoing Spaniards. The conscripted soldiers from Spain could not wait to get home, wreaking vengeance on people and property in Oriente province before they left. Cattle were killed and water troughs filled with manure.[64] The incoming Americans were more fastidious, collecting rubbish from the streets, cleaning the drains and embarking on a campaign against the tropical diseases that were already taking a toll of their troops. Yet the new rulers were disdainful of the Cubans, dismissive of the soldiers in the armies of Gómez and Calixto García and overtly contemptuous of the black population. Official dealings were mostly conducted with the wealthy community of merchants and traders, and with the incoming exiles from New York and Florida – US-educated white Cubans already familiar with American ways and language.

These American-influenced Cubans were soon joined by an influx of American citizens, visiting their newly conquered territory or planning a new life. A *New York Times* correspondent reported in May 1900 how

> Cuba is simply over-run with Americans of all ages, of all conditions of life, of all professions, and of no professions. From the gray-haired nanny, down to the newsboy selling his papers in the street, Americans are in evidence. Years ago the rush was to the west of the United States: now the tide has turned southward to Cuba . . . From appearances, many seem to think that they will find the streets paved with gold to be had for the picking up.[65]

One of the first tasks of the occupying force was to organise a census.[66] The total population was now officially put at 1,500,000, with 250,000 in Havana. The census suggested that the black population had diminished to as little as 32 per cent, the smallest percentage recorded since the first census in the eighteenth century, although the figure may have been influenced by the wishful thinking of its organisers. The census also revealed that some 300,000 inhabitants, a fifth of the population, had disappeared from the earlier figures, with the assumption that this was the death toll of the war. The four-year war had certainly been hugely destructive of human life and property. Disease and battle itself, coupled with Weyler's policy of population 'concentration', had decimated the Cuban people. A devastating account of conditions in Pinar del Rio in the autumn of 1899 was provided by General Fitzhugh Lee, the American commander in Havana:

> Business of all sorts was suspended. Agricultural operations had ceased; large sugar estates with their enormous and expensive machinery were destroyed; houses burned; stock driven off for consumption by the Spanish troops, or killed. There was scarcely an ox left to pull a plow, had there been a plow left. Not a pig had been left in the pen, or a hen to lay an egg for the poor destitute people who still held on to life, most of them sick, weary, and weak. Miles and miles of country uninhabited by either the human race or domestic animals were visible to the eye on every side. The great fertile island of Cuba in some places resembled an ash pile, in others the dreary desert.[67]

A further important task facing the military governor was the creation of a Cuban security force. The soldiers of the Spanish army had left for Spain after their surrender, and those of the Cuban rebel army, some 33,000 of them, were pensioned off in May 1899, each receiving 75 dollars as the price for handing in their weapons. Reluctant to create an actual army, since the US planned to be responsible for the island's defence, a decision was taken to re-create the paramilitary Rural Guard, already existing in embryonic form in the Spanish era. The US introduced segregation into the force, causing considerable resentment and dismay among the black fighters of the independence war. The officers were almost entirely white.

The Guard was designed to mop up some of the demobilised rebel soldiers who had no jobs to go to, and to deal with the chronic problem of banditry in the countryside that continued long after the war was over. Not everyone supported the establishment of the Rural Guard. General James Wilson, a notably progressive US officer in charge of Matanzas, was strongly opposed, fearing that it would lead to a military dictatorship – the pattern in much of Latin America. 'Give me the money', he wrote, 'to spend on oxen and tools and the reconstruction of the peasants' *bohíos*, and I will guarantee peace and order.'[68] He was not listened to.

The lack of a proper army would create serious difficulties in the early years of the Republic, and set the Cuban armed forces apart from comparable institutions elsewhere in Latin America.[69] As Cuba moved towards independence, the Rural Guard was complemented by a tiny artillery force of 150 white Cubans, notionally at the command of the President.

In spite of the Teller Amendment, most Americans running Cuba thought that they had arrived to stay. They had received assurances from President McKinley, who told the US Congress in December 1898 that the military government would remain in Cuba 'until there is complete tranquillity in the island and a stable government inaugurated'. No one knew how long that would be. Most assumed that the occupation would last into the long distant future, or even be made permanent – the fate decreed for Puerto Rico, captured in August. Few imagined it would last barely four years.

General Brooke believed that his government was popular and would continue into the indefinite future. 'There is not a sensible man who thinks we can leave for a long time,' he reported in January 1900 at the end of his year in office. That time would not be 'measured by months but by years'. Brooke claimed that he had 'consulted all classes', but he met only the more conservative elements in Cuban society, who told him what he wanted to hear: that Cubans would support US annexation.

Brooke had no plans to run the country himself, and Cubans were chosen to head the four principal government departments of Interior, Finance, Justice and Education, and Agriculture, Trade and Industry. Only those who had lived in exile in the United States were given ministerial jobs, and all were white. The economy was kept securely in American hands. The important, and income-generating, Department of Customs, run by Major Tasker Bliss, was placed under US military control.

General Brooke was shunted aside in December 1899 in favour of General Wood. Like Brooke, Wood believed that he was there for the long haul. Like all colonial governors, he got little cooperation from the governed, and vented his contempt in private letters to McKinley: 'We are dealing with a race that has been going steadily downhill for a hundred years', he wrote in April 1900.[70] McKinley had told him 'to get the people ready' for a republican form of government, saying 'I leave the details of procedure to you. Give them a good school system, try to straighten out the courts, put them on their feet as best you can. We want to do all we can for them, and to get out of the island as soon as we safely can.'

Ordered to do something about education, and himself still believing in eventual US annexation, General Wood set about organising the country on American lines, adapting existing Spanish schools to the system common in Ohio and building new ones. Textbooks were translated from English and teachers sent to the United States for instruction, both in the US syllabus and in American teaching methods.[71]

Schools were established by Protestant missionaries who flocked to the island from the United States 'to convert Catholics . . . to evangelical Christianity and to bring them into line with American ideas'.[72] Churches were founded by Methodists, Baptists, Episcopalians and Presbyterians. The Methodists specialised in offering segregated education to the children of the white elite.

Racist in most other respects, the American occupiers were happy for labour to be obtained from wherever it could be found. Although few regular jobs were available in the cities, plenty of work remained on the plantations and in the mines. Soon, as in the early years of the Spanish occupation, employers began looking to the Caribbean islands nearby. Plantation owners and mining companies, faced by the post-war shortage, recruited black contract workers from Haiti and Jamaica. A thousand arrived in the first six months of 1900. White Cubans soon revived their old fears of a black island, and the military authorities ordered the immigration to be halted. When a US company planned to import 4,000 workers from Jamaica, to build a new railway line the length of the island, the US authorities were again obliged to step in after protests by Cubans in Santiago. The Americans eventually got the message, and Frank Steinhart, General Brook's aide-de-camp, advocated 'white immigration only', suggesting that workers should be brought in from northern Spain.[73]

The mood in Washington began to change after the first year of occupation. President and Congress grew anxious about the expense of their new imperial responsibilities. Cuba alone was costing half a million dollars a month. The Philippines had to be thought about as well – and budgeted for. The capture of Manila had been welcomed by the local population, but the subsequent occupation had met spirited resistance. The rebellion was not crushed until 1901. The establishment of an American empire in the Pacific was proving expensive. So too was Cuba. Elihu Root, the new secretary for war, described it as 'a burden and annoyance'.

Root, a wealthy Republican lawyer, was the politician in Washington charged with masterminding Cuba's future, selected for the job by President McKinley in 1899. McKinley understood that the new imperial responsibilities acquired by his nation required a competent administrator in the war department rather than a military man. 'No such intelligent, constructive, and vital force' had occupied the post in American history, recorded Henry Stimson, one of his successors.[74]

Root turned his attention to the question of the elections. In the early months of occupation, the American authorities in Washington and in Cuba imagined that Cuba would soon be incorporated into the Union. They sought to ally themselves politically with that small but enduring section of the Cuban population that supported the idea of US annexation. Root shared the view of General Wood that 'sensible' Cubans favoured it, and if elections could so be rigged to ensure that 'sensible' Cubans won, the dream of annexation would be assured.[75] If Cuba were to be given a limited suffrage, Root wrote, the 'mass of ignorant and incompetent' people would be kept out, and it would be possible to 'avoid the kind of control which leads to the perpetual revolutions of Central America and other West India islands'.[76]

The first post-colonial elections in Cuba were held in 1900. Municipal elections took place in June and those for a constituent assembly in December. The electoral regulations were framed by the Americans to give the vote to Cuban males over the age of 20 who were able to read and write. They also had to be the owners of property worth $250, or, an inevitable concession, to have served in the rebel army. Cuban women were not allowed to vote. With these restrictions, the total electorate was barely 100,000 men, some five per cent of the population. The poor and most blacks were effectively excluded from the franchise.[77]

Three parties presented themselves at the municipal elections. Two advocated immediate independence: the Republicans, led by General José Miguel Gómez, the governor of Santa Clara; and the Nationalists, who enjoyed the tacit support of Máximo Gómez and were powerful in Havana. Only the Democratic Unionists, a conservative group including several supporters of the old Autonomist party, favoured annexation. The result, tempered by regional loyalties, was a victory for the independence-minded parties.

General Wood was appalled, recognising that independence was now on the agenda, and deploring the fact that the friends he had cultivated in Cuba had failed to make an impact. 'The highly intelligent Cubans of the land-owning, industrial and commercial classes are not in politics,' he noted gloomily.[78] He had failed to realise that the classes he favoured were not just uninterested in politics, they had other things on their minds. They were entering a period of terminal decline, for the war had destroyed their businesses. The sugar industry was in crisis, plantation owners were bankrupt, the owners of urban property were ruined. The collapse of the Spanish empire had brought down its former beneficiaries with it. The political future of the island was the least of their concerns. Those able to do so wished to pack up and leave.

Root was more optimistic. One of the purposes of securing a narrow electorate was to prevent the black population from voting. A *New York Times* headline the previous year had resurrected the old scare: 'Cuba May Be Another Haiti. Results Of Universal Suffrage Would Be A Black Republic. The Negro Could Carry First Election.'[79] In this at least, wrote Root, the result of the June election had been a triumph, since it excluded a great proportion 'of the elements which have brought ruin to Haiti and Santo Domingo'.[80]

Yet it could not be ignored that the result was a victory for the pro-independence parties. Independence was now inevitable. Understandably dismayed, Wood was obliged to plan for this unwelcome outcome. His new task, and that of the US administration in Washington, was to organise and prepare for a transfer of power that would leave the United States with a substantial measure of control. What could the Americans salvage from this electoral disaster? Wood hoped to be able to hold on to 'the collectorship of customs and the military commander – representing the US – holding, if necessary, the veto power'.[81]

Root had more ambitious ideas, and sought to provide the intellectual underpinning for Cuba's future relationship with the United States after independence. He raised again the question of the eternal historic interests of the United States in the Caribbean, in a letter of January 1901, and invoked 'the traditional and established policy of this country in respect of Cuba'. He recalled the decision, first made in the 1820s, that 'the United States would not in any circumstances permit any foreign power other than Spain to acquire possession of the island of Cuba'.[82] The United States would have to make good this decision in the light of the new circumstances of the twentieth century, with a Cuba that demanded its right to be independent.

Root considered that the United States had a moral obligation to establish 'a stable and adequate government' in Cuba, and he argued that it also had an historic and strategic interest to ensure the island's continued independent existence. Yet how could this be guaranteed when local conditions in Central America and the Caribbean at that time, and more widely in Latin America, were not such as to create much confidence in the likely wisdom, competence and stability of an independent Cuba? Root shared Wood's view of the unsuitable nature of the Cuban political class thrown up by the elections, but hoped for the emergence of 'a better class of people' in the future. He speculated about how they might be able 'to get rid of the adventurers who are now on top'. Yet he was also worldly enough to recognise that this might not be possible. The Americans would have to choose between the creation of an unstable 'Central American Republic' (later to be described in a more pejorative way as a 'banana republic') or the retention of some sort of US control 'for the time necessary to establish a stable government'.

Root well understood that this would not be easy. The people of Cuba, he wrote, had always lived in 'a military colony, 60 per cent of whom were illiterate – and many [of whom were] sons and daughters of Africa'.[83] He had few models to follow, but he was familiar with the story of Britain's occupation of Egypt in 1882, and its subsequent relationship with the government in Cairo. Although the British had been obliged to retain troops in the country, their two lofty ambitions had been to keep out other powers, and to ensure that the Egyptian ruler paid interest on the foreign loans he had been granted. Might not the Americans follow this model in Cuba?

Root's brainwave was to bind the two countries tightly together through guarantees incorporated into the new republican constitution that the Cubans were shortly to start discussing. Such guarantees would provide the United States with a veto power over Cuba's foreign, defence and economic policy; it would also allow the US to retain 'the right of intervention' to preserve 'Cuban independence and the maintenance of stable government'. This latter requirement was eventually to be embedded in the famous 'amendment' put forward in the US Congress by Senator Orville Platt, and incorporated grudgingly by the Cubans into the constitution of their new Republic.

Mortgaged independence: the Platt Amendment, 1902

The Enmienda Platt, the Platt Amendment, has been familiar to every Cuban schoolchild for more than a century, two words that evoke the humiliation of the settlement imposed on Cuba at the close of the US occupation. Orville Platt was an influential Republican politician on the US Senate's foreign relations committee and he stood up in Congress in Washington on 15 February 1901 to introduce the 'amendment' that was to bear his name.[84] Platt himself was of little consequence; he was simply carrying out the orders of Root, who, with descant additions from General Wood, had been composing his country's future relationship with Cuba. Continued military occupation was no longer an option, but the wording of the Platt Amendment would ensure that, even when independence had been granted and the American occupation force had sailed away, the United States would maintain a unique form of colonial control.

With its easy assumption of the superiority of US civilisation, and its blindness to the sensibilities of the Cubans, the Platt Amendment was one of the defining documents of the imperial era. Its influence lasted long after it was formally abrogated in 1934, and it continued to echo in the global perceptions of the United States a century later, notably in the wording of the Helms-Burton Act of 1996. Its purpose, when first outlined in February 1901, was to cement the relationship between Cuba and the United States into a permanent pattern before the Cubans had a chance to give an opinion on the matter. The Cuban constituent assembly, elected to draft a new constitution in December 1900, was obliged to accept it. The Americans insisted that it should be incorporated into the constitution that the Cubans were supposed to be designing for themselves.

The first of the Platt Amendment's seven paragraphs was framed to ensure that Cuba could make no treaty with foreign powers, or permit foreign military bases on its soil, without the permission of the United States. The second indicated that Cuba's public finances would be overseen by the United States. The third gave the Americans the right to intervene in Cuba whenever it felt the need. The fourth forbade any retroactive attempt to question what had occurred during the years of the American occupation. The fifth, suggested by General Wood, obliged the Cubans to continue with the efforts made by the American occupation forces to improve the country's control of disease. The sixth left the legal future of the Isle of Pines pending, while the seventh gave the Americans a right to establish permanent military bases on the island. (For the text of the Platt Amendment, see Appendix B.)

The US base at Guantánamo Bay, still functioning a century later, was the fruit of the seventh paragraph. The US navy had long thought of the bay as a potential coal depot, and there were other strategic developments in the wind. 'In view of the probable construction of the trans-isthmian canal [eventually built across Panama],' John D. Long, the US secretary of the navy, noted in May 1900, 'it is necessary that the US should control the windward passage through which commerce and our transports and warships must pass on the way to the canal from northern parts.'[85]

The Platt Amendment was incorporated into US law on 2 March 1901, and on 12 June Cuba's constituent assembly, with much grumbling, voted to include it as an annex to the Republican constitution they had been preparing. The vote was carried by a vote of 15 to 14. General Juan Gualberto Gómez, once Martí's disciple and one of the black leaders of the independence war, voted against it, declaring that the Amendment had 'reduced the independence and sovereignty of the Cuban Republic to a myth'. Others, those who voted in favour, argued that a restricted independence was better than continued American occupation, which was widely believed to be the alternative.

Although the Platt Amendment was eventually repealed in 1934, it had a baneful effect on Cuba's political development during the first three decades of the Republic and clouded US–Cuban relations until the end of the twentieth century. The United States intervened in Cuban politics with military units from 1906 to 1909, in 1912 and from 1917 to 1923. In some ways yet more disastrous, and inimical to the island's political development, the Amendment enabled Cuban governments to summon American military assistance whenever they were faced with powerful internal opposition – by workers or peasants, or simply by rival political factions. American soldiers often arrived to solve problems in Cuba that a genuinely independent government would have been obliged to sort out on its own. The resentment created was to explode in 1933 and again in 1959.

4

The Cuban Republic, 1902–1952

A Republic for Americans: Estrada Palma and Charles Magoon,
1902–1909

Only his shoes remain. Below, the likeness of a gigantic Greek goddess sits eternally poised on the steps in front of the plinth, laurel-wreathed and sandalled, ever at the ready to write with her sculpted stone pen. Only the barest trace of ceremonial lettering can be deciphered. This memorial to Tomás Estrada Palma, the first elected president of the independent Republic of Cuba, was erected in the Havana suburb of Vedado on one of the great avenues that leads down to the sea. Little now survives. The statue of the man perceived to have betrayed the nation was torn down by a revolutionary mob in 1959. His unforgiveable crime was to have accepted something less than independence from the hands of the US occupying force, and to have presided over the inauguration of a Republic that often seemed to privilege Americans over Cubans.

Cuba's 'pseudo-republic', as *fidelista* historians have described it, was formally proclaimed on 20 May 1902. Leonard Wood, the US military governor, formally handed the country over to President Estrada, a Cuban-born American citizen who had been a veteran of exile politics for nearly three decades. Characterised by endless violence, dramatic corruption, military revolts, gangsterism and sporadic military intervention by the United States, the new Republic also experienced spectacular economic growth and prosperity for a small section of society. With a span of nearly 60 years, it was eventually swept away by Fidel Castro's Revolution in 1959. While 20 May continued to be celebrated in the United States as Cuba's independence day, Castro's Revolution dropped the anniversary altogether.

Estrada, representing the Republican Party, had been elected unopposed at a presidential election in December 1901. Máximo Gómez had refused to put himself forward, while Bartolomé Masó, who was hostile to the Platt

Amendment and would have been more popular than Estrada, withdrew after General Wood had rigged the election against him by appointing five of Estrada's supporters to the electoral commission.[1] Most of Cuba's embryonic political elite threw their weight behind the new President.

Estrada was a man of his time. He belonged to the educated and ruling class that had no prejudice against its US occupiers, and looked forward to a close and continuing relationship with the Americans after independence. Much of the Cuban population might be imbued with an embryonic sense of nationalism, but thousands of them had crossed over to the United States in the previous half century, to work and to study and to establish small businesses. The wars and economic uncertainty of the final decades of colonial rule had led to an immense migration, and the creation of a large Cuban-American population on the mainland was not without repercussions back home. Martí might have had reservations about 'the colossus of the North', but many of his fellow migrants came to admire its dynamism, generosity and modernity.

The migration had been made up over several generations of a vast cross-section of the Cuban people – young and old, men and women, black and white – and many of them moved easily between the mainland and the island. Constant communication was maintained between the two communities. In the early years of the Republic, almost everyone of importance and influence possessed direct experience of living in the United States.[2] American intervention in Cuban affairs was not an insult for such people; they welcomed it, and often requested it.

The people running the Republic's new government might have learnt about the American system that the occupiers had sought to impose, and even admired it, but they had no immediate model to hand for their own use other than the old Spanish colonial practices that allowed the rulers to organise the country for their personal benefit. Estrada, an austere schoolmaster, was himself an honest man, but many officers in the rebel army who translated themselves into candidates for office had no such self-restraint. Even if personally honest, many still received loyalty from their former troops, now impoverished and without work, and were expected to distribute largesse among their supporters.

Corruption was not a simple matter of individual enrichment. Since jobs in the state sector provided an income for many thousands of people, and since their job was dependent on the electoral victory of their chosen party, electoral fraud became entrenched at the very start of the Republic. The armed supporters of the Conservative and the Liberal parties would guard the polling stations to try to ensure the victory of their candidate. If serious disputes arose, as they did at each election, the United States could be called upon to intervene under the obligations it had accepted with the Platt Amendment.

American intervention was welcomed by the Cuban elite in the early years, and supported by the American settlers and businessmen who arrived in considerable numbers. More than 13,000 North Americans had acquired title to land in Cuba by 1905, bringing in millions of dollars of investment. Soon, some 60 per cent of rural properties were owned by American individuals or corporations.[3] Many Cubans who had fought in the independence war – for independence not economic annexation – were disillusioned by this development, but others believed it to be inevitable and desirable, and hastened to associate themselves with the new economic power in the land.

Irene Wright noted sympathetically in 1910 that a population 'suddenly released from colonial conditions' had not 'found itself as a Cuban people, or constituted a nation with an identity of its own'.[4] Her contemporary comment reveals the intrinsic problem. With a bleak colonial inheritance, battered by war and divided by race and class, the Cuban people were hardly prepared to march onto the stage of history. Nor were they ready for what was to come next, for the vacuum created by the absence of a properly constituted Cuban nation was happily filled by American settlers and entrepreneurs, and their allies on the island. Irene Wright had the measure of the tragedy:

> This republic is not a creature of Cubans – it was neither fashioned by them nor by them influenced – but on the contrary it is of all-American manufacture. Americans built it. Americans set it up again when it fell flat. American influence is all that sustains it to this moment. If they discover anything to criticise in it, or its failure, let Americans remember in so criticising that they are dealing with the work of their own hands.[5]

The US Marines returned to Cuba just four years after they had left. Some 2,000 soldiers landed at Havana in September 1906 and established themselves at their old base at Camp Columbia on the outskirts of the city. Soon there were 5,000 of them distributed around the country. They stayed for just over two years, much of the time spent mapping the island, and withdrew in February 1909. The intervention was not a unilateral military action by the United States, but the result of a request by Estrada Palma under the terms of the Platt Amendment. No one could have been more irritated by Estrada's petition than Theodore Roosevelt, now the American President. 'I am so angry with that infernal little Cuban republic,' he declared. 'All that we wanted from them was that they should behave themselves and be prosperous and happy so that we should not have to interfere. And now, lo and behold . . . we have no alternative save to intervene.'

With Cuba, as elsewhere in the early years of the century, except for Panama and the Philippines, the Americans liked to give the impression of being reluctant imperialists. Annexation, or occupation on the European model, was rarely their preferred style, although it was not unknown. The Marines occupied Nicaragua from 1912 to 1925, Haiti from 1915 to 1934, and the Dominican Republic from 1916 to 1930. They returned to Cuba in 1912, 1917 and 1921.[6] Typical of the American attitude towards Cubans was that of Henry Cabot Lodge. 'Nobody wants to annex them,' he wrote in September 1906, 'but the general feeling is that they ought to be taken by the scruff of the neck and shaken until they behave themselves.'[7]

The Americans intervened in 1906 to prevent the Cubans from fighting among themselves, and they were obliged to do so partly because of the inadequate legacy of occupation. When elections were held for Cuba's national congress in February 1904, it was immediately obvious that the state had no capacity to organise a fraud-free contest. With the country divided – between the Republican Party, of conservative and centralist leanings, and the National Liberal Party, which supported local autonomy – the election result was inevitably contested. To the American eye, little of principle distinguished the parties. Both were led by former rebels seeking the spoils of peace.[8]

Estrada's Republicans were in power and proved more successful at fraud than the Liberals, and secured the victory of more congressmen. The Liberals refused to accept the result, and absented themselves from the congress, an unhappy augury for the presidential election in December 1905. Believing that his services were indispensable, and backed by the US minister in Havana, Estrada Palma sought re-election. The Liberals united behind the candidature of José Miguel Gómez, the governor of Santa Clara whose running mate was Alfredo Zayas, a colourless lawyer. Máximo Gómez would have been the more popular candidate, but he had died in 1905. Gómez and Zayas disliked each other intensely, but both were to be dominant figures in Cuban politics for the next 20 years, and both eventually became President.

A violent atmosphere before the December poll, and the certainty that government officials would secure the re-election of Estrada, led Gómez to withdraw, and Estrada was again elected without opposition. The Liberals now turned to the only weapon with which they were familiar, trained in its use since 1868. With machetes in hand, and other simple weapons, they organised an armed insurrection to overthrow the government. Some 24,000 armed rebels, many of them black, assembled in Pinar del Rio in August 1906 and began to march on Havana. They were joined by provincial leaders throughout the country in what became known as the Guerrita de Agosto, the August War. The usual panic broke out among whites in Havana, with calls for American intervention. One excited writer, calling for immediate US annexation, described the Liberal rebellion as the 'first spark' of a race war in which 'the butchers of Africa' would revenge themselves on the whites.[9]

Estrada was faced with a rebellion that he could not easily crush. The Americans had left the Cuban state without a standing army. The Rural Guard had only 3,000 men, distributed in tiny groups around the country. An artillery force was manned by a mere handful of soldiers. Fearing his imminent overthrow, Estrada appealed to Washington for military assistance in September. Everything in his own personal trajectory, as well as in that of other leading Cubans, made his decision inevitable. He had worked closely with the United States throughout the independence war, and had happily entwined the Americans in Cuba's affairs.[10]

Roosevelt agreed to intervene only 'if Cuba herself shows that she had fallen into the revolutionary habit, that she lacks the self-restraint necessary to ensure peaceful self-government and that her contending factions have plunged the country into anarchy'.[11] He sent two emissaries to Havana to seek 'a peaceful solution', and William Taft, the under-secretary for war, and Robert Bacon, the under-secretary of state, arrived in Havana to negotiate between Estrada and the Liberals.

Estrada did not seek negotiation; he wanted US military intervention to keep him in power. He outmanoeuvred Roosevelt by resigning as president and obliging his cabinet to do likewise. The country was left without a government. Roosevelt could not abandon Cuba and its American investors to another round of civil war, and was obliged to fill the vacuum. The Marines were sent to Havana, 'to establish peace and order'.

Some thought Roosevelt should send General Wood back to Cuba, but he chose Charles Magoon instead, a lawyer from Minnesota who became the first civilian captain-general. Magoon was the closest approximation to a typical European colonial governor that the United States possessed; he had just finished a stint in control of the Panama Canal Zone, America's most recent acquisition.[12] His principal task in Cuba was to remedy what had been left unfinished in 1902. Magoon's advisers devised a more reliable electoral system, drew up rules for the state bureaucracy and established a small professional army.[13] They also created a new legal system to replace the codes of the Spanish era.

Magoon ruled Cuba for three years. The new army was trained and ready in 1908, as were the new electoral rules. The task of drafting the necessary reforms was handed to Colonel Enoch Crowder, an American officer who would play an influential role in Cuba at intervals over the following 20 years. Like Magoon, he had acquired some relevant colonial expertise, working in the Philippines as the military governor's legal adviser. Often described as 'a farm boy' from Missouri, 'Bert' Crowder was educated at West Point, and his military experience went back to the campaigns against the Indians: he had fought against the Apache leader Geronimo in New Mexico in 1886 and against the Sioux chief Sitting Bull in 1890.

Crowder organised drafting committees in which Cubans were represented, although they often missed meetings. Sometimes it proves easier to leave detailed work to the occupying power. Municipal and provincial elections were held in August 1908, under the rules devised by Crowder, and won by the Republicans, renamed as the Conservative Party. This, another Magoon creation, was formed from the coalition that had supported Estrada. The Liberals remained divided as usual, but when presidential elections were held in November, they won with Gómez and Zayas, the team deprived of victory in 1906. President Gómez ruled until 1913. 'Once again the Cubans have the destiny of their nation in their hands,' he declared optimistically when Magoon, Crowder and the Marines left at the beginning of 1909.

The renewed American occupation had been a humiliating experience for many Cubans. They had been made to appear to outsiders, and to themselves, as inexperienced, incompetent and divided. It seemed that any dissident group that lost an election, or felt worsted in an argument, could cry 'Foul' and take to the hills, while their opponents would speed off to the US embassy, to request the return of the Marines.

Although the influence of the United States became all-pervasive in the early years of the Republic, much survived of the empire of old Spain. The Spanish collapse had not meant an end to the Spanish grip over many aspects of Cuban society. The new Republic had not started with a clean slate, for many Spanish bureacrats remained at their desks. Those who wanted to stay signed a new oath of allegiance, first to the United States and then, after 1902, to the Republic of Cuba. The country was ruled much as it had been in colonial times. Apart from a few modifications introduced during the American occupation, little really changed. Cuba's Spanish-born population – the *peninsulares* – was still large at the turn of the century, and soon there were to be more. White migration from Spain would continue at a steady rate throughout the first decades of the Republic.

A Republic for white settlers from Spain

High above the tiny streets of the village of Casablanca, on the eastern side of Havana's harbour and close to the looming fortress of La Cabaña, stands a great marble statue of Christ, one hand raised in blessing. Completed in 1958, it is one of the last of the grandiose public works of the Batista era, together with the road tunnel that passes under the harbour entrance. American visitors might be reminded for a moment of the Statue of Liberty in New York's harbour, welcoming Europe's poor and huddled masses.

The reference is not altogether misplaced, for General Wood ordered the construction of an immigrant reception centre in Havana harbour in 1900, modelled on New York's Ellis Island (opened in 1892). The new Cuban centre, called Triscornia, was built on the slopes above Casablanca and remained there until 1959. General Wood's aim, like that of his Spanish predecessors, was to encourage the immigration of white settlers from Spain.

Most of Spain's settlers remained in Cuba after 1898, a reversal of earlier Spanish experience. When their empire had collapsed in Latin America at the start of the nineteenth century, Spanish citizens abandoned the colonies in droves, returning to their Spanish motherland or re-settling in Cuba or the United States. The pattern was similar in the imperial retreat from Europe's African colonies in the 1960s. White settlers in Algeria and Kenya, and later those from Angola and Mozambique, streamed back to Europe. Cuba was an exception to this imperial rule. Not only did Spanish settlers stay behind, they were reinforced over the next 30 years by nearly a million fresh migrants from Spain.[14] The old Spanish ambition to 'whiten' Cuba, to push the white population over the 50 per cent mark, had been achieved by the time the Spaniards withdrew. It was made permanent by the fresh immigration of the twentieth century, during the first three decades of which more Spaniards came to Cuba than in the four centuries of Spanish rule.[15]

Cuba remained a typical settler society with the white colonists still in charge, similar to many of the European colonies in Africa. Politics was left to the Cuban-born, but Spaniards controlled commerce and industry and the retail trade and were well represented in the professions as well as in schools and newspapers. The US-organised census of 1899 revealed the presence of 113,000 white male foreigners on the island, representing 20 per cent of the male adult population of 523,000. Most of that 20 per cent were Spanish born. A further 252,000 white males were defined as Cuban (*nativos*) while 158,000 were described as 'men of colour'.[16]

Spaniards arriving in Cuba after 1898 were driven by tradition and by the deteriorating economic situation, and came primarily, as in the past, from Galicia, Asturias and the Canary Islands.[17] Although some returned to Spain, and others went on to the United States or to Latin America, at least 40 per cent of the half million Spaniards who came to Cuba in the first 20 years of the Republic remained there. Among them was Angel Castro, the father of Fidel.

General Wood made special efforts to respect the rights of the Spanish settlers, hoping that they would stay to run the country. Their individual and property rights were sustained by the military government, guaranteed by the peace treaty of December 1898, and ratified by the Republic in the constitution. Having ensured a steady influx of white settlers, Wood drafted legislation to keep black and Chinese immigration to a minimum. In May 1902, five days before leaving, he signed a law forbidding the import of contract labour, specifically mentioning the Chinese, but preventing a possible surge in black immigration from Puerto Rico. Estrada's new Republic made no break with the old colonial order, and retained the racist legislation imposed by the Americans.[18]

The 'whites-only' policy was not without problems for the landowners, for not all new Spanish immigrants were uneducated farmhands. Some were anarchists or anarcho-syndicalists, typical products of rural Spain. Some were trained agitators soon to be active in Cuba's embryonic union movement.

After the first great sugar strike, in October 1917, with a demand for higher wages and an 8-hour day, the President decreed that all foreign workers connected with the strike were to be expelled from the country. White immigration had become a two-edged sword.

Most Spanish immigrants, moving rapidly upwards in status, made themselves more than at home within Cuban society, happily establishing themseves in the late nineteenth-century *casinos*, or social centres, in Havana, some of the most sumptuous buildings in the city. Just as the blacks once had their *cabildos* to maintain the cultural memory of their original African location, so the Spaniards kept their regional origins alive. The Centro Asturiano, the club of the immigrants from Spain's north coast province, still stands on the south-east side of Havana's Parque Central, a magnificent palace now housing the non-Cuban collection of the Museo Nacional de Bellas Artes. This opulent and competitive building, originally constructed in 1885 to outstrip any possible rival, was a symbol not just of justifiable immigrant emotion but also of white pride, similar to that exemplified by the constructions in Pretoria of Sir Herbert Baker. Across the Parque Central, next to the Hotel Inglaterra, stands the Teatro Tacón, originally built as the Centro Galiciano, by poor immigrants from Galicia made rich in Cuba.

These *centros* were designed as social meeting places, where daughters could be married off to someone from the right region. They had their own theatres and libraries; they created credit and savings banks; they wrote their own newspapers, notably the *Diario de la Marina*. They provided hospitals and schools for their members, everything from the cradle to the grave. The budget of a single Spanish regional *centro* was far larger than that of any provincial government on the island.

The immigrant reception at Triscornia survived until 1959, but Spanish migrants had tailed off long before. Wars and slump made migration to Cuba less attractive, and the mood in Cuba changed after the Revolution of 1933. Spanish migrants were no longer made welcome. The great tide of refugees at the end of the Spanish civil war in 1939 headed for Mexico City rather than Havana.

A Republic denied to blacks: Evaristo Estenoz and the massacre of 1912

White supremacy was the official mood in the early years of the Republic, but the jovial optimism of the settlers could not disguise the fact that the country contained a large population of unhappy blacks. Black Cubans provided the bulk of the soldiery in the independence war, and reaped no reward. As the racist character of colonial society reasserted itself in the Republican era, the *mambises* were soon forgotten. Their great generals had been killed in the war. The new leaders who sprang up to defend the black community came mostly from the middle-class 'men of colour', aspiring politicians who had returned from exile to work within the Liberal Party.

The two most prominent black leaders in the new era, Juan Gualberto Gómez and Martín Morúa Delgado, devoted themselves to the black cause through the promotion of education and integration. Gómez campaigned in the newspapers, and Morúa in the senate. Both sought legislation that would prohibit racial segregation in public places and ban discrimination in employment. In this they were largely unsuccessful, although Morúa secured an end to segregation in the new artillery force.

Yet nothing the two men did in congress or the newspapers could quell the growing sense of disillusion that permeated black communities throughout the country. What had the independence war been about? Rafael Serra, a black journalist returning from exile in New York, gave voice to this feeling in a book of essays published in 1907:

Unfortunate are Cuban blacks if all they will get as a just reward for their sacrifices for the independence and freedom of Cuba is to listen to the anthem of Bayamo and to the false adoration devoted to the memory of our illustrious martyrs. No, my brothers, we deserve justice, and we should no longer continue to encourage a humiliating and ridiculous patriotism.[19]

Arthur Schomburg, the black American historian who visited Cuba in 1905, also wrote about black Cuba's discontents:

During the colonial days of Spain, the Negroes were better treated, enjoyed a greater measure of freedom and happiness than they do today. Many Cuban Negroes were welcomed in the time of oppression, but in the days of peace . . . they are deprived of positions, ostracised and made political outcasts. The Negro has done much for Cuba. Cuba has done nothing for the Negro.[20]

Many of the white liberals who had fought for independence were as patronisingly racist as those who had fought for Spain. Bartolomé Masó, hero of the struggle against the Platt Amendment, was a supporter of white immigration and had firm views about the role of blacks in an independent Cuba. 'Our negroes . . . are mostly uneducated labourers, quite unfitted for holding positions,' he told an interviewer in 1898. 'With sufficient employment [they] will give no trouble . . . Our negroes will work as before in the cane-fields, and I see no reason to anticipate trouble from them. We have no coloured officials in this government, and very few of our officers are black . . .'[21]

Some black war veterans were active within the various associations of veterans created after the war, and many were bought off with discreet payments. Yet the general black discontent continued, and large numbers swelled the ranks of the Liberal army in August 1906, in support of the war of

José Miguel Gómez against Estrada Palma. During the subsequent rule of Charles Magoon, as discussions began about the reform of the electoral system, many black veterans began to consider the possibility of mobilising as blacks and perhaps forming a political party.

Prominent among them was Evaristo Estenoz, a war veteran who had been born a slave, and worked as a private contractor in Havana. Blacks had been the architects of the independence struggle, he argued, and had been robbed of 'all the fruits of victory'. He and his friends had previously supported the Liberal Party; now they expressed their disappointment and hostility. The party had done nothing to improve conditions for the blacks. In 1907, he set up a black political party with a broadly progressive platform, the Independent Party of Colour. It campaigned for more jobs in the public sector to be given to blacks.

Estenoz was the son of a black mother and a white father and came originally from Oriente. He was widely travelled and had visited Europe and the United States. He had gone with Rafael Serra to examine the experiences of American black organisations. If whites could learn from the United States, so too could the blacks. Caught up in the logic of the Platt Amendment, he even called on Magoon, and exchanged letters with Crowder. He hoped the Americans could be persuaded to take up the Afro-Cuban cause.

The new party, and its newspaper, *Previsión*, began to develop what would later be called black consciousness. The paper attacked the obsession of white Cubans with their European origins and took up the issue of Cuba's African heritage, pointing out that Spain had been colonised by Africans in the Muslim era. It called for the whites-only immigration policy to be abandoned, and for the ban on black immigration to be dropped. Unlike the Liberals, who had adopted the cock as their emblem and supported the legalisation of cock-fighting (banned during the American occupation), the new party chose a horse as their symbol. The horse represented both the preferred vehicle of the independence war, but also the god Changó, the Yoruba deity of thunder and lightning.[22]

The new party was the first real political challenge to the rules of the political order established in 1902. As it began to erode the traditional Liberal vote within the black community, it was subjected to campaigns of abuse. The old fears of a Haiti-style revolution were revived in the Havana newspapers, and Estenoz was accused of promoting black racism. He was arrested in 1910, his newspaper was seized and the party threatened with closure. Hundreds of blacks were arrested across the country. Such arbitrary actions increased the sense of white panic and the Havana newspapers began printing alarmist accounts of a coming black rebellion. The blacks had been rightly detained, announced the *Diario de la Marina*, 'because they were threatening the whites, and more precisely the white women'.[23] The imminent arrival of Halley's Comet, scheduled to pass over the island on 19 May 1910, gave rise to stories across a still superstitious community that it foreshadowed a racial catastrophe for the whites.

After the peaceful passing of the comet, the white panic subsided. No trace of an imminent uprising was detected, no arms were found, no black conspiracy was uncovered. Estenoz was released from prison at the end of the year, and the prisoners put on trial were found not guilty and released. But the damage had been done. A mood had been created in which it was easy for congress to agree on a law forbidding any political movement to be formed on the basis of colour. The so-called 'Morúa Law' was put forward by the reformist black senator, who claimed that since Estenoz's party represented only the interests of black Cubans, it would inevitably discriminate against whites – which would violate the constitution. The Independent Party of Colour was banned.

Estenoz had two possible courses of action. He could make common cause with José Miguel Gómez and try to persuade him, given the size of the potential vote his black supporters would normally supply to the Liberals, to lift the ban and provide them with secure jobs. Alternatively, he could play the Platt Amendment card and make fresh overtures to the United States, the self-appointed guarantor of Cuban liberties. He had had a friendly reception from Magoon and Crowder, why should he not expect the same from President William Taft? Estenoz would test whether the American guarantee extended to the blacks.

Negotiations with Gómez produced nothing, and Estenoz now issued an ultimatum. If Morúa's law was not withdrawn, the blacks would fight to save their honour. At the same time, and with the hope of securing the threat of US intervention, he forwarded a petition to President Taft requesting an appointment. The petition was lost in the entrails of the State Department bureaucracy, but the US minister in Havana gave his personal view in a comment to Washington in February 1912. He explained that although the blacks had 'always been the backbone of political uprisings' in Cuba, they had always acted 'under white leadership'. Blacks acting alone would be an insignificant force:

> As practically all the talented negroes and mestizos of political inclinations are well cared for by the Liberal and Conservative parties, the negroes themselves lack the necessary leadership and talent to bring about unaided a widespread revolt. Therefore I do not think that the present agitation will be productive of anything more than the passing excitement which it affords. At the most a few sporadic outbreaks might occur, which could readily be put down by the Army which is not in sympathy with the negro movement.[24]

The US minister underestimated the determination of the black leader. Still hoping to provoke an American intervention, Estenoz launched an armed protest movement on independence day, 20 May 1912. Action took place chiefly in Oriente, with a smaller group in Las Villas. There may have been as many as 4,000 rebels, and some have suggested a figure of 7,000.

US warships did sail for Cuba that month, and four companies of US Marines landed at Guantánamo Bay. This was the first military intervention since Magoon had left in 1909, and General Wood, now the chief of the general staff in Washington, was quick to reinforce the US base at Guantánamo. But the Marines had not come to support Estenoz and the blacks; they were sent to protect the US sugar estates in the region.[25]

President Gómez was not pleased with the US mobilisation. His forces were quite able to conduct a massacre on their own. The repression was fierce, and some 3,000 blacks were killed. This was a race war, crushed by white Cubans. It was over within three weeks. Estenoz was killed on 12 June, surprised by an army patrol. His body was taken to Santiago and laid out in the Moncada barracks.[26]

Much controversy has surrounded these events, a debate similar to that over the 'Conspiracy of La Escalada'. Was this a rebellion by frustrated blacks, or was it a racist massacre organised by the government? For the authorities at the time, it was a black rebellion fortunately crushed by loyal troops. Later historians have been divided. Aline Helg describes it as 'a government-initiated racist massacre' aimed at the annihilation of Estenoz's black party, and has evidence to show that government repression *preceded* the action of the black protesters.[27] Others, notably Louis Pérez, argue that the black protest developed into a violent and uncontrollable black and peasant rebellion. In this version, the discontent and disappointment with the republican settlement of 1902, bubbling away within the black community in Oriente, finally exploded into a peasant *jacquerie* in the hills that took on the colouring, at moments, of a race war. Estenoz lit the tinder that caused the explosion. The violence had a political purpose, but it went beyond the usual breakdown of law and order at election time, and became a more generalised outbreak of anarchy.[28]

The versions are not mutually exclusive. Cuban politics, certainly since 1868, involved groups and individuals taking up arms to make their point, and Estenoz's armed protest of 1912 was no different in principle from that of José Miguel Gómez in 1906. Unfortunately for Estenoz, three things were different. The protest was led by a black for the first time since Aponte's rebellion a hundred years earlier; it took place against the background of widespread racist propaganda in the press; and it exploded chiefly in Oriente, an endemically conflictive part of the island since the first days of the Spanish conquest, very different from the western provinces where Gómez had raised his standard in 1906.

Estenoz might have expected his armed protest to lead to a period of negotiation; instead it sparked off a race war, with a revival of the poisonous atmosphere engendered by Lersundi's *voluntarios* in 1869 and by Weyler's concentration camps in 1896. 'This is the free and beautiful America,' commented the Conservative newspaper *El Día*, 'defending herself against a clawing scratch from Africa.' *El Día* commented favourably on American lynchings as a model for Cuba to keep the black population under control.[29] White militias were organised, martial law was imposed and the general commanding the forces in Oriente organised a special show for journalists of the army's new machine guns. They were directed towards a peaceful peasant village, killing 150 peasant families in their huts.[30]

'The "*reconcentración*" ordered by the Cuban general', wrote the French consul in Santiago, 'will empty the countryside of all indigenous and foreign families. It will hand over all these unfortunate and inoffensive black day labourers, rural workers, coffee pickers, cane cutters, herdsmen, and servants to the pitiless executioners of the military administration's dirty work. I tremble for this black flesh.'[31]

The massacre of 1912 remained etched in the memory of Cuban blacks for decades. They almost never took part in politics again, devoting themselves to music and retreating into their own African religions, and participating in white Cuban society in the only institutions to which they had easy access – the lower ranks of the army and the police force. Maybe they got their own back on the whites during the dictatorship of Machado in the 1920s. A later dictator, Fulgencio Batista, was one of their own.

A Republic for gamblers: Mario Menocal and Bert Crowder

The first decade of the Republic may have been characterised by white racism, violence, corruption and American military intervention, but at another level the country underwent an extraordinary economic recovery. As Cuba moved from the Spanish into the American sphere, new settlers and fresh investment poured in, transforming not just the sugar industry and its associated railway network, but also the mining and tobacco industries and the manufacture of textiles and other consumer goods. Given the prostrate country that existed in 1898, the recovery was a notable achievement.

Its first political beneficiary was Mario Menocal y Deop, Conservative president from 1913 to 1921. His period in office coincided almost exactly with that of Woodrow Wilson in the United States, as well as with the First World War, which created an insatiable demand for Cuban sugar. Income from sugar nearly doubled between 1914 and 1916.

A man who still dreamed in the 1930s of returning to power, Menocal was perceived by his contemporaries as 'more American than Cuban'.[32] Born in 1866 and educated at Cornell, Menocal returned to Cuba to fight in the independence war under Calixto García, later serving in the US military government as the Havana police chief. When the Americans left, he set out to make his fortune, joining the newly created Cuban American Sugar Corporation of New York and becoming the manager of its vast Chaparra estate in Oriente, soon to become one of the most successful sugar enterprises on the island.

A millionaire businessman, Menocal believed that what was good for the Cuban-American Sugar Corporation would be good for Cuba. He was so rich himself that he hardly needed to be personally corrupt, yet he acquired more from the Cuban treasury than from Chaparra's sugar mills. He ruled in an arbitrary manner, as though he were still a Spanish captain-general untrammelled by the demands of democracy, and he presided over a system that worked most effectively by buying people off with the money of the state. He introduced many reforms that bolstered the power of the presidency, including the modernisation of the armed services, with the amalgamation of the army and the Rural Guard, and the creation of a national bank in 1915 that issued a national currency – the Cuban peso – on a par with the US dollar.

While distant battles in Europe had usually had an adverse effect on developments in the Caribbean throughout much of Cuba's colonial history, leading to increased piracy and the collapse of trade, the First World War gave Cuba a gigantic bonanza, as the sugar price went sky high. Cut off from its German suppliers of beet sugar, Britain among others turned to the United States for its sugar supply – and by extension to Cuba.[33] Land was bought up, peasants evicted, forests cut down, plantations laid out, sugar mills constructed, new technologies introduced. Teresa Casuso, scion of the sugar oligarchy, recalled the drama of the environmental destruction in Oriente:

> I remember . . . the great impenetrable forests that were set aflame, whole jungles that were fired and razed to the ground to make way for the sugar cane. My parents were in despair for that lost wealth of beautiful, fragrant tropical wood – cedar and mahogany and mastic, and magnificent-grained pomegranate – blazing in sacrifice to the frenzy to cover the countryside with sugar cane. In the nights the sight of that flaming horizon affected me with a strange, fearful anxiety, and the aroma of burning wood floating down from so far away was like the incense one smells inside churches.[34]

Others were as concerned with uprooted peasants as with cut-down trees, and wrote of rural communities driven from their lands to join the surviving groups of bandits in the hills.[35]

With new lands to plant and harvest, plantation owners grew desperate for labour. Dispossessed peasants would not be turned overnight into a willing workforce. Former black slaves had preferred fighting for independence to working in the plantations, and were still angry over the massacre of 1912. White migration from Spain was at a low ebb in the war years because of shipping difficulties. Recruiting blacks from the Caribbean had been forbidden since the turn of the century, but the inexorable demand for workers led successive governments to override existing legislation. Landowners had to search for labour in neighbouring islands. Ironically, the demand of Evaristo Estenoz for the ban on black immigration to be lifted was granted in the year of his death. The Nipe Bay Company, owned by United Fruit, persuaded the government to allow it to import 1,400 workers from Haiti for its Preston plantation, next door to Chaparra. The wall had been breached, and over the next decade nearly 200,000 workers from Haiti and 80,000 from Jamaica came over to Cuba to work, from islands experiencing no comparable boom.[36]

Many were employed only during the harvest. Landowners preferred Haitians who could be shipped home after the harvest and did not have to be paid during the off-season. Many from Jamaica remained, leaving a permanent trace within the population of eastern Cuba. Americans preferred Jamaicans, since, as one journalist noted, 'they are the only servants in Cuba who can cook American style with any success'.[37] The labour recruiters also resurrected Chinese migration, banned during the American occupation and condemned by the Chinese emperor in 1873. Since the Manchu dynasty was swept away in 1911, the old rules no longer applied, although many new additions to Cuba's Chinese community came from California.

Happy with office, Menocal contemplated his re-election in 1916 and organised the customary fraud to ensure his victory. Magoon and Crowder had devised an elaborate and seemingly foolproof electoral system in 1909, but Cuban presidents would continue to rig the results – to no one's surprise. Much of the population continued to believe in the old nineteenth-century traditions of war and revolution. Another fraudulent election would mean another rebellion, and the violent campaign of 1916 was no exception.

Defrauded of victory, the Liberals organised an armed revolt to protest against the result, which had revealed more votes cast than there were eligible voters, and appealed to Woodrow Wilson to intervene. José Miguel Gómez landed on the south coast in February 1917, while Alfredo Zayas raised a rebel banner with other Liberals who would take their turn as President over the next 20 years – Gerardo Machado and Carlos Mendieta. The rebellion was called La Chambelona, the lollipop, after a Liberal song popular during the campaign.

Gómez was convinced that his American friends, who had come to his rescue in 1906, would do so again. Yet they were now more experienced in Cuban affairs and did not always jump the way that was expected of them. They had intervened reluctantly in 1906 to prop up a regime they had put in power just four years earlier. Fifteen years after independence, and on the verge of entering the great European war, they were yet more reluctant. The Americans condemned the Liberal rebellion, and although they eventually sent 2,000 Marines in 1917, these arrived, as they had done in 1912, to protect the US sugar plantations not at the request of aggrieved parties to an internal conflict. They stayed on the island for six years, 1,600 of them stationed in Oriente and 1,000 in Camagüey.

The Marines did not take action in the battle between Menocal and the Liberals, and Menocal defeated the rebellion through the tough methods of repression that Cuba had inherited from Spain. Along with many of his supporters, Gómez was captured and imprisoned, although he was released in September and the others amnestied in March 1918.

When fresh elections loomed again Menocal invited Bert Crowder to return to Havana to suggest 'amendments to the electoral law'. Crowder was familiar to Cubans and was now famous in America too, as the man put in charge of the draft. Arriving in March 1919, he immersed himself in census returns and electoral rolls, in the search for an ever more perfect electoral system, to be ready for the polls in November 1920.

Alfredo Zayas was declared the winner, and once again the Liberals shouted fraud. Once again they called for US intervention to verify the results of a fresh election. Washington was faced with its usual difficult choice. Treaty-bound to protect lives and property, it knew the situation was unstable, hearing from the US minister in Havana that 'if disturbances or revolution were to come, US interests would be the first to be destroyed'.[38]

The Marines had been on the island since 1917, but President Wilson preferred a political to a military intervention. Crowder was sent back to Havana in January 1921, as his personal representative. He arrived on an American battleship, the *Minnesota*, and remained on board in Havana harbour, engaged in negotiations to prevent further violence and to solve the election dispute.

The campaign for fresh elections in March 1921 took place in such an atmosphere of violence that the Liberals abstained, believing that they would again be the victims of fraud. The ever-hopeful Gómez went to Washington to appeal to the new American president, Warren Harding, for intervention. Harding was not interested, and Gómez died in New York in June. The Cuban leader who had sought US intervention on so many occasions, with such persistence and panache, was finally out of the race. Alfredo Zayas became President in May.

The election shenanigans were now overshadowed by a far more serious crisis. The end of the world war in 1918 affected sugar production and the sugar price. The world price, fixed by an Anglo-American committee, had been kept low during the final year of the war, at 4.6 US cents per pound of raw sugar. Controls were lifted in 1919, and the price soared inexorably in the early months of 1920 – to 10 cents a pound in March and to over 20 cents in May. This miraculous, if ephemeral, moment was dubbed the 'dance of the millions', as immense fortunes were made by the US sugar companies in Cuba, and just as rapidly lost. The peak was reached in the middle of 1920, and then the price suddenly plunged – back to below 4 cents a pound by the time of the election in November.

What the US sugar companies had briefly won was now lost by the Cuban banks. They demanded, and eventually secured, a moratorium on the repayment of debt in October 1920. The political and the financial crisis intertwined and soon overwhelmed the country. The National Bank was forced to close its doors in April 1921. Its controlling shareholder was found hanged on the balcony of his apartment. The entire Cuban banking system collapsed in June, and many bankers fled into exile. Only a handful of foreign, mostly US, banks remained in operation, further enriching themselves by the purchase of sugar mills whose owners had been bankrupted.

Once wealthy, but now impoverished, Cuba was in desperate need of American assistance, not the Marines this time but a large loan. Zayas's new government approached several US banks and they demanded severe conditions – to be guaranteed by the continuing presence of Bert Crowder on board the *Minnesota*. He now took on the role of financial expert and adviser. Crowder wrote the script, while Zayas spoke the words. The government's budget would be cut, existing contracts would be reviewed and future projects would be subject to congressional approval – the American pattern. Crowder and Zayas worked separately and together in yet another attempt to reform the government bureaucracy and to root out corruption. An uphill task. The promised American loan was finally forthcoming in 1922. Crowder remained in Havana as the new US ambassador and as the guarantor for the US bankers.

American military interventions in Cuba in 1906, 1912 and 1917 had propped up unstable and insecure governments to maintain peace and security. Crowder's intervention in 1921 was of a new and different order, more directly concerned with the protection of US investments and loans during a difficult period. Cuba had become a significant producer of immense wealth, in whose activities American companies and individuals were deeply involved. Bankers and traders, mill and plantation owners, railroad operators and simple investors, all looked to the United States to protect their interests. Cuba had become a colony in all but name.

A Republic under dictatorship: Gerardo Machado, the tropical Mussolini, 1925–1933

Elections in 1924, still violent and fraudulent, produced a victory for the Liberals, their first since 1909. Their candidate, Gerardo Machado y Morales was a typical Liberal *caudillo*, little different from the Republic's first generation of corrupted politicians. He saw himself as the political heir of President Gómez. He enjoyed considerable popular appeal with the traditional liberal electorate, but was also at home in the army, the police force, the Liberal Party, the business community and the United States embassy.

Machado would have been well equipped to run any Latin American republic in the nineteenth century, but taking his turn as Cuba's president in the 1920s – with the sugar price collapsing, the stock exchange crashing and the country's finances in permanent disarray – he found the going more difficult than in earlier years, and his government's actions were correspondingly harsh. He coped with the situation by turning his government into an authoritarian dictatorship, the flavour of the era in other areas of the world from whose influence Cuba was by no means immune. Julio Antonio Mella, the Communist student leader, described him in a memorable phrase as a 'tropical Mussolini'.

Machado had humbler origins than earlier presidents. Once a butcher in Santa Clara, the town where he was born in 1871, he came from a family of cattle robbers, cutting up by day what they had obtained by night. A natural recruit to the rebel forces in the independence war, he rose to be a commanding officer, and turned to Liberal politics in peacetime. Elected mayor of his home town in 1900, and a collaborator of José Miguel Gómez, he reaped his reward when the Liberals became the chief beneficiaries of the creation of a Cuban army. He was appointed to be deputy chief of the armed forces in 1909, and was later the minister of the interior. He took an active part in La Chambelona, the Liberal war of 1917.

Machado established himself as a successful businessman while climbing up the political ladder, controlling the electric company in Santa Clara and then the sugar *central* at Carmita. In the 1920s he became a director of the powerful Compañía Cubana de Electricidad, the subsidiary of a US firm and a target of Cuban nationalism for many years because of its high prices. The American boss helped to finance his political campaigns.

Machado's business experience was an asset he put to good use. Bert Crowder noted with approval that he behaved like 'an intelligent executive in a position of semi-dictatorial authority'.[39] Machado soon took a leaf from the American book. If American pro-consuls could summon advisers to Cuba every few years to rewrite the election laws, why should a Cuban President not ask the Cuban congress to do the same? He arranged for a complicit congress to decree the tight control of all political parties. No new ones could be established, and the old ones were forbidden to reorganise. The road to a one-party state was mapped out. Machado's power was based on the army, soon the most powerful party in the land.

The old liberal fear in the nineteenth century was that Cuban independence would follow the pattern of Latin America or the Caribbean, with the emergence of military *caudillos* or the establishment of black rule. In the 1920s and 1930s these fears were realised with what was, in effect, a military dictatorship under Machado. He extended his presidential period in 1928 for a further six years, without troubling to call a fresh election.

Bert Crowder remained as US ambassador in Havana until 1927, watching his protégé's operations with considerable pride. 'Most Cubans' favoured a second term, he wrote in February 1927, and since Machado supported the 'closest possible co-operation' with the United States, the State Department would be well advised to give him an 'informal' assurance that it would not oppose his re-election.[40] In Crowder's eyes, Machado had done well in difficult circumstances, and his economic policies were not unintelligent. Indeed they prefigured some of the programmes of the Roosevelt New Deal. To mop up the unemployed, he embarked on huge public spending projects, among them the central highway the length of the island and the vast *Capitolio* building in central Havana, a copy of the US Congress building in Washington. Construction work on these prestige projects was concentrated in the off season, when no sugar cane was cut. To the thousands of US citizens who flocked to Cuba during the era of Prohibition, the island was an agreeable and fashionable place for a holiday. Enchanted by its rhythmic music, its beaches, its sunshine, and its rum, few visitors knew much about its politics.

Cubans were more critical of Machado than American tourists. The prolonged financial crisis, the economic uncertainty and Machado's manipulation of the political system, created opposition on a scale that any president would have found hard to deal with. Much of it was spearheaded by survivors of the older generation of Liberals and Conservatives, many of them members of the newly created Veterans' and Patriots' Association. Machado's control of congress meant they had little chance of returning to power by legitimate means. General Carlos García Vélez, the son of Calixto García, had organised an armed revolt near Cienfuegos in April 1924 even before Machado took over. He denounced graft and corruption in similar tones to those of Crowder, but his American friends proved of little assistance. President Coolidge sent USS *Cleveland* to Havana to support the government, and the revolt collapsed.[41]

Another rebellion was organised by a similar group a few years later, almost the last of its kind. The former president Menocal joined forces with Miguel Mariano Gómez, the son of the former president Gómez, and with Colonel Carlos Mendieta, a popular mayor of Havana, to revive the spirit of La Chambelona. They formed a right-wing group, the Unión Nacionalista, that sought support against Machado from within the armed forces. They also hoped to secure US support for a coup, and when this was not forthcoming, they turned to armed rebellion. Menocal and Mendieta sailed from the Havana Yacht Club to land at Rio Verde, in Pinar del Rio. Too old for such rash activities, they were promptly detained and imprisoned.

Others fared just as badly. A group of 40 led by Emilio Laurent and Sergio Carbó landed at Gibara on the north coast of Oriente. Advancing by train towards Holguín, they soon came under attack. Although Laurent and Carbó escaped, most of the others were tortured and shot, as were several innocent inhabitants of Gibara, which was bombed from the air.[42] Another group in

Oriente, led by Antonio Guiteras, sought to capture the Moncada barracks at Santiago, but they failed in the attempt and were captured and imprisoned.

The Gibara episode was the swansong of the generation formed by the experience of the independence war and the subsequent small wars that accompanied most Cuban election campaigns. The old figures from the independence war were dead or in their dotage and were widely discredited.

Other forces in society began to emerge during the Machado dictatorship. Cuban workers, for the first time since the slave revolts of the nineteenth century, were not only restless but on the road to creating their own organisations. The early traditions of the workers' movement, as in Spain and much of Latin America, were rooted in anarchism. A small workers' organisation, the Confederación Nacional Obrera Cubana (CNOC), was created by anarchists in 1925, and brought together small groups of anarchists, socialists and communists, all pledged to work on behalf of the working class. The anarchist strain began to fade in the 1920s, partly because of the appeal of the successful Russian revolution, which indicated that a modicum of discipline might be useful to a political movement, and partly because Machado shot or deported prominent anarchist leaders, or fed them to the sharks.[43]

An embryonic Communist Party, formed in August 1925 by socialists attracted by the Russian revolution, was eventually strong enough to take over the CNOC in 1931. Several of the more prominent Cuban Communists were Jews from eastern Europe – a fresh input into Cuba's ethnic mix – some of whom still found it easier to speak Yiddish rather than Spanish.[44] One of them, Yunger Semjovich, was to survive into the early years of the Revolution in 1959, under the name of Fabio Grobart. Distrust of the Communists as 'foreign', 'Jewish' and beholden to Moscow was one of the obstacles facing the Party, distrust as prevalent on the nationalist left as on the right. Mella was one of the Party's early leaders, a brilliant student orator shot in 1929 when in exile in Mexico City, assassinated on Machado's orders. Out walking with Tina Modotti, the Italian photographer, he died in the house of Diego Rivera.

Mella came from the middle class, like most Cuban politicians, but the Communists were more 'workerist' than the other movements that sprang up to oppose the Machado dictatorship. They also took more interest in the blacks than the middle-class parties felt called upon to do. Their principal aim was to organise the working class, in the factories, the sugar and tobacco plantations, and the railways, and this inevitably brought them into contact with the black population. Communists had no prejudice against blacks taking a leadership role in the Party, and at one brief stage in the 1930s they supported the idea of setting up a black republic in Oriente, where the blacks were in the majority.

Machado had little choice, from his perspective, except to clamp down on the various forms of opposition that began to emerge, and he did so with uncommon ferocity. The assassination of Mella was only unusual in that it took place in a foreign country. Cuba had always been a violent society. The tradition of the slave-owner with the dog and the whip had not been obliterated, and the machete had given way to the machine-gun as an instrument of social control. Those who participated in strikes and other oppositional activities in the Machado era put themselves in the firing line. Nor was Cuba an exception to the Latin American rule. The crushing of worker demonstrations with bullets was a common phenomenon elsewhere.

The repression soon affected sectors of society unused to such treatment, notably the middle-class students at the university whose parents did not expect them to be shot. A radical organisation at the University of Havana, the Directorio Estudiantil, was created to protest against the dictatorial behaviour of the Machado government. It grew out of the student euphoria of the 1920s that spread to every country in Latin America, similar to the mood that sprang up decades later in 1968. University students came solely from the middle class, and were more influenced by the Argentine student revolt in Córdoba in 1918 that brought students into the forefront of political change than by the (more distant) Russian revolution. They embraced anti-imperialism with open arms, but were often more circumspect about socialism. The Directorio was disbanded by Machado in 1927, obliging the students to turn to more violent forms of opposition.

A generational change in the 1930s brought new ideas and new leaders to the fore. A wide variety of secret organisations began to proliferate, with widely differing agendas. All were united in their desire to see an end to the Machado era, and individuals moved promiscuously from one to another, seeking effective action rather than ideological purity.[45] This freshly minted opposition to Machado became increasingly violent, matching the repression. After 30 years of nominal independence, Cuba remained corrupt and violent, and in the dark atmosphere of the Machado years, it was often difficult to distinguish between politically motivated gangsters and plain criminals.

The Directorio Estudiantil was re-established as a secret organisation in September 1930 and soon embarked on a campaign of violence, terrorism and assassination. More radical students, with a more overtly socialist orientation, split away six months later to form the Ala Izquierda Estudiantil, supported among others by Raúl Roa. A second opposition group, Unión Revolucionaria, was the brainchild of Antonio Guiteras Holmes, the most radical left-wing figure in the opposition. Formerly a leader of the Directorio Estudiantil, he had abandoned chemistry to become a full-time political activist, and split away from the movement in 1931, working briefly with the Unión Nacionalista.

A third conspiratorial movement, which labelled itself ABC for security reasons, was formed in September 1931, with an emphasis on 'youth' and the need for a clean break with the past. Although Machado himself had followed in the footsteps of Mussolini, the principal right-wing force that opposed him

had been drinking from the same well. The ABC had some of the characteristics of the Spanish Falange, but their political lineage seemed closer to the
Italian Futurists and to Mussolini. They were led by Joaquín Martínez Sáenz
and Carlos Saladrigas, both middle-class lawyers, and Jorge Manach, a
French-educated writer.

The ABC's Manifesto-Programme, issued early in 1932, was consciously
based on the Italian fascist programme of 1919. A national-socialist
programme of the radical right, it was hostile to US business interests,
supportive of producer cooperatives and state control of public services and
an advocate of 'Cubans First'. Its fascist flavour was indicated by its plan to
withdraw the vote from illiterates, inevitably aimed in Cuba against blacks.
No one ever revealed what ABC stood for, but the Communists with some
justice suggested that it meant Asociación Blanca de Cuba, the Association of
Cuban Whites.[46]

The ABC's practice was more significant than its ideology, for all student
groups in the early 1930s were subject to foreign influences of one kind or
another, and few were able to adjust them to Cuban reality. Many individuals
moved seamlessly from one group to the other and the ABC would sometimes
work with the Directorio Estudiantil. Ideologically at odds, the anti-Machado
movements, on the left or the right, were all enamoured of violence, believing
that the tactic of terror against the government – against its buildings and its
servants – was their only effective weapon. In their use of terror they were at
one with contemporary movements in Europe; they were also consonant with
the revolutionary struggles of Cuba's past. The ABC may have hoped that this
would provoke American intervention; Guiteras's Unión Revolucionaria and
the Directorio Estudiantil would have fiercely rejected such an outcome.

The revolutionary violence of the early 1930s grew out of the increasingly
desperate economic situation, which had deteriorated after the Wall Street
crash of October 1929. Almost no regime, however repressive, could have
easily survived the crisis affecting the island. The Depression struck Cuba with
the force of a Caribbean hurricane. Just one economic indicator provides a
measure of the disaster as it affected Cuba. The value of the island's sugar
production slumped from nearly $200 million in 1929 to just over $40 million
in 1932.[47] Not until 1991–4 was the island to experience a comparable catastrophe. Machado's government was bereft of ideas or mechanisms that might
have provided a way through the crisis. As more than a quarter of the
workforce lost their jobs, with a million family members facing hunger,
political unrest exploded beyond the capacity of the state to contain.

The economic gales brought political upheaval and revolution to many
countries all over the world, and Latin America was in the eye of the storm.
A peasant insurrection in El Salvador in January 1932 was famously repressed;
an air force rebellion in Chile in June that year briefly established a 'socialist
republic', led by Marmaduque Grove, the uncle of Salvador Allende. These

were new times, too, in Washington. A fresh government led by a Democratic president, Franklin Roosevelt, was inaugurated in January 1933. Americans were offered a 'New Deal', Latin Americans were promised a 'Good Neighbour' policy. Roosevelt told Cuba's ambassador in Washington that he had 'no desire to intervene' in Cuba's affairs. America's sole duty was to do what it could 'so that there should be no starvation and chaos among the Cuban people'. Nothing else was on offer.[48]

The new ambassador in 1933 was Sumner Welles, who had been part of Crowder's entourage in the 1920s and was no stranger to the sugar industry. He and Roosevelt had been at school together, at Groton, and they had a close relationship not unlike the one Theodore Roosevelt had once had with Leonard Wood. Roosevelt asked Machado if he would receive his old friend as a special envoy, as Crowder had once been, but the Cuban President requested that he should come as the ambassador. Machado cannot have been ignorant of the fact that Welles had instructions to investigate the situation, and permission, if necessary, to ease him from power.

Trouble had been brewing throughout the summer. A strike of bus drivers in Havana in July, protesting against a tax increase on urban transport, led to a bloody confrontation between the drivers and the police. Other workers soon joined the strike: tram drivers, lorry drivers, printers and stevedores at the docks. By August, what had been an ordinary workers' protest had developed into a general strike with insurrectionary overtones.

Welles stood back and took no action. Many wealthy Cubans believed that revolution was in the air and hoped for a US military intervention under the terms of the Platt Amendment. American troops stood ready at their base at Guantánamo Bay, poised to intervene to support the government once again. Other US forces were alerted in neighbouring Haiti, under US military occupation since 1915.[49] But they received no orders to move.

Without US support Machado was doomed. Destabilised by the economic collapse, unable to quell the strikers in the streets and under pressure from senior officers – and finally from Welles himself – Machado was forced to resign. He left the country for Nassau on 12 August.[50] His downfall took place rather sooner than Welles had expected and led to the first Cuban revolution of the twentieth century.

A Republic for revolutionaries: Antonio Guiteras and the Revolution of 1933

The Revolution of 1933 unfolded in three distinct phases, as each of the secretive anti-Machado movements emerged from the shadows to take their turn at government. The first had a semi-fascist tinge, and lasted barely a month, its political support coming from the ABC. The second was a radical,

ultra-leftist experience, that survived for four months and came out of the
Directorio Estudiantil, with Antonio Guiteras as its leading player. The third
phase was a counter-revolution lasting five years, from 1934 to 1939, that took
its political colouring from Fulgencio Batista, a worthy successor to Machado.

At the start, an orderly transfer of power led to the appointment as interim
president, effectively selected by Sumner Welles, of Carlos Manuel de
Céspedes, the pedestrian grandson of the independence leader of 1868. He had
once served as a minister under Machado and was supported by the fascist-
leaning ideologues of the ABC. His right-wing government, with its notably
pro-American cabinet, did little more than preside over the dissolution of the
Machado congress and watch helplessly as the mob took over the streets.

They could do nothing to control or canalise this anarchic explosion of
popular feeling, made more dramatic in Havana by the total absence of
policing. Machado's policemen had sensibly disappeared from the streets
before they were met with popular justice. Many were lynched, and, in the
ensuing chaos, hundreds of people were killed and many houses sacked.

Grant Watson, the British ambassador, described scenes of vengeance that
would 'remain for ever a painful recollection for those who beheld them',
perhaps because it was unusual to observe the Havana middle class taking part
in the looting. Looking out of the embassy window after dinner, he noted a
frenzied crowd sacking the house of his neighbour, a Machado senator. He
found it 'a revolting sight, for while Negroes fought for gramophones and
nursemaids for shawls, well-dressed families drove up in Packards and
Cadillacs, [and] seized Louis XV cabinets and gilded chairs'.[51]

With the pressure of dictatorship lifted, the country beyond Havana experienced a mounting tide of revolutionary fervour, beyond the capacity of any
political group to ride or control. A wave of agitation and unrest swept across
the sugar zones, extending to the most distant mills. Young and old, black and
white, old inhabitants and new immigrants – everyone was caught up in the
revolutionary excitement. A vivid account of that summer's great upheaval
was provided a year later by a group of Cuba experts at the US Foreign Policy
Association, who visited the country to report on the events of the revolutionary year. They described the first seizure of a sugar mill at Punta Alegre in
Camagüey, on 21 August:

> Within less than a month the number of mills under labour control was
> estimated at thirty-six. Soviets were reported to have been organised at
> Mabay, Jaronú, Senado, Santa Lucía, and other *centrales*. At various points
> mill managers were held prisoners by the workers. Labour guards were
> formed, armed with clubs, sticks and a few revolvers, a red armband serving
> as uniform. Workers fraternised with the soldiers and police.
>
> During the first stage of the movement, demonstrations in Camagüey
> and Oriente were often headed by a worker, a peasant and a soldier. At

some of the *centrales* in Santa Clara, Camagüey, and Oriente provinces, the workers occupied not only the mills, but also the company railroad systems, and extended their control to the sub-ports and neighbouring small towns and agricultural areas.

Relief committees supplied food to the strikers and their families, and in some cases became subsistence commissions for the whole population of the strike area. At various points these committees allocated parcels of land to be cultivated by the field workers.[52]

In this continuing atmosphere of revolution in the countryside, with violence on the streets of Havana and political plotting behind closed doors, Céspedes and the ABC could not survive. They were swept away on 4 September by an unplanned and unexpected coup. A rebellion broke out at military headquarters at Camp Columbia, the huge base on the outskirts of Havana. Discontent among a group of army sergeants resulted in a barracks mutiny. The sergeants feared a counter-coup by the surviving Machado officers and moved first. A small group of sergeants, corporals and enlisted men formed themselves into a revolutionary junta.

Pre-eminent among their leaders was Fulgencio Batista Zaldívar, a mulatto typist from Oriente, aged 31. The sergeants' mutiny was a bizarre and unlooked-for development, one of the few occasions in Latin American history when a *coup d'état* has been staged by the lower ranks. It was soon capitalised on by a handful of professors and student leaders from the Directorio Estudiantil who had read their revolutionary manuals and had been busily plotting on their own account. They drove out to Camp Columbia to make common cause with the soldiers and to assist in the formation of a provisional revolutionary government. Céspedes was replaced by a coalition of soldiers and students. Their alliance was explained in a contemporary account of the sergeants' actions by Ruby Hart Phillips, the well-informed wife of the *New York Times* correspondent. Hers is probably a close enough guide to what happened:

> They realised the people of the island wouldn't support a military government headed by sergeants no one had ever heard of, so they sent out cars and called members of the university faculty on the phone, members of the Directorio Estudiantil and some other well-known radicals to hurry up and come to Camp Columbia. All the radicals and students rushed out to Camp, thinking it was their conspiracy; when they arrived they found it was the sergeants', but they decided that was as good as any conspiracy, so long as they were in it, and everyone shouted 'Viva la República'.[53]

The soldier-student gathering in Camp Columbia produced a 'Proclamation to the People of Cuba' that was published the next day. Drafted by Sergio Carbó, the newspaper editor who had taken part in the abortive landing at Gibara in 1931, it was signed by 16 civilians, two former soldiers and Batista, who described himself alongside his signature as the 'Revolutionary Chief Sergeant of All the Armed Forces of Cuba'.[54]

The moderate programme outlined in the Proclamation looked forward to a constituent assembly to write a new constitution, and a tribunal to judge the crimes of the Machado era. It sought the protection of property, of both nationals and foreigners; the recognition of debts incurred by previous regimes; and the re-establishment of peace and justice. It was a triumph for the middle-class students of the Directorio Estudiantil, whose programme it was.

Throughout August, the more radical student leaders had been alarmed both by the alliance between Céspedes and Sumner Welles, and by the fact that Machado's army had remained intact after the departure of Machado himself. The rebellion of the sergeants was a godsend to the radicals. Ordinary working-class soldiers were taking up arms against their corrupt and privileged officers. It was an unexpected but most welcome development. Just in case anyone missed against whom the revolution was directed, Sergio Carbó told the *New York Times* that the Republic had come of age and 'with cries of joy' had 'escaped from the American embassy'.[55]

In their own statement, signed, among others, by Carlos Prío Socarrás and Eduardo Chibás, the Directorio Estudiantil claimed their own part in the revolution, emphasising their hostility to the 'inanimate government named by the US Ambassador', and the need to purge the armed forces:

> With this chaotic state in the country, without principle of authority and with many Machado-stained men still in the armed forces, the Directorio decided to launch its revolutionary action, with the relatively untarnished section of the armed forces who, with great patriotic organisation and responsibility, acted energetically but without needing to fire a single gun, cleansing in this way the glorious uniform of the Army, which was on the edge of dishonour, because of the collaboration of its leaders with the *Machadato.*[56]

The cries of pleasure at the latest twist came from the rebellious black crowds in the streets, and soon caused alarm among the Americans in Havana and among Cuba's own white settler elite. 'Fears of a Negro uprising again took hold of certain sections of the Cuban population,' noted the American researchers from the Foreign Policy Association, who described how 'negroes were among the leaders in seizing sugar properties and making exorbitant demands on mill managers'.[57] Ruby Hart Phillips exemplified the mood among American observers, describing in her diary the scenes on the palace balcony on the day after the September revolution:

> Every negro in town is there, apparently they didn't even go home for lunch, or perhaps they thought the new government would serve lunch.

Sergeant Batista has proved to be a powerful and inflaming speaker. He really is good, but he'd better be careful those negroes don't get the idea that the island is completely theirs, and go out to help themselves to anything in sight.[58]

She need not have worried. The whites soon reasserted themselves, and were soon turning up their noses at the dark-skinned Batista. Batista, too, had made clear where he stood. Abandoning the student revolutionaries on the palace balcony, he took himself off for an appointment with Sumner Welles, apparently at his own request. Welles had panicked the previous day, fearing the worst and summoning more US warships into Havana harbour, but Batista, with his immense personal charm and broad grin, made an excellent impression on the nervous ambassador. They were to meet again, frequently.

Batista's junta chose Dr Ramón Grau San Martín, a wealthy doctor and a university professor who had supported the Directorio, to be the new president. He was sworn in on 10 September, and presided for just four months over a revolution that he was wholly unable to control. Batista and the sergeants remained in the background, while the students fought out their differences among themselves.

Grau's revolutionary government was divided from the start between a radical group from the Unión Revolucionaria of Antonio Guiteras, and more moderate elements from the Directorio Estudiantil. Guiteras was in the most powerful position, appointed as minister of the interior, of war and of the navy, giving him nominal control over the army, the navy and the police. His ally, Gustavo Moreno, took over communications, and Eduardo Chibás was put in charge of public works. Guiteras now took the leading role in the revolution, a link between José Martí and Fidel Castro. His political ideology and practice prefigured that of Castro 20 years later, while his incorruptibility in a venal age and his austere style – he was known to have only one suit – harked back to Martí. All three men were imbued by a sense of patriotism common to few.

Born in 1906 to a Cuban father and an English mother, Guiteras had been partly brought up in the United States. He was a radical Liberal soon attracted to socialism, but never to communism, although the US embassy in Havana routinely described him as such. Like the other student leaders, he had long been organising in secret, breaking away from the Directorio to found Unión Revolucionaria in 1931. Later, in 1934, he was to organise a new movement, Joven Cuba, that called for socialism; advocated land reform, industrialisation and the creation of a national shipping company; and hoped to achieve its aims through armed struggle and the infiltration of the armed forces.

Guiteras's views reflected an eclectic mix of revolutionary influences, from Auguste Blanqui to Jean Jacques Jaurès. He drew inspiration from the Mexican and the Russian revolutions, the struggle in Ireland and Sandino's guerrilla movement in Nicaragua. He shared the anti-imperialist politics of the age and, drawing on anarchist roots, advocated rural and urban armed struggle, assaults on army barracks and the assassination of policemen and members of the government. He was a firm believer in direct action, the propaganda of the deed, derived from Blanqui and the Spanish anarchists, and was much criticised by the Communists for his voluntarism and his predilection for violence.

Grau's government had innumerable enemies. First there were the ousted cadres of the fascistic ABC. Then there were the old Conservatives around Menocal and the Liberals of Colonel Mendieta, grouped together in the Unión Nacionalista. Finally there were the senior officers in the armed forces, the survivors of the Machado era. Many had been humiliated during the August rioting and now they had to choose between staging a coup or escaping into exile. The action of Batista and the sergeants made a coup more difficult and the majority decided to leave the country.

Sumner Welles paved the way to what looked like a solution of their problems. During the panic immediately after the sergeants' coup in September, he told US citizens to congregate at the Hotel Nacional, the great hotel palace on the Malecón looking over the sea. Welles had appealed for US intervention, if only to guard the hotel and the embassy, yet immediate intervention proved impossible. Several US warships hovered off Havana, but none had a complement of Marines sufficiently large to land against possible resistance.

Ignorant of these important details several hundred of Machado's officer corps took refuge in the hotel with the Americans, praying for a speedy intervention and their evacuation. Their prayers were not answered. Soldiers loyal to Batista attacked the hotel with heavy artillery and some 80 people were killed and 200 wounded. The surviving officers surrendered and were escorted across the harbour to the Cabaña, several being killed on the way. A second officers' revolt in November, supported by sections of the ABC and sparked off within the airforce, was also brutally crushed, with more than 200 dead.

The defeat and slaughter of the Machado officers immeasurably strengthened the hand of Batista, who was now the unquestioned boss of the army. Hundreds of sergeants and corporals were promoted to fill the depleted ranks of the officer corps. Backed by this newly constituted army, Batista was now in a far stronger position than Guiteras and the students with whom he was allied.

Yet the radicalisation of Grau's government went ahead. It refused to service the debt on the American loans made to Machado. It nationalised Chaparra and Delicias, the two mills of the Cuban American Sugar Corporation, and it nationalised Cuban Electric.

More controversially, in a decree reflecting the frustrated nationalism of many decades, it ordered all businesses to ensure that 50 per cent of their workers had been Cuban born. The decree was aimed at both Spaniards and blacks from the Caribbean. The inherent racism within Cuban society, never far fom the surface, had been released by the September revolution. So too had the resentment against what was seen as the arrogance of the Spanish immigrants. Spanish immigration had in fact been in decline since the Depression, but the decree was a psychological as much as a physical blow to the powerful Spanish community. The notion that a Cuban government could take such an action against the citizens of the mother country was a grave humiliation. Yet the decree against the Spanish was hugely popular, and Spanish businesses and shops came under attack. English, German and North American companies were also affected.

Harsher still was the impact of the decree on the black migrants from Jamaica and Haiti. Fidel Castro's godfather was the consul of Haiti in Santiago, and Castro recalled in 1985 how the consul had been affected by the decree:

> The so-called revolution of 1933 was a movement of struggle and rebelliousness against injustice and abuse. It called for the nationalisation of the electric company and other foreign enterprises, and for the nationalisation of employment ... Tens of thousands of Haitians were mercilessly deported to Haiti. According to *our* revolutionary ideas, that was an inhuman thing to do.[59]

Inhuman or not, the decree against the immigrant blacks was as popular as the attack on the Spanish community.

These populist measures were not sufficient to protect Grau's government. The final showdown between Batista and Guiteras came in January 1934. Batista had defeated his enemies within the armed forces, and the only enemy in sight was the United States ambassador, who had steadfastly refused to recognise the Grau government. Batista well understood that the United States would only recognise and support a more moderate President. The favoured candidate was Colonel Mendieta, leader of what was left of the old Liberal Party. As the crisis deepened, Guiteras called for a general strike to protect the existing government, but the public mood was changing and the workers were no longer listening. Batista pushed Mendieta into accepting the presidency, and he took over on 18 January, to be greeted at the palace by rapturous crowds.

Batista had judged well. The continuing uncertainty had lost the Grau government the support that it had once had. With a new, more conservative president in place, the United States was content to recognise his government, which it did formally a few days later, while Grau sailed off to exile in Mexico.

A Republic designed for Fulgencio Batista, 1934–1952

Batista had made himself the arbiter of Cuban politics, and he was to dominate the country for the next 25 years. Born on a sugar plantation in 1902, he was more representative of the Cuban people than any of the rulers in their history, before or since, claiming African, Spanish, Indian and Chinese blood in his veins. He had joined the army as a private at the age of 19 and, learning how to use the typewriter, he became a stenographer with the rank of sergeant who participated in the work of military tribunals. He was later to become the single most important political figure in the twentieth century in Cuba aside from Castro. As revolutionary leader, elected president, military dictator and millionaire defender of the Mafia, he left an indelible mark on the history of his country that was only effaced by the Revolution of 1959.

Batista manipulated events behind the scenes during the civilian governments of the 1930s – seven followed in quick succession from 1934 to 1940 – before finally submitting himself for election, successfully, in October 1940. Although he was eventually to join the ranks of the most reviled Latin American dictators of his era, in his years as the country's elected president, from 1940 to 1944, he enjoyed considerable popularity.

His counter-revolutionary blow of January 1934 was effected with ease. He simply transferred the allegiance of the armed forces from Grau to Mendieta, through the offices of the US embassy. The United States reinforced the position of President Mendieta by abolishing the Platt Amendment, the chief grievance of Cuban nationalists. It was formally removed from the Cuban constitution on 29 May 1934 and a new treaty was signed. The United States retained a safeguard, refusing to abandon its great military base at Guantánamo Bay.

Yet in spite of Batista's coup, much of the country was still in a revolutionary mood that Mendieta could do little to counter. Guiteras, released from the cares of government, revived the clandestine movement, now renamed Joven Cuba, with which he had once fought Machado, and welded it into an urban guerrilla movement to overthrow Mendieta. Anti-government protests, work stoppages and strikes continued throughout 1934 and into the early months of 1935. He tried yet again to destroy the government with a general strike in March 1935 and brought the country to a halt. Yet Mendieta and Batista still had a populist wind in their sails, and, imposing martial law in the old Spanish fashion, they crushed the strike. Once again a wave of repression swept across the island, with unions made illegal, the university closed and detention and torture made the norm for political activists.

The island came under increasing military control. The process begun under Machado was consolidated under Batista. The army became the most significant force in politics, a power that seeped rapidly into the culture and remained deeply entrenched in Cuban society. The American researchers of the Foreign Policy Association recorded how, when 'speaking of the need of playgrounds and playground directors in Havana, a Cuban woman told of the children who congregated in a small park near her house. All day . . . the children played at revolution. They lined up and paraded, and shot each other with imaginary guns, and dragged off the victims.'[60]

Writing of the influence of North American films, Louis Pérez has described how the gangster movies of the 1930s became especially popular, influencing the Cuban form of political violence. 'The drive-by machine-gun shooting, so much a part of the film genre, became a prominent motif of political warfare in Havana. The method was familiar to movie-goers: the speeding car, the burst of machine-gun fire, the getaway.'[61] The word *gangsterismo* was coined to describe a new development in the country's politics.

In despair after the failed general strike, Guiteras planned a retreat to Mexico. A farm had been bought there, guerrilla fighters were to be trained to return to Cuba to fight a revolutionary war, on the nineteenth-century model.[62] Guiteras was to sail out from Matanzas in May 1935. The operation was an interesting one, but was not to be up and running for another two decades, and it would not be led by Guiteras. He was killed at the Fortín Morillo in Matanzas as he prepared to sail into exile.

Mendieta did not survive as president for long, and was followed by a succession of minor political figures over the next few years, all relying on the whim of Batista. Elections were finally held in January 1936, but the protagonists were ghosts from the past, former President Menocal losing to Miguel Mariano Gómez. President Gómez barely lasted the year, defeated on the issue of rural schools. Batista had sent soldiers to build and teach in rural schools, considered a dangerously populist measure by the old Liberal elite. When put to the vote in congress, Gómez was successfully impeached for trying to prevent it, and replaced by his vice-president.

As the violence receded, the old order reasserted itself under Batista's watchful eye. Grau San Martín reassembled his old supporters and created a new middle-class movement, the Partido Revolucionario Cubano Auténtico, reviving the name of Martí's old party. The Communists, too, began to emerge from the shadows and to feel their way towards legality, creating the Partido Unión Revolucionaria, led by Juan Marinello, a poet and professor at the university. Since Grau's party had no intention of making common cause with them, the Communists turned towards Batista. If Batista would allow the Communists to organise, they would offer him the party political support that he lacked. A deal was done. The Communist Party was allowed to operate legally, and a party newspaper, *Hoy*, edited by Joaquín Ordoqui, was set up. 'The people who are working for the overthrow of Batista,' the Comintern journal noted piously, 'are no longer acting in the interests of the Cuban people.'[63] The Communists were allowed to form a new union movement, the Confederación de Trabajadores de Cuba (CTC), led by Lázaro Peña, a black tobacco worker, and the CTC became the beneficiary of a close relationship with the Ministry of Labour.

The alliance between the Communists and Batista was understandable in the context of the time, but was jeered at by middle-class radicals, the heirs to the upheavals of 1933, and the legend of Communist Party perfidy remained widespread until long after 1959.

One of the belated achievements of the Revolution of 1933 was the creation of a new constitution. Machado had written one to suit his own convenience, but the constitution of 1940 was the first produced by an elected constituent assembly since the first Republican constitution of 1902, flawed by the inclusion of the Platt Amendment. Elections for the assembly were held in November 1939, and Grau's Partido Auténtico and its allies won 41 seats out of 76. Batista's party and the Communists secured 35 between them. The assembly met in February 1940 and completed its work within six months.

The new constitution had an important progressive formulation for its time and became a significant reference point in later years. It had a strong social-democratic content: workers were given a constitutional right to an 8-hour day, a 44-hour week and one month's paid holiday, plus a pension, compulsory social insurance and accident compensation; freedom of association, and freedom to vote in elections and referendums, was granted to adults over the age of 20; and women received the vote for the first time.

The old nervousness about the black population reasserted itself, and, although segregation was outlawed, political movements based on race were specifically banned – as they had been since 1910. Still influenced by US models, though now those of the Roosevelt's New Deal, the constitution favoured a powerful role for the state in economic and social development, the regulation of property rights and eight years of compulsory education for all children.[64]

When Batista became president himself, during the boom conditions of the Second World War, he ruled as a social democrat. Trade union rights were confirmed and extended, government money was spent on social programmes and local Communists were welcomed into his government (with Stalin perceived as a vital ally against Hitler and diplomatic relations established with the Soviet Union).

The war led to the collapse of sugar production in Asia and Europe and Cuba again received an unexpected bonanza. The sugar crop increased from 2.7 million tons to 4.2 million in the period from 1940 to 1944, and the value of raw sugar production went up from $110 million to $251 million. Although European markets were lost, and even some in the United States owing to the scarcity of shipping, these were balmy years for Batista's government.[65] The high sugar price and a prolonged era of social peace, the product of support for the government from the Communist Party and its allied labour movement, gave the country a positive folk memory of the Batista government.[66] People forgot wartime scarcities, unemployment, inflation and the lack of foreign tourists.

When his four-year period came to an end, Batista hoped that Carlos Saladrigas, his prime minister and a former leader of the ABC, would win the presidency, but the voters chose Grau San Martín and the Auténticos. Invoking memories of 1933, he swept the country. Once in government, he continued along Batista's reformist path, soon disappointing his more radical backers. As the storm clouds of the Cold War began to gather, and with the support of Carlos Prío Socarrás, his minister of Labour, he moved against the Communist Party and against the Communist-dominated workers' union, the CTC.

Grau's move to the right sparked opposition within the ranks of the Auténticos, and in 1947, Eduardo Chibás, another memory from the 1930s, formed a more radical party, the Partido Revolucionario Cubano Ortodoxo. With the Ortodoxos, he hoped to win the presidential election of 1948. He was pitted against Prío Socarrás for the Auténticos, another relic of 1933. Prío was the winner, and his four-year government, from 1948 to 1952, has been described as 'the most polarised, corrupt, violent, and undemocratic' in Cuba's republican history.[67]

At mid-century, Cuba was suffering from a systemic crisis, both political and economic. The generation that had participated in the overthrow of Machado and taken part in the revolutionary events of 1933 had had a fresh chance to run the country and had thrown their opportunity away. All the old politicians were discredited, while the one figure from that era that retained a sense of honesty – Eduardo Chibás – had made a dramatic exit from the scene. He shot himself live on radio, in August 1951, during one of his weekly broadcasts usually devoted to attacking the corruption of the Prío government. Possibly an accident or more probably suicide, Chibás's death marked the end of the era that had begun in 1933.

New players were now hovering in the wings. One of these was Fidel Castro, who, together with half a hundred would-be revolutionaries emerging from the University of Havana, was soon to sponsor a fresh revolutionary movement that would inevitably evoke echoes of that earlier event.

Another contender, first on stage, was the military. Remade under Batista, Cuba's armed forces were closely involved in politics but did not fall into the continent's typical pattern. They were not part of the traditional ruling elite. Junior officers were as aware as anyone in the wider society of the failings of successive civilian regimes. Political corruption and *gangsterismo*, coupled with the luxurious life-style of senior officers that rarely trickled down the pecking order, aroused as much anger in the nationalistic breasts of young officers as it did in students at the university.

In the final years of President Prío, junior officers sounded out General Batista to discover if he would support a coup they had under consideration. The old coup-maker was initially reluctant; elections were scheduled for 1952 and he would again be a candidate. Chibás, the charismatic candidate of the Ortodoxos in 1948, was dead. The candidate of the Auténticos was the uncharismatic Grau San Martín. Batista calculated that he might not win, and the unrest within the military suggested that the elections might not even take place. Discovering that the officers were bent on a coup, with or without him, he put himself at their service.

Batista drove to Camp Columbia in the early hours of Sunday 10 March 1952, and arrested the senior officers who lay sleeping there. Before dawn, he controlled the city, and Prío Socarrás was on his way to the Mexican embassy to seek asylum. Prío's rule was in its final months and his downfall left no regrets among the population. No one took up his call for resistance, and his government collapsed without a shot being fired.

Batista's new regime was widely welcomed. After a perfunctory attempt to preserve the constitutional niceties, and to repeat his experience of the 1930s by finding a figleaf president, Batista appointed himself as chief of state. He invoked the name of Martí in his first public speech and associated himself with the popular aspiration for progress and democracy, and for peace and justice; it was an impeccable performance. Police and army pay was increased, congressmen and senators continued to receive their salaries. Much of the constitution of 1940 was suspended, but most people, with the exception of the Ortodoxos, like Castro and his friends, gave the new government the benefit of the doubt. European and Latin American countries granted swift diplomatic recognition, followed at a decent interval by the United States.

Batista's coup forestalled the presidential election and obliged politicians of all stripes to revise their plans. Some accommodated themselves to the new order, but to a new generation of young political activists the coup came as a fresh political opportunity. Like their politically confused predecessors in the 1930s they had doubts about the value of the electoral process in the Cuba context. Like them, they had already organised themselves into action groups and were involved in the internecine political feuding and *gangsterismo* that characterised the post-war period. Now they were presented with an unexpected opportunity to put their theoretical support of violence into practice. The time seemed right. While Batista's coup received some initial support from those disgusted by the corruption of the parliamentary regime, his subsequent actions showed that there would be no real break with the past. Batista had no fresh recipe for the country other than himself and his record. It was not sufficient.

5
Castro's Revolution takes shape, 1953–1961

Castro's attack on Moncada, 26 July 1953

The Moncada fortress lies just a short drive from Santiago's central square. In the 1950s it stood on the outskirts of the city. A once grey, two-storey battlemented barracks, now painted bright yellow picked out with white, its aboveground entrance is approached via a row of concrete steps. The second largest barracks in the country in the 1950s, second only to Havana's Camp Columbia, it was originally designed to house the Rural Guard during the American occupation after 1898, and often regarded subsequently as a symbol of government repression. A hundred years later, its large courtyards are shared between a number of classrooms and a dusty museum, for the revolutionaries of the 1950s had promised that such barrack buildings would be turned into schools. The cells and the interrogation rooms remain as they once were, bleak testimony to past atrocities.

On 26 July 1953 an armed attack took place at Moncada, led by Fidel Castro, the flamboyant figure then aged 26 who was to dominate Cuban politics and history for more than half a century. The assault on Moncada, and a simultaneous move against the barracks at Bayamo, was designed to secure weapons from the arsenal, but its underlying purpose was to overthrow the Batista government established after a *coup d'état* the previous year. The action itself proved to be a disastrous failure, little more than an ill-prepared putsch, as the Communists described it, showing no more interest in the country's insurrectionary traditions than they had done in the 1930s. Yet Moncada was a challenge to the regime, and would lay the groundwork for a revolutionary organisation, the July 26 Movement, that would sweep to power less than six years later. It also made the name of its leader known across the island.

Castro was regarded at the time as the outstanding figure of his generation, a brilliant student orator and a successful athlete, a man marked for politics from early youth. He was born in August 1926, the son of Angel Castro, a white settler immigrant from Galicia, and his second wife, Lina Ruz, a woman from Pinar del Rio. Angel Castro became a wealthy landowner in Oriente and had several children, but only Fidel's younger brother, Raúl, would play a major role in his life's work. Their childhood was spent in and around their father's estate at Birán in Oriente, close to Mayarí and the Bay of Nipe.[1] Castro was educated at a Jesuit college and trained as a lawyer at the University of Havana, and in 1948 he married Mirta Díaz Balart, the sister of a student friend and the daughter of a wealthy family.[2] He appeared set for a conventional political career, and had been preparing for the elections of 1952 as a possible congressional candidate for the Ortodoxo party, when his plans were interrupted by Batista's coup.

Castro became one of the more extraordinary political figures of the twentieth century and Cuba's history will long be dominated by him. His successful revolution made world headlines in 1959 and created the Cuban nation, giving meaning to the struggles of the past and transforming a troubled but essentially peripheral Caribbean island into a player on the world stage. Under his leadership, the Cuban people 'stood up' – in the vivid expression of Mao Tse-tung – and understood for the first time who they really were. As a leading international presence for more than 40 years, Castro dealt on equal terms with successive presidents of the two nuclear super-powers. As the most charismatic leader of the Third World during its heyday, his influence was felt far beyond the shores of his island. Grey-bearded in old age, he continued to exercise a magnetic attraction wherever he travelled, with an audience as fascinated by the dinosaur from the history books as they had once been by the vibrant revolutionary firebrand.

The Russians were beguiled by Castro from the start (Nikita Khrushchev and Anastas Mikoyan in particular), European intellectuals (Jean-Paul Sartre and Simone de Beauvoir) took him to their hearts, African revolutionaries (Ahmed Ben Bella, Kwame Nkrumah and Agostinho Neto) welcomed his assistance and advice, and Latin American political movements were inspired by his Revolution. Only the leaders of the United States, where nine successive presidents preserved him as an eternal enemy, and of China, which for many years considered his political behaviour to be irresponsible, refused to fall for his charm.

Castro became a world hero in the mould of Garibaldi, a national leader whose ideals and rhetoric would help shape the history of a continent. The ignored countries of Latin America, ruled for the most part in the 1950s by narrow oligarchies inherited from the colonial era, were brought into the global limelight, their governments rudely challenged by the revolutionary rhetoric of the island republic. Whether for him or against him, successive Latin American generations were profoundly influenced by the figure of Fidel.

Cuba under Castro became a Communist country where nationalism was more significant than socialism, where the legend of Martí proved more influential than the philosophy of Marx. Castro's skill, and one of the keys to his political longevity, lay in keeping the twin themes of socialism and nationalism endlessly in play. He gave back their history to the Cuban people, enabling them to see the name of their island stamped firmly on the twentieth-century global story. His timely invocation of the name and example of Martí, the hundredth anniversary of whose birth had occurred opportunely in January 1953, proved particularly felicitous.

For many Cubans, Batista's return to power had ruled out any further journeys along the democratic road to political power. An impatient Castro embraced armed insurrection without a second thought, and began to organise in the wake of Batista's coup. Such a strategy was a staple ingredient of Cuba's own troubled history, as well as in the insecure countries that bordered the Caribbean. Nor was Castro alone. Other small and independent groups, gathering secretly in Havana and other towns, were dusting down the old tradition of political violence and preparing for an assault on Batista's regime.

Castro's charisma, his strategic vision and his organising talents, gave his group a powerful advantage. He assembled more than 150 men, trained them, and raised the necessary funds. Most of them were radicals rather than revolutionaries; most came from the youth wing of the Ortodoxo party. Castro drafted a manifesto that outlined a programme for government, invoking the name of Martí. He also made preparations for guerrilla warfare in the countryside, like Guiteras in the 1930s, lest his planned attack on the Moncada barracks should fail.

The preparations for the Moncada operation went ahead undetected. A small farm was leased near Siboney, outside Santiago, and men and munitions were gradually assembled there, the local peasants given the impression that they were constructing buildings to hold battery chickens. On the chosen day in July 1953, a hundred guerrillas dressed in army uniforms set off from Siboney to Santiago in buses and motor cars. They had surprise on their side, but the defenders of the barracks had the advantage of a superior position. Castro's guerrillas were obliged to fight uphill. Several soldiers were killed in the battle, but the guerrillas were easily repelled. Castro's makeshift troop retired in disarray, leaving more than half of their number behind. Some were dead, while many were captured and subsequently executed.

Fidel's younger brother, Raúl, was among those taking part. His unit successfully seized the Palace of Justice, adjacent to the barracks, but was forced to withdraw when the rest of the plan collapsed. Raúl escaped into the countryside, avoiding the slaughter that followed, but he was eventually captured and put on trial.

Fidel also escaped into the hills, only to be discovered a few days later. His life was saved by a black lieutenant from the Rural Guard, who had the wit to take him to the police station in Santiago rather than to Moncada barracks, where he would certainly have been shot along with the other prisoners. He was later transferred to the hilltop jail of Boniato, outside the city.

The regime exacted its revenge. A senior general arrived from Havana bringing specific instructions from Batista that outlined what was to be done. It was 'humiliating and dishonourable for the army to have lost in combat three times as many men as the insurgents did,' announced the general, according to Castro's account at his subsequent trial. 'Ten prisoners must be shot for each dead soldier.'³ That was Batista's order, and it was followed to excess. The ensuing bloodbath, with more than 70 guerrillas shot in captivity, did much to turn public opinion against his regime. Only the intervention of the Catholic archbishop of Santiago called a halt to the killings.

Castro was put on trial in Santiago in September, along with more than a hundred defendants, many of them local leftists who had had no connection with the Moncada attack. Castro, as a qualified lawyer, took on their defence, basing his case on the illegality of the regime and the inherent right of the citizen to rebel against an illegal government. When asked who was behind the attack, he replied that 'the intellectual author of this revolution is José Martí, the apostle of our independence'.

His defence was so successful that only 26 prisoners were found guilty and most were treated leniently. The Santiago judges still retained their independence. Raúl, however, as one of the leaders, was sentenced to 13 years in prison. Fidel had not been on the first list of defendants and was brought before a different court in October, his own trial being held in the nurses' room of a civilian hospital. According to legend, he made a two-hour speech, justifying his actions and outlining his political programme, but since no record was kept of his words, he had to reconstruct them later. 'Condemn me, it does not matter,' were his concluding words. 'History will absolve me.'

The speech when published became the manifesto of Castro's revolutionary movement. In it, he gave details of the 'five revolutionary laws' that would have been published had the attack on Moncada been successful. The first was 'to return power to the people' and to reinstate the constitution of 1940. The second dealt with land rights, promising that all those holding less than 165 acres, or squatting on them, would receive title to the land, while existing owners would be indemnified on the basis of the value of a ten-year rental. A third law would have given workers in large industrial and mining enterprises the right to a share of 30 per cent of the profits. A fourth granted sugar planters the right to 55 per cent of the profits of their production. A fifth law attacked corruption and would have confiscated the holdings of those found guilty of fraud during earlier governments.⁴ Half the property recovered would be used to subsidise workers' pension funds, while the rest would go to hospitals, asylums and charitable organisations.

Nor was this all. The initial five laws would have been proclaimed 'as soon as the rising was over', and followed by other measures, including the reorganisation of public education, the nationalisation of privately owned utilities and telephones, the control of rents and the pursuit of tax evaders. There were echoes here of the revolutionary demands made by Guiteras in 1933.

Castro's laws also re-emphasised two articles included in the constitution of 1940: one, outlawing feudal estates, would have limited the size of agricultural holdings ('to restore the land to the Cubans'), while the other, providing 'employment to the jobless', would have required the state 'to ensure a decent livelihood to each manual or intellectual worker'.

These liberal but far-reaching reforms were coupled with a declaration that Cuba's future policy in the Americas would be one 'of close solidarity with the democratic peoples of the continent . . .' No specific mention was made of the United States, merely an appeal for Cuba to become 'the bulwark of liberty, and not a shameful link in the chain of despotism'. Castro concluded his speech by invoking the name of Martí in his centenary year:

> It looked as if his memory would be extinguished for ever. But he lives. He has not died. His people are rebellious, his people are worthy, his people are faithful to his memory. Cubans have fallen defending his doctrines. Young men, in a magnificent gesture of reparation, have come to give their blood and to die in the hearts of his countrymen. O Cuba! What would have become of you if you had let the memory of your apostle die!

The flowery rhetoric was designed for history, and it did not impress the court. Castro was sentenced to 15 years in prison. He joined his brother and other surviving comrades in the jail on the Isle of Pines, and there he received the education in radical politics that had been lacking in his early schooling.

Prison provided an opportunity for extensive reading – fiction, history and politics – that would not otherwise have been possible. Castro read about Napoleon and Lenin, and also about Roosevelt. He was sustained by letters from Natalia Revuelta, his lover at the time, with whom he sustained a passionate and revealing exchange of letters. Later, he began to make plans for the future and to organise his embryonic July 26 Movement.[5]

Castro served less than two years of his sentence, the beneficiary of an amnesty. A presidential election had taken place in November 1954, while he was inside, with Batista as the sole candidate. Former president Grau San Martín gave the process some initial legitimacy by putting his own name forward, imagining that he still retained some personal popularity. Realising at the last moment that the elections would be fraudulent, in the Cuban tradition, he withdrew, and Batista declared himself to be the winner.[6] Announcing the return of constitutional rule, with guarantees of a free press, he felt secure enough to promise an amnesty for political prisoners – including the Castro brothers.

Released in May 1955, Castro was welcomed at Havana station by Raúl Chibás, the brother of the dead Eduardo, and he may have expected to be welcomed back into the arms of the Ortodoxo party. It was not to be. The party hierarchy were alarmed by his radical language and made no effort to incorporate him into their political plans – with good reason. A handful of Castro's inflammatory newspaper articles, accusing the barracks commander at Moncada of torture and assassination, and describing Batista as 'conceited, vain, dishonest and corrupt', soon brought back censorship, as well as threats against the old civilian politicians. Batista's democratic opening had not lasted long.

After three months in Havana, Castro could see that there was no future in electoral politics. The only solution to the crisis, he wrote to a friend, is 'armed insurrection', the path laid out by Maceo and Martí.[7] His mind was made up. He flew to Mexico in July 1955, preceded by his brother Raúl. Mexico was a country that had given refuge to earlier generations of Cubans, and to exiles from the Spanish Civil War, and it was still imbued with the mystique of its own revolution. Here Castro would organise a guerrilla force to follow in the footsteps of his nineteenth-century heroes. Armed and trained, they would sail to a Cuban beach once again and raise the torch of rebellion.

Within a week of his arrival in Mexico City, Castro was introduced by his brother to an unknown revolutionary from Argentina who had been living in the city since the previous September. Ernesto Che Guevara, just turned 27, had become friendly with a group of Cuban exiles already living there. They all met for supper at the lodgings of the Castro brothers on 26 July, to celebrate the second anniversary of the Moncada attack. Guevara wrote laconically in his diary that his meeting with 'the Cuban revolutionary' was 'a political occurrence'. He described Castro as 'a young man, intelligent, very sure of himself, and of extraordinary audacity'. In a masterful understatement, he noted 'I think there is mutual sympathy between us.'[8]

The chemistry between the two men, by this and all other accounts, was immediate, and was to have a lasting impact on the history of Cuba. Guevara provided Castro with broader horizons, a wider reading list, an insight into other revolutionary experiments and considerable first-hand knowledge of Latin America. Castro gave Guevara a ready-made political cause, for which he had long been searching, as well as the benefit of his own brief experience in charge of an armed revolutionary movement. Together they were to topple the Batista government and to organise a revolution whose ripples would spread out across the world.

Guevara was born in Argentina in 1928, the child of progressive middle-class parents, indifferently united, who had lived in various provincial towns in search of an agreeable climate for their asthmatic son. Without any notable interest in politics, and brought up in the Argentina of the 1940s, in the nationalist era of General Juan Perón to whom his parents had been hostile, he had studied to become a doctor. Footloose at an early age, he had made two expeditions through the Andean countries of Latin America in the early 1950s, acquiring a direct knowledge of peasant conditions and political movements that was unusual for someone of his age and background.

Before coming to Mexico, Guevara had spent nine months in Guatemala, from December 1953 to September 1954. There he had witnessed the final months of the government of Jacobo Arbenz, a reformist regime – supported among others by the local Communist Party – that had aroused the powerful opposition of the United States. Arbenz's support for a modest land reform, which would have affected the surplus lands of the United Fruit Company, an influential US-owned enterprise devoted to the production of bananas, led to an invasion in June 1954 by a small force of Guatemalan officers, organised and funded by the US Central Intelligence Agency. Guevara was forced to take asylum in the Argentine embassy.

The defeat of the Guatemalan government by an American-assisted putsch was a defining moment for Guevara, hardening the amateur revolutionary. His experience there was to create within him a profound distrust of the United States that was to grow with the years and to last until his execution in Bolivia in 1967, a deed watched over by an agent of the same US intelligence service that had destroyed the Arbenz government.

His fortuitous encounter with the Castro brothers gave him a new role in life, and he was quickly signed up to their embryonic revolutionary movement. Castro had come to Mexico to organise a guerrilla force capable of invading Cuba, but he lacked both cadres and cash. He flew to the United States in October and used his Ortodoxo contacts to raise funds from the Cuban community there, making speeches in New York, Philadelphia and Miami, but little money was forthcoming. These were bleak months. Castro was isolated from events in Cuba, with few people sharing his belief that the route of insurrectionary struggle was the right one. Other groups hostile to Batista were already organising inside the island. Students at the university of Havana, enrolled in the Federación Estudiantil Universitaria (FEU), led by José Antonio Echeverría, were making an impact on the ground. So too were the sugar-workers, led by Conrado Bécquer. Even young officers, led by Colonel Ramón Barquín, the military attaché in Washington, were plotting a coup. They planned to seize Camp Columbia, but their leaders were betrayed and detained in April 1956. By contrast, Castro's July 26 Movement had produced some good pamphlets, but not much else.

Gradually the tide began to turn in Castro's direction. Money slowly flowed in – from Venezuela and the United States, and from Cuba itself. By May he had enough to rent a farm, some 20 miles south of Mexico City, where recruits could be secretly assembled. Castro's supporters, some of them veterans of Moncada, arrived from Cuba in small groups, and Castro secured the services of Alberto Bayo, once a Republican officer fighting against Franco during the Spanish Civil War, to train them in guerrilla warfare.

Even in friendly Mexico, it was not easy to organise a guerrilla force of foreigners in secret, and both Castro and Guevara were arrested in June and the farm was raided. Intervention from the former Mexican president Lázaro Cárdenas secured their release, but future military training had to take place in a more distant part of the country. Difficult political negotiations with messengers from former president Prío Socarrás finally secured significant funds, enabling Castro to purchase a small motor yacht, the *Granma*, from an American living in Tuxpan, on Mexico's Atlantic coast. Towards the end of November, he assembled his guerrilla fighters at Tuxpan and they boarded the boat. Soon they were sailing out across the Gulf of Mexico – to Cuba.

The Granma *landing and the revolutionary war, 1956–1958*

Close to the mangrove swamps south of Playa Las Coloradas, on the south-western point of Oriente province, stands a small museum and a replica of a small motor yacht. A pathway leads through the mangroves down to a sandy beach where the original boat – the *Granma* – ran aground on an offshore reef on the morning of 2 December 1956. In Cuba's history of clandestine landings, this was one of the more disastrous, although it would eventually be celebrated as the most epic, since Castro was the captain of this ancient and leaking craft. A man always conscious of historical parallels, Castro was well aware that José Martí had stepped ashore at the eastern end of Oriente some 61 years earlier, engaged in a similar task. He saw himself as coming to complete Martí's work.

Castro's overall strategy had not changed significantly since 1953. The *Granma* landing was designed to ignite a popular, country-wide insurrection that would lead to the overthrow of the dictator. In spite of an inauspicious beginning, it was an important event not just in the history of Cuba but of Latin America as well. Over the next 25 years, young men and women up and down the continent dreamed of repeating the Cuban experience, and made plans to do so, imagining that a guerrilla war in the rural areas could easily spark an irresistible rebellion. Most Cubans, encouraged by Che Guevara, their first and most eloquent revolutionary theorist, firmly believed that the Cuban model could be repeated. Only years later did it become clear that revolutionaries in Cuba's towns had played an equally important role in organising the eventually successful insurrection, a necessary clarification that was often ignored elsewhere in Latin America.

The *Granma* and its cargo of 82 guerrilla volunteers had sailed from Tuxpan a week earlier. The long voyage of some 1,200 miles across the Gulf of Mexico, in heavy seas, had left most of them seasick, ill-prepared for what lay ahead. The plan was for a small force to be waiting for them on the deserted beach, and from there they would have moved seamlessly inland towards Bayamo and Santiago. The landing was scheduled to coincide with an uprising in Santiago, with a fresh attack on the Moncada barracks and the police headquarters. The action would have diverted Batista's local forces and allowed Castro's men to move into the hills without serious opposition.

The initial planning had not allowed for the vagaries of the weather. Moving slowly in the rough seas, the *Granma* arrived two days later than scheduled. Frank País, the competent young leader of the July 26 movement in Santiago, had launched the urban uprising on November 30, as planned, and his men held much of the city throughout the day. With no word of Castro's landing, and in the face of a fierce counter-attack by government troops, they retired into the hills, and the lorries waiting for Castro's boat to arrive at Playa Las Coloradas were also obliged to withdraw.

To make matters worse, the *Granma's* landing had not gone unnoticed by the authorities. Within hours of its arrival, the embryonic guerrilla group was under attack from the air and on land. Several were killed, while 22 were captured and later put on trial. The sorry remnant struggled through the swamps in disarray. According to legend, just 12 of them had survived, though this biblical number was an underestimate. Reassembling three days later at an estate called Alegría del Pino they fell into an ambush and several more were killed. The survivors wandered around, exhausted, hungry and lost, and it was ten days after the landing before they were able to unite with members of the internal resistance.

Their first contact was with Crescencio Pérez, an outlaw peasant leader who controlled the greater part of the western section of the Sierra Maestra. Heir to the traditions of the *palenques* in Oriente – the illegal settlements of blacks and Indians that dated back to the earliest years of the conquest – Pérez was to be a crucial figure in the recruitment of local peasants and bandits to the guerrilla cause.

A strategy of prolonged guerrilla warfare in the Sierra had not been planned by Castro; he had visited the mountains as a young man but was largely unfamiliar with their detailed geography. 'The only ideas we had about the Sierra Maestra were those we had studied in geography books,' he recalled later. He would have preferred a successful putsch, along the lines of the attack on Moncada. Yet a prolonged war in the countryside must always have been seen as a possible alternative, for he had an intimate knowledge of the drawn-out independence wars of the previous century. 'We are in no hurry,' he wrote to Frank País after six months in the mountains. 'We'll keep fighting as long as is necessary.'[9]

Just as Castro was aware of the legends associated with José Martí in 1895, so too were the Batista authorities familiar with the actions of Valeriano

Weyler, the Spanish general who had crushed resistance in 1896 by 'concentrating' peasants in the towns. Taking a leaf from Weyler's book, Batista's men began 're-concentrating' the peasants on the lower slopes of the Sierra Maestra, clearing them from their fields and homes to prevent them making common cause with the guerrillas. Anyone found in the cleared area would be shot on sight. In a twentieth-century development of an old strategy, they could be bombed from the air.

Batista also recreated the *voluntarios* of the 1860s in the shape of civilian paramilitaries led by Rolando Masferrer, a former leftist supporter who became an overtly fascist organiser in the Batista years. Sporting white baseball caps, Masferrer's death squads, known as *Los Tigres*, were to spearhead the repression in Santiago and the surrounding countryside.

Regrouped in the mountains, the surviving remnants of the *Granma* landing accustomed themselves to the routines of guerrilla warfare. They would attack isolated military garrisons close to the coast to obtain weapons and munitions, and then retreat into the impenetrable hills above. Soon they were able to establish regular contact with the urban network of the July 26 Movement, and Frank País made the journey from Santiago to Castro's headquarters early in February 1957. Plans were drawn up to ensure that a continuing supply of men and guns would be sent up to the mountains and that the propaganda war would not be neglected. País returned later in the month with Herbert Matthews, veteran foreign correspondent of the *New York Times*, who sent news to the outside world of the existence of the rebel army.

Matthews's experiences went back to the Italian invasion of Abyssinia in 1936 and to the Spanish Civil War, and he now told readers of the *New York Times* of the war in 'the rugged, almost impenetrable fastnesses of the Sierra Maestra' where 'Fidel Castro, the rebel leader of Cuba's youth, is alive and fighting hard and successfully'.[10] As in the nineteenth century, the Cubans were well aware of the need to secure the support of the North American press, and Matthews's reports helped create a lasting image, both in Cuba and abroad, of a charismatic and invincible leader:

> The personality of the man is overpowering. It is easy to see that his men adored him and also to see why he has caught the imagination of the youth of Cuba all over the island. Here was an educated, dedicated fanatic, a man of ideals, of courage, and of remarkable qualities of leadership.

Matthews would later describe him as 'the most remarkable and romantic figure . . . in Cuban history since José Martí'.

País and Matthews arrived in the Sierra with several members of the Movement's urban leadership, including Faustino Pérez Hernández, who had been on the *Granma* and subsequently been organising in Havana, and Haydée Santamaría, a veteran of Moncada. This *fidelista* nucleus held detailed discussions with Castro after Matthews had left. They made plans to strengthen the existing guerrilla force, to expand its operations into fresh areas and to form an urban militia in each Cuban province. On the political front they agreed to organise a 'civic resistance movement' on a national scale, to secure the support of both workers and middle-class professionals, and to prepare for a 'revolutionary general strike' to bring down the government.[11] Such a movement was established in Havana, headed by Enrique Oltuski, and it drew in the existing supporters of the July 26 Movement together with middle-class Ortodoxos like Raúl Chibás.

The seeds were sown for the significant division – affecting policy, strategy and tactics – that would eventually arise between the rebels in the Sierra and the activists in the cities. Castro's rebellion was heir to the splits within the independence movement of the nineteenth century. The political demands of the guerrillas in the Sierra undoubtedly became more radical as the months passed. With Che Guevara now an increasingly indispensable guerrilla leader, so his political influence began to grow. Yet his hostility to 'imperialism', and to the government of the United States, was not shared by many leaders of the urban network, who retained the traditionally pro-American view of Cuba's middle class – and indeed hoped for American support against Batista.[12]

Frank País was now the acknowledged leader of the Movement outside the Sierra, with wide-ranging responsibilities. Born into a Christian Baptist family in Santiago in 1930, País had once planned to be a schoolteacher, but Batista's coup in 1952 had turned him into a full-time resistance activist. First with his own group and then, after 1955, as the 'chief of action and sabotage' of the Movement in Oriente, he was an inspirational organiser and political fixer. He had met Castro for the first time in Mexico in August 1956 and together they had planned the uprising in Santiago designed to coincide with the *Granma* landing.

In 1957, with Castro isolated in the hills, País's efforts to secure weapons and ammunition, as well as food and medicine, were essential for the guerrillas' survival. País was also responsible for channelling journalists into the Sierra to report on the war. As the police repression increased in the cities his task became ever more difficult and dangerous.[13]

As important as organising the logistics of a guerrilla war was the political need to secure a measure of agreement among the various opposition movements to Batista's rule. These were divided between the old political parties, who hoped for an eventual electoral outcome – or possibly a military coup – and those from the younger generation who supported armed resistance. The Ortodoxos and the Auténticos, and their various splits and sub-groups, had little appeal for the young, but they tied up a number of political cadres with organisational capacity and experience and they had access to considerable sums of money. Former president Prío Socarrás, in exile in Miami, was himself anxious to return to power, and he gave money both to Castro and to other groups in the hope that armed actions might speed up the dictator's overthrow.

Grouped with the 'old parties', and distrusted by the youthful supporters of the July 26 Movement, was the Partido Socialista Popular (PSP), the Cuban Communist Party, led since the purges in 1934 by its secretary-general Blas Roca, the shoemaker from Manzanillo, and its president Juan Marinello. Its entire leadership had been prominent in politics since that time, and much of the antipathy they aroused within the Movement went back to the period when revolutionary students kept themselves apart from party loyalties, and distrust for foreign and Jewish agitators was rife on the left as well as the right. The political programme of the Communists had always been radical, they had considerable support among workers and blacks, they attracted many intellectuals, but they were simply not trusted politically by groups on the left that came from other traditions.

Like the more conservative parties, the PSP had always been hostile to armed action, and was particularly averse, recalling its differences with Antonio Guiteras during the revolution of 1933, to the kind of sabotage and subversion – let alone guerrilla war – advocated by the July 26 Movement. That was not the Communist style. Well rooted in the Cuban working class, the PSP was disdained and distrusted by much of the middle class. Radicals disliked it because of its remembered role in 1933, and because of its collaboration with Batista at intervals over the previous 20 years. The anti-communist atmosphere of the Cold War era had also worked against it.

Communist leaders over the years had been clever and sophisticated political operators, negotiating with power whenever the opportunity arose and opposing the old Liberal tradition of organising an armed revolt whenever thwarted. Given these repeated Liberal failures, theirs was an honourable and modern position, suited for the twentieth century, and they had not been short of arguments to support it. Yet many thought their stand had been weak and ineffective. The Communists had supported the great strike against Machado in 1933, but had second thoughts when they thought that his overthrow might provoke a US invasion. They had participated in the strike against Mendieta in 1935, but were accused of joining in too late. They had warmed towards Batista in 1937, when, after years of operating illegally, he had allowed them to organise as an ordinary political party.

In 1938 they had started to publish a daily paper, Hoy, edited by Aníbal Escalante, and had soon become Batista's closest ally. The Communist-dominated labour confederation, the Confederación de Trabajadores de Cuba (CTC), had collaborated with the ministry of labour. Two Communists, Juan Marinello and Carlos Rafael Rodríguez, had entered Batista's cabinet in 1942, while Lázaro Peña, the black leader of the tobacco workers' union, had been in close attendance. The alliance with Batista had not survived into the post-war years, and the Communists were purged from the labour movement in 1947, but the memory of their collaboration lived on. The fact that Eusebio Mujal, the anti-Communist leader of the CTC who collaborated with Batista throughout the 1950s, was himself a former Communist did nothing for the reputation of the Party. The Communist response to Batista's coup in 1952 was, at best, ambiguous, and the leadership had denounced Castro's attack on Moncada as 'a putsch'. Technically the description might be considered correct, but the analysis did not endear the Party to Castro's supporters.

By 1957 the Party's leadership had publicly opposed Batista's government, but Marinello still dreamed of a popular front that would organise strikes and demonstrations, and participate in elections, and the Party remained hostile to groups supporting a strategy of armed insurrection. Of these, the July 26 Movement was the most well known, but it had at least three important rivals in towns and cities across Cuba that had been organising against the dictatorship in the years since Batista's coup.

One of them, the Movimiento Nacional Revolucionario (MNR), led by Rafael García Barcena, a philosophy lecturer who had been a prominent student leader in the 1930s, had had considerable early support from the professional classes. The MNR had tried, albeit unsuccessfully, to attack a military base in Havana on Easter Sunday 1953, a few months before Moncada, and García Barcena had been imprisoned. MNR supporters had included Faustino Pérez and Enrique Oltuski, who both subsequently joined the July 26 Movement, as did Armando Hart Dávalos, a lawyer who was to marry Haydée Santamaría.

A second group, the Organización Auténtica (OA), funded by Prío Socarrás, was the armed wing of the Auténticos. They had organised a small guerrilla force, also trained by Alberto Bayo in Mexico, that landed in Oriente to the east of Mayarí in May 1957. Denounced to the army by local peasants, few of them had survived.[14] Prío's hope of backing an alternative to Castro died with them.

The guerrillas of the Auténticos had worked closely with a third group, led by José Antonio Echeverría, that emerged out of the Federation of University Students (FEU) in Havana. A talented orator and organiser, Echeverría was an Auténtico supporter, younger than Castro, who represented a strand in Cuba's revolutionary tradition more akin to the ABC, the fascistic student organisation of the 1930s. Echeverría had formed a clandestine Directorio Revolucionario Estudiantil (DRE), a terrorist organisation dedicated to assassination and sabotage, whose name was designed to recall the Directorio of the 1930s. He had met Castro twice in Mexico in 1956 to examine ways in which the Directorio might cooperate with the July 26 Movement, but the two men had not seen eye to eye. Castro's dislike of Echeverría's urban terrorists was reinforced when they refused to support the *Granma* landing. They had schemes of their own.

Together with the Organización Auténtica, the Directorio worked on a plan to seize the presidential palace in Havana and to assassinate Batista. In March 1957 two groups of 150 men fought their way into the building, while Echeverría seized control of the main radio station. Their brave but ill-conceived putsch ended in disaster. The attackers secured entry to the palace, but were unable to locate Batista, and most were shot during the raid. Unaware of what had happened, Echeverría announced from the captured radio studio that the President was dead, and called for a general strike. Someone had turned a switch, and his words were not broadcast. As he returned to the university buildings in Vedado his car crashed into a police patrol car and he was killed in an exchange of fire.[15]

Echeverría was replaced as leader of the Directorio by Fauré Chomón Mediavilla, formerly its military commander and later a minister in Castro's government. The drama of the palace raid gave Echeverría a place in Cuba's list of martyrs, but it weakened the Directorio's organisation and led to a strengthening of the repression.

Castro's rivals had all been severely weakened or destroyed by the middle of 1957, and his tiny guerrilla army in the Sierra – still with only a hundred men in May – was now the only viable insurgent force on the island. An attack was launched at the end of May on a remote military garrison, at El Uvero on Oriente's southern coast, and although men died on both sides it was a timely propaganda victory for the July 26 Movement, revealing that its guerrilla force was still in the field.

Just as the rebels of the nineteenth century had kept in touch with representatives of the United States, so too did the revolutionaries of the 1950s. Frank País held regular meetings in 1957 with the US consulate in Santiago, and was sometimes joined by Armando Hart and Haydée Santamaría as well as by Vilma Espín, the daughter of the Bacardi rum company's lawyer in the city who had studied engineering in the United States at MIT and been a messenger for the Castro brothers in Mexico in 1956. One CIA desk officer noted that 'my staff and I were all *fidelistas*'.[16] One of the topics discussed was American concern about the country's future stability. País told Castro, in a refrain common from Cuban history, of the American 'fear that Cuba would become another Haiti', a reflection not so much of the old nineteenth-century racist preoccupation with the emergence of another black-ruled state in the Caribbean, as of the prospect of Cuba imitating Haiti's chronic instability.

The relationship with the US consulate may have persuaded País of the need to make contact with the civilian politicians of the Ortodoxo party, and he dispatched Haydée Santamaría to Havana to see if they could be brought on board the frail barque of the July 26 Movement. Her discussions bore fruit, and País brought a group of them to the Sierra in July to discuss with Castro their future relationship with the Movement. They included Raúl Chibás; Felipe Pazos, the former head of the Cuban national bank and a veteran of the student revolution of the 1930s; Roberto Agramonte, the son of the leader of the Ortodoxos; and Enrique Barrosa from the party's youth wing. Together with Castro the group of Ortodoxos hammered out a manifesto, the 'Pact of the Sierra', that called for a 'civic revolutionary front' to force Batista from power and to hold fresh elections. Photographs of Castro with these prominent politicians soon appeared in Havana magazines, a publicity coup comparable with that caused by the visit of Herbert Matthews six months earlier.

This was Frank País's last coup. On returning from the Sierra, he was gunned down on the streets of Santiago at the end of the month. A huge funeral demonstration in the city was followed by a general strike that lasted for five days and spread from Santiago to much of the island.

The death of País was a serious blow to the July 26 Movement, but a number of initiatives were already in train. An attempt to stage a naval coup was made in Cienfuegos in September, organised by a group of young officers led by Dionisio San Román, and coordinated with Emilio Aragonés, the Movement's organiser in the town. This was a well-organised and far-reaching conspiracy with connections in other naval ports. The rebels secured the naval base and held much of the town for a day, but a fierce counter-attack by Batista forces, equipped with weapons recently supplied by the United States, was eventually successful. Aragonés managed to escape, but San Román was captured, tortured and killed.

The student Directorio was also active again, and a guerrilla group led by Faure Chomón landed on the north coast near Nuevitas in February 1958, and made its way south to the hills of the Escambray above Trinidad. They found the going rough and soon retreated to Havana, although other groups of independent guerrillas were able to remain in operation in the zone.

Castro's guerrillas in the Sierra Maestra now felt confident enough to extend their operations, and Raúl Castro left the main camp in March with 65 men to establish a second front in the Sierra Cristál, on the Oriente's north coast. Juan Almeida opened a third front to the north of Santiago in the same month.

Early in 1958 the Communist Party finally agreed to throw its weight behind Castro. A few members of its youth movement had been in the Sierra since the previous year, deployed with the column of Che Guevara. Among them was Pablo Rivalta, a black cadre who had visited China. Carlos Rafael Rodríguez had earlier made contact with Haydée Santamaría after the death of País, but he did not move up to the Sierra until July, remaining there permanently, apart from a brief visit to report to the central committee, until the end of the war. Yet he was not present during the all-important discussions about the organisation of a general strike.

From the early days in the Sierra, whenever the manner of the eventual collapse of the Batista regime was under debate, the notion of a revolutionary general strike was high on the agenda. This, according to folk memory, was what had brought down Machado in 1933. Such a strike would not just be a work-stoppage, but would involve a wide range of anti-regime activities, including sabotage, selective assassination and outbreaks of generalised violence that would develop into an urban insurrection.[17]

Such a strike would inevitably be a higher priority for the Movement in the cities (the *llanos*) than for Castro's guerrillas in the mountains (the *sierra*), and the way in which it would be organised was inevitably a focus of tension between the two groups. Faustino Pérez, leader of the Movement and the 'civic resistance' in Havana, came to Castro's camp in March to discuss the problems associated with the project. Pérez thought the time was ripe, Castro was less sure. The organisation of the insurrection was seriously flawed. The Movement's distrust of the Communists, only recent converts to the cause, was still strong, and the Havana organisers had failed to include the Communist Party, with its large workers' movement, in its preparations. Yet the Movement itself had little access to other workers' organisations. Cold-shouldered in Havana, the Communists were so concerned that the strike would be a failure that a senior official went to the Sierra to tell Castro that the strike leaders had overestimated their strength.[18]

Castro felt that he had no choice but to go ahead, despite these warnings and his own reluctance. He and Pérez signed a manifesto, 'Total War Against Tyranny', that called for a strike and declared that the struggle against Batista had entered 'its final stage'. The country 'should consider itself in total war against the tyranny . . . The entire nation is determined to be free or perish.' The revolutionary general strike, 'seconded by military action', would be the conclusive blow that would bring down the regime.[19]

The manifesto outlined political plans made for the post-Batista period. The provisional president would be Manuel Urrutia Lleó, a lawyer from Santiago already sounded out by Castro for this position. Urrutia was the right kind of anti-Communist liberal to win broad support in Cuba – and to be welcomed by the United States. He had travelled to Washington a few months earlier to rally support. He had always expressed sympathy for the July 26 Movement and in May 1957 he had presided over a case in which 151 men had been charged with anti-government activities, 22 of whom had been captured after the *Granma* landing. Urrutia ruled that the prisoners should be released, declaring that in view of the 'illegal retention of power by Batista and his followers, the defendants had been acting within their constitutional rights'.[20]

The date of the general strike was set for 9 April and preparations were made, with bombs exploding in Havana during the previous month to prepare a mood of incipient chaos. The Movement achieved a coup on the eve of an important motor race in Havana by kidnapping Juan Manuel Fangio, the world champion racing driver from Argentina, and then later releasing him with a fanfare of publicity. The Movement's National Student Front, led by Ricardo Alarcón, secured the shut-down of all state schools.[21] The 'civic resistance' clearly had the capacity to perform flamboyant actions under the noses of the police. The die was cast.

'Today is the day of liberation', announced a broadcast on the morning of 9 April from a radio station seized by the Movement. 'Throughout Cuba at this very moment the final struggle to overthrow Batista has begun.'

Castro's misgivings proved well-founded. The workers were unprepared, the police and the army were armed and ready. The Movement's urban activists had insufficient weapons to stage their various diversionary schemes. Their militia melted away. The insurrectionary action scheduled to bring down the regime was over almost before it began. Castro tried to look on the bright side, writing to Celia Sánchez, his loyal aide in Santiago, to point out that 'a battle was lost but not a war'. Yet he could hardly restrain his anger, recognising the dimensions of the disaster that had occurred. 'I am the supposed leader of this Movement, and in the eyes of history I must take responsibility for the stupidity of others, but I am a shit who can decide nothing at all.'[22]

A meeting was held in the mountains early in May to analyse what had gone wrong and what should now be done. Members of both wings of the Movement were present. Guevara delivered a stinging indictment of the strike organisers, accusing them of 'sectarianism', which meant not including the Communists in their plans, and of military incompetence – organising the militia without 'training or combat morale' or 'a rigorous process of selection'.[23] Changes were made to the leadership in the *llanos*, and several of its members, including Faustino Pérez, were transferred to the *sierra*.

With the failure of the strike, Batista made a further determined effort to dislodge the guerrillas from the Sierra Maestra. Some 10,000 soldiers were deployed in May against Castro's base in the southern mountains, and bombing raids were launched on Raúl's column to the north. The offensive lasted for more than two months, but the guerrillas managed to hold out. 'Every entrance to the Sierra Maestra is like the pass at Thermopylae', Castro told visiting journalists.[24]

Victory over the soldiers who tried to seize the Sierra was a turning point in the war, a triumph for the guerrillas that made up for the failure of the strike. Castro now seized the opportunity to plan the final phase of the war. The time had come to organise the invasion of western Cuba, and to follow in the footsteps of Gómez and Maceo in 1896. Che Guevara was told to head for the central province of Las Villas, while Camilo Cienfuegos was to aim for the westerly province of Pinar del Río, reasserting Castro's authority over the independent guerrillas in the Escambray on the way. They set off together at the end of August with a joint force of 230 men, and Guevara arrived in the hills of Las Villas in October. Castro came down from his mountain redoubt a month later and began the march towards Santiago, while Raúl advanced from the north.

The fighting continued on all fronts throughout the autumn and Urrutia landed at a rebel airstrip in the Sierra Maestra in early December to be ready for the final moment. Cienfuegos bypassed Havana and moved towards Pinar del Rio. Guevara captured the central city of Santa Clara at the end of the month.

After just two years in the mountains, Castro had dominated his rivals elsewhere and was on the verge of victory. He had been fortunate in his field commanders, a mere bunch of amateurs two years earlier. Guevara, Cienfuegos and his brother Raúl had all shown exceptional qualities of leadership and strategic vision and were rewarded by the affection and loyalty of their men. Castro had also been fortunate, or perhaps skilful, in ensuring that United States policy towards his guerrilla band had remained divided and uncertain. Liberal American opinion, exemplified by the *New York Times* and progressive elements within the CIA, had looked favourably on Castro, while the Eisenhower government, as much from inertia as from conservatism or anti-Communism, had contentedly gone on supporting Batista, although with a growing lack of conviction. While continuing to supply weapons, it never provided enough to allow Batista a military victory, nor indeed would his army and airforce have been technically equipped to cope with an influx of more sophisticated weapons.

As Castro's victory grew more probable, the Americans did not wish to antagonise the likely future ruler, although this did not deter the British or the Yugoslavs who continued to supply Batista with weapons until the last moment. The Americans believed that they had little to fear from a Castro victory, since it would surely be followed by the anarchy and political fighting that had occurred after the revolution of 1933. Little in Cuban history suggested that a Castro victory would be followed by half a century of relative stability.

General Batista bowed out on New Year's Eve, flying out of the country from the airfield at Camp Columbia with his family and friends. They hopped across the water from Havana to Santo Domingo, ruled by Batista's friend Leonidas Trujillo. The mulatto sergeant who had dominated Cuba's politics for a quarter of a century made his final, humiliating exit. The man who had once admired Franklin Roosevelt, and kept a bust of Abraham Lincoln on his desk, had been deserted by his American friends. He had imagined at the start of the decade that he was the man to tackle Cuba's systemic crisis, staging a coup to sweep away the corruption of the old political class. He had failed dismally, and succeeded only in making matters worse. Now it was Fidel Castro's turn.

The dawn of the Revolution: January 1959

On 2 January 1959, from a balcony in Santiago de Cuba overlooking the elegant Parque Céspedes, Castro made his first speech at the dawn of the Revolution. He had chosen the city in recognition of its part in the struggle in the Sierra Maestra, and to make the point that the humiliation inflicted on Cuba in 1898 by the US landings just along the coast would not be repeated. 'The Revolution begins now,' he announced: 'This time it will not be like 1898, when the North Americans came and made themselves masters of our country. This time, fortunately, the Revolution will truly come to power.'

On the very first day, the revolutionary leader threw down the gauntlet to the United States – although he took supper that night with the US consul and his wife in Santiago.

A revolution was once seen as the culmination of society's ills, the inevitable outcome of a series of disasters that made an *ancien régime* unworkable. The remembered vision of pre-revolutionary Cuba that prevailed in the early years of the Revolution was one of economic stagnation over many decades, of political failure, corruption, bureaucratic incompetence, gangsterism, violence and social breakdown. Revolution and/or socialism, according to taste, was perceived as the natural outcome of an intolerable situation. The Revolution's task was to re-order society and bind its wounds.

Yet Cuba was not a poor country in 1959, with down-trodden people rebelling against their state of backwardness. It was relatively well off, enjoying the second highest per capita income in Latin America in the 1950s, second only to Venezuela whose income was skewed by its oil revenues.[25] On a range of other socio-economic indicators – urbanisation, literacy, infant mortality and life expectancy – Cuba was among the top five countries in Latin America.[26]

The introduction of universal health care is often considered one of the great triumphs of the Revolution. Yet pre-Revolutionary Cuba was not backward in its provision of medical services. The island had some of the most positive health indices in the Americas, not far behind the United States and Canada. Both in life expectancy at birth, and in doctors per thousand of the population, Cuba was among the leaders. In terms of doctors per person, Cuba before 1959 was eleventh in the world, above Britain, France, Holland and Japan. In Latin America, it ranked in third place after Uruguay and Argentina.[27] The figures, of course, were heavily biased towards the urban population, for most of Cuba's doctors were based in Havana and the large regional towns. Conditions in the rural areas, notably in Oriente, were certainly rough – few doctors, few roads, few schools and little regular employment – while many of the inhabitants of Havana were comparatively prosperous.

Much of this reassessment of pre-Revolutionary history comes from Cuban exiles, and exiles often tend to wax sentimental about the past. An outpouring of romanticised fiction about Cuban life in the 1940s was published in the United States in the 1990s, and the revival of ancient bands such as Buena Vista Social Club – soon a globally popular phenomenon – fitted into this perspective. It would be surprising if the study of history had been immune from the *zeitgeist*. A developed sense of nostalgia might even be considered to be an important strand in Cuban national life, derived from the ancestry of its people coming from distant shores – as black slaves recalling a pre-slavery world in Africa, and as white settlers with faded memories of Europe. In revolutionary Cuba itself in the 1960s, a film like *Memories of Underdevelopment*, made by Tomás Gutiérrez Alea in 1968, could pluck at the heartstrings with its evocation of what once had been, and was now lost. The film showed the angst of a bourgeois member of the rentier class who had remained in Havana after the Revolution and became obsessed by regret for what had gone before.

Yet whatever the wider doubts about the exact state of the economic and societal crisis in Cuba in the 1950s, the repression of the Batista years was a reality that provoked cries of revenge as well as demands for a better future. The struggle against the dictator, for most activists in the July 26 Movement, was motivated as much by a desire to get rid of a foul oppressor as by hopes of a better society to come. This was why Castro initially received such wide support across the deep divisions in Cuban society. When visiting Princeton in April 1959, Castro attributed the success of the Revolution to the widespread 'fear and hatred of Batista's secret police', as well as to the fact that the rebels 'had not preached class war'.[28]

Batista's dictatorship was widely perceived as cruel and vindictive, which it certainly was (though not on the scale unleashed in Latin America's southern cone countries in the 1970s and 1980s). Yet many of the regime's repressive actions were brought on by the need to combat the urban terrorism and the guerrilla war. The crucial element in bringing people to Castro's side was his survival in the mountains, and his subsequent military successes. If Batista had been winning the war in 1958, or not all-too-visibly losing it, popular opinion in Cuba might easily have swung towards him. Hoping to see an end to war and oppression, the majority of the Cuban population moved behind the winning side, as people tend to do in such situations.

In the confusion and uncertainty that surrounds the early days of all revolutions, Castro's rebel soldiers achieved their victory in a political vacuum. No government existed in Havana throughout New Year's Day, as Batista's senior officers measured their chances against the rebel army advancing on the country's two largest cities. Swiftly they realised that they were outnumbered and outclassed. The festivities of the traditional national holiday, coupled with the proclamation of a general strike, put paid to any attempt to create a Batista regime without Batista.

Castro marched into Santiago on 2 January. Cienfuegos arrived the same day in Havana from Santa Clara, moving into the base at Camp Columbia just vacated by Batista. Guevara came at dawn on 3 January to take up his post at La Cabaña, the fortress at the mouth of Havana's harbour. The two rebel *comandantes*, perceived as the most heroic, charismatic and romantic figures in Castro's army, now controlled the two military barracks that dominated the capital.

With a sense of theatre, and an intuition that the passions aroused by victory should be allowed a few days to cool, Castro set out on a stately pilgrimage from Santiago to Havana of the kind that the early generations of Spanish conquistadores had been accustomed to perform. He travelled the length of the island for a week, sometimes in an open jeep, sometimes on top of a tank, stopping frequently to greet the enthusiastic crowds. His triumphal journey was recorded on the nation's black-and-white television screens, nearly half a million of which had penetrated into Cuba by the end of the 1950s.

Not until 8 January did he arrive in Havana, advancing through delirious flag-decked streets to Camp Columbia, where, aware of the immense diversity behind the coalition that supported him, he spoke to a huge audience of the need for revolutionary unity. At the end of the speech – an incident recalled by all who witnessed it – two white doves came to rest on his shoulder, an unexpected but optimistic symbol to mark the start of a new era in Cuban history.[29]

Havana enjoyed a prolonged fiesta. For Giangiacomo Feltrinelli, the radical Italian publisher who arrived in the early weeks of the Revolution, Havana was a magnificent and chaotic city, filled with Hispanics, blacks and Chinese, and humming with life and colour. The rebels from the hills were much in evidence, and 'every so often, scattered here and there, you come across bearded guerrillas, complete with pistols and sub-machine-guns, lounging on big chairs in front of public buildings, guarding against the enemy'.[30] Beards and berets became the symbols of the Revolution.

Castro made his first, disarming political moves, appointing Manuel Urrutia to be president, as promised, and José Miró Cardona as prime minister. Urrutia was a puritan by upbringing, and his immediate concern was to close down Havana's casinos and brothels. Cardona was a liberal lawyer who had once been one of Castro's professors. Only three members of the new cabinet came from the guerrilla army, and only one from the July 26 Movement. Castro himself remained at the head of the rebel army, now called the Rebel Armed Forces, and he acquired a new title as Military Commander-in-Chief, an indication of where real power now lay.

It was as well to have moderates in place, for the initial euphoria with which the Revolution was greeted abroad was quickly replaced with the sombre real-isation that revolutions take their toll of those who had once opposed them.

Several hundred former Batista associates, policemen and torturers were shot by firing squad after perfunctory trials. Portrayed as 'a bloodbath' in the American press, this post-war settling of scores was hardly an unusual phenomenon in Cuban history. The passions aroused during the war were deeply rooted, and similar events had occurred within living memory. 'Thirty years earlier, the hirelings of the Machado regime deemed guilty of similar crimes were simply ferreted out by the mob and killed,' recalled Philip Bonsal, the new US ambassador, in his memoirs.[31] The government argued that all those convicted had been brought to trial under legislation promulgated in the Sierra Maestra, but the executions took the shine off the Revolution for many outsiders.

The bad publicity was made worse by a decision to hold trials of war criminals in the Havana sports stadium, shown live on television. The sight of impassioned crowds demanding revolutionary justice appalled many foreign correspondents in the city. Paradoxically, it was Allen Dulles, the head of the CIA, who gave some perspective to these scenes, explaining to the senate foreign relations committee the realities of political upheaval:

> When you have a revolution, you kill your enemies. There were many instances of cruelty and repression by the Cuban army, and they have the goods on some of those people. Now there will probably be a lot of justice. It will probably go much too far, but they have to go through this.[32]

Raúl Castro, the military commander in Oriente, and Che Guevara, at La Cabaña, were perceived as the hard men. Guevara personally signed at least 50 death sentences, while Raúl was alleged to have presided over the mass execution of 70 of Batista's soldiers, shot down with machine guns in front of an open trench. Always known as a radical, with a toughness that bordered on brutality, Raúl's hawkish reputation was publicly confirmed by his elder brother. Appointing Raúl to be the second-in-command of the July 26 Movement, and the man who would succeed him if he should die, Fidel told a crowd in Havana in January that they should not be concerned about threats of assassination. 'The destiny of peoples cannot depend on one man,' he said, 'behind me come others more radical than I; assassinating me would only fortify the Revolution.'[33] Selected as Fidel's official successor, Raúl was also now the defence minister, responsible for the organisation of a new Cuban army.

Raúl Castro was to remain at the apex of power in Cuba for more than four decades. The youngest of the five Castro siblings, he had followed in his brothers' footsteps to the Jesuit school in Havana, but, without aptitude for religion or athletics, he abandoned his schooling and sought refuge in his father's estate office. Persuaded to return to Havana by Fidel, he studied law at the university and became drawn to the youth movement of the Communist Party. Raúl at the age of 18 was described later by his brother-in-law as being 'very curious, curious about Communism, [and] concerned about justice', and very interested in sociology. 'He had a hunger for knowledge, a hunger for resolving the whole situation, and the Communists gave him everything.' Raúl himself claimed that his early radicalism was the result of returning home for the holidays to find that among 'thousands of peasants, the only ones who could study were those of my family.'

Joining the Communist youth movement, as was common in Latin America, meant opportunities for foreign travel, and Raúl sailed to Europe in February 1953 to attend the World Youth Congress in Sofia, visiting Bucharest and Prague on the same trip. Contacts made then were to serve him well later, and, on the boat back to Havana, he became friends with Nikolai Leonov, a young Soviet diplomat, later in the KGB, who was posted to Mexico. They met there in 1955 and Leonov was conveniently posted to Havana in 1960. The seeds of the future close relationship between Raúl and the Soviet Union had already been sown, with important consequences for the course of the Revolution.

Raúl became one of the most powerful commanders during the guerrilla war. Sent to establish a rebel headquarters in the Sierra Cristál, he organised the semi-bandit forces operating in the area into a disciplined force, many of whose members were to form the officer corps in the new Cuban army. Looking for peasant support, he had made contacts in the Sierra with the leaders of the National Association of Small Farmers, a peasant organisation sponsored by the Communist Party, and held a 'peasants' congress' to secure their support. He was the first to welcome Carlos Rafael Rodríguez, the political brain of the Party, to the mountains in July 1958.

The threat that the pro-Communist Raúl would take over in the absence of Fidel alarmed the many fervent anti-Communists in the July 26 Movement. Carlos Franqui, a *fidelista* but anti-Communist journalist who later went into exile, disliked the younger brother intensely, describing him as 'an operetta-class Hitler'. The people instinctively rejected him, he wrote, 'and Fidel augmented that negative image by saying that Raúl was the bad guy; they complemented each other perfectly, like Laurel and Hardy'.[34] Officers and men in the armed forces, however, had considerable affection for their chief.

Raúl married Vilma Espín in January 1959. A talented and attractive woman, she had been one of the leaders of the revolutionary movement in Santiago. The couple were eventually to separate, but Espín retained control of her power base, the Federation of Cuban Women, the island's principal women's organisation. Fidel was a stickler for bourgeois morality, and those guerrilla fighters who had acquired lovers in the Sierra Maestra during the war were expected to regularise their relationship in peacetime. Raúl was among the first; Guevara soon followed suit, marrying Aleida March at a white wedding in May. Only Fidel was allowed to remain unencumbered by fresh matrimonial ties. He was married, he said, to the Revolution.

The new revolutionary regime moved swiftly in the first six months to use the old government machinery to benefit its supporters in the poorest sectors of society. Where necessary, it created new institutions. Its first actions in January, the personal crusade of President Urrutia, had a high moral tone and marked a sharp break with Cuba's immediate past: brothels, gambling dens and the national lottery were to be closed down. The measure created immediate resistance from prostitutes, croupiers, waiters and entertainers of all kinds. In the first of many interventions, Castro requested a stay of execution, arguing that people could not be thrown out of work until alternative jobs had been found for them.[35] Even less welcome to Urrutia was a decision by Castro that government ministers should accept a pay cut. Urrutia's salary of $100,000 a year was the same as Batista's had been, and he wanted to keep it at that level. Judges had their salaries lowered in February, but junior members of the state bureaucracy were given a pay rise.

Several new ministries were created, of which the most immediately popular was the Ministry for the Recuperation of Misappropriated Goods, an institution run by Faustino Pérez that was designed to deal with the properties and companies of Batista and his exiled friends. Two social ministries were established, a Ministry of Social Welfare and a Ministry of Housing. Early measures included a reduction in rents of houses and apartments, in some cases by half, and a cut in mortgage rates. Landlords were forbidden to evict their tenants and the owners of urban land were obliged to sell vacant sites at low prices to anyone planning to build a house.

The government kept up the pressure of rapid change. Price controls over telephones and electricity were introduced in March, and several utility companies were 'intervened', notably the local branch of the US-owned International Telephone and Telegraph Company. Telephone charges were lowered, and so too, in April, were the prices of medicines. A minimum wage was introduced for the cutters of cane. Popular euphoria remained high and no one in government asked where the money would come from.

Details of the long-awaited land reform were finally announced at a ceremony in May in the Sierra Maestra. The assembled peasants were told by Castro of the start of 'a new era'. The new law put an end to all large estates, as he had foreshadowed in his speech after Moncada in 1953. Landowners were allowed to keep 402 hectares (1,000 acres) of their property, but larger areas were liable to expropriation.[36] A number of large cattle holdings were exempted, as were sugar and rice plantations known to produce exceptional yields. Some of these were as large as 1,375 hectares (3,333 acres). Much of the expropriated land, some 40 per cent of the island's existing farmland, was to be divided into small individual plots of 67 acres, while larger ranches and plantations were to be run as agricultural cooperatives.

The law was designed to be popular with landless peasants, and they were offered a glowing future. 'From now on,' Castro told those from the region around Santa Clara in June, 'the children of the peasants will have schools, sports facilities, and medical attention, and the peasants will count for the first time as an essential element of the nation.' On 26 July, at the celebrations in Havana to commemorate the attack on Moncada, thousands of peasants came riding into the city on horseback – some were bussed in – to listen to Castro speak about the new reform. To give tone to the occasion, Lázaro Cárdenas, the old revolutionary President of Mexico from the 1930s, sat beside him on the stage.

The land reform itself was moderate, only the rhetoric was revolutionary. Yet it was perceived by the powerful landowning class in Cuba and throughout Latin America as the thin edge of the wedge. It caused particular preoccupation in the United States, for one clause stated clearly that land in the future could be owned only by Cubans. The law struck at foreign landowners, of whom the majority were American. There was a promise of compensation, but in many people's eyes the law lent credence to the belief that Castro was a Communist, and he now began to be labelled as such, both outside and inside Cuba. The political struggle within the government became more acute.

A new institution was established to organise the land reform, the National Institute for Agrarian Reform (INRA), and it was soon to become the real headquarters of the revolutionary government. INRA, based in what had once been Batista's city hall, spawned a Department of Industry, run by Che Guevara, a 100,000 man militia, run by Raúl Castro, and a Department of Commerce. By definition, INRA was concerned with everything to do with the land reform, and this soon included road-building and housing, and expanded seamlessly to cover health and education – and defence.

Castro placed himself at the head of INRA, with Antonio Nuñez Jiménez, the principal author of the land reform law, as its director. Nuñez Jiménez was a Marxist economist and geographer, but perhaps more significantly a revolutionary romantic. He was later described by René Dumont, the French agronomist who worked for a while in Cuba, as 'better fitted to organise a meeting, or ride a horse, banners in the wind, to occupy the territory of the United Fruit Company, than to organise, rationally, the socialist sector of agriculture'.[37]

The land reform law was signed by the entire cabinet, but many of its members were hostile to its provisions, considering them to be 'communistic'. President Urrutia and other moderates now defined themselves as anti-Communists, not because of any concern about the Soviet Union, but because of the strong position that members of the Communist Party had secured within the entourage of the Castro brothers. The first serious protest came from Pedro Diaz Lanz, the head of the airforce. Complaining publicly about the 'indoctrination classes' being held within the military, he left in a small boat for Miami in June. Next in line was President Urrutia, who was forced to resign by Castro in July after he had outlined his anti-Communist views in several published interviews. Castro's choice as the new President was Osvaldo Dorticós, a lawyer and the commodore of the Cienfuegos Yacht Club, who was not unsympathetic to the Communists. He had once been the secretary of Juan Marinello, the long-serving figurehead of the Party.

Infighting within the cabinet was a reflection of the growing hostility to the direction of the Revolution from the country's former political and social elite. In voicing their criticisms of the land reform, Cuba's old political class, many members of which were themselves large landowners or beneficiaries of the old economic system, began to behave in the same way as their forebears had done in the course of the previous 60 years. So deeply ingrained was their memory of the Cuba of the Platt Amendment, that had enabled them to call for US help whenever threatened by social forces other than their own, that they assumed that the United States could again be summoned up to protest on their behalf.

The old elite felt itself to be under economic threat, but it was also alarmed by the way in which the Revolution had allowed the black population, hitherto largely invisible, to emerge onto the stage. Many whites could not forgive Castro for championing their cause.

Blacks in the Revolution, 1959

One evening in March 1959, Che Guevara's black bodyguard went with friends to a club in the beach resort of Tarará, east of Havana. Guevara was convalescing there after the exertions of the guerrilla war, and the government had effectively moved to the resort to be with him. His bodyguard, Harry Villegas, nicknamed Pombo, was later to fight with him in the Congo and Bolivia. He recalled years later what had happened when he visited the Tarará club, a place where blacks were traditionally forbidden to enter.

Pombo's black group were refused entry, and General Bayo, the officer who had trained the guerrilla force in Mexico, was sent for to get them out. How was it possible, asked Pombo, that a man like Bayo 'who was so well-respected and so well-liked in the army, could fail to understand that we had not fought so blacks would continue being oppressed'.[38]

The event at Tarará was a tiny but dangerous echo of the situation 60 years earlier, when black soldiers complained that they had not taken part in the liberation war against Spain to find themselves in a peacetime Cuba where the customs of the slave era were maintained. Pombo and his friends left the club, as Bayo had asked them to do, but when they got back to their base and explained what had happened to other members of Che's escort their anger erupted again. Seizing their rifles, they returned to the whites-only club and told everyone there to get out, saying: 'This is now the Rebel Army's club.'

Bayo, according to Pombo's account, explained to Guevara what had happened, and he spoke to them, 'telling us we shouldn't do things like that, because they could be used by the enemy. He said the Revolution had not yet progressed far enough for people to understand that there were neither blacks nor whites, but rather that we were fighting for all Cubans, for equality, against discrimination.'

Pombo reflected on the incident years later, in the 1990s. 'The revolution has created the conditions to end discrimination, and is fighting to do so, but there are still those who will insult you to your face . . . I have known people who have told me, "I'll give my life for you, but I wouldn't let you marry my daughter because you are black"'.

Castro's Revolution was made by white radicals, many of them the children of recent migrants from Spain. A hundred years earlier such people would have joined the *voluntarios* and fought for Spain against black Cuba. In the 1950s they were in the vanguard of revolutionary change. Yet blacks were not prominent in the leadership of the revolutionary war. A handful, perhaps a dozen, had participated in the Moncada attack in 1953, and rather more were recruited to the Rebel Army in the Sierra. Juan Almeida, a mulatto bricklayer's apprentice, became a senior *comandante* and an important revolutionary leader in subsequent decades, but the significant black element that had characterised the *mambí* independence wars of the nineteenth century was not a major presence in the guerrilla war of the 1950s.

Black reluctance to join the rebel cause in large numbers had several causes. One was the lack of a political programme specifically aimed at blacks. Castro's July 26 Movement made no great effort to attract a black constituency, and 'the colour question' was never mentioned in Castro's speeches or programmes before 1959.[39] He only came to realise its importance after the revolutionary triumph. The Communist Party was the only party that went out of its way to encourage black membership. Nicolas Guillén, the poet, and Lázaro Peña, the trade union leader, were both prominent black figures within it. Castro had kept himself publicly aloof from the Communists and could not benefit from this connection.

Another reason for the lack of black support was the emotional and political investment that many blacks had made in the dictator. Batista was a mulatto, a lower-class figure in origin, much despised and ridiculed by the traditional white ruling elite. Blacks could identify with him: he too was barred from exclusive whites-only clubs; he participated openly in the rites of Santeria; and he gave support to the *ñáñigos* ceremonies popular with Afro-Cubans. Batista's role as an outsider, an opponent of the traditional white political system that had never done much to support the blacks, made him something of a role model for many poor blacks. The percentage of blacks in Batista's army and police force was well above the national average.

Many blacks, of course, supported Castro, and took part in the revolutionary war and the urban resistance. Yet just as in 1898, many of them felt bleakly disappointed on the morrow of victory, and Pombo, initially, was one of them. Castro, ever alert to the popular mood, soon got the message, and the Revolution's treatment of the blacks was eventually to become one of its great achievements, though never uncontroversial.

Castro took swift action in response to the incident at Tarará. He made his first speech on the issue in March and called for a campaign against racial discrimination – in education and employment and in all public facilities. Gradations of colour were of no significance, he said, 'We all have lighter or darker skin. Lighter skin implies descent from Spaniards who themselves were colonised by Moors that came from Africa. Those who are more or less dark-skinned came directly from Africa. Moreover, nobody can consider himself as being of pure, much less superior, race.'[40] Not for the first time, he evoked the history of the independence war. 'We also had reactionaries who used to say that independence was not possible because, if we had independence, it would bring about a Republic governed by blacks. So they raised all sorts of fears, the same fears that are surfacing today.'

His speech came to be called the 'Proclamation against Discrimination', and all whites-only facilities in Cuba were subsequently opened to everyone or closed down. Many whites were unhappy about these developments, or, at best, cynical. Teresa Casuso, an erstwhile friend of Castro who later went into exile, described in a memoir how 'employing the Negroes as a tactical weapon' became 'an important part of Fidel's overall strategy in Cuba, where he sought to represent himself as the friend and protector of the oppressed – that is, the Negro and the peasant'.[41] The old elite could not forgive Castro, she wrote, for launching 'these repressed, long-suffering groups into a crusade of spite and hate'. Casuso's words were those of a disgruntled white exile, yet the early years of the Revolution were in no way characterised by black triumphalism.

Castro was a progressive white liberal at heart, and his rhetoric on race was very similar to that of President Kennedy and President Johnson in the United States. He was certainly not going to adopt the black separatist banner of the black radicals of 1912. The Revolution remained as hostile to black separatism as the white government of the early years of the century had been – perhaps more so. Castro's government moved to close down the black societies that had once played such an important role in promoting black and African consciousness during the colonial era. The mutual-aid Sociedades de Color, long channels for the expression of Afro-Cuban cultural and social concerns, were emasculated, for the Revolution could admit no competitors. Their festivities were limited to weekend parties and their funds were confiscated. Their provincial clubs and their national headquarters were closed down.[42] More than 500 of these black societies ceased to exist, and Juan René Betancourt Bencomo, a sociologist who had been the president of their national federation, went into exile.

Yet Castro had his own way of indicating to the blacks that he was in tune with their aspirations. Popularly known in the first years of the Revolution as El Caballo, the Horse, he kept a small model of a horse on his desk that would be seen by viewers when he appeared on television. The origin of this custom is usually credited to a remark by Beny Moré, the great black singer, who heard Castro coming past one night and shouted out 'Here comes the Horse' – and the nickname remained.[43] The popularity of the horse was derived from its pictorial representation as the magic number one in the Chinese lottery. More intriguingly, although few have traced the allusion, the horse was the symbol of Evaristo Estenoz, the leader of the black rebellion of 1912.[44] Castro was opposed to black separatism, but reviving the memory of that rebellion, so deeply etched in the memory of blacks in the Oriente, was a subtle way to show the blacks that he was on their side.

The Revolution was to create avenues of economic progress for the great mass of the black population, but without a programme of US-style positive discrimination their social and political advance remained slow. By 1979 there were still only 5 black ministers out of 34, 4 (out of 14) black members of the politburo of the Cuban Communist Party, and 16 (out of 146) members of the Party's central committee. No black generals served in Angola, although most of the troops were black.[45]

True to white Cuban tradition, the Revolution did not want Cuban blacks to organise as blacks, yet, once made aware of the issue of race, Castro quickly grasped the significance that it had outside the country. Blacks in the United States were already beginning to mobilise in support of their civil rights, and blacks in Africa had been campaigning successfully to secure their independence from colonial rule. The Revolution soon identified itself with both groups, and, on occasion, it facilitated meetings between them. Cuba was to become an important bridge between America and Africa.

The Revolution's impact abroad, 1959–1960

The fresh wind striking Cuba had already been blowing over the long-established military dictatorships of Latin America, and the Revolution itself had an almost immediate impact in countries throughout the world. It exploded at the moment when the French and British empires were nearing their final collapse, and when the United States was on the verge of a new era of student activism and black militancy. In many of the world's major states, where ageing figures from the era of the Second World War (and earlier) were still in charge, the Revolution was perceived as the dawn of a new era. With Dwight Eisenhower in the United States, General de Gaulle in France, Harold Macmillan in Britain, Konrad Adenauer in Germany, Nikita Khrushchev in the Soviet Union and Mao Tse-tung in China – all of them born in the nineteenth century – the old world seemed distinctly old.

Onto this geriatric scene sprang the youthful and, above all, photogenic guerrillas from the Cuban hills, energetic fighting men in their 20s and 30s promising to sweep away the ancient order and bring in a fresh epoch. Their reformist zeal and fiery internationalistic rhetoric was soon seized on by new generations everywhere, dissatisfied – or simply bored – with the post-war settlement. Itinerant would-be revolutionaries descended on Havana from the earliest days of the Revolution. Its initial impact was greatest in Latin America itself, where writers and intellectuals took heart from the fact that their continent, for the first time since the early nineteenth century, appeared now to be again a protagonist in world history. Writers later to emerge as the great Latin American novelists of the twentieth century – Gabriel García Márquez, Mario Vargas Llosa, Augusto Roa Bastos, Carlos Fuentes – were inspired by the cultural energy unleashed by the Revolution. Some of them contributed to the sparkling cultural pages of *Revolución*, an early mouthpiece of the regime, while others wrote for *Prensa Latina*, Cuba's new revolutionary newsagency, founded by Che Guevara and his Argentine compatriot Jorge Masetti, with the ambition of providing an alternative view of the continent to that provided by the 'imperialist' agencies.

Visitors from outside Latin America began to descend on Havana in droves in 1960, the Revolution's second year, with their notebooks at the ready. Intellectuals in the United States were not immune to the heady attraction of the Cuban upheavals, and were concerned by their government's hostility. Their enthusiasm for the Revolution was soon to help inspire the student mobilisations, the black rebellions, the anti-nuclear campaigns and the movement against the Vietnam War that would characterise the politics and culture of the United States in the 1960s. From Europe came a swathe of admirers, including the French writers Jean-Paul Sartre and Simone de Beauvoir, who compared the Cuban Revolution to the Liberation of France in 1944 and saw the guerrillas as the reincarnation of the French *maquis*.

These early revolutionary tourists came with their own agendas and their own expectations and definitions of what a revolution should be. Some looked back to the Russian Revolution of 1917 and pictured Cuba's cane-cutters as an industrial proletariat pioneering an orthodox revolution, Soviet-style. Others invoked the Chinese Revolution of 1949, and dwelt on the vanguard role that the Cuban peasantry had played in the Sierra Maestra. Some looked forward to the battle for economic development in the emerging post-colonial Third World, and saw Cuba in the forefront of a coming struggle.

Sartre, then the most famous philosopher of the post-war world and with whose writings Guevara was familiar, came early in 1960. 'Revolution is strong medicine,' he wrote in his book, published in English the following year as *Sartre on Cuba*. He described what he had seen and gave it his uncompromising approval:

A society breaks its bones with hammer blows, demolishes its structures, overthrows its institutions, transforms the regime of property and redistributes its wealth, orients its production along other principles, attempts to increase its rate of growth as rapidly as possible, and, in the very moment of most radical destruction, seeks to reconstruct, to give itself by bone grafts a new skeleton. The remedy is extreme; it is often necessary to impose it by violence.[46]

Others in the field in the early months of 1960 were independent leftists from the United States, writers like Leo Huberman and Paul Sweezy, the editors of the *Monthly Review*, a well-established Marxist magazine. 'A revolution is a process, not an event,' they wrote prophetically. 'It unfolds through many stages and phases. It never stands still. What is true of it today may be untrue tomorrow and vice versa.'[47]

C. Wright Mills, a distinguished American sociologist on the left, arrived a few months later and wrote a book, *Listen Yankee*, that took the form of a Cuban revolutionary explaining his revolution to an American reader. The book was a paean of praise for the Revolution, but at the end, in his own voice, Wright Mills discussed its chief weakness, its lack of qualified personnel:

I mean this in two senses: first, in the ordinary sense of an absence of enough people with skill and knowledge and sensibility; but secondly, I am referring to this absence combined with the felt menace of counter-revolution and with the fact of a generally uneducated population. This combination could lead to the easy way out: the absolute control of all means of expression and the laying down of a Line to be followed.[48]

Wright Mills died shortly after his book was published, before he could see how far-sighted he had been.

The leftist enthusiasts were soon followed by journalists and academics, notably I. F. Stone, the editor of his own radical political weekly in Washington, Claude Julien from *Le Monde* in France, and young American researchers like Robert Scheer and Maurice Zeitlin.[49] 'The Cuban Revolution', wrote Scheer and Zeitlin, 'is, above all, a revolution for economic development. Like those of revolutionary movements in other undeveloped countries, its leaders hold that economic development is the key to social and cultural progress.'[50] Here too was accurate prophecy, for it was the demonstration effect of the Cuban Revolution – on Latin America and the rest of the newly emerging Third World – that was to alarm the American liberals in the new Kennedy Administration in 1961 almost as much as Castro's inclination to look favourably on Communists.

Supporters of the Cuban Revolution in the United States set up a Fair Play for Cuba Committee in New York in April 1960, and subsidiary committees were formed in cities across the United States and Canada. Among its early supporters were William Appleman Williams, Norman Mailer, Allen Ginsberg and Lawrence Ferlinghetti, as well as old Latin American hands like Carleton Beals and Waldo Frank.[51] The Committee later achieved wider notoriety in 1963 through the activities of one its members, Lee Harvey Oswald, the convicted assassin of President Kennedy.[52]

Ordinary visitors, anxious to catch a glimpse of a revolution at first hand, continued to pour into Cuba until the end of the 1960s. Some came under their own steam, many came as official guests. The Revolution was well aware of their potential as propagandists, staging extraordinary international events, including a Cultural Congress in 1968 that brought writers, artists and subversive political activists to Havana from Europe, the Americas and from Africa. Havana in the 1960s, like Paris in the 1790s and Moscow in the 1920s, became for a brief moment a revolutionary Mecca, the epicentre of a changing and optimistic world.

The United States' reaction to the Revolution, 1959–1960

Castro's Revolution was not welcomed in the upper reaches of President Eisenhower's second administration, then in its declining years. The famous wartime general, with his memories of the invasion of Europe and of relationships with Churchill and Stalin, could not have been expected to take an interest in a Caribbean revolutionary, let alone to look on him with favour. He took himself off to play golf when Castro visited Washington in April 1959. He had already had some experience with such people, for he had ordered the CIA to overthrow the government of Jacobo Arbenz in Guatemala in 1954, a successful US operation perceived as a Cold War model for disposing of regimes judged to be sailing too close to the Communist wind.

Latin America was close to the heart of his brother Milton, but in so far as President Eisenhower had much concern with the continent in the late 1950s, it was because he was affronted by the harsh reception given to Vice-president Richard Nixon when touring the continent in May 1958.[53] In each capital city Nixon had been greeted by demonstrators expressing their hostility to US support for Latin America's military dictators. When Nixon's car was attacked in the streets of Caracas, Eisenhower took immediate military action. 'The moment this news reached me,' he recalled, 'I ordered a thousand United States troops flown to Guantánamo Bay and Puerto Rico', to be ready to rescue the Vice-president.[54] That was Eisenhower's preferred style, to shoot from the hip and ask questions later, although Nixon himself drew the conclusion that a fresh US emphasis on economic development and democracy in Latin America might not come amiss.

Later that year, with Batista's regime on the verge of collapse, the President received disquieting news from Allen Dulles, the CIA chief: 'Communists and other extreme radicals appear to have penetrated the Castro movement. If Castro takes over, they will probably participate in the government.'[55]

Expressing regret that he had not been informed earlier, Eisenhower pinned his hopes on some 'third force' emerging that was neither Batista nor Castro. The immediate possibility of such an outcome was effectively scotched during the interregnum in Havana on New Year's Day 1959, when Batista's generals failed to act, but it remained on the American agenda. It was raised again during a meeting of the National Security Council in March 1959, when the chances of bringing 'another government to power in Cuba' were analysed, but the discussions were inconclusive and were abandoned until June.[56]

Initially the Americans had been reassured by the appointment of Urrutia and Miró Cardona. An intelligence digest on Eisenhower's desk on 7 January reported that 'American businessmen meeting in Havana are urging rapid recognition on the basis that this government appears far better than anything they had dared hope for.'[57] Others urging recognition nearer home included Adam Clayton Powell, the black Democratic congressman from New York. Official diplomatic recognition was extended on the same day, and Philip Bonsal, a fresh ambassador untainted with connections to Batista, was sent out to Havana. Bonsal was an old Cuba hand who had worked there for ITT in the 1920s, and later served in the Havana embassy as consul. His father had been a war correspondent on the island during the US intervention in 1898.

Yet in spite of fair words on both sides, and an initial climate of politeness, considerable distrust existed between the US government and the Cuban revolutionaries, and vice versa. Given the conflictive history of US–Cuban relations since 1898, no radical and nationalist government could have come to power in Havana without causing concern in Washington. Similarly, no radical Cuban government worth the name could have had illusions about its future relationship with the United States. A parting of the ways would arrive at some stage. It came sooner rather than later.

The Cubans, of course, were more familiar with the United States than the Americans were with Cuba. Most Americans had a roseate view of their past relations with the island not shared by the new Cuban government. A disappointed Eisenhower recalled wistfully at a press conference in October how the United States had once fought for Cuba's freedom: 'Here is a country that you would believe, on the basis of our history, would be one of our real friends.'[58] The Cuban reading of their own history was rather different.

Nixon was the first senior figure to meet Castro. The two men talked for three hours during the visit Castro made to Washington in April, the visit Eisenhower had ignored. Nixon later recalled that he told everyone of his conviction that Castro was 'either incredibly naïve about Communism or under Communist discipline'.[59] In June, within weeks of the land reform law, the United States sent an official Note of protest, just as the Cuban opposition had hoped it would. The reform, the US Note claimed, would have an adverse effect on the Cuban economy and would discourage private investment in both agriculture and industry. The compensation that the law indicated was inadequate, and the Note demanded that it should be 'prompt, adequate and effective', a mantra that would be repeated over the following months. The Cubans had based the value of the expropriated holdings on the value that the landowners themselves had provided when submitting their tax returns. These, based on assessments made years earlier, were of course conveniently low, and far below the current price of land.

The Americans had once been modest advocates of land reform, and were later, through the Alliance for Progress, to promote it in Latin America in the 1960s with some enthusiasm. They had provided Japan with a land reform after 1945, and Guevara, who visited Tokyo in June 1959, pointed out that the Japanese reform 'favoured and imposed by the United States' had been the most radical in the world – 'they permit only one hectare [2.47 acres] per person'. How then could the Americans criticise the Cuban reform which allowed private ownership of 400 hectares?[60] The Japanese reform had also given a lower rate of interest on the compensatory bonds.[61]

The land reform was the turning point in the US relationship with Cuba. When the National Security Council revived its discussions on Cuba in June, it decided that Castro would have to go. The US government's privately stated objective was to adjust its actions 'in such a way as to accelerate the development of an opposition in Cuba which would bring about . . . a new government favourable to US interests'.[62] The task was not as easy as it must at first have looked. Roy Rubottom, assistant secretary for inter-American affairs, gave the NSC a summary, at a meeting in January 1960, of what the US administration had been doing in the previous six months:

In June [1959] we had reached the decision that it was not possible to achieve our objectives with Castro in power . . . In July and August we had been busy drawing up a program to replace Castro. However some US companies reported to us during this time that they were making some progress in negotiations, a factor that caused us to slow the implementation of our program. The hope expressed by these companies did not materialize. October was a period of clarification . . .[63]

By the end of the month, Rubottom's report noted, the State Department and the CIA had drafted a new programme that they recommended to the President for approval and which 'authorised us to support elements in Cuba opposed to the Castro government, while making Castro's downfall seem to be the result of his own mistakes'.[64]

The decision arose out of the economic rather than the Communist threat. Prominent figures in Cuba had expressed concern about Castro's willingness to cooperate with the local Communists, but Cuba had no diplomatic relations with the Soviet Union in 1959. The Russians had recognised the government in January, at the same time as the United States, but diplomatic relations were not resumed until May 1960. Six months into the Revolution, and the United States had already settled on its overthrow.

The Soviet Union's reaction to the Revolution, 1959–1960

The Cuban Revolution caught the Soviet Union by surprise. Ignorance of Latin America was deep-rooted in Soviet government and society, and its leaders were wholly unprepared for the possibility of acquiring a socialist ally in the Caribbean. The days of the Comintern, when information flowed plentifully between Communist parties in Latin America and Moscow, came to an end during the Second World War, and the Soviet state had long since accepted that Latin America was an integral part of a western hemisphere dominated by the United States. Not until the years after Castro's Revolution did the Russians feel obliged to remedy their ignorance, establishing a special academy in Moscow, and producing Spanish-speaking Latin American experts on an industrial scale – to work as diplomats, spies and journalists, and as advisers to Cuba's state industries.

The first diplomatic contact between Moscow and Havana had been made during the special circumstances of the Second World War. The first Soviet embassy was opened in Havana in 1943 by Maxim Litvinov, the ambassador in Washington, and Stalin welcomed Batista's foreign minister, Aurelio Concheso, on a visit to Moscow the same year.[65] Andrei Gromyko was the ambassador to both Washington and Havana, though he did not visit the island. The friendly attitude of Batista's wartime government to Moscow and to local Communists did not survive for long. Presidents Grau San Martín and Prío Socarrás swung behind the anti-communist position of the United States at the start of the Cold War, in line with other countries in Latin America. After Batista's coup in 1952, the Soviet Union broke off diplomatic relations.

Castro's attack on Moncada in 1953, and the subsequent guerrilla war, passed largely unnoticed in the higher echelons in Moscow. 'When Fidel Castro led his revolution to victory, and entered Havana with his troops, we had no idea what political course his regime would follow,' Nikita Khrushchev recorded in his memoirs.[66] Jon Lee Anderson, Guevara's biographer, who interviewed several junior Soviet officials involved with Cuba, reveals a different story, and suggests that the Russians were already taking an interest before 1959: 'the Kremlin did not suddenly "discover" Cuba by spinning a globe after reading the news reports of its revolution . . .'[67] This may well be so, but the interest aroused at junior levels in the Soviet bureaucracy had not obviously percolated through to the Politburo. The Russians took little overt interest in the island during the Revolution's first year.

The Cubans were more interested in making overtures to the Soviet Union than the other way round. They needed to sell sugar. In June 1959, as the details of the land reform law became known and as the United States began secretly planning to overthrow the government, Che Guevara was sent on a foreign expedition to garner support, visiting several countries of the embryonic Third World, including Egypt, India, Indonesia and Yugoslavia.[68] He also sought new markets in Japan, and the Soviet Union was in his sights as well. When in Cairo he made contact with the Soviet embassy and the wheels moved fast. The Russians made an initial agreement in July to purchase half a million tons of sugar. This was not in itself remarkable since they had bought a similar quantity in 1955, in the days of Batista.

Yet Soviet curiosity had been aroused, and Alexandr Alexiev, a diplomat and KGB agent, arrived in Havana in October and was introduced to Castro and Nuñez Jiménez at their offices in the INRA building.[69] Alexiev had been in Spain during the Civil War and was a fluent Spanish speaker. He had worked at the Soviet embassy in Buenos Aires and subsequently ran the Latin American department of the Soviet foreign ministry. In 1961, after the restoration of diplomatic relations, he became the Soviet ambassador in Havana.

Nuñez Jiménez had visited New York in July 1959 and had gone to a Soviet trade exhibition there. He now suggested that the exhibition should be brought to Cuba, telling Castro and Alexiev that 'it would open the eyes of the Cuban people about the Soviet Union by showing that the American propaganda about its backwardness is untrue'.[70] The exhibition was scheduled to travel to Mexico City, and it was not difficult for its tour to be extended to Havana. It arrived there in February 1960.

The Russians were now fully awake to the Cuba question. Khrushchev sent his deputy, Anastas Mikoyan, to open the exhibition in Havana. Mikoyan was an old Bolshevik from Armenia who had been on the Soviet politburo since 1935. He signed a sugar deal with the Cubans, agreeing to purchase a million tons of sugar a year over the next five years. The Russians would pay 20 per cent of the price in dollars and 80 per cent in goods – chiefly oil, machinery, wheat, newsprint and various chemical products.[71] They would also provide a $100 million dollar credit for the purchase of plant and equipment. Similar agreements were made in succeeding months with several Soviet allies – the German Democratic Republic, Poland and Czechoslovakia.

Mikoyan had long discussions with Castro, and travelled throughout the country. His son, Sergo, struck up an immediate and lasting friendship with Guevara. Both returned to Moscow with an upbeat account of the Revolution. The relationship had been established just in time, for Cuba and the United States were now locked in battle. This was election year in the

United States, and the struggle took place in full public view. Richard Nixon and John Kennedy outdid each other in their promises to deal with the Cuban menace, while President Eisenhower continued his clandestine planning to destroy the Revolution.

'The First Declaration of Havana': the Revolution changes gear, 1960

The United States' plan to overthrow the Revolution was already in draft at the time of Mikoyan's visit to Havana in February 1960, and the proposal had been presented by Allen Dulles to President Eisenhower in January. The CIA proposed the sabotage of Cuba's sugar refineries, the chief source of Cuba's wealth. Many Latin American countries dependent on a single economic activity were vulnerable in this way – Guatemala's bananas, Chile's copper, Venezuela's oil. All were under threat if the United States disliked the government in charge.

Eisenhower liked the proposal but did not think it went far enough. According to a report by his special security assistant, he told Dulles that 'it was probably now the time to move against Castro in a positive and aggressive way which went beyond pure harassment. He asked Mr Dulles to come back with an enlarged programme.'[72] The 'harassment' proposed by Dulles went ahead while he prepared a more ambitious scheme. Sabotage attacks on the island were soon under way, usually undertaken by CIA-funded exiles in small planes, and aimed chiefly at sugar mills. Other targets were more ambitious. A Belgian freighter, *La Coubre*, bringing in small arms from Antwerp – in the teeth of a US arms embargo – exploded in Havana harbour on 4 March 1960. A hundred people were killed and 300 injured. People at the time invoked the memory of the *Maine*, whose destruction had sparked US intervention in 1898, but the event also furnished the famous photograph of Che Guevara in his beret. He had hurried to the scene and been snapped by Alberto Korda.

In April relations between the United States and Cuba deteriorated further. When the first 300,000 tons of Soviet crude oil arrived, in exchange for sugar, the Cuban government requested the three existing refineries on the island – owned and operated by Shell, Standard Oil and Texaco – to refine it. The interim US plan was to try to break Cuba economically, and the US oil companies in Cuba came under pressure from the US government to refuse to refine the Soviet oil. Faced with their intransigence, the Cubans confiscated their assets on the island in June.[73]

The Americans now turned their attention to the destruction of the Cuban sugar industry. A bill had already been introduced in Congress in January to give the President power to eliminate the existing US sugar quota, which had customarily bought Cuban sugar at preferential rates, and Eisenhower finally signed the act to reduce the sugar quota in July. Cuba was left with 700,000 tons of the year's harvest still to be sold.[74]

'They will take away our quota pound by pound, and we will take away their sugar mills one by one,' said Castro as the bill passed through Congress.[75] American properties in Cuba would be nationalised, he warned, if the quota was cut off. A new slogan appeared in the streets of Havana: *sin cuota, pero sin amo* – without a quota but without a master (*amo* being the old word for a slave-master).

The Russians came immediately to the rescue and offered to buy the unsold 700,000 tons. They were eagerly followed by the Chinese, who offered to purchase half a million tons each year for five years. Khrushchev went further, declaring that the Soviet Union no longer recognised US hegemony over the Americas. 'We consider that the Monroe Doctrine has outlasted its time,' he said, 'has died, so to say, a natural death; and the only thing that you can do with something that is dead is to bury it.'[76]

Castro hit back against the United States, as promised, on 6 August. He announced the nationalisation of all major American properties on the island, including 36 American-owned sugar mills and their adjacent plantations, all the US oil refineries, as well as the electric power and telephone utilities. In September all US-owned banks were confiscated, including the branches of National City Bank of New York, Chase Manhattan Bank and the Bank of Boston. Over the next three months the nationalisation decrees were extended to all American-owned railways, port facilities, hotels and cinemas.[77]

Castro further spelt out his programme a month later, on 2 September, denouncing the United States and placing the Cuban Revolution within the framework of the great liberation struggles of the Latin American continent. His speech became known as The First Declaration of Havana:

> The People of Cuba strongly condemn the imperialism of North America for its gross and criminal domination, lasting for more than a century, of all the peoples of Latin America, who more than once have seen the soil of Mexico, Nicaragua, Haiti, Santo Domingo and Cuba invaded; who have lost to a greedy imperialism such wide and rich lands as Texas, such vital strategic zones as the Panama Canal, and even, as in the case of Puerto Rico, entire countries converted into territories of occupation.
>
> That domination, built upon superior military power, upon unfair treaties, and upon the shameful collaboration of traitorous governments, has for more than a hundred years made of Our America – the America that Bolívar, Hidalgo, Juárez, San Martín, O'Higgins, Tiradentes, Sucre and Martí wished to see free – a zone of exploitation, a backyard in the financial and political empire of the United States, a reserve supply of votes in international organisations . . .

In this fight for a liberated Latin America there now arises with invincible power against the obedient voice of those who hold office as usurpers, the genuine voice of the people, a voice that breaks forth from the depths of coal and tin mines, from factories and sugar mills, from feudal lands where *rotos, cholos, gauchos, jíbaros*, the heirs of Zapata and Sandino, take up the arms of liberty; a voice heard in poets and novelists, in students, in women and in children, in the old and helpless. To this voice of our brothers, the Assembly of the People of Cuba responds: We are ready! Cuba will not fail![78]

In an ominous sentence that prefigured the nuclear crisis that still lay two years ahead, Castro pointed out that revolutionary Cuba now had military support from outside the continent. Cuba 'accepts with gratitude', he said, 'the help of rockets from the Soviet Union should our territory be invaded by military forces of the United States'. Khrushchev's reference to the death of the Monroe Doctrine took on its full meaning.

Petrol was added to the flames that month when Castro arrived in New York to address the UN general assembly, taking up residence in Harlem. Arriving with a delegation of fifty, Castro was first put up at the Shelburne on Lexington Avenue. He walked out the next day, complaining that he had been asked to pay in advance, and established himself at the Hotel Theresa, more usually the haunt of jazz performers, boxers and visiting black musicians. No president visiting the UN had ever stayed in Harlem before.

Castro held court at the Theresa for more than a week, and on one memorable evening he was visited by the Soviet leader. The symbolic significance of their meeting place was well understood by both of them. Khrushchev wrote in his memoirs that 'by going to a Negro hotel in a Negro district, we would be making a double demonstration against the discriminatory policies of hte US toward Negroes, as well as towards Cuba'. The cheering black crowds in Harlem left no one in any doubt about their support for the revolution.

The United States did not like Castro's message, and it struck back in November with the most powerful economic weapon in its armoury: an embargo on US exports to Cuba. It was now forbidden to export anything from the United States to Cuba, except food and medicine. Guevara set off on a round of the socialist countries to seek replacements for what had once arrived overnight from the United States and to look for new markets for sugar. The Soviet Union and the countries of Eastern Europe agreed between them to buy 4 million tons of sugar in 1961, a million tons more than the United States had been buying, and the Russians agreed to plug the import gap. The US embargo was to last until the end of the century – and beyond – creating considerable hardship and major dislocation as the Cubans readjusted the country's entire economic structure.

That structure had now radically changed, with 30 per cent of the farmland now in the social sector, some 80 per cent of industrial capacity under state control, and state enterprises producing 90 per cent of the country's exports.

The economics of the Revolution, 1959–1961

Guevara was not himself an economist but a brilliant autodidact with definitive views about the need for Cuba to escape from the economic embrace of 'imperialism'. From his base at the National Bank after November 1959, and as minister of industry after February 1961, he had been put in charge of economic strategy. He wanted the island to escape from the tyranny of sugar and to develop an independent economy based on industrialisation, yet his programme left many questions for debate. Did an independent economy mean autarchy or self-sufficiency, or simply the possibility of trading with a wider variety of partners? Diversification out of sugar might seem a good idea, but what crops should now be grown? Everyone believed in industrialisation, but did Cuba need a steel works, or small factories to produce consumer goods? Trading with all comers was clearly desirable, but what might Cuba produce that anyone would actually want?

The early years of the revolution were characterised by an earnest discussion about all these questions, while more pressing problems needed urgent decisions. Getting rid of imperialism meant abolishing the economic power of the American companies that owned the commanding heights of the Cuban economy – the sugar mills, the oil refineries, the cattle ranches and most of manufacturing industry. These enterprises, deemed 'imperialist', would in future have to be run by the state. Yet the state itself was in no position to do so, or to provide an endless supply of competent, numerate and well-trained managers. That would come later. Few individual Cuban entrepreneurs or technocrats remained in Cuba after 1959.

Revolutionary Cuba was also short of trained economists. Most of Cuba's existing stock – conservative in outlook, trained in the United States and with little interest in running a state-run economy and rather less understanding of how to do so – had left for Miami. Left-liberal economists were few and far between. Marxist economists could be counted on the fingers of one hand.

Latin America, however, and the United States itself, was replete with radical economists, largely unrequited by governments, many of them working for the United Nations Economic Commission for Latin America (ECLA), based in Santiago de Chile and run by Raúl Prebisch, an Argentinian academic. Cuba appealed to ECLA to send their spare economists to Havana. The Prebisch economic philosophy, dominant within ECLA, sought to promote national industries in Latin America by protecting them behind a variable tariff wall, the common sense of the time.

The ECLA economists, culled from all over South America, set up shop in Havana and were soon helping to run the National Bank, the Ministry of Foreign Trade, the Ministry of Industries, the Ministry of the Economy, and Juceplan, the Central Planning Board. Most were young and enthusiastic, excited by the Revolution and anxious to put their radical theories into practice. Guevara was their charismatic boss. The Revolution relied on Latin Americans in the early years, though later it would receive technical assistance from Russian and East European economists, before its own supply of trained and native-born economists came on stream.

A new period began in 1961, described by Dudley Seers, head of a visiting team of British economists, as one of 'euphoric planning'. Juceplan was given the task of preparing an economic plan for 1962, and drafting a four-year plan for the years 1962 to 1965. Although the phenomenon had long been under discussion in Europe, the only model for an economy brought almost entirely – and rapidly – under state control was the one established in the Soviet Union and the countries of Eastern Europe. Several experts in the matter were invited to Havana, including a team of Czech economists and technicians from other East Europeans countries. Prominent visitors included Michael Kalecki from Poland, who came in 1960, and Charles Bettelheim, a Marxist economist from France, who came in 1961.[79]

The euphoria was provided by Regino Boti, the first head of Juceplan, who announced optimistically in August 1961, just as food shortages were becoming apparent, that the country would soon have a 10 per cent rate of economic growth: 'If we raise our eyes and contemplate the picture of Cuba in ten years time, we conclude . . . that we shall achieve the highest level of living in Latin America by an ample margin, a standard of living as high as almost any country in Europe.'[80]

The optimism was short-lived. Rationing was introduced in March 1962, and a new period of 'economic realism' was initiated. Castro did not hesitate to criticise the optimists. 'Only a few months ago,' he announced when detailing the new measures for rationing on television, 'we made promises that have not been fulfilled.' Food shortages, he said, were caused partly by the lack of experienced managers and partly by the failure of peasants to sell their crops. Since peasants no longer had to pay rent, their interest in production for the market had been seriously undermined.

Most Cuban officials had little notion of the country's relative poverty. When the National Institute of Housing (INAV) was established it built thousands of new apartments and one-family houses that reflected American middle-class standards. Peasant houses were provided with toilets and bidets. Nothing was too good for a new generation of revolutionaries. Individual units, according to Edward Boorstein's account, 'cost about $8,000–$10,000 and were designed with an abundance of fixtures and gadgets, almost all of them of US manufacture'.[81]

The economic blockade imposed in November 1960 affected more than the inputs for public housing. The United States traditionally supplied the raw materials for the factories that produced consumer goods. The country could no longer rely on its existing machinery and technology since most of it came from the United States. No alternative source of spare parts was readily available.

Guevara argued that industrialisation was the only true basis for a socialist economy.[82] Yet Cuba's existing industries, small factories manufacturing bottles, cement, detergents, paint, paper, soap, tyres and tin cans, were mostly owned by US companies and relied on American technology. Guevara initially had a rather simplistic belief that Cuba could import Soviet machines and technology wholesale. He imagined that the Soviet Union would provide Cuba with factories, preferably for nothing, and these could then be set to work to produce goods for Cuban consumers.

The policy was tried, but soon ran into problems, some of them of a cultural nature. Cuban workers were used to modern American machinery and were unfamiliar with the clumsy, 'intermediate technology' produced by the Soviet Union and its allies in Eastern Europe. Yet if more modern and efficient machines were to be imported from western Europe or Japan, they would have to be paid for in dollars, and dollars could only be obtained by selling sugar.

The magnitude of the economic task ahead was not fully appreciated by the government in the early days. To turn a country like Cuba into an advanced industrial economy in a few years, especially in view of the continuing departure of managers and technicians, would have been a most remarkable achievement, wrote Dudley Seers. Everywhere else in the world the change had taken decades 'if not centuries'.[83]

The campaign to eradicate illiteracy, 1961

Cuba did not just lack economists and managers. It had a generally backward and ill-educated population, some 40 per cent of which was illiterate. Castro had identified education as an important area of reform in his speech after Moncada in 1953, and his remarks at that time had concentrated on the abysmal, often non-existent, condition of the rural schools with which he had been familiar since childhood. Few primary school teachers taught in the rural areas. Speaking at the United Nations in 1960, he promised that the Revolution would get rid of illiteracy within a year, a possibility never suggested before in the developing world.

In Havana's western suburb of Marianao lies the spreading former military base of Camp Columbia, an historic camp set up by the Columbia regiment of the US army in 1898, and given over to a huge school complex after 1959, with its former airfields turned into sports fields and running tracks. Tucked away in a distant street within the camp is a tiny museum dedicated to the literacy campaign of 1961 and to the 100,000 student teachers who took part in it. Most of them were teenagers, each given a special uniform to wear and an oil lamp with which to travel in the countryside at night. The museum holds bound copies of their reports, as well as of the letters that the newly literate peasants were encouraged to write. 'Dear Fidel' each letter begins. The campaign was not without danger, and some became the target of counter-revolutionaries. More than 40 were killed. Yet the teenage teachers taught a million people to read and write, and, as Castro had promised, the Revolution abolished illiteracy in a single year. The campaign was one of its great triumphs.

Castro admitted years later that it might have been better, and certainly cheaper, to have bought small radios and embarked on what, by the end of the twentieth century, would have been a slower and more conventional literacy campaign. Yet what was done in 1961 helped to define the image of the Revolution in its early years, at home and abroad. Its impact on the peasantry was electric and it was also a defining moment for the teenagers who found themselves in distant corners of the national territory into which they had never penetrated before. For a generation that had missed the revolutionary war, the experience gave them the right to call themselves revolutionaries.

The literacy campaign caught the imagination of the world, and became the Revolution's most important selling-point in its early years. Its success encouraged the government to engage in a continuing campaign to encourage adult education, helping to produce a workforce that was both better prepared and more politically aware. In later decades, with Soviet assistance and a large budget, Cuba developed an improved educational system without parallel in Latin America – and free to all. A start had already been made in the first year, with the construction of more than 3,000 schools. Some 300,000 children attended school for the first time, and 7,000 additional teachers were recruited and trained.[84] This was not just a matter of devoting large sums to the provision of a free national schooling system for everyone aged six to fifteen. Cuba also became known for its willingness to innovate and experiment.

The Revolution had labelled 1961 as 'the Year of Education', but the year was soon remembered for something yet more significant than the literacy campaign. The thousands of student teachers who headed out to the countryside in April 1961 did so in the tense atmosphere that prevailed on the island on the eve of the US-backed invasion at the Bay of Pigs.

6

The Revolution in power, 1961–1968

The exile invasion at the Bay of Pigs, April 1961

No signpost exists to the Bay of Pigs, but the narrow road off the East–West motorway south of Santa Clara, at the abandoned 'Australia' sugar mill, is marked by a series of small concrete memorials. Each indicates the spot where a militiaman was killed in defence of the island in April 1961. The road continues, between the Bay itself and the Zapata swamplands, to Playa Girón, the sandy beach where a CIA-trained force of Cuban exiles made a landing in an attempt to overthrow the Revolution.

The invasion was yet another in that long series of semi-clandestine landings on the coast of Cuba that have punctuated the island's story over several centuries. Like so many of them, it was incompetently organised and poorly directed, and ultimately unsuccessful. Castro's forces, notably the freshly reinforced militia, were well prepared, and the exile battalions were destroyed within a few days. The landings were organised by the CIA, but US forces played no part in the battle.

The invasion was one of the major strategic errors of the United States in the twentieth century, reinforcing Castro's control over Cuba, ensuring the permanence of his Revolution and helping to drive him into the Soviet camp. The botched landings unprotected by US airpower – the essential element that might have secured an exile victory – were the result of divided counsels and poor planning in Washington, as well as uncertainty about the operation's ultimate goal. They reflected the continuing US ambivalence towards Cuba that had characterised American policy over the previous 150 years.

The defeat of the exile invasion had an impact not just on Cuba but on the whole of Latin America. The world now viewed the Revolution in a new light. For the Cubans their victory meant that the 'annexationist' element in Cuban society, dreaming for more than a century of an American future for the island, was now finally discredited and emasculated. Cuba was now irrevocably independent and all those who sought an alternative future were henceforth regarded as traitors. Castro had harnessed his revolutionary chariot to the powerful forces of a renewed Cuban nationalism and was beyond challenge.

For many Latin Americans, the Bay of Pigs reinforced their ingrained belief that the United States could never be trusted; it showed that their northern neighbour was not as all-powerful as it had once seemed. The grip of 'geographic fatalism', so long an embedded element in Latin America's outlook on the world, was broken. Political groups all over the continent now took Cuba seriously as a model and sought to follow the Cuban road, in the belief that the defeat of US imperialism was possible.

The rest of the world, previously ill-informed about the degree of popular support for the Castro government, came to understand that the claims of the Cuban exiles were a sham: the Revolution was not about to fall. Even with US assistance, the exiles had failed to convert their dislike of Castro into a popular movement to overthrow him. Castro was there to stay. No concrete evidence exists of the private discussions of the Soviet leadership but the Russians must have drawn the same conclusion. Castro was initially perceived as a maverick; now he looked like a man worth banking on.

Hanging over Cuba in 1961 was the memory of a cardinal event in the Caribbean some seven years earlier. Cubans in Havana and Americans in Washington were both familiar with the story of Guatemala, where the leftist government of Jacobo Arbenz had been overthrown by an invasion led by dissident officers and organised secretly by the CIA. The CIA involvement was never openly acknowledged at the time, although widely known throughout Latin America. Eisenhower had been the American president, and Allen Dulles had been the head of the CIA. Both held the same positions at the moment of the Cuban Revolution, and in 1960 they agreed to repeat the Guatemalan project in Cuba.

A formal decision to prepare for the overthrow of Castro, and to train a group of exiles, was taken by Eisenhower in March.[1] The project was to be run by the CIA and to take place in absolute secrecy, and several plans were made to secure the physical elimination of the Cuban leadership. Some of the old Guatemala hands, notably Richard Bissell, the CIA operative given the task of organising the exile force, were reassembled in Washington.[2] Guatemala was the natural choice to prepare the eventual attack.

Initial training in guerrilla warfare was provided for exile recruits in May 1960. Some gathered at the island of Usseppa off the Florida coast, others at Fort Gulick in the Panama Canal Zone. The first group was ready by August to train a larger batch of exiles, assembled at the Helvetia estate in Guatemala, a plantation owned by Roberto Alejos, the brother of Guatemala's ambassador in Washington.

Havana was just as familiar as Washington with the events in Guatemala of 1954. Che Guevara had lived and worked in Guatemala City at the time. His experience there had played an important part in his political radicalisation, creating his later firm belief that the United States would seek to destroy Cuba's Revolution by whatever means necessary. His view was shared by Castro who became convinced in the course of 1960, without the need for secret information from exile sources, that the Americans were planning to repeat the Guatemalan operation in Cuba. Cuban diplomats at the UN repeatedly accused the United States of supporting an imminent exile invasion. Everyone knew it was coming; only the timing and the landing place were in doubt.

The autumn of 1960 was dominated in the US by the presidential election campaign, and Cuba was a major topic on the agenda. Richard Nixon and John Kennedy outdid each other in their interventionist language, with Kennedy invoking the memory of the Monroe Doctrine of 1823: foreign powers should keep out of the Americas. The US would not let 'the Soviet Union turn Cuba into its base in the Caribbean', he said. Kennedy believed it should help 'the forces fighting for freedom in exile and in the mountains of Cuba'.[3]

Bissell had first thought of a guerrilla war to beat Castro at his own game. The initial CIA proposal was to establish a guerrilla bridgehead, on the model of the *Granma* landing of 1956. This advance guard would seek to spark an internal anti-Castro revolt, and rally the people to the exiles' flag. Bissell concentrated his attention on the Oriente, a traditional invasion point. Martí and Castro had come ashore there, in 1895 and 1956, moving rapidly into the hills and melting into the peasant population. Other places considered were the Sierra de Cubitas in Camagüey, the Sierra de los Organos in Pinar del Rio and the Escambray mountains north of Trinidad.

Rejecting the Oriente as too far from Havana, Bissell gave particular attention to the Escambray. Guerrillas could establish a beach-head near Trinidad, and move at once into the mountains. There they would be supplied with food and weapons from the air, and unite with groups of anti-Castro dissidents already present. Bissell's schemes did not go undetected on the island and Castro prepared to thwart them. The existence of armed 'bandits' in the Escambray was common knowledge in Havana in the middle of 1960 and Castro began training a peasant militia to defend the region. Some 800 local farmers were given a two-month training course at La Campaña farm and a physical barrier was formed around the area.[4]

A farmers' militia was ready for action in September, and small platoons combed the area, capturing nearly 200 'bandits' and several of their leaders. Several of the CIA airdrops fell into their hands. Their success obliged the CIA chiefs in Washington to change their strategy. They could not guarantee that a small guerrilla group would be able to generate a wider resistance and the Escambray scheme was abandoned in November.

A plan to stage a conventional invasion was now considered. The exiles would be trained for a limited operation, to capture and hold a slice of territory long enough for members of a provisional, anti-Castro government to be flown in. Such a 'government' would immediately be recognised by the United States and its allies and the Americans would come openly to its assistance.[5] The invasion site chosen was the great sea inlet known as the Bahía de Cochínos, the Bay of Pigs, a name recalling the piratical attacks of the sixteenth and seventeenth centuries when pigs running wild in the countryside were much sought after by European buccaneers. The Bay of Pigs lies on the south side of the island, some way to the west of Trinidad and just to the east of the remote Ciénaga de Zapata, the largest expanse of wetland in the Caribbean.

The Americans were unaware that the zone had recently received development assistance from the revolutionary government. New access roads had been constructed across the swamps and simple tourist accommodation erected at Playa Girón. Castro had visited the area on several occasions in the course of 1960, fishing for trout in the Laguna del Tesoro, inland from Playa Larga, at the head of the bay. The Bay of Pigs might have appeared remote, but it was no longer untouched by the modern world.

In the week before the landings counter-revolutionaries inside the island had stepped up their attacks. A sugar mill was destroyed in Pinar del Rio, and El Encanto, the huge department store in the centre of Havana, was blown up. Two small planes dropped bombs on Camp Columbia on 15 April and on two airbases in Havana and Santiago, destroying most of the Cuban airforce and killing several civilians. Castro was warned that the invasion was imminent and he used a funeral oration for the victims of the bombing to announce the specifically 'socialist' character of the Revolution for the first time. 'This is what they cannot forgive,' he said, 'that we should here, under their very noses, have made a socialist revolution.' He praised the 'admirable' achievement of the Soviet Union, which had just launched Yuri Gagarin into space, and compared it with the United States which had bombed 'the installations of a country that has no air force'.[6]

Two days later, on 17 April, the invasion began. 'Before dawn,' announced a statement prepared for the CIA by a public relations firm in New York, 'Cuban patriots in the cities and in the hills began the battle to liberate our homeland from the despotic rule of Fidel Castro.' One group of exiles came ashore on the beach at Playa Girón, at the eastern entrance of the Bay of Pigs, while a second landed at Playa Larga.

The local militia took the brunt of the invasion, but word soon got out to Havana and Castro alerted what was left of his airforce. The exile force came under attack from primitive training planes armed with machine guns and from Sea-Furies capable of launching rockets. The troop carriers used by the exile force had no air defences and several were disabled. Castro drove down from Havana and made his headquarters at the Australia sugar mill, near Jaguey Grande.[7]

Before he left Havana, Castro had ordered the arrest of anyone suspected of counter-revolutionary activities, and 35,000 people were detained in the capital alone, including the auxiliary bishop of Havana. The CIA's hope that thousands would rise up against the Revolution were thwarted on the first day. Castro also drafted an appeal to 'the people of America and the world', to express their solidarity with Cuba's struggle against US imperialism and 'its mercenaries and adventurers who have landed in our country'. Khrushchev sent a diplomatic note to Kennedy with a clear message of support for Castro: 'We shall render the Cuban people and their government all necessary assistance in beating back the armed attack on Cuba.' The message was welcome, but not strictly necessary.

The fighting was fierce around Playa Larga, and 160 Cuban defenders were killed, but the eventual outcome was clear almost from the start. The invasion was crushed within two days. Of the 1,500 exiles who took part, more than 100 were dead and 1,200 were captured. The survivors were paraded at the packed Sports Palace in Havana and interviewed on television each night by a panel of journalists. The commanders had mostly been officers in Batista's army, according to General José Ramón Fernández who was interviewed in 1997: 'When we took them prisoner, I knew all the commanding officers by name. A good number of them had been my students before the revolution, when I was an instructor and assistant director of the school for cadets.'[8]

Castro himself took part one evening, to argue about the merits of the Revolution with the captured exiles – who represented a cross-section of the nation: army officers, peasants and blacks. When Castro suggested that their fate should be put to the vote of the Cuban people, the audience shouted out 'Paredón' – 'to the wall' – and he was obliged to backtrack, saying that to condemn everyone would be to 'belittle our victory'.

Only five officers were executed, and a further nine were sentenced to 30 years in prison, but the majority of the prisoners were detained in Cuba pending their transfer to the United States. Castro suggested to Washington that they should be exchanged for 500 tractors, and Eleanor Roosevelt, widow of the former US president, agreed to chair a 'tractors' committee'. Washington did not have the stomach for such a proposal and negotiations dragged on for more than a year. The prisoners were eventually exchanged in December 1962, not for tractors but for $53 million dollars worth of food and medicine.

In the wake of the Bay of Pigs disaster, the Kennedy administration revised its strategy but did not abandon its attempts to destroy the Revolution. The April fiasco, according to one American history of the operation, led to the development within Kennedy's inner circle of a 'personal animus' against Castro. President Kennedy himself, and his brother Robert, the attorney-general, even more so, 'longed for some redeeming opportunity'.[9] Fresh clandestine planning was soon underway. Bissell was in disgrace, and the baton was passed to General Edward Lansdale, a counter-insurgency specialist formerly active in the Philippines. He was put in charge of a scheme known as 'Operation Mongoose', closely overseen by Robert Kennedy. Covert operations, under the Mongoose umbrella, were designed to stir up trouble in Cuba and bring down the regime, and some speculated on the assassination of Castro.

Four hundred CIA officers worked on Lansdale's project in Washington and Miami. A presidential directive of November 1961, establishing the Mongoose project, declared that the United States would 'help the people of Cuba overthrow the Communist regime from within Cuba and institute a new government with which the United States can live at peace'. Lansdale presented an operational plan to the White House in January 1962 that called for 'a six-phase effort' to undermine Castro from within. His project was designed to conclude 'with an open revolt and overthrow of the Communist regime' in October 1962.[10]

No mention was made of possible US military action, and a second presidential directive in March put Lansdale's plan on the backburner, noting regretfully that final success for 'Operation Mongoose' would indeed require 'decisive US military intervention'. President Kennedy remained hostile to direct US involvement. Richard Helms, the new CIA director, later claimed that General Lansdale's team, 'under constant badgering from the younger Kennedy', had only come up with 'nutty schemes'.[11]

Nutty they may have been, but the memory of Mongoose was to cause damage beyond its authors' wildest imaginings. For Castro was well aware of its existence and of the dangers that it posed, and he was now to embark on a perilous venture – dreamt up by the Soviet Union – to ensure that his Revolution would never again suffer an attack like the one at the Bay of Pigs.

The missiles of October 1962

The world did not wake up to the Cuban missile crisis, officially, until the evening of Monday 22 October 1962, when President Kennedy first spoke on television to announce the detection of Soviet missiles on Cuba and to declare his intention of imposing a naval blockade. A US overflight had photographed an R-12 missile launch site in the San Cristóbal region of Pinar del Rio more than a week earlier, on 14 October, and Kennedy had been informed of this development two days later. The information had been kept secret for a further six days while the President and his advisers made plans to deal with the crisis. Fortunately for historians, he secretly recorded their deliberations.[12]

'My guess is,' President Kennedy told the small group that handled the crisis on Monday 29 October, after the immediate crisis had subsided, 'well, everybody sort of figures . . . *in extremis,* that everybody would use nuclear weapons.'[13]

That was the general belief during the crisis week. For the first time since the United States dropped atomic bombs on Hiroshima and Nagasaki in 1945, hundreds of millions of people all over the globe feared that nuclear weapons might be used again. Several decades later it seemed possible that the threat might have been more apparent than real – for both Kennedy and Khrushchev were level-headed negotiators during the actual crisis – but the international anguish aroused at the time was genuine.

The nuclear panic aroused in many countries was not noticeably present in Cuba itself. Most Cubans were preoccupied more by the prospect of an imminent conventional invasion by US forces than of a generalised nuclear war. The Cubans were not privy to remarks made by Dean Rusk two weeks earlier, at the first crisis meeting in the White House on Tuesday 16 October, but the line of thought followed by the US secretary of state almost certainly mirrored their own: 'I think we have to think very hard about two major courses of action as alternatives,' Rusk told his colleagues. 'One is the quick strike . . . I don't think this in itself would require an invasion of Cuba . . . Or we're going to decide that this is the time to eliminate the Cuba problem by actually eliminating the island.'[14]

The possible elimination of the Revolution – if not of the island itself – by United States action lay at the heart of the October crisis, and it had been the chief item on the agenda of both Cuba and the Soviet Union ever since the Bay of Pigs invasion of the previous year. During that first crisis meeting on 16 October all the historic US antipathies to Cuban independence rose to the surface. Maybe we might have to 'sink the *Maine* again, or something', suggested Robert Kennedy.[15] Others discussed a possible US air strike against the island.

Castro had felt under continuing threat from outside forces ever since the previous year – and not without reason. The Cuban victory at the Bay of Pigs had not put a stop to the campaign to get rid of the Revolution by Cuban exiles and the United States. The planners of 'Operation Mongoose' were still working away. US-backed counter-revolutionaries were again active in the mountains of the Escambray. Years later it was recognised that Kennedy's administration had no intention of sponsoring a fresh invasion by exiles or by American forces – the Bay of Pigs fiasco had cured it of such an ambition – but the Cubans had to take that possibility into account when considering their own defence. The American military had certainly made contingency plans for such an invasion, as would become clear during the October crisis.

Short of invasion and war, the Americans had sought the downfall of Castro by all means, and had busily orchestrated an international coalition against the island in Latin America. The Organisation of American States, under US pressure, had voted to expel Cuba from membership early in 1962.[16] Latin America's governments were now lined up against the Cuban Revolution, leaving the island in diplomatic limbo.

Castro made a long and emotional speech in February in response to the OAS decision, the 'Second Declaration of Havana', in which he underlined the continental ambitions of the Revolution with a new slogan. Cuba considered it to be 'the duty of every revolutionary to make the revolution. It is known that the revolution will triumph in America and throughout the world, but it is not for revolutionaries to sit in the doorways of their houses waiting for the corpse of imperialism to pass by . . . ' A green light was given to Cuban-style guerrilla movements all over the continent, to subvert the existing regimes and to help Cuba escape from its isolation.

Cuba also continued to make overtures to the Soviet Union. Castro had already declared Cuba to be a 'socialist' country on the eve of the Bay of Pigs. Later that year, in December 1961, he announced – hoping to further ingratiate himself with his new friends – that he was, and always had been, 'a Marxist-Leninist'. Orders were sent out to construct a new Communist Party in Cuba along Soviet lines, to be created from the ashes of the uneasy political alliance of parties that had been cobbled together to run the Revolution in the early months. Having signed his application for membership as a socialist comrade, Castro now hoped to secure the guarantee of Soviet military support that such membership should surely entitle him to.

The imperial powers involved with Cuba's affairs over the centuries invariably followed up their initial seizure and settlement with a preoccupation about the island's defences – although results were often slow in coming. The Spanish in the sixteenth century took steps to fortify Havana and other ports along the coast in the wake of attacks by French and English privateers. Then, in the aftermath of the British occupation in the eighteenth century, they began the construction of the great Cabaña fortress at the entrance to Havana harbour. The Americans, for their part, during their occupation of Cuba after 1898, had secured the base at Guantánamo for themselves, believing it to be useful for local intervention as well as for continental defence.

Now it was the turn of the Russian empire to assume the historic role of Cuba's defender. Controversially, it tried to do so with the twentieth century's new phenomenon, the nuclear missile. The reasons for its decision, and the course of the international crisis that resulted from it, have been exhaustively covered in historical debate. Memoirs have been written and volumes of official documents compiled. Surviving participants met at intimate conferences between 1987 and 2002 – in Washington, Moscow and Havana – to re-examine what happened and to publish their findings. Yet often lacking from the published versions of the story is the particular viewpoint of Cuba, the epicentre of the crisis although not the place where crucial decisions were made.

Castro's continuing overtures to the Soviet Union were followed with considerable concern by the United States government, which was inevitably obliged to imagine the worst. Yet the Russians took their time to welcome Cuba into the communist fold. Throughout 1961 and the early months of 1962 Moscow showed signs of understandable anxiety – and division – about the political reliability of their new-found Caribbean friend. This was the time of the Soviet Union's escalating ideological dispute with Mao Tse-tung's China, and, for many orthodox Communists in Moscow, Castro's revolutionary rhetoric – particularly when he championed guerrilla struggle and peasant revolution – appeared dangerously close to the line espoused by the Chinese leader. When Castro turned against some members of Cuba's old Communist Party in March 1962, attacking and dismissing Aníbal Escalante, a veteran from the 1930s and the very man chosen to create the new Communist Party in the Soviet image, several senior Russians wondered about the judgement of their new partner.[17]

Others were more sanguine. Khrushchev and Mikoyan – both of whom were genuinely attracted to Castro and retained some of the revolutionary enthusiasm of the first generation of Bolsheviks – saw the advantage to the Soviet Union's global ambitions in recruiting this charismatic leader to the cause of world communism. They could hardly allow Castro to be overthrown. If that were to happen their own claim to revolutionary leadership would be seriously undermined, not just in China but in that emerging Third World of states recently released from colonial rule where Cuba had already achieved emblematic status. A policy of accepting Castro as their strategic ally, defending and embracing Cuba within the Communist family, appeared increasingly attractive. The decision was taken some time in April or May 1962.

The Soviet motive in escalating their military assistance to Cuba to the nuclear level, and the timing of that decision, is still a matter for debate. The defence and survival of Cuba was now perceived to be important to the Soviet Union, but the desire to achieve a more equal balance of strategic nuclear forces with the United States may well have been of paramount consideration. Predominant in space exploration at that time, but behind in the production and deployment of nuclear missiles, the Soviet Union had some catching up to do. Cuba provided them with a unique opportunity for a breakthrough.

Sergo Mikoyan claimed that his father and Khrushchev had first discussed sending nuclear missiles to Cuba at the end of April 1962.[18] It was certainly not a Cuban idea. Cuba had been asking for military protection against a possible US attack, but without being specific about how this would be done. 'We were then in discussions with the Soviets,' Castro told the American reporter Tad Szulc (without mentioning a date), 'and we were discussing what measures should be taken. They asked us our opinion, and we told them in so many words – we did not speak of missiles – that it was necessary to make clear to the United States that an invasion of Cuba would imply a war with the Soviet Union.'[19]

This initiative, Castro told Szulc, asking for 'measures that would give Cuba an absolute guarantee against a conventional war, and against an invasion by the United States', had certainly come from Cuba, but 'the idea of the missiles, concretely, was Soviet'.[20] A definitive Soviet decision on missile placement was already in evidence in May, according to an account by Alexandr Alexiev, the senior Soviet diplomat in Havana in 1962. Summoned back to the Kremlin, Alexiev attended a meeting with Khrushchev towards the end of May at which half a dozen senior Soviet figures were present – including Mikoyan, Andrei Gromyko and Marshal Rodion Malinovsky, the Soviet defence minister. Khrushchev had startling news, according to Alexiev's account (as told to Guevara's biographer Jon Lee Anderson): 'Comrade Alexiev, to help Cuba, to save the Cuban revolution, we have reached a decision to place [nuclear] rockets in Cuba. What do you think? How will Fidel react? Will he accept or not?'[21]

Alexiev said he did not think the Cubans would agree, but he found the Soviet leadership undeterred by his negative response and deduced that the decision had already been taken. He returned to Havana on 29 May, accompanied by Marshal Sergei Biryusov, the newly appointed commander of the country's strategic missile forces. Once in Havana the marshal began discussions with the Castro brothers on military cooperation. 'What would be necessary to prevent a US invasion?' the marshal asked Castro, according to the official Cuban account.[22] Castro replied with a simple formulation: 'The adoption of measures that tell imperialism unequivocally that any aggression against Cuba would mean a war not only with Cuba.'

Biryusov asked him how this could be done 'concretely', and Castro replied that he thought that a simple Soviet–Cuban military pact would be sufficient, pointing out that the United States had many of these pacts and that they were respected.

Biryusov then brought up the question of whether nuclear missiles would be considered as a tangible sign of support, and he gave details of Khrushchev's proposal to deploy them on the island. Castro asked what kind of missiles these might be, and how the Russians imagined that their installation might be carried out. Biryusov explained 'the principal characteristics of the missiles, their range, and the explosive force of their nuclear warheads'. He also indicated that their deployment, of necessity, would have to be done 'quickly, in secret, and under cover'.

This preliminary Soviet encounter with the Castro brothers was followed by a more formal meeting between Biryusov and an accompanying Soviet official and the six-man Cuban secretariat of the recently formed Organiz-aciones Revolucionarias Integradas (ORI), the forerunner of the new Communist Party.[23] This was the ruling group of the Revolution at that time, consisting of the Castro brothers, Che Guevara, Osvaldo Dorticós, Emilio Aragonés, and Blas Roca. As a result of the purge of Escalante three months earlier, Roca was the sole representative of the old Communist Party.

Castro had made up his mind, and became an advocate of Khrushchev's plans, presenting the Soviet case for installing missiles on the island to his country's top leaders with the expectation that they would agree. He argued that the installation of missiles, in his opinion, would strengthen the socialist camp – according to the version given in the official Cuban account: 'If the Party took the stand that the socialist camp should be willing to go to war for the sake of any socialist country, then it should not give the slightest consid-eration to any dangers for Cuba that this decision might entail.'[24]

Those present agreed that Khrushchev's proposal would contribute to Cuba's defence and would be 'a powerful deterrent that the US rulers would have to weigh before undertaking any military action.'

Castro had swallowed the Soviet proposal, but commented years later that the Cubans did not like the missiles and if it had been a matter only of their own defence they would not have accepted their deployment. The decision was difficult, 'not because we were afraid of the dangers that might follow', but because it would 'damage the image of the Revolution, and we were very zealous in protecting the image of the Revolution in the rest of Latin America'.

Castro was also aware that the missiles would turn the country into 'a Soviet military base', and that in turn would entail 'a high political cost' for the country's image.[25] The presence of foreign military bases all over the world was much under discussion at that time, and the Belgrade conference of non-aligned countries in 1961, at which Cuba had been an active participant, passed an overwhelming vote condemning the bases maintained by the super-powers.[26] Cuba had long fulminated against the US presence at Guantánamo.

Yet despite the impact on the international image of the Revolution, the Cuban leadership felt obliged to go ahead. Raúl Castro and Marshal Biryusov went off together to explore the different places in the island where the Soviet missiles and their accompanying units might be deployed. 'On that tour,' records the official history, Raúl was told 'in detail' about the nature of the military equipment and the number of Russians that would have to be accom-modated in Cuba.[27] The Russians were anxious to make an impression, and the military package they proposed was gigantic. Some 42,000 soldiers would be sent to start with – four Soviet combat regiments. The military hardware would be on a comparable scale, with 16 intermediate-range ballistic missile-launchers and 24 medium-range launchers, each equipped with two missiles and a nuclear warhead. In addition there would be 24 advanced SAM-2 surface-to-air missile batteries, 42 MIG interceptor fighters and 42 Ilyushin-28 bombers as well as 12 Komar-class missile-carrying submarines boats and numerous coastal defence cruise missiles. No such treasure fleet, no such armada, had ever been seen in Cuban waters before.[28]

The Cubans expressed an obvious concern: how could such a vast arsenal be transported across half the world without arousing the suspicions of the United States? Raúl Castro asked whether the Soviets could really transport these 20-metre-long missiles to Cuba without being discovered 'by the enemy's intelligence services', and he discussed his worries with Fidel. The Cuban leadership was clearly uncomfortable about this possibility and remained so throughout the months of preparation, although the official account blithely records their 'confidence in Soviet expertise in such matters'.[29] They were to be seriously disillusioned.

The Cubans had good cause to be worried. The moment the actual construction of the missile sites began in October, the United States caught sight of them – from the photographs produced by their reconnaissance planes overflying the island. The Americans knew exactly what a Soviet missile site looked like, since they had made similar flights over the Soviet Union. Supremely over-confident, it had not occurred to the Russians to change or modify the design.

With hindsight the Cubans regretted their servility towards their Soviet ally. 'If we had known what those missiles were like,' Castro told his colleagues a few years later, in 1968, 'and if the question of camouflage had been posed to us, it would have been easy to decide what to do. In a country where there are so many construction projects, so many big chicken barns and all sorts of [other] things, it would have been the easiest thing in the world to build all those installations under roofs or something else, and they would never have been discovered.'[30]

In spite of these Cuban misgivings, unvoiced at the time, the Russians went ahead. A formal decision to begin missile deployment was taken in the Kremlin on 10 June. The Russians calculated that the installations would be completed within five months, just after the mid-term elections in the United States. The Cubans, still hoping that a public and formalised relationship with the Soviet Union would be a less provocative guarantee of their future security, continued to argue in favour of a simple military pact. The Russians played along with this idea and Raúl Castro travelled to Moscow early in July to initial a draft treaty.

Still worried by the possible discovery of the movement of missiles across the Atlantic, Fidel told his brother to ask Khrushchev just one question – what would happen if the operation were discovered while in progress?[31] Fidel may have understood rather better than Khrushchev that it would not be easy to keep the secret, or maybe the ever-reckless Khrushchev did not really much care. According to the Cuban account, he gave Raúl a typically crude reply:

'Don't worry, I'll grab Kennedy by the balls and make him negotiate. After all, they have surrounded us with their bases, in Turkey and other places.'[32]

Raúl and Marshal Malinovsky initialled the draft military agreement, scheduled for renewal after five years. It included the nuclear installations, and among its clauses was a stipulation that the nuclear-tipped missiles would remain under the sole command of the Soviet military.[33] Plans were made for the pact to be formally signed in Havana in November when Khrushchev hoped to visit the island – to unveil the missiles to an astonished world.[34] Reconnaissance work in Cuba began in the middle of July. A group of Cuban speleologists selected caves suitable for storing arms and ammunition, while 'peasant families living in some of the places selected' had to be moved away and given new land and housing.[35]

The Russians involved in the project, code-named Operation Anadyr, were initially told that they were to take part in an exercise in the far north of the Soviet Union, along the river Anadyr. Years later, the project's commander, General Anatoly Gribkov, explained the nature of his unprecedented task: he was to 'assemble and outfit nearly 51,000 soldiers, airmen and sailors; calculate the weapons, equipment, supplies and support such a contingent would need for a prolonged stay; find 85 freight ships to transport men and gear; put them to sea and ensure them the right reception and working conditions on their arrival in Cuba'. He was also required to 'conceal the entire operation and complete it within five months'.[36]

Soviet units started to arrive early in August, unloading at seven different harbours around the Cuban coast: at Santiago, Nuevitas, Casilda, Havana, Bahía Honda, Cabañas and Mariel. 'The troops landed, regrouped, and left at night in caravans of thirty to forty vehicles. To make sure that they could travel, Soviet and Cuban engineering units had to repair roads or build new ones, and prepare fords in order to detour around bridges unable to withstand such heavy loads.'[37]

The nuclear warheads, the last deliveries to arrive, came early in October. This sensitive cargo was loaded on two ships, the icebreaker *Indigirka*, which arrived on 4 October, and the *Alexsandrovsk*, which docked on 23 October. Colonel Ivan Shishenko, the Soviet officer in charge of their storage, explained that the *Indigirka* moved the bulk of the warheads, while the other ship transported supplemental munitions that were never actually unloaded.[38] Both ships sailed from Murmansk and docked at Mariel.

The warheads were stored initially at a depot in Bejucal, in Havana province, and remained there until moved to the launch sites on 26 October, the day before the crisis was finally resolved. One of the problems of transporting them in Cuba's tropical climate was to keep them at a temperature less than 20 degrees Celsius, and air-conditioned vehicles had to be prepared.[39]

Castro made one last effort to persuade Khrushchev to make a public announcement about the defence treaty, sending Guevara and Aragonés to

Moscow in August to argue the case. Ostensibly the two Cubans were bringing the Cuban revisions to the military pact initialled by Raúl in July, but they also hoped to persuade the Russians to go public. They still hoped that if Khrushchev were to sign the treaty and publish it, this might in itself be enough to deter a possible US invasion. The Cubans could then insist on their right to accept a Soviet base, just as the Turkish government had done when US nuclear bases were established in Turkey.[40]

Visiting Khrushchev at his summer dacha in the Crimea, Guevara and Aragonés encountered a brick wall. Khrushchev insisted that the agreement should remain secret until the missiles were safely installed. The Cubans were obliged to fall in with his wishes. Significantly Khrushchev made no move to sign the defence pact, saying he would do so when visiting the island later in the year. Maybe he realised that a crisis with the United States might arise at some stage, and that it would be easier to negotiate with the Americans bilaterally (or to 'grab them by the balls', as he had so graphically imagined) without the Cubans muddying the waters. When Guevara asked him what would happen if the Americans were to make a premature discovery of Operation Anadyr, Khrushchev was all smiles. 'You don't have to worry,' he said blithely, 'there will be no problem from the United States.'[41]

Khrushchev was wrong. There was a big problem. By the time Guevara and Aragonés returned to Havana, early in September, the United States was already aware of the increased Soviet build-up on Cuba. High-level reconnaissance planes had revealed the existence of the SAM-2 missile sites and of increasing numbers of Soviet soldiers. On 7 September Kennedy asked the US Congress for approval to call up 150,000 reservists, and the announcement of a military exercise, to take place in the Caribbean in October, fuelled fears of an imminent US invasion.[42] On 26 September the US Congress adopted a resolution that would authorise the President to take armed action against Cuba if necessary – to prevent the establishment of military power on the island that might endanger the security of the United States. The worst fears of the Cubans were being realised.

When President Kennedy's crisis committee met in the White House on Tuesday 16 October and asked aloud whether an air strike should not be launched against the island, Robert McNamara, the defence secretary, introduced a more sober note of realism into the discussion. No air strike could be launched against the Soviet missile bases, he said, if they had already become operational:

> *If* they become operational *before* the air strike, I do not believe we can state we can knock them out before they can be launched. And if they're launched there is almost certain to be chaos in part of the East Coast [of the United States] or the area in a radius of 600 to 1,000 miles from Cuba.[43]

McNamara also explained that air strikes would have to be extended to airfields and storage dumps, and this would involve 'potential casualties of Cubans – in, at least in the hundreds, more likely in the low thousands – say two or three thousand'. McNamara concluded with firm opposition to the whole notion of such strikes: 'I would strongly urge against the air attack, to be quite frank about it, because I think the danger to this country in relation to the gain that would accrue would be excessive.'[44]

The crisis group then moved on to examining a possible invasion. McNamara thought it might be necessary 'to invade to reintroduce order into the country'. Such an invasion, said General Maxwell Taylor, chief of the general staff, could be mounted with 90,000 men, by air and sea, taking place over five to seven days.[45]

President Kennedy made his first and most important decision: 'We're going to take out these missiles.' That was the most basic American position. He did not specify how this was be to be done, nor did he take sides in the debate about air strikes versus invasion. He simply requested that preparations should be made for both. Five to seven days were what General Taylor required to be ready.

In Havana, the Cubans knew nothing of this decision, but they were alerted over the weekend of 20/21 October to a possible escalation of the crisis by developments at Guantánamo. Unusually large US troop reinforcements had been arriving at the US base, and civilian families living there had been ordered to leave. 'The United States Prepares an Invasion of Cuba' was the headline of *Revolución*, the Cuban daily, on the morning of Monday 22 October. Without waiting for Kennedy's television speech, publicly scheduled for that evening, and still uncertain whether it presaged an imminent invasion, Castro placed the Cuban armed forces on alert that day and mobilised some 270,000 reservists that night. Cuba's UN ambassador was told to request an emergency session of the Security Council.

The Soviet commander in Cuba received orders from Marshal Malinovsky in Moscow the same day 'to take immediate steps to raise combat readiness and to repulse the enemy together with the Cuban army and with all the power of the Soviet forces' – with the important exception of the R-12 missiles and the nuclear warheads.[46] The Russians, like the Americans, did not wish the crisis to slip out of their control.

After a week of secret discussions in Washington, Kennedy appeared on television on the night of 22 October to announce that close surveillance of the Soviet military build-up had revealed 'a series of offensive missile sites' that were 'in preparation on that imprisoned island.' Each medium-range missile, capable of carrying a nuclear warhead for 1,000 miles or more, he said, would be 'capable of striking Washington DC, the Panama Canal, Cape Canaveral, Mexico City, or any other city in the southeastern part of the United States, in Central America, or in the Caribbean area'. Other, intermediate-range, missiles would be able to reach twice as far, 'capable of striking most of the major cities in the western hemisphere, ranging as far north as Hudson Bay, Canada, and as far south as Lima, Peru'. Cuba, Kennedy went on, lies 'in an area well known to have a special and historical relationship to the United States', and the stationing of missiles was 'a deliberately provocative and unjustified change in the status quo which cannot be accepted by this country'.

Kennedy had decided what to do, and had rejected both the air strikes and the invasion. He chose a third option, announcing a naval blockade of the island: 'All ships of any kind bound for Cuba from whatever nation or port will, if found to contain cargoes of offensive weapons, be turned back.'

He also requested the Security Council to consider a US resolution calling for 'the prompt dismantling and withdrawal of all offensive weapons in Cuba'. Such an action would require inspectors; it was required to take place 'under the supervision of United Nations observers'.

Kennedy concluded with an emotional appeal 'to the captive people of Cuba', describing how he had 'watched with deep sorrow how your nationalist revolution was betrayed and how your fatherland fell under foreign domination. Now your leaders are no longer Cuban leaders inspired by Cuban ideals; they are puppets and agents of an international conspiracy.'[47]

Castro replied to Kennedy's speech on the following evening, and he too spoke on television. Recent events, he said, were the culmination of the policies pursued by the United States since the triumph of the Revolution. Like Kennedy, he delved into history, explaining how their 'special and historical relationship' went back to the last years of the previous century, when 'our progress, our independence, and our sovereignty' had been 'undercut by the policy of the Yankee governments'. The Americans, he went on, had tried everything: diplomatic pressure, economic aggression, and 'a Guatemala-type invasion: the invasion at Playa Girón'. Now they were embarked upon a new adventure, 'trying to prevent us from arming ourselves with the assistance of the Soviet camp'. Castro dismissed all talk of UN intervention, and with reference to the UN's continuing crisis in Central Africa after the death of Lumumba, he said: 'We refuse all inspection: Cuba is not the Congo.'

Invoking other more distant elements in Cuban history, Castro claimed that Kennedy was not a statesman but a pirate, a word with a special resonance for Cubans. He asked why the Americans had proclaimed a blockade when 'they own the seas already. [Henry] Morgan is the owner of the seas. I don't say [Francis] Drake, because Drake was a person of some renown . . . They can search through the archives . . . but in the history of piracy they will not find a precedent of any kind for this sort of action. It is an act of war in time of peace!'

The only precedents, Castro continued, might be found in the history of fascism. 'The United States today is unfortunately the refuge of world reaction, of fascism, of racism, and of all the most retrograde and most reactionary currents in the world. This is a historical fact. Once it was a country of liberty. But those days of Lincoln are gone – from Lincoln to Kennedy is quite a long stretch.' Castro concluded by brandishing his very own, borrowed, nuclear deterrent: 'The people should know the following: we have the means with which to repel a direct attack . . . We are running risks that we have no choice but to run . . . We have the consolation of knowing that in a thermo-nuclear war, the aggressors, those who unleash a thermo-nuclear war, will be exterminated. I believe there are no ambiguities of any kind.'[48]

The mood in Cuba that week was relatively relaxed, in spite of Castro's rash threats. Kennedy had addressed a postscript in his speech to the 'captive peope' of Cuba, yet this did not reflect the mood in Havana at that time, well summarised by the American historian Robert Quirk in his biography of Castro:

> The overwhelming majority in October 1962 stood by their government in the crisis, as they had done at the time of the Bay of Pigs invasion, some because they supported the social and economic reforms, others because for them a sense of national pride came before economic well-being. As men in high places in both Moscow and Washington debated the fate of millions, for most Cubans life went on as usual. They rode Czech buses to their workplaces. They crowded into the popular coffee-houses and refreshment stands and waited in queues to buy rationed foodstuffs – some, perhaps, buying more than they should have. During the day children learned their lessons in the schools. Along the Malecón men and boys fished from the shore.[49]

In Washington, meanwhile, Operation Mongoose had been dusted down again. On Tuesday 16 October, after the morning meeting of the National Security Council, Robert Kennedy held a meeting with those involved in the project, and referred to 'the general dissatisfaction' of the President with progress thus far. He focused discussion on a new and more active programme of sabotage just prepared by the CIA. Pressed by Richard Helms as to what the ultimate objective of the operation might be, and what could be promised to the Cuban exiles, Robert Kennedy hinted that the President might be becoming 'less averse to overt US military action'. He wondered aloud how many Cubans would really defend Castro 'if the country were invaded'. The Mongoose specialists went on to discuss the possibility of using Cuban exiles to attack the nuclear missile sites, but, perhaps fortunately for all concerned, Robert Kennedy 'and the rest of the group agreed that that was not a feasible option'.[50]

The US naval blockade began on Wednesday 24 October and the next day the Soviet government ordered its ships' captains to stay outside the blockaded zone – the order affected ships carrying R-14 nuclear missiles, and their submarine escorts, scheduled to dock that day. Although the following days were fraught with anxiety, the eventual solution to the crisis was relatively simple. A letter sent from Khrushchev to Kennedy on Friday 26 October said that his purpose in sending to Cuba what he referred to as 'defensive' missiles was to prevent a repeat of the Bay of Pigs. He would happily withdraw them if the United States would agree not to invade the island. Since, prior to the crisis, the United States had had no intention of supporting another invasion by the exiles, Kennedy and his advisers were happy to accept this offer. They did so in a letter sent the following day. To save face they insisted that UN inspectors should verify the Soviet withdrawal, a request that was acceptable to Khrushchev but rejected furiously by Castro. The US–Soviet agreement also contained a tacit understanding that US missiles in Turkey, judged to be obsolete, would be withdrawn.

Entirely adjacent to these events and decisions was Castro, whose Revolution lay at the heart of the crisis. He had not asked for the missiles to be placed in Cuba. No one requested his permission when they were removed. To cover over his humiliation, he issued a statement on 28 October to indicate that he had a voice and a point of view, even if no one was listening. Kennedy's guarantee that there would be no invasion of Cuba would, he said, be ineffective unless other measures were taken, as well as the withdrawal of the naval blockade. Castro listed five demands: an end to the economic blockade; an end to subversive activity against Cuba launched from the United States; an end to 'acts of piracy' carried out from US bases; an end to the violation of Cuban airspace and territorial waters; and an end to the US occupation of Guantánamo. Implicit in his statement was the belief that the five demands should have been included in the bargain that Khrushchev made with Kennedy.

When the immediate crisis was over Mikoyan was sent to Havana by Khrushchev to patch up relations. He arrived on 2 November and was obliged to stay for three weeks to placate the Cuban leader.[51] Mikoyan not only had to discuss inspection, to which the Cubans remained adamantly opposed, but also the withdrawal of the Soviet Il-28 bombers from Cuba, a demand that the Americans had added as an afterthought. Mikoyan had no power to negotiate with the Cubans, for the decisions had already been taken in Moscow. His task was to persuade Castro to accept inspection, and after three weeks he had to admit failure. Castro was adamant. There would be no inspection.

President Kennedy announced a formal end to the crisis at a press conference on 20 November: 'We will not, of course, abandon the political, economic, and other efforts of this hemisphere to halt subversion from Cuba, nor our purpose and hope that the Cuban people shall some day be wholly free. But these policies are very different from any intent to launch a military invasion of the island.' McNamara announced the lifting of the naval blockade on the same day.

Soviet ships sailed away from Cuba, carrying the nuclear missiles and their troops. The United States dropped its demand for inspection and agreed that aerial surveillance (which the Cubans could not prevent) would be just as good. In Cuba the mood was grim. The missiles crisis was one of the few major events in the history of the Revolution that Castro was not able to turn to his advantage. He was not accustomed to failure and humiliation, least of all at the hands of the ally that he had so recently been courting.

'The events of those days left behind feelings of disillusion and bitterness,' wrote Tomás Diez Acosta, the official Cuban historian of the crisis, whose account reflected the views of Castro. The sense of disillusion came from 'the poor political role of the Soviet Union' in accepting all the demands of the United States. This had left Cuba 'in a very complicated situation', since it had to oppose 'the humiliating US demand for on-site inspection'.

Even worse was the public handling of the proposed swap of missiles in Cuba for the US missiles in Turkey. In any proposed exchange, it would have been more honourable for the Soviets – and a matter of elementary justice for the Cubans – to have demanded first of all the return of territory illegally occupied by the Guantánamo naval base and the withdrawal of US troops stationed there.

After this bitter but instructive experience – in which Cuba was neither consulted nor taken into account as it should have been – Cubans never again had the same trust in the Soviet political leadership's ability to handle international problems.[52]

Successive United States governments kept Kennedy's (never officially revealed) promise not to invade Cuba. Other countries in the Caribbean suffered from the attentions of US troops – the Dominican Republic, Grenada, Panama, Haiti – but Cuba remained sacrosanct. Even when the Soviet Union collapsed in the 1990s, and hopes rose among Cuban exiles that a more active movement to overthrow Castro might receive the support of Washington, the promise was kept.

The anti-Castro rhetoric was of course maintained. The island was kept in diplomatic isolation, and the exiles were encouraged to continue their programmes of harassment. Kennedy presided over a ceremony at the Orange Bowl in Florida in December, to welcome the returning prisoners captured at the Bay of Pigs and now finally released. Accepting from them their battle flag, he promised that it would be returned to them in a 'free Havana'.

The CIA's fingers could still be found in many pies, and although Operation Mongoose was officially wound down, it continued in all but name. A new unit in the State Department – the Coordinator of Cuban Affairs – was set up to recommend 'new courses of action' with regard to Cuba, and it reported in April 1963 that the 'present covert policy' involved continuing support for exiles. These still believed that the Castro government could be 'overthrown from within', and planned sabotage attacks against Cuban shipping.[53] Kennedy authorised the CIA to support a limited programme of 'hit and run attacks' against suitable targets in June, and the programme was extended in the autumn to include the sabotage of power plants, oil refineries and sugar mills.

'We caught on right away,' Castro later recalled, suggesting that the historical period marked by 'pirate bases in Central America and pirate raids on our coasts' had now returned. This modern form of piracy, he said, was

> carried out with impunity by vessels equipped with the most modern electronic devices . . . So, in the great and extraordinary era of proletarian internationalism and intercontinental missiles, we were forced to go back to the time of the Dutch pirates, Drake, Jacques de Sores, and all those gentlemen whose exploits we have read about in history books.[54]

These attacks along the Cuban coast were to continue throughout the 1960s, a perpetual irritant to the government and to the population, and an excuse for the Cuban government to maintain an ever more powerful and intrusive secret service. As in the days of Spain, the island's captain-general was obliged to take strong-arm measures against the 'pirates' – and those who supported them on the island.

Castro's early honeymoon with the Soviet Union, May 1963

In the wake of the disastrous breakdown in trust between Havana and Moscow after the missile crisis, Khrushchev sought to re-establish a fresh relationship with Castro, sending a long and seductive letter in January 1963 and inviting him to pay a visit to Moscow in April. To impress the Cuban leader the Russians sent their new aeroplane to Havana to collect him. The Tupolev-114, described as the largest and heaviest airliner in the world at that time, was a turbo-prop that could fly directly from Havana to Murmansk in twelve hours. Castro took a team of reliable *fidelistas* with him, including Emilio Aragonés (the man appointed to organise the new revolutionary Communist Party after the dismissal of Aníbal Escalante), Sergio del Valle, José Abrantes (the chief of state security and formerly of the Communist Youth Organisation) and René Vallejo. Apart from Abrantes, there was hardly a Marxist among them.

At Moscow airport on 28 April Castro was greeted by Khrushchev and Leonid Brezhnev, and by the cosmonaut Yuri Gagarin. The Cuban visit was important for Khrushchev. In trouble at home, he needed to bask in the reflected glory of Cuba's revolutionary leader, to prove to his Party and his people that he had been right to back this newest recruit to the Soviet camp. He also needed to ensure that the wayward Castro, with his ideologically undisciplined supporters, did not move into the Chinese sphere, at a time when the Sino-Soviet dispute was still a matter of intense debate.

The Castro visit was a huge success. The popular welcome for the Cuban party was spontaneous and enthusiastic; Castro was fêted wherever he went. The Russians were beguiled by this attractive hero from the distant tropics.[55] Castro attended ceremonial dinners and a performance at the Bolshoi, but he also escaped from his minders and wandered unguarded through Red Square, enjoying the plaudits of the crowd. On 1 May he appeared there on top of the Lenin mausoleum, at Khrushchev's side, and watched while Soviet missile-launchers were driven across the cobbles.

Castro stayed in Moscow for a week, and then went travelling for a month through the Soviet Union, to a punishing schedule. He visited Tashkent and Samarkand, and went on to Irkutsk to walk by the shores of Lake Baikal. Picking up some phrases in Uzbek, he delighted the audience at a collective farm. He returned to Leningrad, via Krasnoyarsk in Siberia and Sverdlovsk in the Urals, and then on to Kiev and back to Moscow, to a final rally at the Lenin Stadium. Even then the visit was not over. Castro and Khrushchev went off together to the Soviet leader's dacha by the Black Sea, and visited Tbilisi. Not until June did Castro return to Moscow, in time to catch the large Soviet turbo-prop back to Havana from Murmansk.

Discussions during the Soviet visit were to have an important impact on the Revolution's economic policies. Cuba would now abandon Guevara's visionary projects of economic diversification, and – with Soviet assistance – would concentrate on sugar production. The Cuban government, noted one Soviet columnist approvingly, had refused to take 'the adventurist path of autarky', a crack against the Chinese, but also an attack on the alternative policies favoured by Guevara.[56] On the Sino-Soviet dispute, Castro had already made a choice defined by economic necessity. China sent Cuba rice, circuses and condoms, while the Soviet Union sent the wherewithal for the construction of entire factories, as well as farm machinery and weapons – and, of course, the Russians bought large quantities of sugar.[57]

The prolonged Soviet visit put paid to any hope of a rapprochement with the United States. 'No satellite leader has ever spent forty days in Russia,' President Kennedy pointed out to journalists, 'basking in such glory and getting so much of Khrushchev's personal attention.'[58] Far from trying to establish 'channels of communication' to Castro, as a committee of the National Security Council recommended in June, the US government's emphasis was again on a programme of sabotage – of 'major segments of the Cuban economy'.[59] The public rhetoric continued on both sides, as did the attacks along the Cuban coast, yet Castro and Kennedy both privately expressed interest in exploring alternatives strategies. Jean Daniel, a French journalist of *L'Express*, interviewed both men in October and November 1963, and wrote a hopeful report. Yet whatever might have been was too late. On

1 Hatuey, Taino chief who attempted to resist the Spanish conquest but was burnt at the stake in 1512, recalled on the sheet music of a 1920's popular song by Elísio Grenet

2 Diego Velázquez (1465–1524), the Spanish conqueror of Cuba in 1511 and the island's first governor

3 Entrance to a coffee estate, *Harper's New Monthly Magazine*, vol. 6, 1852

4 The beach at El Morrillo in Pinar del Rio where Narciso López (1799–1851) landed in 1851, hoping to annex Cuba to the United States, *Harper's New Monthly Magazine*, vol. 6, 1852

5 A Plea for Cuba. 'The Spanish rule in Cuba is a history of bloodshed, tyranny and brutality.' The Marquis of Lafayette and Baron von Steuben ask Columbia what America's fate would have been had they not intervened in the war of independence. Victor Gillan in *Judge*, 19 October 1895

6 (*above left*)   José Martí (1853–1895), writer and independence leader, painted in exile in New York by Herman Norman

7 (*above right*)   Máaximo Gómez (1836–1905), soldier from the Dominican Republic who became the commander-in-chief of Cuban forces in the independence wars

8 (*right*)   General Valeriano Weyler (1838–1930), Spanish captain-general of Cuba, 1896–7, and pioneer of the concentration camp

9 Fort Gonfaus, manned by Spanish forces at Guáimaro, and captured by Calixto Garcia in October 1896

10 Children waiting for food outside the office in Matanzas of the US consul Alexander Brice, 1898

11 Officers in the army of Máximo Gómez at the town of Remedios, 1899

12 General Leonard Wood (1860–1927), American military governor of Cuba, 1899–1902, photographed in 1901

13 (*above*) Indian children at Yara, outside Baracoa, photographed by the American ethnographer Stewart Culin in 1901

14 (*left*) Tomás Estrada Palma (1832–1908), the first president of Cuba, 1902–08, photographed in the presidential palace in Havana in 1902

15 (*above*) Fulgencio Batista (1901–1973),
president of Cuba 1940–44 and 1952–8,
photographed with his wife and members of
her Women's Legion, *c.* 1935–6

16 (*right*) Fidel Castro and the Soviet leader
Nikita Khrushchev at the United Nations in New
York, September 1960

17 Medium-range ballistic missile base installed by the Soviet Union at San Cristóbal in Pinar del Rio, photographed by a US reconnaissance plane in October 1962

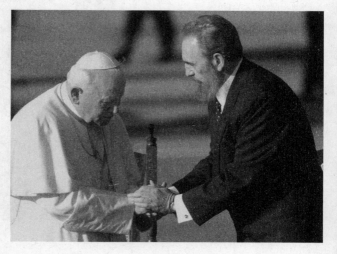

18 Fidel Castro and Pope John Paul II on the occasion of the Pope's visit to Cuba in January 1998

22 November, the day Daniel lunched with Castro, President Kennedy was assassinated in Dallas, Texas. The fantasy of a possible improvement in US–Cuban relations vanished, never to reappear.

Castro made a second visit to the Soviet Union in January 1964, for Khrushchev needed reassurance that the Cubans were committed to the Soviet policy of peaceful co-existence and would not cause problems with the new administration of President Johnson in the United States. Castro, for his part, wanted to get a better sugar deal. After ten days, the two leaders had settled both points. Khrushchev agreed to purchase Cuban sugar at the favourable rate of 6 cents a pound, at least until 1970. The Russians would buy 2.1 million tons in 1965, 3 million in 1966, 4 million in 1967 and 5 million thereafter. The Revolution, which had once sought to escape from the tyranny of sugar production, was now tied to it for the foreseeable future.

As for peaceful co-existence, Castro and Khrushchev agreed that revolutionary movements should be allowed to travel along both peaceful and non-peaceful roads towards the eventual liquidation of capitalism, a nod to the Chinese but also a recognition that Cuba still had hopes of promoting successful revolutions in Latin America.

The first exodus: Camarioca, 1965

The Revolution's embrace of Communism increased the numbers of Cubans seeking to leave the island, yet since commercial flights between the island and the United States had been stopped after the missile crisis the flight into exile had become increasingly difficult. In the early years of the Revolution, the procedure for leaving the island was relatively simple, though not always easy. Would-be exiles needed an air ticket, an exit permit from the Cuban government and a US entry visa from the US government, standard practice for citizens of Latin American countries at the time. US visas were often difficult to obtain and were only granted to known leftists in exceptional circumstances. Securing a Cuban exit permit was often a bureaucratic nightmare, delivered only after the payment of all income and property taxes had been verified. Yet in spite of the obstacles, tens of thousands of Cubans left the island.

Portions of the Cuban population had been accustomed to exile over the centuries, a phenomenon nurtured by traditions of poverty, oppression and political disagreement with whatever regime happened to be in power. Middle-class opponents of Spanish colonial rule throughout the nineteenth century found refuge in Europe and the United States; thousands of workers in those years – notably in the tobacco industry – moved to Florida and established flourishing communities that remained Cuban in outlook and inspiration. Activists during the wars of independence often found themselves languishing unexpectedly in Spain's African jails at Ceuta, on the Moroccan coast, or on the island of Fernando Po. Politics moved seamlessly between communities in Cuba and the mainland of Europe and America. The independence wars were orchestrated and funded by Cubans in exile, as was the war against Batista. The exodus from Cuba during the Castro era created similar patterns of life abroad to those experienced by earlier generations.

First to leave after the Revolution were those involved in the Batista government – its beneficiaries and prominent supporters. The Revolution had specifically targeted them, and the early executions of known killers and torturers was a signal that they would not be welcome in the new Cuba. Estimates suggest that slightly more than 40,000 people left in the first two years.[60]

A second and rather larger group was formed by those unhappy with the Revolution's radical turn. Many people from Cuba's liberal middle class felt they had participated in Castro's war, if only from the sidelines, but they did not approve the subsequent lurch towards socialism, let alone communism. Catholic believers, and those sufficiently affluent to keep their children in private schools, were early opponents of the Revolution's move to the left. Such people usually assumed that Castro's hold on government would be brief, and many flew out to Miami in the sure knowledge that they would soon return. Estimates indicate that 80,000 left in 1961 and nearly 70,000 in 1962.[61]

'Many of those who departed', wrote US Ambassador Bonsal in his memoirs, 'did so in the conviction that they would soon return to find their country and their way of life restored to them without the need to exert serious effort on their part.'[62] These willing migrants had underestimated the tenacity of the Revolution, but some were children and had no choice. Some 14,000 children in 1961 and 1962 were sent off on their own, in an airlift that became known as 'Operation Pedro Pan'.[63] Parents were often desperate for their children to escape what they perceived as Communist indoctrination, and thought that they would be better off in Florida. What was expected to be a brief separation in many cases lasted a lifetime.

The initial departure of Batista supporters was of considerable benefit to the Revolution, effectively exporting the social and financial basis of the counter-revolution and leaving any internal opposition without focus or leadership. Some historians claim that the Revolution's political stability can be largely explained by the fact that potential opposition was siphoned off.

Exile may have been less traumatic for Cubans than for those caught up in other revolutions, since the existence of flourishing Cuban-American communities in Florida, established since the nineteenth century, provided a ready welcome for the first generation of exiles.[64]

The rate of exodus went into a sharp decline after the missile crisis, when flights between Cuba and the mainland stopped entirely for three years. Those seeking to leave could escape only by boat, a risky and uncertain enterprise. Anxious to establish a more orderly exodus, Castro announced a new policy in September 1965, declaring boldly that participation in the Revolution was strictly voluntary. Anyone who wished to leave the island for 'the Yankee paradise' was free to do so, he told an assembly of the formidable Committees for the Defence of the Revolution. The fact that people were escaping in small boats, 'and many of them were drowning', was being used by the Americans 'as propaganda'. The Voice of America claimed that Cuba was 'a prison island' from which its people wished to escape.[65] Something needed to be done.

Since there were no direct flights, the solution was to make a harbour available from which legal and orderly departures might take place. Camarioca, a fishing port to the west of the beach resort of Varadero, was selected as the site. It would be open from October, said Castro, to the boats of Cuban exiles who wanted to come to pick up their relations. The terms were harsh: those leaving were obliged to leave their homes and property to the government. The response was immediate. Several thousand Cubans converged on Camarioca from all parts of the island and hundreds of small boats came over from Florida to collect them.

Many never arrived at the other side. Wayne Smith, a US diplomat working on the Cuba desk in Washington, wrote later that the US coastguards did what they could to keep the boats under surveillance, but it was a losing battle. 'Too many people totally inexperienced in handling boats were putting to sea in small and unseaworthy craft.' A dozen boats were sunk, and the exhausted coastguards were soon predicting 'a major tragedy' unless the operation was halted.[66]

The humanitarian problem was serious enough, and given much publicity by the media. More damaging politically for the US administration was the unscheduled arrival of unregulated refugees. Something had to be done to staunch the flow before it became a major political issue, and the US government now requested talks with the Cubans, the first such official contact for several years. Castro agreed to halt the impromptu 'boatlift' from Camarioca on 15 November. During the month-long exodus, nearly 3,000 Cubans had been taken off the beach, while some 2,000 remained.

The Americans suggested that a regular airlift should be inaugurated to ferry to Miami the Cubans who had asked to leave and whose applications had already been processed by the US 'interests section' of the Swiss embassy in Havana. Much to their surprise, Castro agreed.

President Johnson signed a new immigration law on 3 October, the US–Cuban Adjustment Act, and told the would-be exiles in ringing tones 'that those who seek refuge here in America will find it'. He asked the US Congress to provide $12 million to help fund the expected influx. The Americans suggested that priority should be given to the 15,000 to 20,000 Cubans who already had relations living in the United States. They also declared their willingness to accept Cuba's political prisoners, then estimated rather vaguely by the United States at somewhere between 15,000 and 30,000.

The 'freedom flights' negotiated by Johnson and Castro began in December, with two flights a day from the airport at Varadero, five days a week. The 2,000 migrants left stranded on the beach at Camarioca were eventually taken to Florida on boats chartered by the US government. The flights continued for six years, until August 1971, when President Nixon called a halt. Castro was also willing to see an end to the flights, considering them to be 'an unnecessary drain on the workforce'.[67]

The US government paid for the flights and provided a $100 dollar grant to each family. The total expenditure for the six-year period was $50 million and during that time 3,000 flights had brought more than a quarter of a million Cubans (260,561) into exile in the United States.[68] By the end of the 1980s the total Cuban migration was close to a million, roughly 10 per cent of the population.[69]

The social composition of this immense diaspora changed over time. The exiles of the early 1960s came chiefly from the white middle class, and received a ready welcome in the United States. By the 1970s and 1980s they came from other sectors of society as well, with lower grades and fewer skills, and many were black. These, like their fellow migrants from Puerto Rico, the Dominican Republic and Haiti, found themselves on a lower rung of the ladder of opportunity when they arrived in the United States, affected by unemployment, discrimination and reduced access to education and social services.

President Johnson's US–Cuban Adjustment Act granted automatic residency to any Cuban without documents who landed on American soil. Later migratory accords, signed by President Clinton in 1994 and 1995, required that all Cubans intercepted by the coastguards at sea would be sent back to Cuba. A new phenomenon arose in those years as a result. Illegal speedboats would collect migrants from Cuba for a large sum, and, avoiding the Cuban and US coastguards, would land them on the Florida shore, where they would immediately be eligible for US residency.

The departure over the years of more than a million Cubans was a tragic experience for the migrants and a lasting hurt for the Revolution. The Cuban opposition to the Revolution that existed abroad, funded and supported by the US government, showed its teeth at the Bay of Pigs, and remained a serious threat to the Revolution until the end of the century. Yet the subversive actions of the exiles were largely without legitimacy in their original homeland and served only to further solidify the Revolution.

For the Cuban government, the large-scale emigration in the early years meant a serious loss of professional and technical skills, though it was not without its political – and even economic – advantages. Dudley Seers, a British economist, discovered on a study trip in 1962 that it provided 'the government with a supply of large houses and cars, since refugees who ran these had to give them up. It also reduced the demand for consumer goods, and at the same time it changed the composition of this demand, since those who left were in large part consumers of luxuries.'[70]

Many houses were taken over by government institutions and others by students from the provinces, foreign advisers and slum resettlement programmes, happily bringing black families into bourgeois areas where they had previously been forbidden to live. Forty years later, great areas of central and suburban Havana were still inhabited by people who appeared to be squatting, and still looked as if they could not quite believe their luck.

Havana's questionable loss was Florida's certain gain, where some 700 dollar millionaires of Cuban origin flourished by the mid-1980s. Exiled Cubans were worth nearly $1 billion in the local economy, the proud owners of thousands of small businesses including grocery stores, restaurants, drugstores, jewellery stores, furniture factories, bakeries, garment factories, private schools, cigar factories, record plants, publishing houses and radio stations. Thousands of Cuban doctors and hundreds of lawyers and bankers were well-established in Florida, with just as many entrepreneurs in the construction industry.[71] Florida and Cuba had been united under the Spanish flag during the first centuries of conquest; in the late twentieth century the two sectors of the Cuban community were irrevocably separated, yet forever united by ties of kinship, history and memory.

Exporting the Revolution: Latin America, 1962–1967

While disgruntled Cubans sailed for Miami, rather smaller groups left Cuba to help foment revolutionary movements in Latin America. Ever since the early months of the Revolution, Cuban leaders had talked of toppling the dictators of the Caribbean and extending their rebel army's operations to the Latin American mainland. Che Guevara outlined the implications of the Revolution's success in its first month: 'The example of our revolution for Latin America, and the lessons it implies, have destroyed all the café theories. We have shown that a small group of resolute men, supported by the people and not afraid to die if necessary, can take on a disciplined regular army and completely defeat it.'[72]

Guevara was not alone. The continental possibilities of the Revolution were the theme of one of Castro's earliest speeches, in January 1959: 'How much do the peoples of our continent need a Revolution like this one which has been made in Cuba!' Later he talked boldly of how the Andes might be turned into the Sierra Maestra of the Latin American revolution.

Like other revolutionaries the Cubans dreamt that their individual experience would change the world; their internationalist rhetoric was exemplary. Yet it was not until 1962 that they made a conscious decision to put their revolutionary theories into practice and to actively promote guerrilla warfare in Latin America. Encouraged by Guevara, Castro made plans to accelerate history.

After the radicalisation of the Revolution, in the wake of the Bay of Pigs invasion of 1961, Cuba became ever more isolated within the Latin American hemisphere. Every government, with the exception of Mexico, broke off diplomatic relations and joined in the US economic embargo. Cuba planned to escape from its isolation by overthrowing these governments through the strategy of guerrilla warfare that had proved so successful against Batista.

Guevara was the most outspoken advocate of this policy and its principal inspiration. He had travelled up and down the continent in earlier years, and was the only revolutionary in Cuba with direct and intimate knowledge of its geography and its contemporary history. He believed with passion that small groups of armed men could defeat established armies, as they had done in Cuba. He deployed a compelling argument, although he ignored the great gulf that existed between the frail mini-states of the Caribbean and Central America, and the substantial economies and armies of South America. The first had little more than a paramilitary police force to protect them, the second had centuries of experience in the crushing of native rebellions.

The political possibilities of irregular warfare, conducted in the rural areas of Latin America – and later of the Third World – became Guevara's principal preoccupation, and he eventually left Cuba to seek proof of the correctness of his theories. These were elaborated in his first book, *Reminiscences of the Cuban Revolutionary War* published in 1960, which gave his personal account of Cuba's successful war. This was followed by a second book, *On Guerrilla Warfare*, a handbook for guerrilla fighters, published and reprinted all over Latin America. 'In the conditions that prevail, at least in Latin America and in almost all countries with deficient economic development,' he wrote, 'it is the countryside that offers ideal conditions for the fight.'

The theme was taken up in Castro's speech of February 1962, the Second Declaration of Havana, which emerged as a lyrical invocation of the idea of revolution itself, and the inevitable and coming explosion in Latin America:

The signal sounds clearly from one end of the continent to the other. The anonymous masses – this America of colour, sombre and taciturn America, whose songs echo through the continent with grief and reproach – are beginning to inscribe the pages of history with their own blood, to suffer and to die. They are beginning to shake the world . . . to seize the rights of which they have been deprived by one group or another for almost 500 years. They are rising from the fields and mountains of America, from the slopes of the sierras, from the plains and the forests, from isolation and from the city's traffic, from the seashore and the river-bank . . . For this great humanity has cried 'Enough'! and has finally begun to move.[73]

Recruits to Cuba's guerrilla programme were not lacking. Thousands of young people all over Latin America were inspired by the *barbudos* of Cuba and many now hoped to reproduce the Revolution in their own countries. Cuba provided a modicum of financial assistance, a supply of weapons, some military training and advice and even, on rare occasions, a handful of Cuban fighters.

The Cubans were not operating in a political or historical vacuum. The violent overthrow of dictatorships had been discussed in Latin America throughout the twentieth century by each new generation coming to years of political discretion. General Bayo, the Spanish veteran, described how he had had 'thousands' of conversations in earlier years 'with utopian idealists who dreamt of organising guerrillas – to overthrow Franco, Somoza, Pérez Jiménez, Perón, Cárias, Odría, Batista, Stroessner, Rojas Pinilla, and so many others'. Bayo recorded dryly how 'these conversations, once spoken, dissolved in the air like cigarette smoke'.[74]

Small-scale expeditions were launched from Cuba in the early months of the Revolution – against Trujillo in the Dominican Republic, against Somoza in Nicaragua, and against Panama. These were piratical expeditions in the Caribbean style, refined over the centuries, and often merely tit-for-tat exchanges. Most were freelance operations, without the blessing of the Cuban state, although sometimes a compromising letter of encouragement from Che Guevara might be found in a dead guerrilla's rucksack. Trujillo was an obvious target – he had welcomed Batista to Santo Domingo as an exile and given assistance to other exiles to launch attacks on Cuba – though he was eventually assassinated with the help of the CIA.

Guatemala, to which Guevara was linked by experience and friendship, was also on the list. So too was Peru, where Ricardo Gadea, the brother of Guevara's first wife, was planning an insurrectionary war.[75] Nicaragua was in Guevara's sights, and he was alleged to have provided 20,000 dollars in 1961 to Carlos Fonseca and Tomás Borge, two revolutionaries who founded the Sandinista movement. Nor were Venezuela's leftists, who had sent help to the Cuban guerrillas in 1958, forgotten. They received considerable Cuban support.[76]

Top of Guevara's priorities was his homeland of Argentina. In 1962 he began planning for a guerrilla movement to be established in its northern provinces with the hope of expanding it across the continent. With the cooperation of the Cuban secret service three Argentinians were recruited to organise it – Jorge Masetti, Alberto Granado and Ciro Bustos. This was a mainstream Cuban operation and Abelardo Colomé Ibarra, the Havana police chief, was put in overall charge with José Martínez Tamayo as the chief liaison officer between Cuba and the Argentininian force in the field. General Francisco Ciutat, another old Spanish Republican with 25 years in Moscow, joined as a guerrilla trainer.[77]

The Argentinian group called themselves the People's Guerrilla Army and began their training in Cuba in the autumn of 1962. They moved to Czechoslovakia after the missiles crisis and to Algeria in January 1963. In May they travelled to Latin America and assembled at a farm in eastern Bolivia before crossing into the Argentinian province of Salta. Jorge Masetti was their leader, called Comandante Segundo because he was waiting for Guevara – Comandante Primero – to arrive.

It was not an optimum moment to launch a war of liberation. The group arrived in Argentina just as a civilian government was re-installed after a period of military rule. After six months of recruitment and exploration they were betrayed, surrounded and destroyed.[78] Guevara himself remained in Cuba and this first attempt to start a continental revolution ground to a halt. Yet all was not lost. The Salta experience was built on two years later when a guerrilla movement was again established in the eastern lowlands of Bolivia, in the same geographical location and with some of the same people.

The Cubans now concentrated their efforts on Venezuela, where the local Communists had agreed to support an armed insurrection. Several senior Cuban officers were involved, including Ulises Rosales del Toro and Arnaldo Ochoa. They helped to land small units on the coast of Lara and Falcón at intervals between 1963 and 1967. Although a handful of Cuban fighters took part in the Venezuelan war the principal focus of Cuba's assistance programme was concentrated on training and supply. Some 300 Venezuelans may have passed through the Cuban training camps in this period, and possibly some 2,000 Latin Americans learnt the basic techniques of guerrilla warfare in Cuba in the 1960s. The figures are inevitably imprecise.[79]

The Venezuelan Communists began to change tack after presidential elections in December 1963 in which the country voted overwhelming for the candidates of the conventional parties. Many erstwhile revolutionaries began to re-examine their commitment to guerrilla warfare and in November 1965, after much internal debate, the Venezuelan Communist Party recommended 'the suspension of armed action'. The war continued in a sporadic fashion until the end of the decade and received Cuban assistance at least until 1967, but it lost much of its political support in the cities.

About to host a 'tricontinental' conference in Havana in January 1966, celebrating the successes of revolutionary guerrilla warfare all over the Third World, Castro was enraged by the decision of the Venezuelan Communists to abandon the armed struggle. He spent the next two years denouncing them for their pusillanimity and praising the surviving guerrillas in Venezuela who had fought on, though this was not what his new friends in the Kremlin wanted to hear.

Cuba's guerrilla strategy was put into theoretical form by a French writer, Régis Debray, who, after discussions with Castro and Guevara, produced a series of articles on the subject that were widely distributed in Latin America.

His most striking contribution, an extended polemic entitled *Revolution in the Revolution?*, was published early in 1967. In it, he argued from the Cuban experience that the small motor of a guerrilla group in the countryside would set in motion the larger engine of revolutionary struggle in the cities. Yet by the time of publication the theory was already wearing thin.[80] It was clear by the mid-1960s that the counter-revolution had got the upper hand. Revolutionary groups formed in the Cuban image had been crushed in Peru in 1965; the revolutionary movement in Guatemala had received serious setbacks, including the assassination of the Communist Party leadership in 1966; and the long-standing insurgency in Colombia, which went back to the early 1950s and had been given a fillip by the Cuban Revolution, had been driven back into mountain and jungle fastnesses far from the country's urban centres.

Physical involvement by Cubans in Latin America's struggles had always been small, limited to Argentina, Bolivia and Venezuela. As the South American dream dwindled the Cubans embarked on a fresh venture in another continent. More Cuban soldiers were to go with Guevara to the Congo in 1965 – just over a hundred – than had gone to all the Latin American guerrilla groups put together.

Exporting the Revolution: Black Cuba's return to Africa, 1960–1966

Aware that the revolutionary fires in Latin America were burning low, Cuba made a strategic decision in 1965 to involve itself directly in what was perceived as the unfolding African revolution. 'Africa is rising from the ruins,' *Verde Olivo*, the Cuban army magazine, announced in December 1964: 'The fire of national liberation is burning in Angola. The Zairean patriots are raising the flag of independence on the points of their guns. Rebels are fighting heroically in Mozambique. The people of Southern Rhodesia are rejecting false independence that would only perpetuate the rule of the racist minority.'[81]

The time had come for the Cuban Revolution, still aflame with the spirit of internationalism, to lend a hand. The initial battlefield was not any of the countries mentioned by *Verde Olivo*, but the geographically central state of the Congo.[82] A unit of a hundred Cuban blacks, well trained in the techniques of guerrilla warfare and commanded by Che Guevara, was sent there in 1965 to join the rebels fighting in the east of the country. 'It was the first time that I had seen so many blacks together,' said one of the Cuba guerrillas. 'Blacks, only blacks, we were all blacks. It baffled me. I wondered, "Shit! What's going on?"'[83] It was a serious affair.[84]

When it was withdrawn six months later, Cuba concentrated its assistance on a rebel movement in Guinea-Bissau, a group led by Amilcar Cabral that was fighting for independence from Portugal. Cuba also sent a group to

Congo-Brazzaville, to train the soldiers of the Popular Movement for the Liberation of Angola, the MPLA, led by Agostinho Neto. Black solidarity across the Atlantic was often emphasised. 'I don't believe there is life after death,' Cabral told Cuban soldiers in Brazzaville in August 1966, 'but if there is, we can be sure that the souls of our forefathers, who were taken away to America to be slaves, are rejoicing today to see their children reunited, and working together to help us to be independent and free.'[85]

At the time of the Revolution's triumph Cuba's black population was less than a century away from slavery. Most of Africa, from which their recent ancestors had sprung, was still controlled by Europe's colonial powers and only a handful of countries were independent: Egypt and Ethiopia, and Ghana – freed from British rule in 1957. South Africa was a white-ruled apartheid republic.

Within a couple of years, the scene had changed out of all recognition. General de Gaulle returned to power in France in 1958, a few months before the Cuban Revolution, and offered independence to all French colonies south of the Sahara. The British and Belgians felt obliged to follow suit, and sixteen of Europe's colonies in Africa received their independence in 1960. Radical new governments in some of them believed that their own struggle for freedom should be extended throughout Africa, and they provided active support for the liberation movements in white-ruled countries engaged in that pursuit. Armed resistance to colonial rule now began in Portugal's colonies – Angola in 1961, Guinea-Bissau in 1963 and Mozambique in 1964.

The Cuban Revolution had appeared at an opportune moment and was seen by many Africans as part of the emancipatory wave affecting Africa and much of the globe. By 1961 Castro and Guevara had made common cause with the more radical African leaders and had offered to help them towards their revolutionary goals. The Cubans were the experts and arch-exponents of guerrilla warfare and the Africans wanted advice. No one guessed in those early years how far these initial contacts would eventually go.

Guevara was the first Cuban leader to take an interest in Africa and the first to visit the region. He stopped off in Cairo in June 1959 to salute President Nasser, then the nationalist hero of the Arab world. Cuba had had no diplomatic links with Africa before the Revolution, except a consulate in Egypt. Raúl Castro followed Guevara to Cairo in July and diplomatic relations were established in the autumn. Ambassadors were also exchanged with Kwame Nkrumah's Ghana and with Sekou Touré's Guinea.

Sékou Touré was the first African to make a state visit to Havana and he was greeted in October 1960 by thousands of enthusiastic black Cubans, shouting 'Africa! Africa! Africa!' He was later to be a valuable link with the liberation movement in Guinea-Bissau.[86] Contacts with the Algerian revolutionaries of the Front de Libération National (FLN) were made a year later, a few months before the eventual Algerian triumph in July 1962, when the

French finally withdrew. Unrolling since the mid-1950s, Algeria's revolutionary struggle had aroused particular interest among Cuba's own revolutionaries in the years before January 1959. The anti-Batista activists in Cuba had been fascinated by the reports from Algeria printed regularly in the pages of the weekly *Bohemia*. Algeria's experience seemed to parallel their own.[87]

Cuba's first emissary to the FLN headquarters in Tunis, in October 1961, was Jorge Masetti, the journalist who was later to lead Guevara's guerrilla movement in Argentina. He arrived in Tunis with an offer from Castro to the FLN of a shipload of American weapons – captured from the Cuban exiles at the Bay of Pigs in April. It was a nice touch. The Algerians gratefully accepted and the weapons – rifles, machine guns and mortars – were unloaded at Casablanca in Morocco in January 1962 and subsequently transferred to the Algerian frontier. On its return journey to Havana the Cuban ship carried 76 wounded Algerian guerrillas and 20 orphan children from the refugee camps. More than 53 public health workers were sent out to Algeria in 1963. This was the start of the Revolution's unprecedented programme of humanitarian solidarity with Africa that would continue and grow over subsequent decades.[88]

Cuba's relationship with Algeria was based on Castro's personal friendship with Ben Bella, prime minister at independence in 1962. Many of Castro's decisions about foreign affairs – for good or ill – were based on how he sized up foreign leaders he met. If some powerful African caudillo took his fancy – Ben Bella, Agostinho Neto, Amilcar Cabral, Mengistu Haile Mariam of Ethiopia – Castro would back him to the hilt. The same was true of his relationship with prominent Latin American figures. Salvador Allende of Chile, Tomás Borge of Nicaragua, Maurice Bishop of Grenada, Juan Velasco of Peru, Hugo Chávez of Venezuela – all enjoyed his warm personal approval. So powerful was the attraction and commitment that Castro often did not seem to care or notice that his particular friend of the moment was not wholly in control of the situation in his country. This instant capacity to sum up an individual did not always serve him well when trying to analyse the situation in a specific country with whose history, customs and culture he was largely unfamiliar.

Ben Bella flew into Havana from New York on 16 October 1962, just three months after independence. He was greeted by Castro, with the orphaned Algerian children carrying flowers. 'The two youngest revolutions of the world met and compared notes,' Ben Bella later recalled. For the next three years, until his overthrow in 1965, he was to be Cuba's guide to the politics of the African continent, although Nasser of Egypt, Julius Nyerere of Tanzania and Alphonse Massamba-Débat of Congo-Brazzaville also played important roles. Algeria provided a home to several leaders of the African liberation movements and facilitated their contacts with the Cubans. Ben Bella also provided assistance to Cuba's favourite guerrilla movements in Latin America, notably those in Venezuela and Argentina.

Cuba's ambassador in Algiers, Jorge Seguera, was well connected and kept in touch with everyone. He had fought in the Sierra Maestra and was a close friend of the Castro brothers and Guevara. Although he was active and knowledgeable, his opinions were not always sensible. Piero Gleijeses, historian of Cuba in Africa, suggests that his advice may have contributed at certain moments 'to Havana's overestimation of the revolutionary potential of the region'.[89]

The Cubans were on a learning curve in Africa and they followed events in the Congo with particular interest – like everyone else at the time. When Castro spoke at the UN General Assembly in September 1960 he addressed the theme of the day – Africa's independence – and declared his support for the Algerians, the blacks of South Africa and Patrice Lumumba of the Congo, which had become independent six months earlier and subsequently fallen prey to UN intervention and separatist wars. 'The people of the Congo are on the side of the only leader who has remained there to defend the interests of his country,' said Castro, to show where he stood on the issue that had polarised the UN. 'That leader is Lumumba.'

The Congo occupied the world's headlines for several years, as the return of the Belgians and the arrival of UN forces was accompanied by civil war, and later by the involvement of mercenaries from South Africa and the United States, some of them Cuban exiles. Lumumba was captured and killed in January 1961.[90] A fresh development occurred in July 1964 when Moises Tshombe, a conservative leader from Katanga, supported by Belgium and the United States, seized power, sparking a rebellion by a radical group that claimed to be the heirs to Lumumba. Their rebellion was knocked out by a Western intervention force in November, when Belgian paratroopers carried in US transport planes from the British base on Ascension Island destroyed the rebel headquarters at the town of Stanleyville in the north of the country.

Guevara travelled to New York in December to denounce Western intervention at the UN General Assembly and to offer support to the rebels on behalf of the Revolution. 'All the free men of the world must prepare to avenge the crime of the Congo,' he declared. Castro sent him out to Africa to discover what could be done to help the Lumumbist rebels, and to assess the needs of other liberation movements. Guevara's tour lasted for the first three months of 1965, and he met the Lumumbists from the Congo, the MPLA from Angola, Cabral's Party for the Independence of Guiné and Cape Verde (PAIGC) from Guinea-Bissau, and the Front for the Liberation of Mozambique (Frelimo).

He flew first to the three former French colonies with radical governments: Algeria, Guinea and Congo-Brazzaville. In Algiers he made plans with Ben Bella; in Conakry, Sékou Touré arranged for him to meet Cabral, who had his headquarters in the city; and in Brazzaville, he met Angola's leaders for the first time. Congo-Brazzaville, bordering both the Congo and the Cabinda enclave of Angola, had the most radical government in Central Africa, led since August 1963 by Alphonse Massamba-Débat, a former schoolteacher who had studied in France and absorbed much of the rhetoric of the French left. He had given early support to the rebel Lumumbist movement in the Congo and to the MPLA. Brazzaville was an important base for both movements, and he was concerned that this might lead to destabilisation by the West. He asked Guevara for Cuban troops to be sent to stiffen his presidential guard, and Guevara transmitted the request to Havana.

Massamba-Débat introduced Guevara to the three most senior MPLA leaders – Agostinho Neto, Luis de Azevedo and Lucio Lara – who were organising a guerrilla war against the Portuguese in Angola. At that stage the Angolans only wanted instructors from the Cubans, rather than weapons or troops. 'The war was getting difficult, and we were inexperienced,' Lara later recalled. 'We wanted Cuban instructors because of the prestige of the Cuban Revolution, and because their theory of guerrilla warfare was very close to our own.'[91] Guevara explained the Cuban plan to send instructors to aid the Lumumbist movement, and agreed that some could be sent to Brazzaville, to help the Angolans, and a team led by Jorge Risquet arrived later in the year.

Moving on to Dar es Salaam in February, after a side trip to Peking, Guevara made contact with the Lumumbists and with the Mozambican movement, Frelimo. His chief contacts with the Lumumbists were Gaston Soumaliot and Laurent Kabila, the man in charge of the rebel forces in eastern Congo. Che offered them thirty instructors 'and all the weapons we could spare'. Kabila accepted 'with delight', and Soumaliot asked that the instructors should be black.

The meeting with Eduardo Mondlane and Marcelino dos Santos from Frelimo was more difficult. Frelimo had recently begun its liberation war and Guevara clearly believed that the claims of battles won were exaggerated. The Frelimo leaders, understandably, were not enamoured by the priority that Guevara gave to the war in Congo and did not wish their guerrillas to be trained there, as Guevara was advocating. There was no meeting of minds. The Cubans never established the close relationship with Frelimo that they had with the MPLA. Guevara eventually gave away and agreed that a number of Frelimo fighters should be sent for training in Cuba. Assistance with weapons would also be provided.

Guevara held a stormy meeting with a group from other liberation movements and explained why he thought the war in the Congo to be of fundamental importance – 'victory there would have repercussions throughout the continent'. He also repeated his argument in favour of establishing a training centre for African freedom fighters, run by the Cubans, inside the Congo. The trained fighters would be expected to assist in the liberation of the Congo before returning to the struggle in their own countries. Guevara had taken the verbal enthusiasm of the Africans for pan-African unity at face value, imagining that African aspirations to continental unity were similar to those in Latin America. This was not the case. Most Africans did not share Guevara's internationalism. They were prepared to fight only for the liberation of their own country, not for the continent.

The African reaction to Guevara's utopian scheme was wholly negative. According to Guevara's own account the assembled Africans argued fiercely that their peoples, 'abused and degraded by imperialism', would not accept casualties occurring as the result of 'a war to liberate another country'. Guevara had a wider view. 'I tried to show them that we were talking not of a struggle with fixed frontiers, but of a war against the common enemy, present as much in Mozambique as in Malawi, Rhodesia or South Africa, the Congo or Angola. No one saw it like that.'[92]

These were crucial differences. The Cubans came to Africa with their own set of experiences and distinct views about what should be done. The Africans, closer to their own reality, had another view. Guevara glossed over their differences and flew back to Havana to give Castro an optimistic report. A troop of black soldiers had already been training and was ready to leave. Guevara returned to Dar es Salaam in April, leading the first group of 14 black Cuban guerrillas across Lake Tanganyika into eastern Congo.

The Cubans had underestimated the divisions and the difficulties. There was trouble from the start. No senior Congolese political figures were present at Dar with whom to discuss future plans. Kabila and Soumaliot were away in Cairo, patching up the political differences within the Congolese revolutionary movement – a discouraging indication of what was to come.

The Africans had some excuse; they had not been told that the Cuban soldiers were to be led by Guevara. They had been informed that there would be a training mission. They had no idea that it would be led by a world-famous guerrilla leader. Yet it was clear that they and the Cubans were not going to see eye to eye. Local politicians, however hard-pressed, rarely like outsiders to come and tell them how to run their liberation movements. The Cubans were internationalists in the purest sense: they had come to combat US imperialism wherever it appeared, and to further the interests of the world revolution. The Congolese had no such ambitions and were circumscribed by their own petty nationalisms, their internal feuds and their lack of knowledge about the politics of the wider world. As a revolutionary movement they were not altogether serious.

The Cubans were to remain in the Congo for seven months, reinforced each month by another small group, bringing the eventual total to over a hundred. They did not speak the language and they were unfamiliar with the terrain. They withdrew in November 1965, defeated militarily and politically. They were driven out by a force of South African mercenaries and undermined by a decision of a meeting of African heads of state to withdraw support from the Lumumbist groups. With the overthrow in June of Ben

Bella, Cuba's principal African ally, the international support for the Congolese operation from radical African countries had begun to unravel.

Guevara sounded the final retreat on 20 November and organised his men to cross the lake back to Tanzania. 'All the Congolese leaders were in full retreat, the peasants had become increasingly hostile. Yet the idea of finally abandoning the territory, going out by the way we had come in, and leaving the peasants defenceless . . . all this made me feel pretty bad.'[93]

Castro, on the other side of the world, was less engaged. 'In the end,' Castro explained later, 'it was the revolutionary leaders of the Congo who took the decision to stop the fight, and the men were withdrawn. In practice, this decision was correct: we had verified that the conditions for the development of this struggle, at that particular moment, did not exist.'

After a few days in Dar es Salaam, the bulk of the Cuban contingent returned home, but Guevara remained behind in the Cuban embassy to write a painful memoir: 'Victory is a great source of positive experiences,' he wrote, 'but so too is defeat, perhaps more so, in my opinion, when both participants and observers are strangers who have gone to risk their lives in unknown countries, with a different language, to which they are bound solely by the ties of proletarian internationalism, embarking in this way on a unique chapter in the history of modern wars of liberation.'

Unique it was, and seemingly unrepeatable, at least by the Cubans. Guevara's next revolutionary experience took place in Bolivia, a country that was more familiar and whose language the Cubans understood. Castro was not altogether convinced by Guevara's account of African defeat, and he would embark on a yet more dramatic African intervention ten years later, in Angola in 1975. First he was to take an interest in other black revolutionary movements nearer home, led by people, like the black population of Cuba, whose ancestors came from Africa and had once been slaves.

Exporting the Revolution: mobilising black Americans

Castro first took a public interest in the black movement in the United States when he stayed in Harlem, at the Hotel Theresa, in September 1960. He met black journalists and talked to Malcolm X, the black Muslim preacher. He expressed his solidarity with the struggle of American blacks. His early rhetoric on the race issue was flamboyant, enabling him to voice criticism of the American social model as well as its foreign policy.

'What of the blacks?' he asked in the speech of February 1962, known as the Second Declaration of Havana, reflecting on the Alliance for Progress, a programme for Latin American development that the United States had put forward. Castro expressed his doubts whether blacks in Latin America, any more than the poor and the Indians, would be much attracted by it. 'Into what kind of "Alliance" can he be invited by the US system of lynching and brutal discrimination? Latin America's 15 million blacks and 14 million mulattoes know to their horror and anger that their brothers to the north cannot ride the same buses as their white compatriots, or attend the same schools, or even die in the same hospitals.'

Yet to move from stirring rhetoric to something more concrete was never contemplated seriously by the Cubans. As the years went by Cuba's relationship with black revolutionaries in the United States became more problematic. Castro was influenced both by the continuing ideological debate within his government, fuelled by the ever-closer relationship with Moscow, and by his need not to further inflame relations with the United States.

When riots swept American cities in the early 1960s, and several black ghettos destroyed themselves in the process, the Cubans watched from the sidelines. The Watts rebellion in Los Angeles in August 1965, in which 34 people were killed, was closely followed in the Cuban press, and Castro invited persecuted US blacks to seek asylum in Cuba, but no action was taken.

Successive US administrations made efforts to remove some of the most odious elements of discrimination, and even – rather prematurely – praised the blacks for their protests. 'The real hero of this struggle is the American negro,' said President Johnson in March 1965, before the Watts explosion, outlining his plans for voting rights for blacks. 'His actions and protests – his courage to risk safety and even life – have awakened the conscience of the nation. His demonstrations have been designed to call attention to injustice, to provoke change and stir reform. He has called upon us to make good the promise of America.' Johnson was speaking during the celebrated civil rights march from Selma to Alabama, which itself had been launched by Martin Luther King to test the real impact of the new Civil Rights Act. The Johnsonian rhetoric and the new Act, however emasculated it became after passing through the US congress, did much to deprive black radicals of a wider audience.

With the exception of the Guevara expedition to the Congo, and later to Bolivia, Cuba's revolutionary activities in Africa and in Latin America depended largely on local initiative. Cuba helped out, with money and training, but only where others were prepared to plan, organise and fight. Many American blacks had the necessary enthusiasm, but the Cuban revolutionaries had little to no experience of dealing with this particular culture. Those that visited Cuba or came to live there did not help themselves much, for they were notably disunited and held no firm ideological convictions of their own that they could sustain for any length of time. A CIA investigation in July 1967 noted that the Cubans were giving 'moral support to radical African-American groups,' but had been careful 'not to provide them with any material assistance, and certainly not military training'.[94]

Cuba had a further difficulty with American blacks. Many of the black groups advocated a black nationalism that verged on separatism, something that was anathema to the old Communists of Cuba and to the trend of white Cuban republican ideology since the start of the century. The Cuban leadership wanted to express its support for American blacks, but it certainly did not want them to proselytise in Cuba, nor to allow their ideas to percolate Cuba's large black population.

The outcome was much propaganda rhetoric favouring the black struggle in the United States, notably in the period up to 1968, and the active discouragement of revolutionary black leaders, notably Robert Williams, Stokely Carmichael and Eldridge Cleaver, who arrived in Cuba expressing enthusiasm for the Revolution and then were swiftly (except in the case of Williams) sent on to other destinations, usually Africa.

Castro had met Williams, an opinionated black nationalist from North Carolina, during his stay in Harlem in 1960. Williams had visited Cuba on a trip organised by the Fair Play for Cuba Committee and, according to his own account, had received some encouragement from Castro. He returned to the island in 1961, by then in flight from the attentions of the FBI, and took up permanent residence in Havana, the first of many black revolutionaries from the United States so to do.[95] He was the first and the most difficult – not to say tiresome – American black nationalist with whom the Cubans had to deal, and he stayed in Havana for five years, until 1966.

Williams had begun his political life in the National Association for the Advancement of Colored People in the 1950s, but, dissatisfied with its pacifistic stance, he had organised armed self-defence units to protect his local community against the Ku Klux Klan. A US military veteran, he was one of the first American blacks to call for the formation of a Black Liberation Front, and to envisage the possibility of urban guerrilla warfare inside the United States.

Williams became an influential figure in Havana, meeting the handful of prominent black figures in the Revolution as well as Che Guevara and Manuel Piñeiro, the security chief in charge of foreign operations. Piñeiro spoke excellent English, having studied and lived in the United States and married a woman from Texas. Similar in outlook to the many Latin American leftists in the capital in the early 1960s, Williams was an early convert to Guevara's 'foco' theory of guerrilla warfare and discussed how it could be adapted to the United States. Although he was notionally the chairman in exile of a group in the United States called the Revolutionary Action Movement, he had few followers.[96] Piñeiro made it clear to him that Cuba preferred the integrationist approach of Martin Luther King to the separatist black nationalism espoused by Williams.[97]

Way to the left, Williams was inevitably caught up in the ideological infighting of the period. He took the Chinese side in the Sino-Soviet dispute,

just at the moment that the Cubans came down firmly in support of the
Soviet Union. He left for China in July 1966 after five years in Cuba, and the
Chinese, for their own purposes, were happy to publish his attacks on the
Cuban 'racism' to which he felt he had been exposed. The Cubans responded
by forging Williams-style newsletters (allegedly masterminded by Osmany
Cienfuegos) that accused Mao Tse-tung and his 'arrogant, power-mad under-
lings' of having 'betrayed the Cuban Revolution', and of encouraging 'ethno-
centric fanaticism' and 'discrimination against Africans' in China.[98]

Different and less ideological than Williams's group, a new generation of
black radicals began to emerge in the United States in the middle of the 1960s.
They had one thing in common: a willingness to abandon the pacifism and
non-violence of the traditional black organisations. They called their
movement Black Power. Stokely Carmichael, who became their most charismatic spokesman, was one of the first supporters of this new group to visit
Havana. A radical West Indian by origin, who had been the chairman of the
Student Non-Violent Coordinating Committee (SNCC), he was invited to
Cuba in August 1967 and spoke at the meeting of the Organisation of Latin
American Solidarity conference (OLAS). 'Castro is the blackest man I know,'
he told *Time* magazine.[99]

As cities in the US blazed away in that hot summer, notably in the black
ghettos of Detroit, Carmichael called for blacks to continue burning and
pillaging, with the aim of creating 'fifty Vietnams in the United States' –
echoing the image made famous by Guevara. He assured the Cubans that the
US blacks were ready 'to destroy US imperialism from within, as you are ready
to do it from without. We can't wait for them to murder us, we must be
prepared to be the first to kill.'

Castro gave Carmichael a warm welcome, and told the audience at the
conference that the imperialists were angry 'because of the rapprochement
between the revolutionary movements in Latin America and the revolutionary
movement inside the United States'. Then, with more than a sigh of relief,
Castro added that 'we would be more than honoured if he chose to live here,
but he doesn't wish to stay in Cuba because he considers the struggle at home
to be his fundamental duty'.[100]

Carmichael asked the Cubans if they would help him to go to Conakry,
where Amilcar Cabral had his headquarters. Many black leaders like
Carmichael were on a personal pilgrimage that led them from black nationalism to Pan-Africanism, a revival of an earlier concern of the black movement
in the United States. Cuba was a useful way-station, but many were to be
happier in the all-black environment of Africa than in Cuba's hybrid society.
Carmichael hoped that African-Americans would be allowed to fight
alongside the guerrillas in Guinea-Bissau – to atone for their participation in
the Vietnam war.

The Cubans sent him on to Guinea in September, and Carmichael
discussed his proposal with the PAIGC. Cabral was lukewarm, at best, but he

agreed to accept some 20 or 30 African-Americans as fighters, provided they were trained somewhere else. Carmichael and his Cuban escort travelled on to Dar es Salaam, to secure the support of Julius Nyerere. The Tanzanian president also rather surprisingly agreed, but when Carmichael returned to Conakry he met the South African singer, Miriam Makeba.[101] Love triumphed over revolution, and he eventually married Makeba and settled down happily in Conakry. He effectively said goodbye to Cuba in a speech in 1968 where he argued that communism and socialism were not 'ideologically suited' for black people. 'The ideologies of communism and socialism speak to class struggle, but we are not just facing exploitation. We are facing something much more important, because we are the victims of racism.'[102] Subsequently, presumably under Makeba's influence, he withdrew his earlier hostile remarks about Cuba and became a steadfast supporter, albeit from afar. Makeba was treated with great respect when she came to Cuba in 1972 and was granted honorary Cuban citizenship.

Castro had always kept a close eye on changing American opinion. Immediately after Americans had staged their first major anti-war protest in April 1967 – the Mobilisation to End the War in Vietnam – he spoke about the event in a speech celebrating the sixth anniversary of the Bay of Pigs:

> It is really impressive to see hundreds of thousands of US citizens marching through New York, some of them with pictures of Ho Chi Minh . . . and . . . along with the pictures of Ho Chi Minh, and some of the martyrs in the civil rights cause, the news dispatches reported that there were also pictures of Che Guevara.[103]

That same year, (white) emissaries came to Cuba from the radical US student movement, Students for a Democratic Society, bringing news of a new black movement, yet more radical than Black Power. They brought pamphlets with them from the Black Panther Party for Self Defense, as well as a new book, *Soul on Ice*, written by Eldridge Cleaver, the Party's minister of information.[104]

Cleaver eventually arrived in Havana in December 1968, yet, as with Carmichael, the Cubans found him to be a difficult and argumentative comrade. He left after five months on the island for Algiers where he was allowed to set up an international office for the Black Panthers.[105] The Cubans were not altogether sorry to see him go. Huey Newton, the founder of the Black Panthers, came to live in Cuba later, in 1973, but he, like others who came in subsequent years, kept a deliberately low profile.

With the collapse of black militancy in the United States in the 1970s, largely as a result of harsh police action but also through ideological division and uncertainty, the freshly Sovietised Cuba established easier relationships with the various sectors of the American black movement. The perfect intermediary was Angela Davis, an attractive and intelligent black American communist, much fêted when she came to Cuba in October 1972. Educated as a Marxist philosopher at Brandeis university and later in Frankfurt, Davis was a member of the Che-Lumumba Club of the US Communist Party, and hostile to the putschist tactics of the Black Panthers. Her reception by Cuban blacks at a mass rally was so enthusiastic that she was barely able to speak. Carlos Moore described the extraordinary impact that she made, not so much by what she said, as by her presentation as a role-model for Cuba's blacks:

> Starved as they had been for over a decade for positive symbols of self-identity, black Cubans had reacted to Angela Davis's beautiful, unstraightened 'Afro' hair. Here was someone everyone could identify with, without fearing being tagged as 'counter-revolutionary', or as a 'black racist'. Angela Davis was a Communist, a heroine, a 'runaway' Negress, approved of by Cuba. She wore a lovely, 'loud'-coloured, tight-fitting dress, and did not straighten her hair. She was black. She was defiant. She was revolutionary. She was beautiful, in a sense that Afro-Cubans understood in their secret code of blackness.[106]

If Davis's visit marked a milestone in white Cuba's long struggle to come to terms with the island's black population, it also marked the beginning of a more relaxed attitude by American blacks towards the Revolution. The fact that Cuba was a Mecca for African heads of state inevitably aroused interest among US blacks, and throughout the 1970s a stream of prominent African-American cultural figures visited the island – including Sidney Poitier and Harry Belafonte.

Yet old ways took time to change, and black Cubans took time to adjust to the agenda of North American blacks. The novelist Alice Walker, who came to Havana in 1977, was saddened to find that young Cubans took no special pride in being black. 'The more we insisted on calling ourselves black Americans,' she wrote, 'the more distant and confused they grew.' She had the impression that Huey Newton was still the only black man with an Afro in Havana.[107]

Although interested in US blacks, the Revolution had little to do with the burgeoning black power movement in the Caribbean. Several Caribbean intellectuals visited Cuba in the late 1960s, and wrote about their experience, but none related the Cuban process with anything that might prove possible elsewhere in the Caribbean at that time. Riots exploded in Jamaica in 1968 when the Guyanese-born historian Walter Rodney was expelled, and the rioting spread into the shanty towns of the city. Yet Cubans showed little interest in the question of black power in the islands of the Caribbean, and the internecine rivalries that it provoked, until the revolution in Grenada years later, in March 1979, when Castro took a personal interest in Maurice Bishop, its ill-fated leader.

Exporting the Revolution: Che Guevara's expedition to Bolivia, 1966–1967

The Tricontinental Conference held in Havana in January 1966 marked the high tide of Cuba's advocacy of guerrilla struggle and the notion of Revolution for export. An impressive range of delegations had arrived from all over the world, and Castro, with his eternal emphasis on the need for revolutionary unity, had even invited those groups attracted by the siren calls of Maoism, although he had made a point of criticising China's hostile attitude towards Cuba.

An unseen presence at the conference, though not himself in Havana, was Che Guevara, the acknowledged prophet of revolution. Still recovering in Dar es Salaam from the disastrous Congolese venture, he was writing his memoir of the expedition, though not for long. The Cuban Revolution still had need of his services, and a metaphorical pin had been stuck into the map of Latin America – in the central and landlocked Republic of Bolivia – a place perceived as the epicentre of a potential new revolutionary wave.

Bolivia had already received Cuban attention in 1963, when Masetti's group had launched their Argentine venture from a farm in its south-eastern corner. It had provided the launch pad for a Cuban-backed guerrilla group, led by Hector Béjar, that headed into Peru in the same year. Now Bolivia was again the focus for Cuba's hopes of continental revolution. Several young members of the Bolivian Communist Party had arrived for military training towards the end of 1965, and 'Tania', a Cuban intelligence agent, had been stationed in La Paz since the previous year.

Guevara returned secretly to Havana in July 1966 and selected a small group of Cuban troops for his new mission. Some he had known since the Cuban guerrilla campaign, others had fought with him in the Congo. Some were survivors of Masetti's debacle, notably Martínez Tamayo. The enterprise had the tentative support of the Bolivian Communist Party and a group from the youth movement, led by Roberto 'Coco' Peredo, had bought a small farm in eastern Bolivia, along the rugged banks of the river Ñancahuazú. Guevara arrived there in November.[108]

For several months, the embryonic 'foco' survived undetected in the foothills of the Andes, but it faced a serious political problem from the start. Castro's continuing arguments with the old Communists in Cuba, and with the Soviet leadership in Moscow, now came to dominate the Cuban expedition to Bolivia. Mario Monje, the leader of the Bolivian Communist Party, had initially agreed to the Cuban project, partly because he thought it was directed at promoting guerrilla movements in Argentina and Peru, as in earlier years. He preferred the peaceful road for his own country. Elections had been held in Bolivia that year, albeit to ratify a military coup in 1964, but the

Communist Party had been allowed to participate and had secured a creditable, though minuscule vote. Monje told Guevara in December, when he visited the guerrilla camp, that if there was now to be a guerrilla war in Bolivia, he should clearly be the commander. The idea was absurd, and Monje knew that he would meet a refusal. After his experience in the Congo, Guevara would tolerate no debate about who should be in charge. Monje retreated from the camp and his Party offered no further assistance. Only the handful of individual young Bolivian Communists, who had already expressed their loyalty to Guevara, remained with him.

Guevara was now marooned in the Bolivian bush with no visible means of support, except for 16 Cubans, 3 Peruvians and 29 Bolivians. Castro had been faced with a similar paucity of numbers when he first retreated with the survivors of the *Granma* landing into the Sierra Maestra, but at least he had had an embryonic resistance movement in the towns of Cuba. Guevara had nothing, and even his communications with Havana depended on wireless technology that was rudimentary, inefficient and heavy to handle.

While Guevara was in Bolivia, the mood in Cuba was changing. Absent since 1965, he was no longer a key player in the councils of the Revolution. Although his advocacy of guerrilla struggle in Latin America, and his personal involvement in the Cuban campaign in Bolivia, had received the solid support of the revolutionary high command in Havana, he had not been without his critics. The Soviet Union, and its supporters within the old Cuban Communist Party, were notably hostile. Castro had been riding two horses at once for some years, actively backing Guevara's guerrilla projects and stretching out a hand to the Soviet Union. Since the horses were galloping off in very different directions, the acrobatic act could not have been indefinitely sustained.

A Soviet warning was delivered to Havana in the middle of 1967 when Aleksei Kosygin, the Soviet premier, paid a surprise visit. The dour and uncharismatic Russian arrived in June, just as the Cubans were preparing for the first conference of the Organisation of Latin American Solidarity (OLAS), a gathering of paid-up supporters of Cuba's strategy of armed struggle. Guevara's presence in Bolivia was by then an open secret, and his final great polemic, 'Create Two, Three, Many Vietnams', in which he expressed his expectation that the struggle in 'our America' would soon achieve 'continental proportions', had just been published. In a splendid peroration, he had written his personal requiem:

> Our every action is a battle cry against imperialism, and a battle hymn for the people's unity against the great enemy of mankind: the United States of America. Wherever death may surprise us, let it be welcome, provided that this, our battle cry, may have reached some receptive ear, and another hand may be extended to wield our weapons and other men be ready to intone

the funeral dirge with the staccato singing of the machine-guns, and new battle cries of war and victory.[109]

Guevara's hymn, intoxicating to the cohorts of the Latin American left, was harsh music to the ears of the Soviet premier, fresh from a visit to President Johnson in the United States, where the leaders of the two superpowers had been singing songs of peaceful co-existence. In Soviet eyes, the world was too dangerous a place to be disrupted by unstable visionaries promoting revolution. Kosygin travelled to Havana to wag a powerful Soviet finger at its recalcitrant Caribbean ally, giving due warning that Soviet economic assistance, notably the oil lifeline, might dry up if Cuba were to continue exporting revolution to Latin America. Castro heard the message, and it sank in, though he could take no immediate action. He was waiting for news from Bolivia.

When the OLAS meeting assembled in July, under its inflammatory banners – 'The Duty of Every Revolutionary is to Make the Revolution' – Castro reiterated his familiar themes, and was cheered to the echo. He kept to the line established a few months earlier, when a Cuban guerrilla contingent had been captured on a Venezuelan beach: 'We are lending assistance, and we shall continue to do so as often as we are asked, to all movements that are struggling against imperialism in whatever part of the world.'

Yet the Kosygin visit had cast a chill over the proceedings. If Washington and the Soviet Union were to get together, if the two superpowers were to act in concert, what chance did a small country like Cuba have to plough a separate furrow?

In the perspective of history, Cuba's guerrilla war in Bolivia in 1967 appears as a tragedy foretold. Discovered by the army in March, and accidentally divided into two small groups in April, Guevara's guerrilla bands wandered aimlessly through the flooded lands of eastern Bolivia, each one crossing and re-crossing the Rio Grande in a vain attempt to reunite. One group was betrayed in August as it tried to cross the river and annihilated, while Guevara's platoon was surrounded by Bolivian troops in October. Guevara himself was wounded and captured, and executed the following day. A handful of Cuban fighters survived, and made their way across the country to safety in neighbouring Chile early in the following year.

The collapse of the Bolivian expedition led to a change in Cuban policy. Castro now felt obliged to obey Kosygin's request to abandon the strategy of armed struggle. The dream of reviving the ambitions of Simón Bolívar, and sparking a continental revolution, finally drew to a close. The strategy had already begun to look threadbare long before October 1967. None of the Cuban-backed movements in Argentina, Venezuela, Colombia, Guatemala and Peru – operating for the most part without the support of the local Communist parties – had shown signs of success. Some had already been destroyed. Only Guevara's personal charisma, and the hope that the great guerrilla theorist and warrior could triumph where others had failed, kept faith alive in the possibility of a favourable outcome to the Bolivian struggle. Now he was gone.

With his death, a new realism dawned in Havana. Latin American guerrillas in training in Cuba found themselves inexplicably put on hold. They did not understand that Castro, after a decent interval, was looking for an opportunity to abandon them. Guerrilla struggle in Latin America was off the Cuban menu.[110]

Guevara wrote his own epitaph in a farewell letter to his parents before setting off for the Congo in March 1965: 'Once again I feel under my heels the ribs of Rocinante. I return to the trail with my shield on my arm.'

Rocinante was Don Quixote's horse, and Guevara imagined himself as a twentieth-century Don Quixote. Many will call me an adventurer, he wrote, 'and indeed I am', but he saw himself as an adventurer of an unusual type, to be counted among those 'who put their lives on the line to demonstrate their truths'. Therein lay his lasting appeal, a man who participated in one successful revolution and threw it all up to start again from scratch.

Inside the Soviet camp, 1968–1985

The Prague Spring, and the decisive turn to the Soviet Union, 1968

The defeat of the Cuban expedition to Bolivia in 1967, and the death of Guevara, marked a new stage in the development of the Revolution. Its history was to unroll over the next 20 years in close alliance with the Soviet Union – in foreign affairs, economic policy, cultural matters and the very structure of government. Cuba was to subject itself to a make-over in the Soviet image.

The moment of decision came the following year, in August 1968, when Warsaw Pact forces led by the Soviet Union invaded Czechoslovakia and established a new pro-Soviet government in Prague. Many Cubans, including several close to Castro, assumed that such an intervention would provoke Cuban hostility and criticism. They were in for a rude surprise.

All over the world 1968 was a pivotal year, from Vietnam to the United States, from France to Mexico, and from Czechoslovakia to Cuba. The 'Tet offensive' in Vietnam at the end of January, in which tens of thousands of Vietnamese troops attacked American bases throughout South Vietnam, provoked demonstrations throughout the United States. A seismic shift occurred in US public opinion, which now grew hostile to the war. Lyndon Johnson announced in March that he would not stand again as president and peace talks with the Vietnamese Communists began in Paris. The gathering sense of the United States as a society in crisis was accentuated by the assassination of Martin Luther King Jr. in April, followed by rioting in several American cities and the deaths of many black demonstrators. Robert Kennedy, a Democratic presidential candidate, was assassinated in Los Angeles in June.

In France an explosion of student unrest in May resulted in the occupation of the Sorbonne. The 'Paris events', a youth rebellion that spread to universities all over the world, echoed the militancy of Mao Tse-tung's Cultural

Revolution that had broken out in China two years earlier. Hundreds of students were killed in Mexico City in September, during a police attack against a demonstration before the opening of the Olympic Games. These revolts had specific local causes, but opposition to America's war on Vietnam was a common theme, as was support for Castro and the Cuban Revolution and for Alexander Dubček and the 'Prague Spring'. Photographs of Guevara were a notable presence in all the student demonstrations of 1968. Korda's snapshot of the guerrilla commander in a beret became an iconic image of protest on a global scale.

Castro's initial contribution to this revolutionary euphoria was to expand the activity of the state. In March he crushed the 'counter-revolutionary' remnants of the Cuban private sector, small in economic weight but large in terms of the number of people employed. The time had come, he said, to deal with that 'small segment of the population that lives off the work of others, living considerably better than the rest, sitting idly by and looking on while others do the work; lazy persons in perfect physical condition who set up some kind of vending stand, any kind of small business, in order to make fifty pesos a day'. These parasites had to go, and the full fury of the Revolution was unleashed on small commercial enterprises. 'Thousands of party members secretly on alert throughout the country spread out to confiscate all private businesses', according to the account of José Luis Llovio-Menéndez. The measure affected 'bars, groceries, garages, small stores, the shops of self-employed artisans and other independent workers, from carpenters to masons to plumbers'. Two days later, not a single private business was operating in Cuba 'except for the few remaining private farmers, the owners of freight trucks, and cab drivers'.[1] For those like Llovio-Menéndez, contemplating exile, the crackdown heralded a new era: 'Life in Cuba became only duller and more onerous without the amenity of the occasional bottle of beer or cocktail, the convenience of a corner laundry, the expert assistance of the self-employed handyman, or the casual availability of *croquettes*, *pan con tortilla*, and cold drinks from street peddlers.'[2]

Revolutionaries, of course, believed that the counter-revolutionaries who operated in Havana's café culture had finally been dealt a death blow, but it was a high price to pay. Some 30 years were to pass before the country recovered some of the bourgeois vivacity created by small-scale private enterprise.

Elsewhere, the belief of the world's students that the old politics were being visibly undermined was heightened by developments in Czechoslovakia, widely perceived as a signal of possible changes in the rest of the Soviet bloc. Antonin Novotny, the old Stalinist leader, was voted out in January and replaced by Alexander Dubček, a more youthful figure who began promoting a 'socialist democratic revolution'. An 'action programme' published in April declared that socialism could not be constructed without 'an open exchange of views, and democratisation of the entire social and political system'.

Outsiders referred to the process as 'the Prague Spring', and described Dubček's project as 'socialism with a human face'.

The world watched with fascination as the Czechs struggled to secure a measure of internal freedom. Communist states in Europe with anti-Soviet leaders – President Tito of Yugoslavia and President Ceauşescu of Romania – gave support to the Czech Communists. In the other countries of eastern Europe, and in Cuba, the details of the process were followed with intense interest, as the Soviet Union put pressure on the Dubček government to change course. Would there be a repeat of the Hungarian tragedy of 1956, when Khrushchev feared the loss of a satellite to the West and felt obliged to intervene? Or would Russia's leaders, this time, allow their Czechoslovak ally a measure of autonomy?

The brutal answer came in the morning of 21 August, when Soviet troops moved across their border into Czechoslovakia through the hills of Ruthenia. With them came an army of half a million, with soldiers from Poland, Hungary, East Germany and Bulgaria. Several hundred Soviet tanks were deployed in the streets of Prague. Dubček and other Czech leaders were arrested and taken to Moscow. The 'Prague Spring' turned to winter overnight.

In Cuba a long silence ensued while Castro decided what to say. No revelations emerged, even years later, about the internal debate within the Cuban leadership. Most Cubans imagined, given the euphoria the Czech struggle had sparked around the world, that Castro would reiterate the Revolution's traditionally independent line and condemn the Soviet invasion. Had not Che Guevara, whose ideas were so fondly remembered in the emotional months since his death, been a trenchant critic of the Soviet model?

Two days after the Russians drove into Prague, Castro finally appeared on television. To the amazement of his listeners at home and abroad he spoke out in strong support of the Soviet action, coupling his message with a powerful indictment of the Dubček reforms:

> A real liberal fury was unleashed; a whole series of political slogans in favour of the formation of opposition parties began to develop ... [suggesting] that the reins of power should cease to be in the hands of the Communist party ... Certain measures were taken, such as the establishment of a bourgeois form of 'freedom' of the press. This meant that the counter-revolution and the exploiters, the very enemies of socialism, were granted the right to speak and write freely against socialism.[3]

Castro was addressing his local audience and had little concern with outside opinion. He had drunk deeply at the well of Soviet orthodoxy and made his choice. Cuba would take a similar, though less outspoken, stand a decade later, in support of the Soviet invasion of Afghanistan in 1979. There was to be no third way for Cuba, no alternative version of communism. Cuba from now on was to be an irreproachable Soviet supporter, and would reconstruct its society in the Soviet mould. It would take time, and not until the middle of the 1970s did Cuba achieve the status of a recognisably orthodox Soviet satellite, but the path had been chosen.

Castro was convinced of the importance of Soviet strategic power, and a believer in the strength of its institutions – until the Soviet Union vanished suddenly in 1991. He came to believe that a disciplined Communist Party in Cuba was a necessity, and even when the Soviet Union disappeared he continued to insist on the importance of a single party. Yet something of the old sense of independence remained. Castro dutifully took his Soviet medicine, yet he often claimed that the Cuban recipe for socialism was an improvement on the Soviet model. He considered that Cuba was more adept at supporting Third World revolutions than its Soviet mentor.

Castro had tried to go it alone in the 1960s. Cuba was not a fully Sovietised society during its first revolutionary decade. The country benefited from Soviet assistance in many areas, but it persevered with its home-brewed programme. Yet by 1968 Castro's regime was intellectually bankrupt and he fell gratefully into the Soviets' warm embrace. The attraction of the alliance with the Soviet Union was not so much the armaments, and the military guarantees that came in their train, as the ideological blueprint that the Soviet and East European experience provided them with.

A large percentage of Cuba's population had happily backed a dramatic break with the past in 1959, but the ideas behind the revolutionary programme were never spelt out clearly, nor did they seem to be the most important factor in mobilising people to support the Revolution. Much of the ideology came from Castro himself, a charismatic 'populist' leader well versed in articulating ideas and motivating people. Important in the unfolding of the revolutionary process was his sense of history, his ability to pull out the more radical skeins from Cuba's historical fabric, and to weave them into a fresh account of the past that emphasised Cuba's 'imagined community' as an independent and prosperous nation. His 'History Will Absolve Me' speech of 1953 was a crucial intervention, highlighting the future changes in politics and society that would be necessary, and hinting implicitly that such changes would only be possible outside the existing capitalist system.

The guerrilla leadership spent time on military strategy and tactics, but it never gave much thought to the nature of a future government beyond the tactical demands of the moment. The theoreticians of the July 26 Movement in the cities produced plans and blueprints that were frequently disavowed by the leadership in the hills. Beyond the outlines of a moderate reformist programme, involving land tenure, education and improved conditions for the workers, little had been sketched in.

Once in power in 1959 the July 26 Movement was less than prepared for government. It controlled the country, but with little idea of what might come next. A vague and literally half-baked ideology, derived from Castro's published speeches and articles, was of little use. A vacuum existed where there should have been a political philosophy.

In the circumstances it was not surprising that Castro and his closest colleagues should have chosen to ally themselves eventually with the local Communist Party and with the Soviet Union. They needed to do so for obvious strategic reasons – the United States was only 90 miles away, and the example of the US intervention in Guatemala in 1954 was ever-present in their minds. Soviet military support was essential.

Yet was it really necessary for Castro to purchase the entire Soviet package, lock, stock and barrel? He had never been a traditional Communist himself, he owed nothing to the old Communist Party and he was rapidly making friends with radical, non-Communist regimes in the embryonic Third World. Many of these, while happy to be fellow-travelling with the Russians as the most sympathetic of the two superpowers, did not subscribe to the Soviet Union's version of socialism. Castro had gone beyond the simple nationalism of Nasser's Egypt or Nkrumah's Ghana, but might he not have followed the independent trail blazed by Tito in Yugoslavia and later by Ceauşescu in Romania?

He did not choose to do so, nor does he seem to have even considered the possibility. The reason can be found precisely in his Movement's lack of ideology. When the Cuban revolutionaries came to run the country they were at a loss. They were essentially pragmatic. First they tried one thing, then another: they imported foreign economists; they tried import-substitution; they sought diversification; they nationalised everything in sight; they listened to the siren songs of those suggesting economic autarchy. Finally they turned to the Soviet Union, the source of innumerable advisers, much fresh technology and seemingly limitless amounts of cash. The Russians had run a revolution for half a century. They were the experts. They knew the answers. The attempt to find an alternative way forward was a chimaera. Dubček had got it wrong.

Castro's denunciation of the Czech reformers was followed by a clampdown on the open-minded political debate that had existed in Cuba in the early years, much influenced by radical currents in the American and West European left. Soviet orthodoxy would gradually impose itself during the 1970s and many independent-minded intellectuals who had not already taken the chance to leave began to seek exit visas. A steady haemorrhage of talent was soon under way. Cuba would recover its particular strengths in art and music in the 1990s, but its high reputation in literature and drama was lost for the duration.

Castro's attack on the Prague Spring was the final straw for many external supporters of the Revolution. West European liberals, and socialists in France and Italy, began to distance themselves from their earlier encomiums. Castro's solidarity with Moscow was also a blow for Trotskyists, the supporters of the anti-Stalinist tradition of Communism. Many of them in the United States had been supporters of the Fair Play for Cuba Committee that championed the Revolution as a socialist alternative to Soviet-style communism. Coming as it did during a year of political upheaval in the United States and rebellious fervour in Western Europe – a reminder of 1848 when established regimes felt the chill wind of revolution blowing through their palaces – Castro's speech appeared to many of his former supporters as an attempt to douse popular radicalism. More measured, even hostile, critiques of the Revolution began to appear abroad, where once there had been nothing but praise and adulation.

'Ten million tons': the failure of the sugar target of 1970

One last episode of the revolutionary spontaneity that had characterised Castro's first decade in power took place in the early months of 1970. In a final flight of fancy before the grey evening of Soviet economic orthodoxy closed in, Castro sought to defeat the laws of nature and economics by producing a miracle in the cane fields. *Los diez millones van!* was the slogan that electrified the nation. Yes, we shall bring in a 10 million-ton sugar harvest!

Sugar production had returned to its traditional place at the heart of the economy after Castro's first visit to the Soviet Union in 1963. Earlier utopian debates about possible diversification, favoured both by Guevara and less radical revolutionaries, were rapidly brought to a close. Soviet economic wisdom dictated that sugar was the principal crop with which Cuba had a comparative advantage in the world market and that the income it provided was the best way to pay the country's import bills. Capitalist economists had long since embraced the same conclusion. Cuba would be dependent on sugar for the foreseeable future – for just 30 more years as it turned out.

Sugar was the only Cuban product that its new friend and ally actually wanted for its own consumers, and the island was soon producing more than ever before. Sugar production grew by 40 per cent from 1960 to 1990, by which time sugarcane had come to occupy 45 per cent of Cuba's arable land – a vast expanse that should perhaps have been growing food for the Cuban consumer, though such arguments lay in the future. The sugar industry was also a large employer with 235,000 people working on the agricultural side of production at the end of the 1980s, and 140,000 on the industrial side.

Under a follow-up deal in 1966 Cuba agreed to provide a regular supply of raw sugar to the Russians in the years ahead – 5 million tons in both 1968 and 1969. Cuba had a guaranteed market and a guaranteed price, much as it had had with the United States before the Revolution, although the terms were now more favourable. An ambitious investment programme to modernise the industry was soon under way, with Soviet assistance. The existing mills, some built in the nineteenth century, were antiquated and needed attention. Cane-cutting was still done with machetes and would benefit from the introduction of machinery. The railway system that moved the cane was in serious disrepair. Ports to harbour the ships arriving from the Soviet Union needed enlargement and modernisation. Existing warehouse facilities were wholly inadequate. Cuba had dealt almost exclusively with small American coastal traders before 1959; now it needed room to store the imports that flowed in from the other side of the globe.

Yet however large the investment, an increase in sugar production was bound to be slow. Cuba was unable to deliver the amounts that the Soviet agreement had specified. The harvests of 1968 and 1969 produced only 3.7 million tons. Castro, still in ultra-revolutionary mode, was dissatisfied and thought the country could do better. Plucking a round number from the air, he proclaimed a fresh and more ambitious target for 1970. A 10 million-ton harvest was to be the country's aim, a figure that had never been achieved before.

If such a target could be attained, Castro argued, Cuba's economic problems would be at an end. The Russians would purchase the agreed figure of 5 million tons, at a premium price above that of the world market. A further 2 million would be offered for sale on the world market, at the world price, and the remainder would be sold on the domestic market or mopped up by other socialist countries. Everyone would be happy.

The round number caught the public imagination, as doubtless it was intended to do, and the country was shaken up as it had been in the early years of the Revolution. The 'battle for sugar' took place during the harvest months between November 1969 and July 1970. The Party, the trade unions, the military, bureaucrats, students and schoolchildren – everyone was mobilised to secure the target. Holidays were abandoned, Christmas abolished, schedules disrupted. The efforts of the entire country were directed towards the sugar plantations and the cane was harvested in the chaotic, holiday atmosphere of carnival.

Yet it was soon evident in the early weeks of 1970 that the target would not be achieved. Many outside observers had thought it over-ambitious from the start. Jeremiads had been voiced from within the government, notably by some of the old Communists whose disquiet echoed that of Cuba's Soviet patron. Some were already arguing in 1968, when the idea was first mooted, that it was an impracticable ambition, declaring that 'to judge by the present size of our sugar-cane crop, the years that remain, and the difficulties we have met, it will be almost impossible to reach 10 million tons by 1970'.[4] Castro took no notice. When Oswaldo Borrego, the sugar minister and an old comrade of Guevara's, suggested gently that to achieve the target might not be possible, he was accused of faint-heartedness and dismissed from his job.

The final figure for the harvest was in fact a major achievement. At 8.5 million tons it would have been a highly creditable result in any other year. Yet given the great propaganda build-up with which it had been invested it was a severe disappointment. No amount of work in the cane fields, no amount of willing labour by volunteers, could make up for poor organisation – in transport, communications and timetables. Not only did the great mobilisation fail to produce the required amount of sugar it was also detrimental to the rest of the economy as other branches of production suffered considerable disruption.

The following year's figure, 5.9 million tons, although not brilliant was perfectly respectable and sugar production settled down to a more regular rhythm in the 1970s. It accounted for three-quarters of Cuba's foreign currency earnings throughout the decade. The Soviet quota provided Cuba with its bread and butter, while sugar sold elsewhere brought in much-needed dollars.[5] Sugar exports to Western markets earned between $200 and $350 million a year during most of the 1970s, but a huge hike in the world price in 1974 and 1975 increased Cuba's earnings to around $800 million for 1974 and $1,200 million for 1975 – something of an *annus mirabilis*.[6]

The return to sugar remained a subject of much debate. Some economists believed, as Guevara had done, that it was a historic error. Others concluded that the forced redirection of Cuba's sugar trade from the US to the Soviet Union gave the island 'an historical reprieve' by substituting an expanding export market for a shrinking one.[7] Only when the Soviet Union itself collapsed in 1991 were the Cubans obliged to rethink their strategy, substituting tourism for sugar production.

Everyone agreed that the attempt to secure 10 million tons had been a mistake for which the responsibility was Castro's alone. He had mobilised the population to achieve what became a personal project and it had proved impossible. Yet his economic policy-makers had gone along with the scheme. A decade after the Revolution, they appeared as bankrupt of ideas as their political counterparts. Many experiments had been made, but little had come right. Several significant social advances had been secured for the poorest section of society – in health, education and housing – but a vacuum still remained at the heart of government where an economic policy should have been. Production was blighted, the economy was stagnant and uncertainty prevailed about the direction in which the country should go.

Castro now turned the economy over to a new team of Soviet advisers, backed up by some of the old Cuban Communists who had long been out of favour. The political turn signalled by the attack on the Czech reformists was followed by an economic turn in 1972, when Cuba joined Comecon, the Council for Mutual Economic Assistance, the economic union of Communist countries that controlled the multifarious trading relationships between the Soviet Union's closest allies. Cuba was formally enrolled as a member of the

Soviet camp, and for more than a decade the country reaped the benefit of this relationship. Only years later, in the mid 1980s, did its advantages begin to seem less obvious.

'The Brezhnev Years': restructuring the country in the Soviet image, 1972–1982

The task of reorganising the Cuban economy in the 1970s took time, and much of the work occurred behind the scenes. Its course was punctuated by many Cuban trips to Moscow and innumerable visits to Havana by Soviet advisers. Their presence became increasingly noticeable in the summer of 1971, with 'perhaps as many as ten thousand' Russians to be seen in the city, according to Robert Quirk's estimate. 'Small boys on the street learned to say *tovarich* and begged in Russian for Chiclets and ballpoint pens.'[8] Advisers worked closely with managers of factories producing goods for export and attended meetings to help introduce Soviet methods into the planning process. The dominant role of English in Cuba's business discourse between 1902 and 1959 subsided.

Kosygin returned to Havana in November 1971, on a friendlier visit than in 1967. Castro was now safely ensconced within the Soviet camp, the Soviet oil lifeline was flowing smoothly and Soviet weapons were arriving by the regular shipload. A visit earlier that year from Marshal Andrei Grechko, the Soviet defence minister, was followed by a large shipment of military equipment, including surface-to-air missiles. Kosygin and Castro travelled together through Cuba for a few days, looking at factories and agricultural projects. 'Socialism is winning,' said the Soviet leader in an optimistic mood.

Castro spent two months in 1972 on an extensive tour of Eastern Europe, preparing for the country's entry into Comecon and meeting his new trading partners in Bulgaria, Romania, Hungary, Poland, Czechoslovakia and East Germany. He was fêted by Leonid Brezhnev and Kosygin in Moscow in June, and Cuba was formally admitted as a Comecon member in July. He returned to Moscow in December, to sign a 15-year economic agreement with Brezhnev that Soviet and Cuban economists had been working on throughout the year. This provided for a substantial increase in the Soviet subsidy to the economy and was described by Castro in glowing terms as 'a model of truly fraternal, internationalist, and revolutionary relations', as indeed it was. The Russians agreed to increase the price they paid for Cuban sugar; all debt repayments were to be deferred for 15 years (to be repaid subsequently over 25 years without interest); and fresh credits for capital investment ($350 million over the next three years) would be available at low interest rates. The Kremlin, Castro admitted honestly and gratefully, had 'worked out most of the ideas'.[9] No one could have foreseen that Mikhail Gorbachev would be in power in the

Soviet Union 15 years later, at the moment when the Cuban debt would have to be repaid.

With the assistance of the Soviet advisers, the government created solid institutions of economic planning. The first five-year-plan under the new system was introduced in 1976, with the industrialisation of the country as its declared aim. Its chief Cuban architect was Humberto Pérez, a Moscow-trained economist who would remain in charge of economic strategy for the next ten years, running Juceplan, the Central Planning Board.[10] Cuba's new planning system, the SDPE (Sistema de Dirección y Planificación de la Economía), was modelled on the reforms introduced into the Soviet Union in the previous decade. Its aim was to help state enterprises to become self-financing, to introduce the notions of profit and incentives and to promote decentralisation and efficiency.[11]

Over a 10-year period, from 1975 to 1985, the Revolution entered the sunny uplands of economic growth. The annual rate of growth between 1970 and 1988 was 4.1 per cent, with a significant improvement in the early 1980s. The comparable figure for Latin America was a meagre 1.2 per cent.[12] The Cuban population began to appreciate the improvement.

The Soviet advisers had an additional task, to assist in the creation of new political institutions. The Revolution had been controlled for more than a decade in an improvised and haphazard manner by Castro and a handful of friends. The 10-million ton fiasco showed how necessary it was to take decision-making out of the hands of one man. The Revolution needed a more formally democratic theatre through which the will of the people could, at least in theory, be institutionally enshrined. The embryonic Communist Party needed to be larger and more representative. The country deserved a proper constitution.

The first reform affected the Council of Ministers, which was provided in 1972 with a powerful executive committee of eight members. The three most trusted members of the existing leadership were charged with ironing out problems with the Soviet ally: Raúl Castro's task was to maintain close relations with the Soviet military, a job at which he had already proved himself to be more than capable; Osvaldo Dorticós was appointed to look after planning and trade; while Carlos Rafael Rodríguez would handle foreign affairs. All three made regular visits to Moscow and the capitals of Eastern Europe.

The second reform involved the writing of a new constitution and the development of a system of popular participation in government. A committee was set up under Blas Roca to prepare the draft of a new constitution that was sent out for public discussion in Party cells as well as in factories and farms. While the constitution sought to codify the structure of a new legal system it also mapped out fresh arrangements for a form of democratic decision-making. *Poder popular*, or people's power, envisaged a three-tier system of municipal, provincial and national assemblies. Although based on the Soviet system it had a number of Cuban particularities.

The third reform affected the Communist Party itself. Efforts had been made over the years to construct a political party that would group the movements that originally supported the Revolution, resulting in an idiosyncratic organisation that called itself 'the Cuban Communist Party' created in the 1960s. This party was now organised on more orthodox Soviet lines. Its first congress was inaugurated in December 1975 with a speech by Castro in which, in the presence of representatives of Communist parties from all over the world, he admitted that the Revolution had

> failed to take advantage of the rich experience of other peoples who had undertaken the construction of socialism before we had . . . Had we been humbler, had we not over-estimated ourselves, we would have been able to understand that revolutionary theory was not sufficiently developed in our country . . . to make any really significant contribution to the theory and practice of socialist construction.[13]

A year later, in December 1976, everything was in place for the first meeting of the National Assembly, the apex of the system of People's Power. Castro formally announced the start of a new era:

> At this moment, the Revolutionary Government transfers to the National Assembly the power it has exercised up until today. In this way, the Council of Ministers places in the hands of this Assembly the constituent and legislative functions which it exercised for almost 18 years, which is the period of the most radical and profound political and social transformations in the life of our fatherland. Let history judge this era objectively.

After years of revolutionary turbulence, Cuba was now a well-established, well-organised and well-armed Communist state. Few people, not even members of the old Communist Party, had imagined such an outcome in 1959. The decade after 1976 was to be remembered warmly by many Cubans as 'the Brezhnev years'. Few other countries have celebrated the rule of the grey and increasingly geriatric Soviet leader, whose palsied hand controlled the fate of the Soviet Union and Eastern Europe for nearly two decades. Yet the Soviet relationship in the days of Brezhnev, who died in 1982, suited Cuba quite well, providing almost unlimited funds and few political shocks, in a manner reminiscent of the old Spanish empire in its better moments. The money went to the armed forces and to the island's education and health programmes, but it also produced rising living standards and a more general availability of consumer goods.

Other revolutions had been less fortunate. Twenty-five years after the French Revolution, the revolutionaries were mostly gone to early graves, while Napoleon, their heir, was about to be defeated at Waterloo. The Russian revolutionaries suffered a similar fate in the same time span, and the survivors of Stalin's purges, 25 years after the Russian Revolution, were in the midst of a genocidal war inflicted on them by Nazi Germany. By contrast, the Cuban Revolution had remained remarkably peaceful; it surrendered to the Soviet empire, but unlike the French Revolution, in the remark attributed to the Girondist Pierre Vergniand, it did not devour its own children.

Opposition to the Soviet line, at home and abroad, 1968–1972

Not everyone was content with Castro's definitive turn to the Soviet Union at the end of the 1960s. Many external supporters of the Revolution, once attracted by its originality and spontaneity, deplored its descent into Soviet orthodoxy. Many Cuban intellectuals were also led to protest, and suffered for their opposition. The most famous case, and the one given most publicity at the time since no one quite understood the rules of the game, was that of Heberto Padilla, a provocative writer and poet who disliked the pro-Soviet trend – and was led to court political martyrdom.

Like many of the Cuban intellectuals prominent during the first decade of the Revolution, Padilla was of middle-class origin and spent several years as a young adult in the United States. Later, as a worldly cosmopolitan and an enthusiastic supporter of the Revolution, he had enjoyed a reasonably privileged life. He had worked in London for *Prensa Latina* and served in Cuba's embassies in Moscow and Prague. He came to dislike what he perceived as the hypocrisy of the Soviet system and, returning to Havana in 1967, he made no secret of his disappointment that Cuba seemed likely to construct its society on a similar model. Some of his contemporaries had already chosen exile – Carlos Franqui, the former editor of *Revolución*, had left in 1964; Guillermo Cabrera Infante, Cuba's wittiest writer, in 1965. Others had chosen a quiet life, accepting the Revolution's framework for artistic activity. Padilla also stayed behind, but he went on the attack. His poems were imbued with the idea, common in the West but anathema in Cuba at the end of the 1960s, that an artist should be a free spirit, independent of politics.

The Revolution's attitude towards culture had been laid down by Castro in a speech to a group of artists and writers and assorted intellectuals delivered in June 1961. There would be creative freedom in Cuba 'within the Revolution', he declared, but nothing would be permitted 'against the Revolution'.

Most supporters of the Revolution accepted the rubric at the time. The country had been under attack, war still threatened and elementary patriotism demanded a degree of restraint, affecting the normal rules of artistic licence. While some writers chose exile, most of the intellectuals who returned to Havana to serve the Revolution in 1959 had remained there, happily producing their poems, novels, plays – and, most notably, their films.

Artists and film-makers flourished. The productions of ICAIC, the state film institute directed by Alfredo Guevara, were the most striking cultural creations of the Revolution. The documentaries of Santiago Alvarez became world-famous. Yet in the late 1960s, under the shadow of Soviet conformity, the cultural margins began to narrow.

In 1968 a collection of Padilla's verse, implicitly critical of the Revolution's treatment of artists, won one of the annual prizes awarded by the Casa de las Americas, a cultural institution dedicated to promoting the Revolution's pan-American mission. One poem in particular, 'Outside the Game', had a local resonance that any Cuban reader would have detected:

> The poet! Kick him out!
> He has no business here.
> He doesn't play the game.
> He never gets excited
> Or speaks out clearly.
> He never even sees the miracles
> But spends his days finding fault.

Padilla's poem was dedicated to Yannis Ritsos, a Greek Communist poet who was imprisoned in 1967 by the Greek junta, but the authorities were not fooled. Immediate and harsh criticism appeared in the pages of *Verde Olivo*, the weekly news magazine sponsored by Raúl Castro and the armed forces.[14] Battle was joined about the merits of the poem, though not for long. Padilla himself retreated to the sidelines, and he and others with a comparably independent and non-conformist position soon found their work, hitherto popular and attracting prizes, was no longer accepted for publication by the various state publishing houses.

Padilla kept in touch with visiting European writers and journalists, and the Cuban secret service kept in touch with him. As foreign press coverage of Cuba became increasingly less favourable after 1968, Padilla was fingered as an important source of hostile commentary. Arrested in March 1971 he was accused of writing counter-revolutionary poems. Many of the world's well-known writers sprang to his defence, signing a letter to *Le Monde* that expressed their 'misgivings', and called for his release. Among the signatories were Sartre and Simone de Beauvoir, Octavio Paz and Carlos Fuentes, García Márquez and Vargas Llosa, and Julio Cortázar – a formidable list of well-known supporters of the Revolution. (García Márquez and Cortázar later made their peace with Castro, and withdrew their support for the letter.)

Castro fought back. In a speech to the National Congress on Education and Culture, held in April, he attacked Cuban and foreign intellectuals for their lack of faith in the Revolution. The worst offenders – 'despicable agents of cultural imperialism' – came from Western Europe. The Congress soon echoed his words, calling for art to serve as a weapon of the Revolution:

We reject the claims of the mafia of pseudo-leftist bourgeóis intellectuals to become the critical conscience of society. They are the bearers of a new colonialism . . . agents of the metropolitan imperialist culture who have found a small group of mentally colonised people in our country who echo their ideas.[15]

The Congress condemned 'every expression of bourgeois ideology' and proclaimed that 'culture, like education, is not and cannot be apolitical or impartial'. Padilla's supporters were dismayed by the tone of the Congress. The Revolution had come a long way from the generous, open-hearted welcome offered to intellectuals of Cuba and the world, both in 1961 and again at the Cultural Congress in Havana in 1968.

Padilla was released after a month, and, to the consternation of his friends, he made a public statement of 'self-criticism'. Further fury was aroused abroad, with a fresh letter in *Le Monde* with added signatories, including Susan Sontag, the American writer, and Juan Rulfo, the Mexican novelist, which claimed that Padilla's treatment recalled the 'most sordid moments of the era of Stalinism'. Padilla was to remain in Cuba for ten years, working as a translator, and eventually left for the United States in 1981, where he published his memoirs.[16] He died in Alabama in 2000.

Cuban cultural affairs were eventually reorganised in 1976 with the creation of a ministry of culture, established along Soviet lines at the same time as the refurbished Communist Party and the National Assembly. Run by Armando Hart, an old revolutionary, the new ministry left Cuban culture open to global influences confined largely to Eastern Europe.

An opening to the mainland: Castro's visit to Allende's Chile, 1971

Outsiders disillusioned with the Revolution's close association with the Soviet Union after 1968 were able briefly to transfer their affection for Third World nationalism from Cuba to Chile. Salvador Allende, Castro's supporter and close friend, many times the presidential candidate of the Chilean Socialist Party, was elected president of Chile in September 1970. Chile became the fresh revolutionary flavour in the early 1970s and the Chilean road to socialism was soon being contrasted favourably with the Cuban way.

Castro arrived in Santiago de Chile in November 1971 to see the new regime for himself and to exchange experiences with his old friends. The Cuban Revolution was officially in favour of other revolutionary regimes on the Latin American mainland. Guerrilla movements had been promoted for precisely that purpose. Yet when victory was achieved the Cubans were invariably nervous – both with Chile in 1970 and with Nicaragua in 1979.

Chile posed a serious political problem for Castro. Allende's election victory occurred just as he had decided to take the Soviet road. Chile had a powerful, Moscow-line Communist Party, about which Castro had often made unfriendly comments. Allende's Socialist Party, however, was way to the left of the Communists, and possibly the warmest supporter of the Cuban Revolution in Latin America. Allende had been a patron of the Organisation of Latin American Solidarity, the Cuban movement supporting guerrilla struggle set up in 1967. He was not an advocate of such a strategy for Chile itself, but both he and his party supported Castro.

The problem for Castro was that he no longer supported them. As a loyal ally of Moscow, he was now closer to the Chilean Communist Party. Its leaders were keen to damp down the flames of revolution, anxious lest the Chilean revolution should get out of hand. Castro's visit to Allende was necessary and inevitable, but a serious embarrassment to both men. The existence of a Marxist competitor in the Americas, with a very different history and politics to Cuba's, was not an easy concept for Castro to absorb. Allende found Castro's presence unnerving. It irritated and inflamed the opposition to his government, only two years away from the military *coup d'état* that was to destroy his experiment with socialism and Chilean democracy for years to come.

Castro had little experience of bourgeois democracy, Chilean-style, and although he was received with enthusiasm by the supporters of Allende, half the country was not on his, or Allende's side – and said so whenever they got the chance. The Chileans expected him to come for a week, but he stayed for more than three and had a rough time as he moved through the country. Unfamiliar with student hecklers and tabloid newspapers, he was made uncomfortable by the treatment he often received. A large and hostile demonstration held in Santiago, organised by the right-wing parties, and made up largely of women from the wealthy suburbs who banged empty pots and pans – with which many of them were surely unfamiliar – to indicate that socialism was a harbinger of hunger. 'We don't want Castro here' was the least offensive of their slogans.

The march produced an inevitable reaction from Allende's supporters: the workers would not permit 'the fascist hordes to control the streets again', said the Communist leader of the trade union movement. The night ended with rioting, and the imposition of a state of emergency in the city. Order was restored by General Augusto Pinochet, the officer in charge of the emergency zone.

Castro was left with a pessimistic view of Chile's future. Pleased by his reception in working-class areas, he could not understand Allende's reluctance to arm the workers, little realising the limitations of the president's power. Castro was reported to have said when he got back to Havana that he considered Allende 'very stubborn' and living 'in a world that is too full of illusion and poetry. He is tied to his constitutional ideas. He trusts in the impartiality of the military. And he is certain that they will always defend the legitimate government.'[17]

Castro was not convinced that this would happen. 'They'll try to screw him the first chance they get,' he said, and General Pinochet took his chance less than two years later, on 11 September 1973.

Castro stopped in Lima on his way home, intrigued by a different phenomenon. He visited General Juan Velasco, the radical president of Peru who had staged a coup three years earlier and then gone on to promote land reform and the state ownership of foreign oil companies and to establish diplomatic relations with Havana and Moscow. 'Within the tradition of Latin American military coups,' Castro told a group of friends when he got home, 'there's never been anything like a group of military men proposing to apply agrarian reforms and to nationalise North American companies. Their daring has gone beyond the simple adoption of progressive or reformist measures.'[18]

Castro thought Velasco's military government had revolutionary potential, but identified its obvious weak spots: the fear of the military to give 'greater participation to the masses', and 'their inclination to take advantage of power to get rich'. Castro's analysis was sharp and to the point, and Velasco's regime would collapse swiftly after his death in 1976. He was a strong nationalist leader, but he clamped down on his internal opposition, ignored all civilian politicians and left no lasting legacy. Yet Castro clearly felt more at home in Velasco's Peru than in Allende's Chile.

Castro leaps to the defence of Angola, 1975

Castro had taken the Soviet shilling, but he retained the capacity to operate on his own account. To the surprise of both Moscow and Washington in 1975, he jumped back into the African arena that Che Guevara and his Cuban troop had left so abruptly ten years earlier. Equally brusquely he ordered a large troop contingent to be sent by emergency airlift to the Angolan capital of Luanda, to rescue the revolutionary army of Agostinho Neto from almost certain defeat at the hands of a South African invasion force.

The Cuban intervention – secret, sudden and entirely without selfish motivation – was conceived as a limited operation to protect Neto's Movimento Popular de Libertaçao de Angola, the MPLA, from defeat, and Castro planned to withdraw his troops when the immediate crisis was over. It was not to be. Cuban forces were still actively engaged in Angola 15 years later, with commitments far in excess of anything envisaged in 1975.

Angola was an African country for which many Cubans, both black and white, could conjure up considerable sympathy. The ancestors of many Cuban blacks came from the banks of the Congo river and from the shores of that section of Africa's coast. The Luso-Hispanic traditions that once linked Cuba with the Atlantic slave trade – with Brazil and Angola, and with Spain and Portugal – were a powerful element in Cuban history. White Cubans were also intrigued, for Angola, like Cuba, was a white settler country, a continuing destination for migrant families from Europe. Thousands had arrived in Luanda from Portugal after 1945. The country's population of some 6.4 million in 1974 included 320,000 whites, although many were to leave in 1975.

The MPLA was founded by a group of left-wing intellectuals, and it had been engaged in a small-scale guerrilla war against the Portuguese colonial power since 1961. Cuba had made direct contact with them when Guevara met Neto in Brazzaville in 1965. A handful of Cuban instructors were sent that year to the MPLA's camps in the Cabinda enclave, in the north of Angola. The experience was unsatisfactory for both sides: the Cubans were overly optimistic, and found the Angolans politically backward and slow to learn; the Angolans found the Cubans arrogant and overbearing. Neto visited Havana in January 1966 to take part in the Tricontinental Conference, subsequently recording his impression that 'Fidel and the other Cuban leaders were disappointed in the African liberation movements, and wary of them, because of their bad experiences in Zaire.'[19] Guevara's failed expedition of 1965 cast a long shadow.

The Cuban instructors withdrew their assistance to the MPLA in 1967 and concentrated on the PAIGC of Amilcar Cabral in Guinea-Bissau. This proved a good investment, since the defeat of the Portuguese army in Guinea-Bissau provoked a revolution on the Portuguese mainland in April 1974. A group of young officers, radicalised by military failure in their African wars, overthrew the inert regime in Lisbon of Marcelo Caetano, successor to that of Salazar, the old dictator.

The new military government in Lisbon, in which the Portuguese Communist Party played an influential role, ordered a swift withdrawal, decreeing independence for Guinea-Bissau in September 1974 and for Mozambique in June 1975. Angola was more problematic. Three rival independence movements, each with its international sponsors, were all jockeying for power – through negotiation if at all possible, through violence if need be. Neto's left-leaning MPLA enjoyed the political support of Moscow and Havana as well as that of several individuals in the Portuguese government. Among them was Admiral Rosa Coutinho, known to the western press as the Red Admiral. Sent to Luanda, he was under orders to liquidate the colony and hand it over to the MPLA.

Such an outcome was opposed by a second independence movement, the National Front for the Liberation of Angola, the FNLA, led by Holden Roberto, who received military aid from China, political support from President Mobutu of the Congo and had long been in receipt of a small wage from the CIA.[20] A third, rather smaller movement, UNITA, led by Jonas Savimbi, was discredited by its links with the former government in Portugal of Salazar and Caetano, and was soon to be backed by South Africa. The Portuguese government sought a coalition government that would prepare the way for independence in November 1975, and the rival groups met at Alvor in Portugal in January and notionally agreed to settle their differences. Long before the agreed date Angola was plunged into civil war.

Cuba had been asked by Neto for military instructors in the autumn of 1974, but the Cubans, after their earlier experience with the MPLA, were cautious. They sent two officers to examine the situation on the ground before any decisions could be made. No urgency was apparent since the MPLA hoped to secure help from Yugoslavia and the Soviet Union, its traditional supporters. When Neto told Castro of his modest military requirements, he asked him to use his influence with his friends in the Soviet camp to secure 'useful and timely aid'.[21]

Cuba took no further action until the middle of 1975, by which time the position of the MPLA was rather bleak: Portugal had withdrawn Rosa Coutinho from Luanda; the implicit guarantee that the MPLA would take over at independence was now no longer valid; the threatened civil war was now under way, with the imminent possibility of intervention by South Africa. The MPLA's need for assistance was now acute, but Havana had not been focused on African affairs. Castro was preoccupied with internal developments, with the reorganisation of the country's political and economic structure. The first congress of the freshly minted Cuban Communist Party was scheduled for the end of the year. In August he agreed to assist Neto with training: some 480 military instructors would be sent to Angola, to staff four training centres. Their work would start in October and they would turn out trained recruits over three to six months.

Other countries began to express an interest in the Angolan civil war. Gerald Ford, the US President, authorised the CIA to increase its covert assistance to Holden Roberto and Jonas Savimbi in July to the value of $24 million, the start of an operation that would last for the next 20 years.[22] American money and weapons poured in before the Soviet Union or Cuba were able to begin their own rather meagre operations on the MPLA's behalf. South African troops moved north into southern Angola in August, almost certainly with US knowledge, under the pretext of protecting the hydro-electric project on the Cunene river that South Africa had helped to fund. The Portuguese authorities protested, but South Africa claimed it was protecting its investment.[23]

Henry Kissinger, Ford's secretary of state, had been more concerned in the early months of 1975 with the left-wing revolution in Portugal than the future government of its former colonies, and secured the downfall in August of the pro-Communist prime minister, General Vasco Gonçalves, who, with Admiral

Coutinho, had been the figure most sympathetic to the MPLA. With the threat of Communism lifted from Western Europe, US attention was more closely focused on Angola.

Cuba was now aware that the MPLA might soon require emergency military assistance, since the Angolan recruits would not emerge from the training programme until early the next year. The MPLA's Luanda base was now under serious threat. Colonel Otelo Saraiva de Carvalho, the most radical figure of the Portuguese revolution, was in Havana for the customary celebrations on 26 July and Castro asked him to ensure that a Cuban arms shipment being sent to Luanda would be speeded through by the Portuguese authorities. Now alert to the delicate military situation, Castro sent a message to Brezhnev in August indicating that Cuban special forces might be needed, and that if so Cuba would need Soviet help with transport.[24] The Soviet leader, bent on a wider rapprochement with the United States at the time, was initially reluctant. Soviet transport assistance was not made available to the Cubans until the following year.

Cuba's promised contingent of 480 instructors arrived at Angolan ports at the beginning of October, in a fleet of three merchantmen. They moved swiftly to their four training camps: one was at Ndelatando, 30 kilometres east of Luanda; another at the port of Benguela, further south; a third in the eastern province of Lunda; and a fourth in the enclave of Cabinda.

Kissinger claimed later that Cuban combat troops had arrived in August, but the evidence suggests that this was not so.[25] MPLA forces were successful in their defence of Luanda in October, repelling attacks by Holden Roberto's FNLA, but they did not do so with Cuban troops. The nature of the war did not change until 14 October, when South Africa invaded in strength in the south. The civil war had become internationalised and the Cuban instructors were soon caught up in the struggle.

The invading force from South Africa, 'Operation Zulu', was made up initially of 1,000 FNLA guerrillas trained in South Africa, together with 150 white soldiers and officers, soon to be reinforced by 1,000 soldiers from the South African Defence Force. The invading column moved north at speed, reaching the outskirts of Benguela, south of Luanda, where the Cubans had their second training camp, at the beginning of November. The Cubans were inevitably drawn into the battle that took place at Catengue, 43 miles southeast of Benguela, and lost more than 20 men – dead, wounded or missing.[26] Their efforts were not sufficient, for Benguela fell to the South Africans on 6 November. The fall of Luanda now appeared imminent. Holden Roberto thought his FNLA units would capture it before independence day, scheduled for 11 November.

Hearing news of the defeat at Catengue, Castro decided on 4 November that he would have to send troops to defend Luanda. He consulted no one, except his brother Raúl, and made no attempt to talk to Moscow. Time was of the essence and the Russians would almost certainly have prevaricated, as Brezhnev had done in August. Castro gave the Cuban deployment the code-name 'Operation Carlota', after a slave woman who had led one of the slave revolts on the sugar plantations of Matanzas in 1843, and died with machete in hand. Anniversary celebrations of the revolt had been held in Cuba in 1973, and her name had remained in Castro's mind.[27]

Cuban special forces were flown out to Luanda on Cuban turbo-prop planes, with no assistance from the Russians. The flights lasted 48 hours, with refuelling stops in Barbados, Bissau and Brazzaville. One hundred soldiers left on the first plane, 150 on two flights the next day. Luanda was under threat from the FNLA in the north, assisted by white mercenaries and elements from the army of Mobutu's Congo, and from the South African units moving in from the south. Some of the Cubans arrived in time to take part in a decisive battle against the FNLA at Quifangondo, north of Luanda, on 10 November, manning half a dozen Soviet multiple rocket launchers.

Stiffened by the Cubans the MPLA forces held out, and the FNLA's motley force, trying to advance on the capital, was routed. Neto was able to proclaim Angola's independence at midnight on 11 November, as the Portuguese high commissioner quietly slipped away to a ship in the harbour.

The main force of South Africans was still advancing towards Luanda from Benguela, and Cuban soldiers were now sent south to join the surviving instructors from the Benguela camp to halt its seemingly inexorable advance. They held the line against the South Africans north of Novo Redondo, blowing up bridges to slow them down. A handful of Cubans had turned the tide. They were reinforced later in November when Cuban troop ships docked at Luanda with more than a thousand soldiers.

Several Cuban units went north to defend Cabinda against the FNLA and an invasion of Mobutu's troops from the Congo. One Cuban reservist, sailing on the *Sierra Maestra* and destined for Cabinda, wrote in his diary of Castro's final message before they left:

> Then he spoke to us about the importance of Cabinda and said that we were going there, that our task was to prevent the enemy from entering that province and also to protect our Congolese brothers from a possible attack from South African troops . . .
>
> He told us to be careful, that he didn't want corpses or suicidal missions, and that he trusted us because most of us were workers and students. He kept talking to us; he told us some stories about the Cuban Revolution, he compared Cabinda with Girón, he compared Mobutu with Pinochet, and then he compared the ship *Sierra Maestra* with the yacht *Granma*.[28]

Some 4,000 Cuban soldiers had been sent to Angola by the end of the year. The Russians did not collaborate until January 1976, when they helped to organise an airlift between Havana and Luanda. Soviet assistance was now vital, since the United States had prevailed upon the government of Barbados to withdraw landing rights from Cuban planes flying out to Luanda.

With no prospect of swift military victory, and with no international support, the South African forces withdrew from Angola after four months, in March 1976. The Cuban intervention had been dramatic and effective and the language and symbolism of the island entered into the imagination of the continent. Castro had compared Cabinda with Playa Girón. A retired South African general had the same message, writing in a newspaper that 'Angola may well be regarded as South Africa's Bay of Pigs.'[29]

Castro flew to Guinea in March, and met Neto in Conakry to discuss a schedule for Cuban withdrawal. They decided that Cuba would leave behind sufficient military units to help organise a strong and modernised army in Angola. They would stay 'for as long as necessary'. Neto's principal requirement was an army capable of securing internal security and national defence without the need to call on outside help. Given the guerrilla forces operating in the country, it was a tall order.

Castro was no longer planning a quick withdrawal. The veteran Cuba-watcher Herbert Matthews wrote perceptively in March how the Angolan enterprise had opened up new horizons for Cuba:

> Vistas that might seem dazzling to Fidel Castro's eyes will open up with the victory in Angola . . . For Fidel Castro there is no 'darkest Africa'. It is all ablaze with lights – the campfires of fellow revolutionaries . . . So long as Castroite Cuba exists there will be armed Cubans in Africa, and they will be much more than shock troops for the Russians. Fidel Castro sees them as standard bearers for the non-aligned countries of the third world.[30]

The impact of the Cuban intervention on the mood in Africa could hardly have been foreseen, yet it raised issues rarely posed so starkly. As noted by a columnist in the *Rand Daily Mail* in February 1976:

> Whether the bulk of the offensive was by Cubans or Angolans is immaterial in the colour-conscious context of this war's battlefield, for the reality is that they won, are winning, and are not White; and that psychological edge, that advantage the White man has enjoyed and exploited over 300 years of colonialism and empire, is slipping away. White elitism has suffered an irreversible blow in Angola, and Whites who have been there know it.[31]

Blacks too had taken notice of the changing climate. The principal of a black high school in Soweto, the immense African township outside Johannesburg, told the *New York Times* in February that Angola was 'very much on the minds' of his 700 students. 'It gives them hope,' he said.[32] Four months later, in June 1976, the immense Johannesburg township of Soweto exploded in one of the great urban rebellions of South African history. The Cuban intervention in Angola had been one of the detonators. Among the heroes of the young revolutionaries in Soweto were Malcolm X, Mao Tse-tung and Che Guevara.

The nomadic road to socialism: Castro and the Ethiopian revolution, 1977

Castro's long-standing interest in Africa had been revived by the Angolan intervention, and he continued to be fascinated by its revolutionary possibilities, often giving it a higher priority than Latin America. He was still captivated by the idea of black Cuba recovering its African roots, but he was also now a leader of the Third World, appointed to be a dynamic chairman of the Non-Aligned Movement in August 1976 as a result of his successful, high profile assistance to Agostinho Neto.

Africa looked more promising to Castro than Latin America, where right-wing military dictatorships had entrenched themselves with brutality and terror in Chile, Argentina, Bolivia and Uruguay. A visitor to Havana in 1978 heard Castro argue that Latin America's 'rigid social structures' and 'organised interest groups' made rebel activity more difficult there than in Africa, which was 'poor and lacked such forces'.[33] Castro considered the countries of Latin America to be caught up in a web of immobility and conservatism spun by the military and the Church and reinforced by business corporations, trade unions and political parties. Africa, by contrast, was a blank sheet of paper. This simplistic notion, reflected in Castro's reluctance to engage with the complexities of Africa, was an outstanding characteristic of his continuing involvement in its affairs. He was not alone in this; his misunderstandings were shared by others.

As well as helping Angola and the other former Portuguese colonies, Cuba had been providing assistance to other regions of Africa ever since Guevara's mission to the Congo in 1965. Requests from African liberation movements were rarely turned away. Some were based in Somalia and received training from Cuban instructors. The secessionists in Eritrea, fighting to free their country from Ethiopian occupation, were helped by Cuba. So too was the socialist republic of South Yemen, across the Red Sea, where 100 military instructors had been stationed since 1973.

The Horn of Africa, from which Somalia looked over the waters that led to the Suez Canal and the Gulf, had long been perceived as a sensitive spot by both East and West. A Cold War balance had existed in the area for some years and affected the politics of South Yemen and Ethiopia as well as Somalia. President Mohammed Siad Barre, the ruler of Somalia since 1969, was considered to be in the Soviet sphere, and he provided the Russians with access to the Somali naval base at Berbera. Ethiopia, across the desert frontier of the Ogaden, ruled by Emperor Haile Selassie since the 1930s, was closely allied to the United States and housed several US military bases. The emperor was overthrown in September 1974 and uncertainty about the country's political future had reigned for some years.

At the end of February 1977 Castro made a surprise tour of Africa that lasted for several weeks. The cause of his renewed interest was his old-fashioned enthusiasm for what looked to him to be a genuine revolution, breaking out in unfamiliar territory. The uncertainties in Ethiopia had been resolved by Colonel Mengistu Haile Mariam, a hitherto unknown Ethiopian officer, who seized power in Addis Ababa on 3 February in a bloody coup. Mengistu announced his intention to establish a Marxist–Leninist regime and he requested Soviet assistance, prompting the United States to declare that it would reduce its existing aid programme to Ethiopia because of its human rights' violations.

Ethiopia had long been a major player in Africa and Addis Ababa housed the headquarters of the Organisation of African Unity. A left-wing revolution there would be of cardinal importance for the continent and would cause Ethiopia to change sides in the Cold War, affecting the fortunes of Cuba's existing allies, the Somalis and the Eritreans. Colonel Siad Barre had long had plans for a 'greater Somalia', and his ambition, and that of earlier Somali regimes, was to incorporate into Somalia the large but desert territory of the Ogaden, lost during the colonial era and still occupied by Ethiopia. The change of regime in Addis Ababa would certainly thwart that ambition.

This was no blank sheet, but a region where the complications were writ large. Castro needed to examine the terrain, and to take the African pulse. He set off at once, accompanied by a small group of his closest advisers, those familiar with some aspects of Africa, like Osmany Cienfuegos and José Abrantes, as well as Carlos Rafael Rodríguez, his Communist guru.

He also sought African advice, pausing at Algiers airport to embrace Houari Boumedienne and stopping in Libya to talk to President Gadafy and to attend a meeting of the People's Congress in Tripoli. Then he flew to Aden, the capital of the avowedly socialist state of South Yemen. After two days of talks with President Salim Ali Rubayyi he moved on to Mogadishu, the Somali capital, for discussion with Siad Barre.

Castro needed all his diplomatic skills. Cuba and Somalia were friends, yet the revolution in Ethiopia was, by all reports, far more radical. Addressing a Somali crowd in the football stadium in Mogadishu, Castro spoke uncontroversially of 'the great spirit of collaboration and fraternity' that existed between the Cuban and Somali peoples, 'fighting side by side against imperialism'.

He flew to Addis Ababa the following day to meet the new revolutionary leader. Castro was impressed by Mengistu, and they talked for many hours. He had encountered a revolutionary soul-mate and support for the Ethiopian revolution was now to become a Cuban priority. 'I know Mengistu well,' he

told the magazine *Afrique-Asie* on his return to Havana. 'He is calm, intelligent, bold and brave, and I believe that he has exceptional qualities as a
revolutionary leader.'[34]

Castro waxed lyrical about Ethiopian developments. 'The events of 3
February were decisive,' he explained. 'The leftists and the true revolutionary
leaders took over the reins of power, and the process assumed a truly revolutionary course.' He was excited by what he perceived as a profound revolution
of great historical significance that reminded him of the French and Bolshevik
revolutions. An 'intense class struggle' had been unleashed 'between the
workers and the peasants, on the one hand, and the proprietors and
bourgeoisie on the other'. Surely the fact that Ethiopia's revolution was 'being
criminally attacked from abroad by Arab reactionaries and imperialism' was
proof enough of its radical credentials?

Castro and Mengistu remained closeted together for several days,
discussing ways in which Cuba might provide support and examining how a
clash with Somalia over the Ogaden might be avoided. Castro thought it
intolerable that two socialist peoples might be about to go to war. He outlined
a plan for a conference to be held, designed to unite the 'progressive forces' of
East Africa, and he persuaded Mengistu to join together with the Somalis and
the Yemenis for discussions.[35]

The emergency conference, chaired by Castro, took place in socialist Aden.
Castro sought to persuade the three *soi-disant* Marxist leaders to form a loose
anti-imperialist federation that would be provided with assistance from the
Soviet Union. Such an arrangement would leave open the possibility of some
kind of autonomy for the Somalis in the Ogaden and – the other Cuban difficulty – for the Eritreans in the north.

The task was not possible; the wide gap between the contending parties
could not be bridged. Siad Barre went home to complain about Mengistu's
intransigence; the Ethiopians remained concerned by the Somali leader's
expansionist plans. The conference collapsed with no agreement and was
followed by a straightfoward request from Mengistu to Castro for military
assistance from Cuba against a probable Somali attack.

Castro gave no immediate repy. Such a decision would require the support
of others, and not just in Africa. For the moment he continued his African
tour – consulting with the leaders of Tanzania, Mozambique, Angola and
Algeria – before moving north to Berlin and Moscow. His personal excitement
about the Ethiopian revolution continued to register in press interviews. 'One
could say that I discovered Africa,' he told a reporter in Algiers, 'just as
Christopher Columbus discovered America.' It was a revealing statement. His
first-hand African experience had provided Castro with fresh and surprising,
not to say unusual, insights into the nature of the contemporary world.

'Travelling around the world a bit,' he told an audience in East Berlin, 'you
learn a lot, not just about Marxism–Leninism, but about imperialism and

colonialism and neo-colonialism.' He went on to describe how he had seen countries in Africa that were going 'from tribalism and nomadism to the construction of socialism, and these are truly interesting phenomena that enrich our doctrine and tactics'.[36]

'Africa is imperialism's weakest link today,' he explained to *Afrique-Asie*, when he got back to Havana. 'Perfect opportunities exist there for the transformation from quasi-tribalism to socialism, without having to go through the various stages that were necessary in other parts of the world.'[37]

Castro had invented a wonderful new Marxist theory: a simple leap could be made from nomadism to socialism. He explained his startling thesis to an astonished audience of Germans in Berlin, and doubtless to the Russians as well. Stopping in Moscow on his way home, he was greeted by the entire Soviet leadership: Brezhnev, Podgorny, Kosygin and Gromyko. Nothing was too good for their Cuban ally. Brezhnev toasted Castro at a banquet, saying that they had all followed his travels through Africa with 'comradely interest'.

Castro gave his Soviet allies an account of his meeting with Mengistu and his appreciation of the Ethiopian revolution, doubtless furnishing the Russians with the views he was to explain to the readers of *Afrique-Asie*: 'it is a powerful mass movement and a profound agrarian reformation in a feudal country where the peasants were practically slaves. Urban reforms have been implemented, and the major industries in the country have been nationalized.' The success and consolidation of the Ethiopian revolution, he said, would be 'extremely important for Africa'. With Mengistu, the country had 'a true revolutionary'. And, of course, he would be a worthy recipient of Soviet support.

As Castro had prophesied, the Ethiopian revolution moved ahead rapidly. Mengistu ordered all US military facilities in the country to be closed down in April, and in May he followed Castro to Moscow for the red carpet treatment. Castro despatched General Arnaldo Ochoa, Cuba's commander in Angola, to Addis Ababa to assess Ethiopia's military needs.

War came in July. Somali forces launched an invasion of the Ogaden, with 40,000 troops and 250 tanks. They had been given the green light by the United States, which hinted at a commitment to provide weapons. 'By saying you would give Siad Barre arms,' Castro told a US diplomat a year later, 'you helped touch off the war, and since you obviously would have been delighted if Somalia had won and ousted Mengistu, it is difficult not to believe that you did it deliberately.'[38]

The Cubans agreed initially to help Ethiopia by sending a group of military instructors; 200 were operating by September. Later that year, after a fresh Somali offensive in the Ogaden, Mengistu asked Castro for large-scale military support. Siad Barre, meanwhile, expelled all Cubans and Russians from Mogadishu in November. Like Ethiopia, he had changed sides in the Cold War.

Cuba started to send combat troops to Ethiopia in the autumn and to supply weapons in January 1978, as they had done earlier to Angola. On that occasion, the initiative had been entirely Cuban. This time, the Soviet Union was backing the decision. A joint Cuban–Soviet operation was organised, with the Soviets providing the transport and the Cubans supplying the soldiers. Some troops were sent out from Havana, others were transferred from Angola and from Congo-Brazzaville. Some 24,000 Cuban troops were deployed in Ethiopia over a period of two years.

Cuba's intervention was as decisive in Ethiopia as it had been in Angola, and it broke the back of the Somali advance into the Ogaden. General Ochoa's combined force of Ethiopian and Cuban troops forced their way through the Jijiga Pass in March 1978 and the Somalis were obliged to withdraw. Mengistu came to Havana in April and was welcomed with a triumphal reception. The Cuban troops withdrew slowly after their victory and some 16,000 were still stationed in Ethiopia in January 1979.

Castro's Ethiopian excursion was not without problems. The fighting in Angola had been popular with Cuban troops – Luanda was a European city where the inhabitants spoke Portuguese and Cubans could feel relatively at home. The same enthusiasm was not summoned up for the war in the Ogaden. Cuba had no historic links with the east side of Africa, apart from slaves brought from Mozambique, and Cubans had nothing in common with Ethiopian civilisation. The fact that Ethiopia, previously regarded as the enemy by the groups that Cuba had helped in Somalia and Eritrea, was now an ally was confusing at best.

The Eritrean People's Liberation Front, advocating secession from Ethiopia, had been supported by Cuba since 1970, and now Mengistu's success in the Ogaden had enabled him to turn his attention to crushing its resistance. Cuban soldiers were not asked to fight against the Eritreans, but their presence on the Somali border, keeping guard against attacks from the troops of Siad Barre, was of considerable service to Mengistu, allowing him to transfer his troops in safety to the Eritrean front in the north.

Cuba's soldiers were finally withdrawn from Ethiopia in September 1979 and Mengistu was to remain in power for another twelve years, during which he presided over a long separatist war and years of terrible famine. His revolution did not survive the end of the Cold War and the collapse of the Soviet Union, by which time the strange history of Cuba's military adventures in Africa had drawn to a close.[39] He had been regarded in the West as just another African dictator whose fall from power was widely welcomed, yet Castro once perceived him as a Jacobin revolutionary who would change the face of Africa. Castro's African wars had a considerable impact on Africa, but they were not on balance of great service to Cuba and a possible rapprochement with the United States during the presidency of Jimmy Carter was certainly made more difficult by these extensive African deployments.

Havana, Washington and Miami in the Carter years, 1976–1979

On 6 October 1976 the Cuban fencing team was returning to Havana from a successful contest in Venezuela. Their plane from Caracas stopped at Trinidad and Barbados, and ten minutes after take-off from Barbados, it exploded. A time bomb had been placed in the baggage compartment. This was the first occasion on which a civilian airline had been blown up by terrorists and all 73 people on board were killed.[40] Until September 11 it was the single worst act of air terrorism in the Americas. Two Venezuelans were charged with placing the bomb on the aircraft, but those thought to be behind the operation were Cuban exiles – Orlando Bosch and Luis Posada Carriles – who had formerly worked with the CIA. They were arrested in Caracas and charged with the crime, but Bosch was acquitted and Posada was sprung from jail. Both remained active in the anti-Cuban cause through the following decades.

In the month after the bombing the United States elected a new Democratic president. The government of Jimmy Carter was widely perceived as a new broom. Something of the kind was needed after the drama of President Nixon's resignation over Watergate, the inertia of the interim presidency of Gerald Ford and the anti-climactic conclusion to the Vietnam war. Carter's likely impact on relations between Havana and Washington – in the doldrums since Cuba's expedition to Angola in 1975 – was debated widely in both capitals, although advocates of a rapprochement can have had no inkling that the time available to reach an agreement was to be impossibly short – less than three years. A revolution in Nicaragua in 1979, and the election of Ronald Reagan in 1980, put paid to the premature hopes of the optimists.

Continuing discussions between the two capitals had always concentrated on very specific issues. Bilateral negotiations had taken place in February 1973 to deal with 'air piracy', and both countries had agreed to prosecute hijackers, or to return them to their country of origin for prosecution. The Barbados bombing now gave a fresh urgency to Cuba's desire to see an end to CIA support for the terrorist organisations of the exiles.

When Richard Nixon was president, all possibility of a generalised improvement in relations had been blocked. Of Castro, Nixon was alleged to have told an assistant, 'There'll be no change toward that bastard while I'm president.' The Cuban newspaper *Granma* exchanged the compliment by spelling his name with a swastika in the middle instead of an X.[41] Yet even before Nixon's resignation in August 1974 attitudes in Washington had mellowed. The US senate foreign relations committee had voted in April for the restoration of diplomatic relations and for an end to the trade embargo.

With Nixon gone even Henry Kissinger appeared friendly. Having brought Communist China in from the cold it was thought that he might wish to cap that with an agreement with Cuba. He said he saw no virtue in 'perpetual antagonism'.[42] Senior officials at the State Department began secret negoti-ations with Cuba in January 1975. The main issues for discussion were the same as always: the US trade embargo, compensation for Cuban losses attrib-utable to the embargo and compensation for US properties nationalised in the early years. In the background were other controversial subjects: the future of the Guantánamo base, a reunification programme for Cuban families and the release of political prisoners. Hints were dropped in September that the talks had been fruitful and that the United States might now be ready to 'enter a dialogue' with Cuba.[43] It was not to be. The Cuban intervention in Angola in November put such a possibility on hold and the secret talks were halted.

Jimmy Carter was inaugurated in January 1977. He was committed to exploring the possibilities of a deal and his first act was to order a halt to US reconnaissance flights over the island and to ease restrictions on US citizens travelling to Cuba.[44] The secret talks were resumed in March and discussions about maritime boundaries led eventually to a decision in September to re-open embassies in Havana and Washington.[45] These would continue to be known as 'interests' sections', but in most respects they would operate as normal embassies. Starting with ten diplomats in 1977, the US 'interests section' had become the largest foreign embassy in Havana by the 1990s with a staff of more than fifty.

The reopening of the embassies was the high point of Carter's attempt to come to terms with Castro's Cuba. Further efforts were sabotaged by strategic disagreements within his team, by Castro's military commitment to Mengistu and by the US failure to take action against the terrorist groups sponsored by the Miami exiles.

A political division arose in Washington between Zbigniew Brzezinski, the national security adviser, and Cyrus Vance at the State Department. Brzezinski was a Soviet specialist concerned with the balance of power in the wider Cold War and largely ignorant of the historic specificity of US–Cuba relations. He perceived Cuba as a Soviet pawn. Although Cuba had been withdrawing some of its troops from Angola it had sent military instructors to Ethiopia in the autumn of 1977, and soldiers began arriving there in January 1978 to participate in the fighting in the Ogaden. Brzezinski argued that the military build-up in Africa would make attempts to normalise relations with Havana impossible.[46] Wayne Smith, an old Cuba hand who became the head of the 'interests' section' in Havana, accused him of a tendency to interpret political and military events 'in terms of some Soviet blueprint for world conquest'.[47]

Cyrus Vance had a different point of view from Brzezinski. He thought that the United States had laid the way open to Cuban intervention in Angola by not recognising Neto's government. 'The reason the Angolans kept the Cubans in Angola', he wrote in his memoirs, 'was because they feared further incursions by South Africa and South African support for UNITA.'[48] Cuban support for Mengistu was less easy to defend and Vance lost the internal argument in Washington.

Attempts to improve the bilateral relationship were now downgraded. While a deal might possibly have been done no urgency was displayed on either side. The State Department would have liked to tidy up the tiresome quarrel, for that is the task of diplomats, but it was under no great pressure to do so. The Cubans were also in no hurry. Castro's principal interest lay in securing US help to control the terrorist groups in Miami, yet that never seemed to be forthcoming. Cuba's military and economic security was tied up with the Soviet Union and they basked in the warmth of new friendships found in the Third World.

While the American people were not much concerned with Cuba either way, most American businessmen were fed up with the economic embargo and would have liked to see the resumption of trade. They had no reason to be frightened of Castro, they no longer had investments in Cuba that needed protecting and the larger companies that had lost money 20 years earlier had long ago written off those losses. A new generation was looking for fresh trading opportunities. The representatives of more than 100 US companies, including Boeing, Xerox, International Harvester, John Deere, Caterpillar Tractor, Prudential and Honeywell, went to Havana in the course of 1977 to weigh up the possibilities.[49] Castro welcomed them all, but showed no sign that he was prepared to make humiliating concessions to bring the embargo to an end.

Yet even if the commercial pressure had swayed Washington a raft of legal difficulties made a Cuban deal problematic if it were to involve a lifting of the embargo. Successive foreign trade acts obliged the US government to refuse all assistance unless there was 'prompt, adequate and effective compensation' for nationalised properties. US officials were obliged to oppose loans being given to Cuba by the World Bank or the International Monetary Fund.[50] No relaxation of the embargo would be possible under the terms of the Trade Expansion Act of 1962 unless the President officially 'determined that Cuba is no longer dominated or controlled by the foreign government or foreign organisation controlling the world Communist movement'. Though not perhaps 'dominated' or 'controlled' Cuba was undoubtedly a member of the Soviet camp.

Cuba would have liked an agreement on its own terms, but it was not desperate. Castro saw no reason to kowtow to the Americans. For the Soviet Union, as the alternative superpower, it was well-nigh essential to have an understanding with the United States, but Cuba had no such pressing need. The country was making its own way in the world. While the blockade was tiresome, Cuba had long learnt to live with it, and knew how to circumvent it.

Cuba now had new friends in the Third World. Much effort was put into sustaining relationships with these countries in the 1970s, recovering the friendships that proved so successful in the early years and reviving the old rhetoric. The policy was remarkably effective. Bridges had been rebuilt earlier in the decade with the countries of Latin America. The useful friendship established with Allende's Chile had been ended by the Pinochet coup, but relations were re-established that year with the new, vaguely leftist, Peronist government in Argentina. A trade agreement promised beneficial exchanges, including for Cuba the chance to buy US automobiles manufactured in Argentina. By 1975, embassies had been reopened Venezuela, Colombia, Ecuador, Panama and Honduras, and established for the first time in the Caribbean islands of Barbados, Jamaica, Trinidad and the Bahamas and in the mainland territory of Guyana.

Distinguished foreign visitors began to descend on Havana: some were Communists like Brezhnev, Erich Honecker and Pham van Dong, others came from the western camp, including Pierre Trudeau from Canada and Olof Palme from Sweden. President Luís Echeverría of Mexico arrived in August 1975 with a mariachi band.[51]

Cuba's military support for Angola and Ethiopia might be frowned on in Washington, but it gave Cuba much credit in Africa. Cuba was perceived to be in the front line of the continuing battle against western colonialism in the continent. Where Cuban military assistance was inappropriate, Castro sent doctors and sports instructors and teachers, and such programmes gave Cuba immense prestige in the Third World. After much work done by sophisticated Cuban diplomats at the UN in New York and in many foreign capitals, Cuba was the natural choice to lead the Third World and its Non-Aligned Movement. In September 1979 its regular summit conference was held in Havana.

Enchanted by his new role as a revolutionary leader of the Third World, Castro no longer had a driving interest in patching up relations with Washington. The two specific interests he had on the American mainland could be dealt with more easily in Miami. Castro needed to put a stop to the freelance terrorism like the Barbados bombing that was directed from Miami and had become a permanent irritant to life on the island. Operation Mongoose, the CIA programme of the Kennedy years, had long been abandoned, and the US government was no longer officially engaged in active schemes of destabilisation. Yet the exile organisations in Miami, once funded and assisted by the CIA, had remained in being and taken on a life of their own.

Castro's other need was a rapprochement with the Miami Cubans, to re-unite the Cuban family across the Florida straits and bind old wounds. The two Cuban needs were intertwined, for if some deal would be made with exiles in Miami who would be happy to see a normalisation of relations, then there would be less support in their community for the radicalised terrorists. Since the US government showed little interest in curbing the Miami terrorists, the best Cuban strategy would be to seek to undermine their support within the exile community, and the first initiatives were taken in the middle of 1978.

Cuba had its own intelligence service in Miami and Panama, and had long been cultivating a prosperous Miami banker, a prominent Carter supporter, who had originally gone into exile in 1960. Bernardo Benes was a prominent member of the Cuban community in Miami who had rejected the dominant exile strategy of trying to isolate Cuba. Contacted by senior figures in Cuban intelligence (including José Luis Padrón and Tony de la Guardia), during a business trip to Panama in August 1977, Benes discussed a possible visit to Cuba.[52] He was invited to Havana to talk to Castro in February 1978, and they discussed the possible unilateral release of political prisoners. Benes informed the White House that secret negotiations with Havana on this issue, a permanent preoccupation of the President, would meet with a satisfactory response.

The initiative again came up against the granite resistance of Brzezinski, who met Benes and refused to have anything to do with the idea. No official meetings with the Cubans should take place unless the withdrawal of their troops from Africa was on the agenda. Vance was more interested and since Castro was not asking for anything in exchange from the Americans he ordered his adviser on Cuban affairs to keep in touch with developments.

The initiative now remained with Castro and he continued to use Benes as his eye into the world of Miami exiles. He announced in September 1978 that representatives of the exile community in Miami had been invited to Havana. They would discuss two outstanding matters: the release of political prisoners, and an increase in family visits – by exiles to see their families on the island. Benes the banker had been working away in Miami and had put together a group of like-minded exiles who were willing to accept the challenge.

At a meeting with Benes and six Cuban-Americans in Havana in October, Castro outlined his own views on the subject. He said he recognised that not all the exiles could be dismissed as 'counter-revolutionaries'.[53] He also said that he favoured 'expeditious procedures' for the release of prisoners held in Cuba, as well as for the reunification of families. Benes was able to return to Miami with 46 political prisoners on the plane. The event was portrayed as a triumph for the exile community, yet it was also a significant breakthrough for Castro.[54] He was able to deal with Miami on his own account, not via Washington.

Benes came back to Havana in November for a further meeting with Castro. This time he brought a larger group of Cuban-Americans with him, known as the Committee of 75. Their discussions were fruitful. According to Castro's figures, 3,238 prisoners were being held for crimes against the state and a further 425 were being held for crimes committed in the Batista era. They would now be released at the rate of 400 a month.[55]

Castro also told the Committee of 75 that he would now permit visits to Cuba from all Cubans living abroad, provided that they were not terrorists who wished to wage a holy war nor agents of the CIA. At the same time, a relaxation of the rules permitting Cubans to travel abroad would be introduced.

One obvious difficulty that lay ahead was the bomb threat associated with the sending of packages.[56] From this problem sprang the idea of establishing dollar shops in Havana where visiting exiles could buy presents for their families. Benes was already under threat from anti-Castro groups in Miami, and the memory of the Barbados bombing was still raw for everyone in Cuba. The visitors and the dollar shops were also a wonderful new source of hard currency for the government.

A new era now began in the relationship between Cuba and Florida. More than 100,000 Cuban-Americans took up Castro's offer in the course of 1979 and travelled to Cuba to see their families. Half a dozen airliners flew in each day. Eventually they were able to transmit large sums of money to their families in Cuba, similar to the remittances that hundreds of thousands of Latin American immigrants would soon be sending back from the United States to their families in Central and South America. Cuba earned over $100 million dollars from the visits in 1979 and 1980 and would benefit hugely from remittances over the following decades.[57]

The new deal did not end Cuban-American hostility to Castro, which waxed and waned over the next quarter of a century. Nor did it altogether put an end to the terrorism sponsored by small groups in Miami and elsewhere. Yet something had been done, not just to reduce the prison population but to ease the heartache of thousands of families wrenched asunder by the inexorable logic of revolution.

The visits of the exiles were also, and perhaps unexpectedly, to have a profound and destabilising effect on Cuban society. The Cuban-Americans brought US dollars with them and US magazines, and they bought presents and consumer durables. The vision of an alternative way of life to that offered by the Revolution was now on show and would become increasingly tempting to some members of a younger generation familiar only with socialist austerity. Many of them now seized the opportunity to leave.

The second exodus: the Mariel boatlift, 1980

The port of Mariel is an unattractive industrial town to the west of Havana, at the end of a motorway from the capital. With the largest cement works on the island, a shipyard and a large electric power station, it is scarcely a tourist resort. Some 125,000 Cubans embarked on small ships here in a six-month period between April and October 1980 and sailed off for a new life in Florida.

Their exodus became known as the Mariel boatlift. Taking place at the same time as the creation of the Solidarity movement in Poland, the trade union opposition led by Lech Walesa to the communist government, this extraordinary Cuban episode appeared to pose a considerable threat to the stability of Castro's government and was perceived in the United States as a further sign of the internal political decay within the world communist movement.

The year 1980 was not an easy one for the Cuban government, and for Castro in particular. Celia Sánchez, his closest friend, secretary, assistant and vital political adviser since the time of Moncada, died of lung cancer in January, leaving the Maximum Leader bereft of comfort and good counsel. Wider concerns included the Soviet invasion of Afghanistan in late December 1979. Castro's overtly pro-Soviet stand served only to undermine his leadership of the Non-Aligned Movement that he had proudly assumed in 1979. The economic outlook was also gloomy. The sugar crop was down and so too was the world price. Rationing was tightened, and austerity was again the prevailing trend.[58]

Simmering internal dissatisfaction broke out at the beginning of April. A small group of Cubans, seeking asylum, crashed a lorry into the grounds of the Peruvian embassy in the Miramar district of Havana. The Cuban guard on duty was killed. The Peruvian ambassador refused to hand over the asylum-seekers, as was his right, and the Cuban authorities withdrew their protection of the embassy. Within days, some 10,000 Cubans had sought asylum within its precincts.

Castro, in the manner of the old Spanish captain-generals, took personal control of the crisis from the start and moved to a house in Miramar to direct operations. An editorial in *Granma* claimed that the asylum-seekers were, for the most part, 'criminals, lumpen, and anti-social elements, loafers and parasites'. None of them were subject 'to political persecution, nor were they in need of the sacred right of diplomatic asylum'.[59] A government statement called them 'scum', people who had renounced the ideals of the fatherland for the lure of consumerism. The Communist Party now organised *mítines de repudio*, demonstrations of hostility, outside the homes of those who had entered the embassy, and a large protest demonstration was assembled to march there.[60]

After prolonged negotiations, the 10,000 would-be migrants in the embassy were permitted to leave by air for Costa Rica. There they were welcomed by the international media before continuing their journey to Lima, which was not of course their desired destination. The United States was closed to most of them, since President Carter had agreed on a limit of only 3,500. It was as difficult to get into the United States as it was to get out of Cuba.

The crisis took a more dramatic turn two days later when Castro stopped the airlift to Costa Rica and announced that anyone who wished to do so would now be allowed to leave. Thousands of Cuban immediately seized the opportunity with alacrity, indeed rather more than Castro had bargained for. President Carter, equally foolhardy, now declared that the United States would receive them with open arms. 'Ours is a country of refugees . . . We'll continue to provide an open heart and open arms to refugees seeking freedom from communist domination.'[61]

An impromptu exodus, organised by the Miami Cubans with the agreement of Castro, was soon under way. Hundreds of small boats came over from Florida and nosed into the harbour at Mariel. On 24 April 94 came, then 349 on 25 April and 958 on 26 April. As thousands of Cubans sought to leave special offices were set up to process their departure. Prisons, detention centres and mental hospitals were emptied of many of their inmates.

After four months the United States had had enough. The political implications of this mass migration were negative for the Carter government, soon to be seeking re-election in November. The arriving Cubans were no longer confined solely to Florida. The 'lumpen' and criminal element in the migration were spread around American prisons, from Arkansas to Atlanta, and the whole country was affected. A fresh series of negotiations was soon under way and the exodus eventually came to a halt in October. The episode was a disaster for Carter and was a contributing factor to his loss of the election to Ronald Reagan.

Nearly 2,000 Cuban prisoners from the Mariel exodus were still housed in the Atlanta state penitentiary years later, in March 1986. According to reports from prison officials there had been 9 homicides, 7 suicides, 400 serious but unsuccessful suicide attempts and more than 2,000 serious incidents since 1981.[62] Castro's capacity to open the taps of unlimited migration was a powerful weapon to use against the United States, though with some of the characteristics of the boomerang, since it rebounded against Cuba. The Mariel boatlift was poor publicity for the Revolution, with its obvious implication of widespread discontent. What was left of the understanding forged between Havana and Washington in the previous three years now melted rapidly away. Carter knew there were no votes in a rapprochement with Cuba, now perceived as an unhappy country that many people wanted to leave.

Western journalists descended on the island in great numbers for the first time in many years, to tell the story with considerable glee. The Cuban government ensured that the demonstrations hostile to those leaving kept up a steady momentum, to show that most of the population remained faithful to the Revolution. The migrants were officially described as 'lumpen', yet the motives of most of them were little different from those leaving other Caribbean islands, or Central America, in those years. They simply sought a better life in the United States.[63]

Their reception in Florida was not as welcoming as they might have hoped. Many of the Mariel generation of migrants were mulatto or black, and came from the poorer segment of Cuban society. They took their chance because they wanted to improve their economic opportunities, but most had nothing but praise for the free services – health and education and sports facilities – to which they had been accustomed on the island. This was not a message that the old generation of exiles wanted to hear and the new arrivals served to increase the existing divisions within the exile community, already unsettled by the initiatives set in train by Bernardo Benes.

Revolutions in Nicaragua and Grenada, 1979

In July 1979, in the year before the Mariel exodus, the Sandinista revolutionaries of Nicaragua drove triumphantly into the city of Managua after a short insurrectionary war. The violent overthrow of the dynastic dictatorship of the Somoza family seemed like a carbon copy of Cuba's Revolution, the fulfilment of Guevara's dream of a successful guerrilla struggle. Like Cuba, a small band of fighters had overthrown the forces of a regular army and seized power. Like Cuba, the people had risen up to overthrow a hated dictator. Like Cuba, the country had once been occupied by the United States and bore similar scars. The US Marines had been entrenched there from 1912 to 1933, under attack from 1927 to 1933 by the guerrilla forces of Augusto César Sandino, the country's José Martí.[64]

The victory in Nicaragua in 1979 aroused a fresh interest in Latin America, as Cuba had done in the 1960s and Chile in the early 1970s. Foreign visitors flocked to Managua to imbibe draughts of the intoxicating liquor of Revolution, as once they had travelled to Havana and Santiago. The Cubans might have felt for a moment that history was again on their side, but Castro himself was more circumspect. The Revolution had abandoned its public support for guerrilla struggle in Latin America after the death of Guevara in 1967, but it could hardly prevent others from picking up the revolutionary banner.

The leftist movements that formed and re-formed in the 1960s and 1970s in Central America owed more to the dynamic of their own historical experience than they did to the Cuban example: Guatemala, El Salvador and Nicaragua all had long histories of revolutionary struggle. The guerrilla groups active there received a certain measure of comfort and assistance from a section of the Cuban secret service, led by Manuel Piñeiro, but his particular department was of dwindling importance, kept alive largely for sentimental reasons.[65] Individual revolutionaries would spend time in Cuba, notably Tomás Borge from Nicaragua, and Castro kept a personal eye on a number of groups, but his chief task was to persuade their opinionated and self-centred leaders that they would never be successful without unity.[66]

When the Sandinistas triumphed the Cubans were uneasy. Castro had not expected their swift victory, and was quick to point out that the differences with Cuba's Revolution were as important as the similarities. Yet the Sandinistas threw themselves into his arms, somewhat to his embarrassment, and without so much as a formal request several senior members of the Sandinista leadership flew to Cuba after their victory to participate in the annual Moncada celebrations on 26 July, held that year in Holguín. Castro joined in the general atmosphere of rejoicing, but his words urging moderation were those of a cautious elder statesman:

> Each country has its path, its problems, its style, its methods, and its objectives. We have ours and they have theirs. We did it in a certain way – our way – and they will do it their way ... No two revolutions are the same. They cannot be ... Our problems are not exactly their problems. The conditions in which our Revolution was made are not exactly the same conditions in which their revolution was made ... In other words, things in Nicaragua are not going to be exactly the same, or anything like what they are in Cuba.[67]

The Sandinista victory posed a dilemma for Cuba. They welcomed it for its own sake and because Nicaragua would be a useful ally on the mainland. Yet its very existence created additional problems, both with the United States and with the Soviet Union. One similarity with the Cuban experience, visible to all on the first day, was the possibility of US intervention, and Castro was at pains to caution the Sandinistas not to antagonise the United States unnecessarily. He recommended them to concentrate on establishing a mixed economy and a pluralist political system, and to try to retain good relations with the Catholic Church, more influential in Nicaragua than it had been in Cuba.[68] Castro did not want Nicaragua's middle class to melt away, as Cuba's had done.

The Sandinistas listened to Castro's advice, but the dynamic of their own revolution lead ineluctably to a clash with the United States. When Carter was replaced by Ronald Reagan in January 1981, the United States sought to sweep back the tide of revolt spreading through the isthmus. This was a tough moment for Cuba too, as the mirage of a possible US rapprochement that had hovered over the island during the Carter years evaporated overnight.

The inexperienced Sandinistas had an even tougher time. The political unity that had brought them to power soon disintegrated and the more conservative members of the ruling group dropped away. As the revolution radicalised, thousands of professionals left the country to re-establish themselves in Miami and in Costa Rica. Soon counter-revolutionary forces – the *contras* - organised themselves to fight a guerrilla war against the government. Advised and funded by the CIA they maintained a low-intensity conflict throughout the 1980s that would slowly grind down the Sandinista defences.

Castro had promised to provide teachers and doctors in his first speech to the Sandinista leaders, but soon he had to send military advisers and weapons.

So too did the Soviet Union. Yet as in Angola, substantial differences soon emerged. General Nestor López Cuba, the leader of Cuba's military mission to Managua, reported years later:

> The Sandinistas had both Cuban and Soviet military advisers, and we didn't always agree on our advice ... The Soviets argued for a large, professional, technically sophisticated, regular army. We, on the other hand, believed Nicaragua needed an army capable of eliminating the irregular forces they confronted internally, and that this could not be accomplished by a regular army.

The Cuban view was based on their experience in Angola, and in the Escambray in the early 1960s. The Soviet Union harked back to its experiences in the Second World War. 'These differences over the conception of the struggle and the structure of the army', said López, 'were ones we also faced in Angola and elsewhere in Africa.' An irregular struggle had to be fought with irregular forces, not with large units of regulars. 'It had to be fought by volunteers.' That was how Cuba had defeated 'the bandits' in the Escambray.[69]

Although the Sandinista victory secured the world's headlines, an earlier revolution that year in the tiny island of Grenada was more to Castro's taste. The New Jewel Movement that led the revolution of March 1979, on an island with a population of only 100,000, was a political organisation modelled on the Cuban example.[70] The dawn raid that toppled the corrupt regime of Eric Gairy was even described as Grenada's 'Moncada'. Maurice Bishop, its leader, was a Marxist radical in the Cuban mould and he looked to Castro for inspiration and assistance. The Grenadan revolutionaries threw themselves at Castro's feet. Cuba is the best example in the world, Bishop told the non-aligned conference in Havana in September 1979, 'of what socialism can do in a small country – for health, education, employment, and for ending poverty, prostitution and disease'.[71]

Later, when the Reagan administration expressed its anxiety at Grenada's close friendship with Cuba, Bishop produced a rhetorical flourish similar to Castro's: 'No country has the right to tell us what to do, or how to run our country, or who to be friendly with ... We are not in anybody's backyard, and we are definitely not for sale.'

Castro had been cultivating the islands of the British Caribbean as they became independent, and had had considerable success with Michael Manley, the prime minister of Jamaica from 1972 to 1980. Manley shared a similar outlook on the world and had similar difficulties with Washington. When he increased the taxes payable by US bauxite companies the Americans cut off his sources of economic assistance. Cuba provided him with considerable technical and medical help and the two leaders met often.[72]

Grenada was a similar case. Castro was delighted and impressed with Bishop and established a close personal relationship with him, similar to his friendship with Manley and Mengistu. Possibly their *rapport* had its downside, since it may well have blinded Castro to the fact that, although Bishop was the pre-eminent figure on the tiny revolutionary island, his leadership was not always unquestioned within the revolutionary ranks.

Castro promised medical assistance and a direct air link was established between the two islands. Cuba provided scholarships for Grenadan students, and soon some 250 of them were studying in Cuba. The Cubans also supplied some military equipment and a handful of advisers. The most eye-catching project they developed was the construction of a new airport at Point Salines, designed to help Grenada to participate in the Caribbean tourist boom. Cuba offered to provide construction workers and machinery to the value of $40 million – a large part of the total cost – and the agreement signed in September 1979 indicated that the project would be completed in March 1984. The airport caused immediate controversy, soon referred to by the United States as a Soviet–Cuban base. 'It is not nutmeg that is at stake in the Caribbean and Central America,' claimed President Reagan, referring to Grenada's chief export, 'it is the national security of the United States.'[73]

Threats from the United States were not the only problems facing the government of Grenada. Internal divisions reached such a pitch in October 1983 that Bishop was placed under house arrest by a radicalised section of the New Jewel Movement, led by Bernard Coard. Castro, on the sidelines, could do little to help his protégé, sending a message to say that the government split would 'considerably damage the image of the revolutionary process'. Bishop is 'well-regarded in Cuba,' he wrote, 'and it will not be easy to explain these events'. Worse was to come. When a crowd of Bishop supporters came to rescue him, he was seized by soldiers and shot, along with several other senior members of his cabinet. Castro was appalled, the personal loss as grievous as the political: 'No doctrine, no principle, no opinion calling itself revolutionary, and no internal split, can justify such atrocious acts as the physical elimination of Bishop and the prominent group of honest and dignified leaders who died yesterday.'[74]

Less than a week later, on 25 October, a US force was sent to invade Grenada. Little resistance was offered and several Cubans were killed. Cuban workers at the airport site were rounded up and deported. A promising attempt to seek an alternative path to development in the Caribbean was utterly destroyed, serving as yet another reminder to Cuba of the hard road it had chosen in a particularly unfavourable location.

8

Cuba stands alone, 1985–2003

Mikhail Gorbachev: the new broom in Moscow: 1985

Revolutions within the Spanish government in the nineteenth century often led to serious trouble and dislocation in its Caribbean colonies. Something similar happened to Cuba after the collapse of the Soviet Union in 1991. The country that had provided the financial backing for Cuba's socialist experiment for 20 years, and the source of its military security over three decades, disappeared for all time. The writing had been on the wall ever since the Soviet Union acquired a new leader in March 1985, the third in as many years. Mikhail Gorbachev, a relatively young man with a reputation as a reformer, was appointed secretary-general of the Soviet Communist Party after the deaths in quick succession of Yuri Andropov and Konstantin Chernenko.

The arrival of Gorbachev on the Soviet scene, even at the time, was seen as a seismic change likely to cause problems in its Cuban semi-colony. For a seasoned operator like Castro, following Soviet developments closely for more than quarter of a century, a new man at the top with a fresh agenda was bound to be greeted with some concern. Yet few foresaw the extent of the catastrophe for Cuba that lay ahead.

The Cubans had received an unpleasant surprise two years earlier, when the Russians explained formally that the Soviet defence guarantee, operative since the missile crisis of October 1962, could no longer be extended to their island. Trouble for the Cubans began with Andropov, the Soviet leader after the death of Brezhnev in November 1982. While Brezhnev had consolidated the Soviet relationship with Cuba over more than 20 years, Andropov was to unravel much of his work. Raúl Castro, the man in charge of Cuba's defences, was summoned to Moscow in March 1983 and told some elementary truths by Andropov that Brezhnev had avoided discussing.

Andropov explained to Raúl, according to Yuri Pavlov, a Latin American specialist in the Soviet foreign ministry in the 1980s, that the Soviet strategic guarantee was no longer operative. 'Owing to the geographical factor and the practical impossibility for the Soviet Union to maintain such extended lines of communication with Cuba in conditions of war, it would not be possible to engage Soviet armed forces in the defence of the island.'[1] Soviet nuclear missile systems were also, of course, excluded.

Raúl Castro returned home with nothing other than a promise of additional conventional weapons that the Russians could provide relatively cheaply, and, according to Pavlov, an increased volume of Soviet weapons were indeed shipped to Cuba between 1983 and 1990. Now lacking the Soviet guarantee, Raúl began organising Cuban defence in terms of a 'people's war' to resist a possible American attack. The mobilisation of the entire population was to substitute for the Revolution's earlier reliance on Soviet assistance.

Andropov had spelt out the new strategic reality. Gorbachev was to do the same for the economy, but Fidel planned to forestall him. The Cubans had taken orthodox advice from Soviet economists ever since the early 1970s. As a member of Comecon since 1972, Cuba had tightly bound its economy to the Soviet bloc. The overall picture had been relatively positive for more than a decade, with a long period of sustained economic growth, averaging 4.1 per cent from the mid 1970s to the mid 1980s. Yet by the middle of the 1980s the economy was beginning to falter and Cuba was faced with a serious crisis in its economic relationship with the non-Communist world. The country was dangerously short of hard currency. The low price of sugar on the world market and years of drought and hurricane, in addition to growing protectionism in western markets, had reduced Cuba's foreign currency earnings.[2]

In February 1986 Castro presented a new and revised economic programme that rejected much of the old Soviet model. Some saw it as a return to the 'command' economy, popular during an earlier era in Soviet thinking and unlikely to be welcomed by the revisionist Gorbachev. Framed within a document presented to the third congress of the Communist Party, the new programme was uncompromisingly entitled the 'Rectification of Errors and Negative Tendencies'.[3] Symbolic of the new mood was the abandonment of the national plan, drawn up ten years earlier by Humberto Pérez, head of Juceplan, and now perceived to be out of touch with reality. Pérez was replaced.[4]

The new programme addressed three problems: the immediate need to deal with the foreign exchange crisis; the longer term need to restructure the economy to reduce the country's dependence on imports; and a more controversial and political need to rectify the previous strategy, replacing material incentives with the moral incentives once advocated by Che Guevara. The first and second problems involved technical solutions: the service of foreign debt was suspended, mechanisms were devised to re-establish centralised control of foreign trade and a campaign to promote non-traditional exports was started, as was an austerity programme.[5]

The specific rectification campaign had several elements. The return to a more centralised command system over economic decision-making was designed to increase international competitiveness and economic efficiency. Subsidies would be reduced and more accurate measures of profitability and more streamlined government administration would be brought in. By reviving the Guevarist vision of a more moral society, the government hoped that citizens would take greater responsibility for their actions.

The programme was controversial in that it involved the abolition of several initiatives introduced in the previous decade that had proved markedly popular. These were the farmers' so-called 'free markets'; the handicrafts markets; the provision of 'motivation bonuses' awarded for productivity increases; the introduction of private enterprise into a wide range of goods and services; and the private selling, renting and construction of houses. If the farmers' markets were to be abolished, the state would have to provide something similar if not better.

The government had long been concerned by the country's over-dependence on food supplies from abroad, and the need to produce more food locally was one of the forces driving the rectification. The food programme now introduced was an attempt by the state to produce food more cheaply than the free farmers' markets had been able to do. 'If it was a question of producing bananas, tubers, vegetables and fruit,' Castro explained later, 'let the state do it, since it has all the necessary resources.'[6] The new mechanisms to gear up local food production took some time to settle in, but fortunately for Cuba they were in place when the link with Cuba's traditional suppliers in the Soviet Union and Eastern Europe was broken in 1990.

The rectification programme was an implicit rejection of the reforming experiments – the expansion of the role of the market and the increased reliance on material incentives – that had been tried and tested in the socialist economies of Eastern Europe. Cuba was again moving out of step. The changes were under way when Castro held his first long conversation with Gorbachev in March 1986. The fresh direction of Soviet policy was already clear and, in speeches and in private conversations, Castro had begun to register his discontent with Gorbachev's message. Now he was obliged to listen to it at first hand, and he did not much like what he heard.

Gorbachev's use of the key words of *glasnost* and *perestroika* – the promotion of political openness and economic restructuring – could be dismissed as an internal affair of the Soviet Union with little necessary effect on Cuba, but other items on the agenda were more alarming. The Soviet leader's pursuit of East–West détente with President Reagan was certain to have an adverse impact. Castro had had just this kind of bumpy ride before – with Aleksei Kosygin in the 1960s – and had not enjoyed the experience.

When Castro met Gorbachev, the Cuban leadership had not formulated an agreed policy toward the policy changes within the Soviet Union. Carlos

Rafael Rodríguez, the old Communist stalwart now on the verge of retirement but still one of Cuba's vice-presidents, had made favourable comments about *perestroika* earlier in the year. At a Comecon meeting held in Bucharest he had referred to 'the mood of imaginativeness and flexibility now abroad among the Moscow allies', with which he would like 'to associate the Cuban process'.[7]

Rodríguez's emollient view was not shared by Castro, and his concerns about Soviet developments were eventually spelt out in December 1988: 'We sincerely support the peace policy of the Soviet Union, but peace has different meanings for different countries. It is almost certain that the way the [American] empire conceives peace is with the powerful: peace with the Soviet Union, but war with the small, socialist, revolutionary, and progressive – or simply independent – countries of the Third World.' Castro was outlining his differences with Soviet foreign policy.

Gorbachev had other global priorities and he did not make his first visit to Havana until April 1989. He behaved politely throughout but was blunt, giving full warning of what was to come on the economic front. 'As life moves ahead,' he informed the Cuban leadership, 'new demands are being made on the quality of our interaction. This applies particularly to economic contacts – they should be more dynamic and effective, and bring greater returns for both our countries.' In public the two presidents signed a fresh treaty of cooperation, to last for 25 years. In private Gorbachev made clear that the old economic relationship, with the price subsidies that had long helped to keep Cuba relatively prosperous, would have to be phased out. There was more to come. The Russians, in future, would expect payment for their goods in US dollars.

The news was worse than Castro had been expecting and he returned to the subject of Cuba's differences with the Soviet Union in a speech in Camagüey in July, warning the country of its possible isolation. He criticised the 'pro-capitalist policies' being adopted in Poland and Hungary, comparing them unfavourably with Cuba's rectification. Reforms in the Soviet Union, he said, with his eye for accurate prophecy, might even lead to its disintegration or to civil war.[8] He was preparing the Cubans for a rocky road ahead.

Cuba's victory at Cuito Cuanavale, 1988

The Cuban people could look after themselves, but the future of their bridgehead in Angola was more problematic. Thousands of Cuban troops were still stationed in Africa and their safety depended on the weapons that the Soviet Union provided for the Angolan armed forces. In Gorbachev's view *perestroika* abroad and a gradual withdrawal from Angola by the Cuban and the Soviet armies would mean a more friendly relationship with the United States, as well as greater resources for the Soviet consumer at home. These were new times.

Dissatisfaction with the reformist winds of change in the Soviet Union was not confined to Havana. Cuba's close African ally, the Angolan government of José Eduardo Dos Santos, was also worried. Dos Santos had been president and leader of the MPLA since the death of Agostinho Neto in 1979. The long war in defence of his government, sustained by 25,000 Cuban soldiers and with a heavy strategic input from Soviet advisers, had been going well in 1986. But vigorous attacks by the guerrilla forces of Jonas Savimbi's UNITA movement, funded and armed by the United States and backed by South Africa, had caused the MPLA's army a series of setbacks in 1987. The Russians had never had much heart for battle, and now had lost it altogether. In his search for détente with the West, Gorbachev was anxious to clear up some of these Cold War conflicts.

Perceiving Soviet weakness, the South Africans prepared an offensive in southern Angola, their most ambitious initiative since 1975. Men and weapons assembled along the frontier in northern Namibia, poised to seize control of the territory across the border. The nearest Cuban forces were based at Menongue, some 125 miles to the west of Cuito Cuanavale, a strategic town surrounded by an area of dense bush. South African and UNITA troops attacked in November 1987, forcing MPLA units to retreat to Cuito Cuanavale. If the town were to fall the entire southern zone of Angola would come under South African control. Angola needed additional help and it needed it soon.

High strategy had been in the hands of Russian officers, but in a moment of crisis Dos Santos was more likely to get extra troops from Cuba than from the Soviet Union. Faced with imminent defeat in the south, he asked Castro for assistance. The new request came just twelve years after the original Cuban intervention in Angola had turned the tide in 1975. Prompt Cuban intervention on this second occasion, as before, was to change the history of Africa. Cuba rescued the Angolan government from South African attack and paved the way to an end to apartheid in South Africa itself.

Cuba's campaigns in Africa had always aroused Castro's personal interest and his geo-strategic ambitions. A year earlier, in Harare, he had pledged that Cuba would remain in Angola 'until the end of apartheid' in South Africa.[9] Later, in Luanda, he reminded a gathering of Cubans that they had been there for eleven years and would be there, if necessary, for 'one hunded times eleven years'. On his return in Havana, he promised that Cuba was prepared to stay in Angola for 'ten, twenty, or even thirty more years'.

Now he was to take a direct part in the strategic planning for the defence of Cuito Cuanavale. Cuba's first action was to send its most experienced pilots to Angola. Based at Menongue, they were to attack the South African forces besieging Cuito Cuanavale. Subsequently combat units and weapons were sent from Cuba 'to meet the situation and foil enemy plans'.[10]

Thousands of Cuban troops were mobilised and the new campaign brought back to Luanda some of the generals who had been in the Angolan war in

1975, and others who had fought in Ethiopia. Their commander was General Arnaldo Ochoa, a veteran of the earlier Angolan and Ethiopian conflicts, described by one authority as a legendary and heroic figure 'second only to Fidel Castro for the Cuban soldiers in the field'.[11]

Castro himself had a lower opinion of Ochoa's strategic talents, and serious disagreements arose between the commander in Angola and the commander-in-chief in Havana. Castro reinforced the Cuban command by sending out another experienced and reliable officer, General Leopoldo 'Polo' Cintra Frías. While Ochoa remained at the principal Cuban base in Luanda, liaising with the Angolans and the Russians, Cintra Frías was placed in command of the southern front.[12]

In the early weeks of 1988, with the arrival of the first 9,000 Cuban reinforcements, the military tide began to turn against the South Africans. The total Cuban contingent was now more than 50,000. Castro noted that Cuba's army in Angola – in proportion to population – was equivalent to the United States sending more than a million men abroad.[13] The Cubans moved inland to the misty hills and forest of Malange in the north, to distant Luena near the border of the Congo and Zambia, and to Cuito Cuanavale in the south, where they were soon to be notably engaged.[14]

The strategic disagreement between Castro and Ochoa, over the tactics to be adopted around Cuito Cuanavale, continued into the new year. Castro demanded an urgent and immediate reinforcement of the garrison there, while Ochoa argued that the town's defence could be assured with mines and air-power, using the Cuban pilots, flying Soviet Migs, who were based at Menongue. So acrid was the debate that Castro demanded Ochoa's return to Havana at the end of January 1988 for face-to-face discussions. Ochoa then went back to Luanda, bearing Castro's detailed instructions about how the Cuban reinforcements were to be deployed at Cuito Cuanavale.

The long-awaited South African attack came on 14 February, and their soldiers, in support of the CIA-funded guerrillas of UNITA, penetrated the suburbs of the town. The Cuban forces fought back and Cuito Cuanavale soon turned into a resounding Cuban victory. After several weeks of heavy fighting the South African advance was halted. Cuito Cuanavale was to become a symbol across Africa, indicating that apartheid and its army was no longer invincible.[15]

The South African defeat obliged its army to withdraw from Angola. This in turn was followed by the withdrawal of South African troops from Namibia, leading to a diplomatic solution – orchestrated by Chester Crocker, the United States secretary of state for African affairs – that allowed both for the withdrawal of Cuban troops from Angola and for the Namibian liberation movement SWAPO, the South West African People's Organisation, to come to power in Windhoek.

This strategic collapse in southern Africa was eventually to lead to the end of the apartheid state itself. In February 1990, two years after Cuito

Cuanavale, Nelson Mandela, the black South African leader, was released from prison. He came to Havana in July 1991 to thank Castro personally for Cuba's assistance in the anti-apartheid struggle:

> The decisive defeat of the racist army in Cuito Cuanavale was a victory for all Africa . . . [It] made it possible for Angola to enjoy peace and establish its own sovereignty . . . [and] for the people of Namibia to achieve their independence. The decisive defeat of the aggressive apartheid forces destroyed the myth of the invincibility of the white oppressor. The defeat of the apartheid army served as an inspiration to the struggling people of South Africa'.[16]

The Cuban victory accelerated an East–West agreement on southern Africa, and the continuing negotiations between the United States and the Soviet Union, conducted by Crocker, were joined by Cuban and South African representatives. All four countries signed an Angola agreement at the UN in New York in December. South African troops would be withdrawn from Namibia, whose independence would now be internationally recognised, while Cuban troops would withdraw from Angola.[17] Cuban soldiers came home from Angola, as Spanish soldiers had once returned from fighting in Morocco, to form a group of nostalgic veterans with bitter-sweet memories of their service in Africa, tending increasingly forgotten memorials to their fallen comrades in towns throughout the island. The internationalist spirit of the Revolution lived on, not with soldiers but with doctors and teachers, deployed in ever-increasing numbers throughout Africa.

Nine Cuban generals with Angolan experience were present at the signing ceremony in New York that marked the end of the intervention, but General Ochoa was not among them. In January 1989 he was recalled to Havana, with the promise of promotion to command the Western army in Cuba, but history had reserved for him another, more sombre fate.

The execution of Arnaldo Ochoa, 1989

Six months after the signing of the Angolan peace agreement, the Revolution faced its most serious internal crisis in 30 years. Four senior figures were arrested in June 1989 and brought before a military tribunal on charges of corruption and drug smuggling. Two were executed and two were sentenced to long prison terms. The number of those on trial eventually rose to fourteen. The trial and death sentences caused shock waves through the island and far beyond, sparking an epidemic of rumours and sowing doubts about the official story. Corruption was a crime that threatened the entire moral basis of the Revolution, for Castro's original July 26 Movement had been cemented together by its principled rejection of the corrupt order that had preceded it. Rumours suggested that the corruption case had more to do with politics than with financial irresponsibility. The arrests occurred just two months after Gorbachev's visit to Havana. Might there have been a plot to replace Castro with a reformist leadership, favourable to the introduction of *glasnost* and *perestroika* into Cuba?

Some believed that the prisoners were executed because of their involvement with corruption and drug trafficking. Others thought they were shot because of the political challenge they appeared to represent. Those abroad questioned whether Castro himself was implicated in the drugs trade, and every tiny piece of evidence was assembled to try to prove this allegation.

The rumour of a possible political threat to Castro was given some credibility by the fact that the principal figure in the frame was General Ochoa, the officer recently in charge in Angola. Ochoa was a popular soldier known to be out of favour with the regime. His strategic talents in the Angolan campaign had already been questioned by Castro. Two other senior figures, Tony and Patricio de la Guardia, had been pillars of the secret service for decades. The fourth man arrested, Diócles Torralba, was minister of transport and a close friend of Ochoa. Tony de la Guardia was his son-in-law. Everything initially seemed to have been kept cosily within one extended, but highly influential, family.

The subsequent arrest of General José Abrantes, the powerful minister of the interior (MININT) since 1986, was a further indication of the gravity of the crisis. A former leader of the Communist youth organisation, Abrantes had been involved with state security since the earliest years of the Revolution. His detention was a sign that the Ochoa crisis had affected the very structure of the state. MININT, with its own paramilitary force, was a rival to the defence ministry of Raúl Castro. Abrantes was also known as an independent figure who spoke his mind. He had made favourable references to the Gorbachev reforms in a recent speech to the Writers' and Artists' Union in Havana.

The leading figures had all worked at the highest level over many years, involved in some of the Revolution's most hazardous foreign operations. Ochoa, born in 1941, had taken part in the revolutionary war and become a professional soldier after 1959, trained at the military academy in Moscow. He took a prominent role in the guerrilla war in Venezuela in the 1960s and later joined the Cuban contingent in Congo-Brazzaville in 1965, helping to train the guerrillas fighting in Angola and Mozambique. He had been with the Cuban tank troop in Syria in 1973–4, defending the Golan Heights against the Israelis after the Yom Kippur war.

Ochoa was again in Africa in the 1970s, first in Angola in 1976, and later, in December 1977, in Ethiopia, commanding the Cuban force in the Ogaden. Returning to Latin America in 1983 he helped with Nicaragua's fight against the contras, and most recently, in 1987–8, he had been in Luanda. He was one of the most well-known and most decorated figures in the Cuban army and, since hundreds of thousands of Cubans had passed through Angola between 1975 and 1989, he had many friends.

The de la Guardia brothers had been active in the Cuban secret service over the same period. Regarded as wealthy playboys in the late 1950s, they had become active supporters of the Revolution and caught the eye of Castro in 1961. They were the chief contacts with the guerrilla movement in Guatemala in the 1960s. Patricio de la Guardia had a relatively unadventurous career, working at a high level within MININT, latterly as its chief representative in Luanda, where he was in close touch with Ochoa.

Tony de la Guardia's life was more flamboyant. One of the scarlet pimpernels of the Cuban Revolution, he had been in charge of Castro's security in Chile in 1971 and had stayed to train Allende's protection squad. In 1975 he helped launder the money secured by the Montoneros, the Argentine guerrilla movement, after they had kidnapped the directors of the grain-dealers Bunge y Born, and in 1978 he was a Cuban contact with the Sandinista guerrillas. He established a relationship with Robert Vesco, the discredited American financier who had been President Nixon's friend and backer, and brought him to Cuba in October 1982. Vesco's financial expertise was useful to MININT's foreign operations.

Tony de la Guardia's task in the 1980s, based in Havana, was to run a secret department within MININT that sought to find ways to thwart the US blockade. Known by its initials as MC, standing for *Moneda Convertible*, or 'convertible money', the department was part of CIMEX, the government corporation dealing with all import–export transactions. MC's specific task was to purchase weapons, electronic equipment and medical products from Western countries, and to find markets for Cuban cigars. Much of its work was done through Panama, whose free trade zones were a centre of illegal operations. The governments of Omar Torrijos and Manuel Noriega were notably friendly towards Cuba.

Suddenly, in June 1989, these apparently non-corruptible paladins of the Revolution were in prison and on trial. The ill-defined corruption charges produced on the first day of their detention were soon expanded to include moral corruption, defeatism and drug smuggling. Ochoa and officials within MININT were accused of using the MC department as a cover for dealings with the Medellín drugs cartel in Colombia, and they were charged very specifically with the trans-shipment of cocaine to Florida via the military airport at Varadero.[18] Not just the individuals involved but the Revolution itself was on trial. Just how much did the Cuban government know about the operations of the international drugs trade? To what extent was the top leadership involved in it? At what level in the revolutionary hierarchy was the decision made to take part? Everyone in Cuba posed the same questions.

Cuba and the surrounding Caribbean sea had been a centre for pirates and smugglers since the sixteenth century. Illegal trade had been the background to its entire history. Not a creek or inlet or harbour had not witnessed the silent entry over the centuries of small ships with experienced crews, bringing in goods from abroad and taking away the products of Cuban farms and factories. In the final decades of the twentieth century the most valuable commodities making their way from South to North America were marijuana and cocaine, and Cuba was plumb in the centre of the route. The *lancheros*, or boatmen, running drugs across the Caribbean were the latest players in a 500-year-old game.

Cuba had the largest and most sophisticated intelligence service in the region, except for that of the United States, and the service had been involved in assisting guerrilla movements in Colombia and Central America over many years, shipping men and arms across the water. Its knowledge of what went on, in and around the shores of the Caribbean, was second to none. So how much of all this did Castro care to know about?

The specific drug-running story that led to the Ochoa affair began three years earlier when a Cuban exile, Reinaldo Ruiz, contacted the Havana Cubans running the MC's office in Panama in 1986.[19] Ruiz was a businessman and minor criminal who had left Cuba in 1962. He had no love for the Revolution, but had his eyes open for business opportunities. He was married to a wealthy Colombian, allegedly with links to the drugs trade, notably to Pablo Escóbar, the head of the Medellín cartel.

Ruiz had teamed up with a Cuban cousin, Miguel Ruiz Poo, who had remained loyal to Cuba and was a senior operative in MC's Panama office. The two men had engaged in a mutually profitable business, smuggling IBM computers to Cuba to break the blockade. The actual smugglers, the *lancheros* who took the goods from Panama to Cuba, were also engaged in drug smuggling, and conversations between the Ruiz cousins turned to the possibility of Cuba entering the lucrative cocaine trade.

They flew to Havana to discuss the matter with Tony de la Guardia and were authorised to transfer cocaine to the island for subsequent re-shipment to Florida. Reinaldo Ruiz asked de la Guardia, according to the account by Andrés Oppenheimer, a correspondent for the *Miami Herald*, whether '*el señor*' (Castro) knew about the situation and received the reply 'of course'.[20] No evidence exists to prove that Tony de la Guardia discussed these cocaine-trafficking plans with Castro, but it is reasonable to assume that they were approved by Abrantes, the minister responsible for the MC department.

The first cocaine trans-shipments were made in April 1987. A cargo of 300 kilos was flown in by a small plane from Colombia to an airstrip near Varadero. There the consignment was picked up by *lancheros* for forward transmission to Miami, but disaster struck before they reached their destination. The *lancheros* were intercepted by a US coastguard patrol.

The suspicions of the US Drug Enforcement Agency, the DEA, were aroused, though their attention was initially focused on Noriega's Panama rather than Cuba. In February 1988, just weeks after Noriega had been indicted in Florida on drug smuggling charges, Reinaldo Ruiz was detained by the Panama authorities at the request of the DEA and flown out to Miami. Accused of using Cuban government facilities to help smuggle cocaine, and of landing a drug smuggling plane at Varadero on at least one occasion, Ruiz sang his heart out in court.

This was disquieting news for Cuba, for these were not the first allegations made about its possible participation in the drugs trade. When questioned by a US television reporter, Castro dismissed the allegations as 'lies from top to bottom', and pointed out that similar accusations had been made in 1982. These had been seen as part of the ongoing war of words between the United States and Cuba, and those of 1988 appeared at first sight to be more of the same. This time, however, the story was to pan out in a different fashion. The Cuban drug smuggling allegations were covered regularly in the Florida newspapers throughout the year, indicating that Cuba was clearly involved and that the Americans knew all about it.

No direct evidence exists to indicate when Castro himself discovered the truth about what had been going on. The Ruiz trial dragged on in Miami for more than a year. Castro had his own means of securing information, and it may well be that the Americans were also keeping him informed of what they knew. One possibility, raised years later, was that he was informed of Tony de la Guardia's activities by Robert Vesco.[21]

The Castro brothers took action early in 1989. Fidel requested Abrantes to make an investigation into the Ruiz allegations, while Raúl ordered a separate investigation into the activities of Abrantes's ministry. The two enquiries understandably caused alarm among those being investigated, and led to the arrests carried out in June. The case against Tony de la Guardia was clear-cut. By using his MC department to engage in covert drug smuggling operations that were both incompetent and involved Cuban exiles, he had overstepped whatever ground rules may have been established for its operation. An assumption that Castro knew what he was engaged in was not available as a defence. Less clear was the case against his twin brother Patricio, or that against Ochoa. Both had been in Luanda at the time of the Ruiz operation at Varadero, but what was the connection between Angola and the drug smugglers of Panama?

The trial began on 25 June, first before a tribunal of 47 high-ranking officers, and then before a military court of three, presided over by General Ulises Rosales del Toro, another veteran of the Sierra Maestra and of the Venezuelan guerrilla campaign of the 1960s. The proceedings were recorded on tape and shown nightly on television.

The dark side of the Cuban operation in Angola soon emerged, a sorry tale of ivory- and diamond-smuggling in which both Ochoa and Patricio de la Guardia were involved. Ivory and diamonds were collected in Angola and then laundered through Tony's department in Havana. At one level such activity was both normal and defensible. Like any responsible general in foreign parts Ochoa was concerned to see that his men were adequately fed, clothed and armed. If the bare minimum was not always available, as was often the case in Angola, the general would have to cope as best he could. In Ochoa's case that meant illegal trading. By importing Cuban sugar into Luanda and selling it on the black market Ochoa soon acquired funds with which to buy diamonds and ivory. These, in turn, could be exported to Panama, with the help of Tony de la Guardia's team, and exchanged for weapons and ammunition.

Further incriminating details soon emerged. Among those on trial was an aide-de-camp of Ochoa involved with the Panama end of the operations. He was charged with making contact with Colombian drug smugglers, and through them with Pablo Escóbar. Ochoa himself, according to evidence produced at the trial, had given him permission so to do.

Two questions were asked in Washington and Miami, and the debate engendered abroad soon filtered through to Havana. How much did Castro know? Was the trial engineered to ensure the dismissal of a popular officer with political ambitions? 'The level of detail Castro gets involved with is nothing short of extraordinary,' argued Jacqueline Tillman, a former adviser to the US national security council. 'It really strains the imagination to think he didn't acquiesce to the drug trafficking.' John Fernández, a spokesman for the DEA in Miami, was more circumspect, pointing out that there was 'no reason to believe that Fidel Castro or people in the presidential palace were in sympathy with the smugglers'.[22]

The charge that the purge of Ochoa might have been politically motivated was supported by statements from General Rafael del Pino, a Cuban airforce officer and Angola veteran who had defected to Miami in 1987. Del Pino claimed bluntly in June 1989 that Ochoa had been detained to prevent disgruntled officers from carrying out 'an uprising against the regime'.[23] The implication of Del Pino's claims was that Ochoa was an officer with political ambitions, and stories were later produced to suggest that he supported the introduction of Gorbachev-style reforms into Cuba.

After a trial lasting two weeks Ochoa, Tony de la Guardia and two others (including Ochoa's aide-de-camp) were sentenced to death. Patricio de la Guardia and Ruiz Poo received prison sentences of 30 years, as did four of Tony de la Guardia's aides who had assisted the *lancheros* at Varadero. Six others received lighter sentences.

On 9 July the 29 members of the Council of State assembled to discuss and ratify the verdicts. Two hastily came back from an official visit to Pyongyang; a third was told to cancel a trip to Argentina. Each spoke up in favour of the death penalties that had been ordained. Those sentenced to death were executed on 13 July.

Subsequently, in separate trials, Abrantes was sentenced to 20 years in prison, charged with 'tolerance of corrupt behaviour', and Torralba received the same sentence. Abrantes died in prison two years later of a heart attack. Before he died he reportedly told Patricio de la Guardia that he had indeed approved of some of the drug shipments. Patricio told his wife of this conversation and she transmitted the gist of it to Andrés Oppenheimer. According to Oppenheimer's account Abrantes claimed that Castro was aware that cocaine shipments occasionally went through Cuban territory, and on one occasion had authorised the sale of cocaine captured by the Cuban coastguards. He had, however, been furious when he realised the scale of what was being done behind his back.[24]

Friends and relatives of the Ochoa and de la Guardia families were never able to bring themselves to believe that the activities of the accused men had not been known to Castro and the rest of the Cuban high command, yet the evidence of Patricio's wife is all that exists to substantiate the allegations that Castro was aware of the drug smuggling engaged in by his officials. Patricio's daughter and son-in-law subsequently went into exile, to Paris, and repeated the allegations, writing books that denounced Castro and claimed that their relative was innocent.[25]

In several Latin American countries allegations of extensive drug smuggling might have been nearer the mark, but the particular history of the Cuban Revolution, with its emphasis on ethical standards, suggests that the extent of what had been going on may well have been a surprise to Castro. Quite possibly he was genuinely ignorant, but the politicised sector of the Cuban population (a very large percentage) were undoubtedly shocked and dismayed, both by the trial and by the executions. Nothing comparable had occurred in the previous 30 years.

Castro's government worked hard to limit the damage caused by the episode. Senior generals lined up behind the government. 'We regretted having to shoot someone who had once been a revolutionary,' said General Enrique Carreras of the Cuban airforce, interviewed years later in 1997. 'But a revolutionary cannot stain his hands, or take the wrong road in order to obtain funds for things our people need. Here there can be no contraband, no drugs. *Not here.*'[26]

Another senior general, José Ramón Fernández, Bay of Pigs veteran and minister of education in 1989, and a member of the Council of State that ratified the death sentences, expressed his shock at the revelations.[27] In his eyes it was unimaginable that Cuba could condone drug smuggling. It was also dismaying for old revolutionaries like him to have had revealed to them the scale of corruption and personal enrichment that appeared from the Ochoa affair to be endemic. The trial and executions were difficult medicines for the Cuban population to swallow.[28] The country was polarised by the episode, with no room for objective interpretation, and its damage to the 30-year-old

Revolution might well have had further repercussions had the Revolution itself not encountered fresh difficulties, in the face of which Cubans were now obliged to unite.

The 'Special Period in Peacetime', 1990

The political hurricane that developed in Cuba in the course of 1989, foreshadowed by the Ochoa trial and the Gorbachev reforms, took physical shape towards the end of the year after dramatic events in Europe. The collapse of the Berlin Wall in November was quickly followed by the 'velvet revolution' in Prague, and December saw the operatic finale to the rule of Nicolae Ceauşescu in Romania, chased from office by a popular demonstration and then captured and executed on television with his wife beside him. Exiles in Miami wondered aloud whether this might not be a possible model for the end of the Castro era.

The American invasion of Panama in December – the deployment of 24,000 troops made it the largest US military intervention since the Vietnam war – was also perceived as a possible alternative ending to the Cuban Revolution. General Noriega, who had provided one of Cuba's lifelines to the capitalist world, sought asylum in the Vatican embassy, to be bombarded with rock music from loudspeakers before handing himself over to the US authorities. More than a thousand Panamanians died in a bombardment that was rather more lethal. Noriega's ramshackle government met a violent end. Might Cuba suffer a similar fate?

Worse was to come. In February 1990 the Sandinistas were defeated in elections that President Ortega had felt obliged to hold – against Castro's advice. Ortega thought he could win, but the Nicaraguan people, oppressed and exhausted by the long, US-orchestrated, intervention by the contras, believed that the return of the Sandinista government would mean endless war. They were probably right. Bullied into voting for peace, they took the non-Sandinista choice. Another close Cuban ally – a revolution on which Cuba had expended much effort and emotional energy – was suddenly gone.

More serious for the economic health of the Revolution was the demise of the Communist states of Eastern Europe in the course of 1990, coupled with the disintegration of the Soviet Union itself after the failed coup against Gorbachev in August 1991. The final and definitive blow for Cuba came on 12 September 1991, a few weeks after the coup, when Gorbachev gave in to pressure from the United States and announced that the 7,000 Soviet troops stationed in Cuba would be withdrawn. As usual in the dealings between the two superpowers the Cubans were not consulted.

The real crisis began in 1990 when the oil supplies that the Soviet Union was contractually obliged to deliver failed to arrive. Cuba's domestic economy was seriously disrupted. The regular flow of Soviet tankers bringing cheap oil had been the Revolution's economic lifeline since the 1960s. In 1989 some 13 million tonnes of fuel had been imported from the Soviet Union (at very favourable rates). A year later, the figure had dropped to only 9.9 million tonnes. The downward trend continued and in 1993 Cuba received only 5.3 million tonnes. Replacements had to be purchased on the world market, at a higher price payable only in US dollars.

Cuba was also still heavily dependent on the Soviet Union for its food imports, of which the Russians supplied 63 per cent in the immediate period before the crisis. They were also the source of 80 per cent of Cuba's imported machinery. In addition the Soviet Union had purchased 63 per cent of Cuba's sugar exports, 95 per cent of its citrus and 73 per cent of its nickel.[29] This entire exchange was now at risk, posing the greatest threat to the Cuban economy since the break with the United States in the 1960s.

That trouble was in store had been clear since Gorbachev's visit to Havana in 1989. The long-term Soviet subsidy was to disappear. Future trade deals would take place in convertible currency, and, in the case of sugar, at the world market price. The average price earned by Cuba in 1990 (with sugar sold both to the Soviet bloc and on the world market) was $602 per tonne. By 1992 the world price had slumped from $277 per tonne (in 1990) to $200, the price at which Cuba was obliged to sell virtually its entire crop. The dimension of the economic disaster for Cuba was without precedent.

Gorbachev himself was under pressure from the United States to cease Soviet support for Castro. Cuba had become an expensive irritant. Soon the other Comecon countries would follow where Gorbachev led. They too demanded dollars. Although the Soviet leadership maintained a friendly but realistic stance towards Cuba, other Russians did not disguise their contempt for their former ally. *Glasnost*, meaning a freer press in the Communist world, unleashed torrents of criticism against Cuba. Semi-independent Soviet magazines, like *Moscow News*, became so hostile that they were banned in Havana. The new media in the East European countries were equally outspoken, reflecting years of pent-up resentment of the spendthrift golden boy of 'tropical socialism'. One Hungarian newspaper noted caustically that Cubans could afford to be ideological radicals because they were 'eating the bread of others and building socialism at the expense of another country'.[30]

Castro was as aware as anyone that Cuba had been dependent since the Conquest on its economic relationship with the outside world, and had always been affected by the vagaries of world politics and world trade. The oscillations of the world sugar price over the years, even when cushioned by the US quota in the first half of the twentieth century, were often the cause of political upheavals in Havana. Yet socialist Cuba's close relationship with the Soviet Union, and its integration into Comecon, had brought a certain

stability to the economy over the years. The historical experience was long
forgotten, and maybe even Castro did not realise how rocky the road ahead
would be.

The economic disaster that swept the country was the most dramatic and
significant change since the island had first become a sugar-based economy in
the wake of the revolution in Saint-Domingue in 1791. The island had
received other jolts in earlier years – at the end of the independence war in the
nineteenth century, during the world slump of the 1930s and at the time of
the transformation to socialism in the 1960s – yet none could compare with
its virtual collapse in the early 1990s.

Few societies have been able to confront such an economic catastrophe and
emerge unscathed. Import capacity fell by 70 per cent between 1989 and 1992
– from $8.1 billion in 1989 to $2.3 billion in 1992. (About one third of gross
domestic product had been spent on imports before the crisis.) The root cause
of the collapse was the loss of the sugar subsidy (with sugar earnings down
from $4.3 billion in 2000 to $1.2 billion in 1992 and only $757 million in
1993), and the loss of external financing, mostly provided in the past by the
Soviet Union (down from $3 billion in 1989 to nothing in 1992). The effect
on the domestic economy was multiplied by shortages of inputs – principally
fuel, but also spare parts, chemical fertilisers, and animal feedstuffs.

From 1989 to 1993, the external shock pushed the economy into free fall.
GDP declined by 2.9 per cent in 1990, 10 per cent in 1991, 11.6 per cent in
1992 and 14.9 per cent in 1993.[31] The Cuban future looked unimaginably bleak
and, for the first time since the nineteenth century, people began to mention
Cuba and Haiti, regarded as the poorest country in the western hemisphere,
in the same breath.[32] The extent of the crisis was soon visible in Cuba's towns
and countryside. Horse-drawn carts and carriages replaced cars and lorries;
half a million bicycles circulated in the streets of Havana, courtesy of the
Chinese; 300,000 oxen replaced 30,000 Soviet tractors.

Priority was given to securing essential food and fuel supplies. Food
imports were halved between 1989 and 1993, but the purchase of foreign food
still absorbed a larger proportion of the country's foreign exchange resources
than before. (Food accounted for 25 per cent of the total spending on imports
in 1993, compared with only 12 per cent in 1989.) In the same period the
import of fuel declined by 72 per cent and overall imports by 76 per cent. The
amount of hard currency available to purchase goods other than food – spare
parts, fertiliser and consumer goods – was reduced in 1993 to 17 per cent of
what it had been in 1989. Food and fuel were both in desperately short supply
and, although outright starvation was kept at bay, malnutrition – unknown in
Cuba for generations – became widespread.

Abroad, the widespread expectation of an imminent Cuban implosion in
1990–91 was at fever pitch. The triumphalism of the Cuban exile community
in Miami knew no bounds. Foreign journalists and writers descended on

Havana in the autumn of 1991 to witness what they imagined would be the final weeks of the Castro government and to write its obituary. 'The signs of popular discontent were telling and extensive,' wrote Marifeli Pérez-Stable when summarising the reports from Cuba appearing in the Miami press:

> Signs of 'Abajo Fidel' [Down with Fidel] painted on walls; clashes between youths and the police; dock workers refusing to load sacks of rice for export because of domestic scarcities; the film institute challenging a party directive to merge with state television; intellectuals signing an open letter to the leadership demanding reform; purges at the University of Havana and other higher education institutions; citizens raiding planted fields; near-riots in front of the special hard-currency stores; workers refusing to join the rapid response brigades the government created to quell dissent.[33]

Castro himself, ever alert to the changing world scene, gave several warning speeches about the probability of tough times ahead, explaining to a meeting of the Cuban Workers' Federation in January 1990 how the government had long been prepared for threats of war:

> For 10 years we have been reinforcing our defences, we have applied the concept of the war by all the people . . . We have drawn up plans for every contingency, including a possible total blockade . . . , in which not a single bullet would reach our country . . . Men, women, children, youths, senior citizens, the people at large, have organised to make the aggressors pay an unpayable price.

He emphasised that the country now faced a different problem: 'There may be other forms of aggression for which we must prepare. We have called the total blockade period "a special period in time of war". Yet, in the face of all these problems we must prepare . . . plans for "a special period in time of peace".'[34]

The crisis came sooner than expected, with an interruption to the flow of Soviet oil. In March 1990 the government was obliged to respond with its first 'economic defence exercise', when gas, water and electricity were cut off for short periods in all areas of the country. In August, when it became clear that normal deliveries of Soviet fuel would not be resumed, the government outlined the immediate measures to be taken to deal with the crisis. One of the nickel plants would be closed and the opening of a new oil refinery delayed. Oil and gas deliveries would be cut by 50 per cent across the island and electricity consumption by 10 per cent. Farmers were urged to use draft animals.[35] The historic socialist achievements of the Revolution – free education and free medical attention – would be preserved, but the austerity programme would inevitably bear down on the great mass of the population. Food and clothing were rationed, industries dependent on foreign imports were closed down and thousands of urban workers were sent to the countryside to engage in the labour-intensive task of growing food.

Much of the country's agricultural land had been given over to cattle and sugar for centuries, and Cuba had relied since the Revolution on food from Eastern Europe to feed the nation. The country faced starvation unless alternative sources of supply could be found. Since no dollars were available to pay for food imports from the West, it was vital to increase food production at home.[36]

A number of initiatives were set in train: a 'food programme' was launched in October to encourage local production; scarce funds were put into research and development in bio-technology, with a plan to make the country self-sufficient in medical products; a recycling campaign was introduced; and a far-reaching austerity drive halved the number of officials working for the Communist Party and made inroads into other areas of the state bureaucracy.

Cuba now had to plan for a future in which sugar would no longer be its principal earner, and the government soon made the inevitable decision taken by every Caribbean island faced with a similar predicament: it would seek to satisfy the growing demand by European and Canadian consumers for beach holidays in the sun. Foreign tourists were to become Cuba's principal source of foreign currency. The Cuban state invested heavily in the new tourist industry, and the government searched for foreign partners, principally from Spain, France and Canada, to help to finance, manage and market it.

Many state bureaucrats felt the cold winds of reform after the administration of central government was radically reorganised. The reform had a particular impact on the tourist industry, where the central government agency was replaced by a smaller ministry, overseeing the work of nine new autonomous, and competing, tourist corporations, but many other ministries and state institutes were rationalised and slimmed down.

The restructuring of the external sector looked to some like the beginning of a return to capitalism, with state companies seeking the participation of foreign private capital. The state monopoly over foreign trade was abolished in 1992, and the constitution was amended to permit the transfer of state property to joint ventures with foreign partners.[37] A new foreign investment law was drafted to appeal to such partners. Under its generous terms a foreign enterprise could own up to 49 per cent of the joint venture, hire foreign executives, be exempt from most taxes and repatriate its profits in hard currency.[38] The number of joint ventures jumped from just 2 in 1990 to 112 in 1993.

The economic policy-makers assumed initially that they could reform the external sector without making dramatic internal changes – supporting capitalism abroad but socialism at home. They wanted 'an isolated enclave of foreign investment and tourism' that would provide the hard currency needed to maintain the social structure without changes.[39] This was soon revealed to be wishful thinking, and the government was obliged to address the question of the internal sector.

Early in 1993 it became clear that the economic reforms introduced in the 'special period' were inadequate to cope with the scale of the crisis. They had done nothing to deal with the growth of the black market, the shortage of dollars, the monetary imbalance and the problem of unemployment. The economic system was on the verge of collapse and two officials from the International Monetary Fund visiting Havana declared that the Cuban decline since 1989 was far worse than the deterioration suffered by the former socialist countries of Eastern Europe in the same period. New measures were now introduced to reconstruct the internal economy, masterminded by a fresh economic team led by Carlos Lage, the youthful vice-president with Castro's ear. José Luis Rodríguez was brought in as the minister of finance, Francisco Soberón was moved to the Central Bank and Raúl Castro kept a close eye on the changes suggested. The reforms were outlined by Castro in his Moncada speech on 26 July 1993.

The first measure, economically essential and politically significant, was the legalisation of the US dollar, authorised by Decree-Law 140 in August 1993. Unable to cope with the burgeoning black market in dollars the Cuban authorities surrendered to economic realism. Long a familiar, though unofficial currency in the rest of the Caribbean, notably in the tourist trade, the dollar was to become Cuba's principal currency for traded goods and services, as it had been during the first years of the century. The Cuban peso remained in use for salary payments, for all purchases on the ration and for all internal transactions by the government.

The return of the dollar was a serious blow to revolutionary pride. First introduced during the US occupation after 1898, the US dollar had replaced the existing Spanish coinage and continued to be used in Cuba until 1915, when the creation of the Cuban National Bank permitted the introduction of the peso. For most business transactions, the dollar had remained supreme until the Revolution. 'Through boom and depression, revolution and moratorium,' wrote Henry Wallich in 1950, 'the dollar gave Cuba an externally stable monetary system with a complete absence of exchange difficulties.' The American business community loved it, since it 'could neither be stretched nor bent'.[40]

Acceptable in economic theory, and necessary in the circumstances, the reintroduction of the dollar had a damaging effect on the political consensus that sustained the Cuban system. Its increasing dominance within the internal economy – and the government opened retail stores trading in dollars to mop up any surplus on the black market – created deep divisions in Cuban society in the course of the 1990s between those with access to dollars and those without. Those with dollars – obtained chiefly through the tourist trade, the black market and remittances from Miami – became significantly wealthier than those who had none. The egalitarian ethic that had been such a proud boast of the Revolution was further undermined, although it had already been weakened by the developing black market exchange.

The second significant reform was the introduction of self-employment, under Decree-Law 141 of September 1993. For the first time in a quarter of a century, more than a hundred small-business activities in the service sector were opened up to private initiative. (All private bars and restaurants had been closed down since March 1968.) Permission was granted to hairdressers, electricians, plumbers and mechanics to work legally on their own account. By the end of 1995 more than 200,000 Cubans were registered as self-employed, more than 5 per cent of the workforce, and in June 1996 the government published a list of a further 40 activities that would be open to the self-employed.[41] Under-employed Cubans jumped at the opportunity offered, especially as it was often possible to charge for services in dollars. The downside for these embryonic private businessmen was that they moved for the first time into the tax economy. Their small businesses had to be registered, and they were soon to be taxed.

The most dramatic change under this rubric was the reintroduction of private bars and restaurants, known as *paladares*. The term *paladar* came from a Brazilian tele-novela, or soap opera, that had played on Cuban television screens in the 1990s. The heroine, who migrated to Rio de Janeiro from the provinces, sustained herself by selling sandwiches on the beach, and her venture was so successful that she eventually returned to her home town and opened a *paladar*, or restaurant. These proved so successful that Castro almost immediately ordered them to be closed, although they were revived again two years later with rather more stringent regulations. Castro justified this in a speech in December 1993 by discussing what had happened in a Havana neighbourhood:

> A restaurant was opened with 25 tables and 100 chairs and a cabaret. Some guy found himself a spot and charged 15 pesos to let people in ... He charged in dollars, pesos, and whatever. He had all the clients he needed. People from abroad would come in and bring friends and even family. I have already calculated how much the happy owner was making. He was making no less than 1000 pesos a day – and this is a conservative estimate. At least 1000 pesos a day! And all this because things had opened up a bit.[42]

Such rapacity had offended Castro's sense of revolutionary morality. When the *paladares* were allowed to reopen they were restricted to 12 tables and were supposed to be family-run. They soon became a popular and established institution.

The third significant reform in 1993 involved the establishment of agricultural cooperatives to replace the old state farms. Known as Unidades Básicas de Producción Cooperativa (UBPC), they were introduced under Decree-Law 142 of September 1993. The state agricultural sector – which had previously controlled 75 per cent of the agricultural economy – dropped to 30 per cent after three years.[43] While the land technically remained in the hands of the state the UBPCs were granted the permanent right to use it and owned what they produced on it outright. They also had managerial autonomy, elected their own leadership, controlled their own bank accounts and were able to relate wages to productivity. This was the most important shake-up of the countryside for 30 years, although since the UBPCs still had to produce quotas at prices fixed by the state, and finance was still allocated by the agencies of central government, their autonomy was not quite as extensive as it first appeared.

One reform, designed to make an immediate and visible impact, secured the return of the private farmers' markets that Castro had abolished in the rectification campaign of 1986.[44] Markets were established on almost every block in Havana by the end of the decade, providing a wide variety of fruits, vegetables, salads and meat – a cornucopia not seen in the city for many decades.[45]

While presiding over these major reforms, Castro kept up his familiar socialist rhetoric, pretending that nothing very much had changed. The reforms were designed 'to improve and perfect socialism', he told the National Assembly at the end of 1993. Their aim was to 'make it efficient, not to destroy it'. Socialism, he argued, was not simply 'more just, more honourable, and more humane in every sense', it was 'the only system that would provide us with the resources to keep our social conquests'.

As for capitalism, it was 'an illusion' to imagine that it would solve Cuba's problems. It was 'an absurd and crazy chimaera for which the masses will pay dearly'. Castro dismissed the experiments with the free market being made in Eastern Europe and Latin America out of hand and began developing arguments that he would deploy at international gatherings over the following decade. 'The neo-liberal model adopted in Latin America, characterised by price liberalisation, the reduction of real wages and welfare programmes, was never consulted with the people, and increased dramatically the already terrifying levels of inequality in those countries.' Cuba, he implied, would be different, and its reforms would be successful.

The Cuban leadership felt itself to be at war and it would have been easy to push through the essential economic decisions with little regard for popular opinion. Yet the reforms were so politically sensitive that they were put out for discussion in every workplace. Some 3 million members of the Cuban Workers' Confederation gathered together to discuss them from January to March 1994. Their social impact was analysed at meetings in 80,000 workplaces and were further debated at a special session of the National Assembly in May.

The popular mood favoured greater participation in the economic reform process, and the government was quick to take account of it. This was undoubtedly a form of guided democracy, but it proved a successful political move in securing support for reform. The discussions enabled the wider population to understand what was at stake, allowing people to feel that they had had some say in what was to come next.

The Party elite had already paved the way at the Communist Party's fourth congress, held in October 1991 at the start of the crisis. This was the first congress, one observer noted, 'where not all the votes were unanimous', and where debate was heard on issues like the free farmers' market, crime and its causes, the electoral system and the press.[46] The authorities were quite prepared to open the door to discussion, divergence of opinion and criticism.[47]

The government's next step was to bring life back to the National Assembly through the appointment of Ricardo Alarcón, one of the Revolution's brightest stars, as its new president. Alarcón had helped run Castro's foreign policy throughout the 1980s – usually from his position as Cuba's representative at the United Nations in New York – and his new task was to preside over what were, in effect, Cuba's fledgling attempts to install a new kind of 'participatory democracy', and also to sell the programme of the 'special period' to the workers.

As the government's leading intellectual after the retirement of Carlos Rafael Rodríguez (who died in 1997), Alarcón's task was to elaborate and propagate the Revolution's latest ideas about democracy. Since the United States, and, to a lesser extent the European Union, were now demanding that Cuba conform to the Western practice of representative democracy, it was important for Cuba to reply in kind, to defend its own definition of democratic practice.

Such a defence was all the more necessary in that much of the outside world assumed that Cuba's single party democracy was a mere cardboard copy of the system employed in the now discredited countries of Eastern Europe. This was not altogether unwarranted since the Cuban constitution of 1976, and the system of popular power to which it gave rise, had been formulated during the period of maximum Soviet influence. The Cubans needed to show that they could think for themselves. Alarcón soon articulated an intelligent defence, losing no opportunity at the same time to point out the flaws in the Western formula – characterised by low turnouts and considerable popular hostility towards existing political elites, particularly in the United States.

The 1976 Constitution was modified and rewritten in 1991 and approved by the National Assembly in July 1992. The new system permitted the direct election of deputies to the Assembly, chosen from a list of candidates (that continued to be approved, of course, by the Party). At the same time, references in the constitution to Marxism–Leninism were quietly dropped and the ban on Christians joining the Party was also abandoned.

Alarcón's return to Havana to participate more fully in debates at the top, coupled with the promotion of Carlos Lage, the talented Castro protégé charged with overseeing the economic reforms, brought a younger generation into the top Cuban leadership – a direct result of the demands of the 'special period'. Some changes had already been made after the economic rectification in 1986, but now there were fresh faces in the Politburo. Although the Castro brothers remained, Cuba was no longer run exclusively by the Sierra Maestra generation.

Very slowly the Cuban economy began to turn the corner. The GDP, at 0.7 per cent in 1994, had stopped falling, and after 1996 it would average out at 3.5 per cent a year.[48] The mood in parts of the country began to change. Visiting a rural cooperative in the Oriente in 1996, Solon Barraclough, a UN economist, found that peasant farmers had plenty to complain about but had no difficulty in accepting their situation:

> Even though there had been some economic improvement since 1993 in [the province of] Granma, one could see deserted modern poultry batteries, half-empty milking parlours, and a huge milk processing-plant operating at only one fifth of capacity. Peasant farmers tended to have better access to food than many other groups. They complained mostly about their lack of machetes, hoes, and files to sharpen them, as well as of shoes, trousers, shirts and skirts. These indispensable basics for peasant production were becoming worn out, but replacement was extremely slow and difficult, when possible at all. Schools had almost no paper, pencils or books. Clinics and pharmacies lacked many basic medical supplies, such as antibiotics or even aspirins.

Yet in spite of their problems the farms were able to shelter refugees from the collapse of the urban and international economy. Barraclough encountered a young barefoot woman tending her baby and chickens in front of her cottage, thatch-covered and dirt-floored but very clean. It also had electricity and a television set. 'In our conversation I learned that she had spent seven years in Prague, learning the techniques of textile manufacture in both schools and factories. She spoke both Czech and Russian. There were now no job openings for her speciality, which was why she had returned to the farm.' In spite of these upsets and privations Barraclough was impressed by the resilience of those he met. 'The philosophical good humour with which most rural people seemed to confront their difficulties was impressive.'[49]

An unexpected result of the country's economic restructuring was the increase in the power and influence of the armed forces in the internal affairs of the country. Raúl Castro announced at an early stage in the crisis that the army would aim to feed itself, and the experience gained enabled the military to oversee the civilian food programme. The military began to acquire a new prominence in the economic affairs of the nation and played a leading role in the drive towards self-sufficiency in food.

One general later recalled that although the armed forces had been 'very professional and technically proficient' in the 1980s, there were 'gaps in the areas of administration, finances, and production'. In the circumstances of the 'special period', Raúl Castro had addressed these problems in 1990, ensuring that army cadres acquired the 'basic skills of food production and agriculture', and 'a rudimentary knowledge of economic affairs'. The cadres 'don't need to be economists,' said the general, 'but they do need to know where each peso we spend comes from, and how to use it effectively'.[50]

Soon, as in many Latin American countries, Raúl Castro's officers took responsibility for several economic areas. General Ulises Rosales del Toro, one of the reliable and experienced members of the old guard, was put in overall charge. Under the trade name Gaviota the military ran hotels and promoted tourism. Almacenes Universales, another military company, was in charge of warehousing, free zones and industrial areas. Construcciones Antex dealt with construction and real estate. Banco Metropolitano was the military's banking and financial arm. The military were also responsible for mobilising labour in the agricultural sector, running parts of the transport industry, and looking after the government's dollar stores.[51]

The expansion of these businesses was stimulated by sharp cuts in the military budget in 1994. The army's new role arose from necessity. State spending on the armed forces was drastically reduced, and they were no longer able to acquire new weapons or even to modernise their existing ones. Heavy spending in the old days had been underwritten by the Soviet Union. Interviewed in 1997 General Nestor López told an instructive anecdote, recalling how, when the collapse of communism was already under way, the Soviet Union had provided Cuba with a final squadron of Mig-29 fighters. Six of them were delivered and, years later, the Russian government enquired whether the Cuban government would like to buy some more. 'How much do they cost?' asked Raúl Castro. 'Twenty million dollars' was the Russian reply. In which case, said Raúl, 'we'll sell you back the six we already have'.[52]

In the 1980s the Cuban military had fought in Africa and helped to train the Nicaraguan army. Now they had other priorities. 'Times have changed, and we have changed,' said Castro in January 1992. 'Military assistance outside our borders is a thing of the past. The most important task is to see that the Cuban Revolution survives. Abroad we intend to live by accepted norms of international behaviour.'[53]

US Marine General Charles Wilhelm, head of US Southern Command, agreed. Cuba's armed forces have been 'dramatically reduced', he told a reporter from the *Miami Herald* in 1998. 'Seventy per cent of the armed forces' effort is involved in their own self-sustainment, in things like agricultural pursuits,' he said. 'It doesn't even begin to resemble the Cuban armed forces we contemplated in the 80s.' General Wilhelm said he thought the 130,000 troops of the 1980s had been reduced by half, and that the reservists had also been cut. Much military equipment was unusable and the number of airworthy tactical aircraft was now 'very small'. The general concluded that the Cuban army no longer had any capacity to project itself beyond its own borders. It was 'really no threat to anyone around it'.[54]

Cuba was not alone in facing a new situation in the 1990s. Other former communist countries had to make adjustments to the world market, and many Third World countries that had once looked to the Soviet Union to provide an alternative model of development were obliged to embrace the neo-liberal belief system (to become familiar as 'globalisation'). Cuba, together with Vietnam and China, was almost alone in its determination to keep to the socialist path, and Cuba's relations with China improved markedly in the 1990s. Official missions were sent to Beijing to study the Chinese model. The Chinese provided free cloth for school uniforms and supplied more than a million bicycles, as well as the wherewithal to construct five bicycle assembly plants. By 1994 China had become Cuba's third largest trading partner.

Yet Cuba's experience was rather different from that of the other countries confronting change in that it faced renewed and implacable hostility from the United States to its go-it-alone strategy. Trade and investment were affected, as well as access to international finance. Specific clauses in the US embargo legislation blocked all funding from US sources, as well as from multilateral sources controlled by the United States, like the World Bank and the International Monetary Fund. Cuba was obliged to rely on short-term trade finance and foreign direct investment and a tiny trickle of aid.

Just when Cuba might have benefited from the end of the Cold War and a possible relaxation in the American attitude the US government tightened the economic screw. Successive presidents were to increase the pressure, seeking to crush Cuba's attempts to achieve economic independence and hoping to overthrow the island's leader. The perceived crisis in revolutionary legitimacy was the staple material of every visiting journalist; books were written with titles such as *Castro's Final Hour* and *Fin de Siècle à l'Havane*.[55] Yet the predicted outcome failed to materialise. The regime fought back and Castro soldiered on regardless. Years later, in 1998, *Time* magazine noted his pride at defying 'world predictions of his imminent demise, as satisfying a triumph to him as any that went before'.[56] Outside observers had jumped to conclusions that seemed obvious at the time, but proved profoundly misplaced. They assumed too readily that Cuba would fall like the countries of Eastern Europe. In so doing they misread the attitude not just of the Cuban leadership, but of the Cubans themselves.

The historical experiences of Cuba and Eastern Europe were very different. Cuba had experienced a Revolution of its own, one of the great upheavals of the twentieth century, the product of specific struggles over more than a century. Whatever its failings, Castro's Revolution was 'Made in Cuba'. The countries of Eastern Europe had also had revolutions of a kind after 1945 – in the wake of Nazi occupation, resistance and the Second World War – but their socialism was permanently defined by the fact that it had been brought to them through the powerful agency of the Soviet army. When their regimes imploded in 1989 and 1990 no one assembled in the streets to protect the old order.

The Cubans had more to defend – their history, their sense of their own identity and their *amour propre*. Most Cubans supported their government because, although they were aware of its failings, they could also identify its successes.[57] In spite of its many inadequacies they were familiar with its solid achievements. Yet not all Cubans thought that way. A minority had never accepted the Revolution and had dreamt of leaving. As the economic situation deteriorated during the 'special period', many grew desperate and sought to escape across the 90-mile channel to Florida.

The third exodus: riot on the Malecón, August 1994

The problem of economic migrants seeking access to the United States – part of a larger issue in the Caribbean and Latin America – had been an awkward and unresolved question in Cuba since the 1960s. Major explosions of pent-up resentment had occurred in 1965 and 1980. A resolution of the problem could never be finally achieved without the cooperation of both Cuba and the United States, yet their two governments were rarely able to communicate with each other.

A riot in the heart of Havana in August 1994 brought the migration issue to the top of the agenda. This was not just a display of discontent by people who wanted to leave the island, it was the first large public protest against the government since the early years of the Revolution. The riot had several causes. One was the 'demonstration effect' created by the flight of thousands of 'boat people' from the prolonged crisis in Haiti in the early months of 1994. Another was the continuing ambivalence about migration policy shown by both the Cuban and the US government. Yet the root of the problem lay in the prolonged economic hardship of the 'special period'.

Late in the afternoon of 5 August an angry crowd of several hundred had gathered on the Malecón, Havana's splendidly decaying boulevard along the ocean. Earlier that morning a group of people trying to escape to Florida had sought to hijack a boat in the harbour and had been prevented from so doing by dockworkers and the police. This had been the second such event in two days and a police officer had been killed during the first hijack attempt. Soon the angry protesters on the Malecón were throwing rocks and bottles at the police and – a special target of irritation – a nearby hotel dedicated to foreign tourists.

The authorities quickly mobilised a much larger counter-demonstration of several thousand to smother the crowd of hostile protesters. Castro was among them and, in the traditional manner of a Spanish captain-general of the colonial era (the Marqués de Someruelos in 1810 and General Dulce in 1869), he waded into the crowd to talk to the protesters, after giving strict instructions to the police to handle them gently. His personal intervention ensured that the immediate crisis was averted and two days later half a million people assembled to attend the funeral of the killed policeman – perceived as a gesture of support for the Revolution.

This specifically Cuban drama was enacted against the background of events in Haiti, where the elected ruler, President Jean-Bertrand Aristide, had been overthrown by a military junta three years earlier, in September 1991. His overthrow, and the subsequent repression, had led to a spiralling migration of Haitians, departing in small boats for the American coast. Some 5,000 were at sea in June 1994, and 6,000 in the first week of July. The United States refused them permission to land and the majority were picked up by US coastguards and taken to the US military base at Guantánamo. By September more than 14,000 Haitians were held there in makeshift camps.[58]

The number of Cuban *balseros*, or rafters, arriving in the United States had also grown, increasing every year since the start of the 'special period': 467 in 1990, 2,203 in 1991, 2,548 in 1992, and 3,656 in 1993. If picked up in US waters by US coastguards these Cuban migrants were granted automatic asylum – in marked contrast to the treatment of the black Haitians, unceremoniously dumped in camps in Guantánamo, in transit for a return to Haiti. In normal circumstances the US government office in Havana granted only a handful of visas to Cubans who sought to emigrate, yet they would be granted asylum if they arrived in US waters. The Cuban government claimed that the US refusal to permit would-be migrants legitimate entry served only to encourage the *balseros* and the hijackers. Exasperated by US policy the Cubans told their coastguards early in 1994 to take no active measures to discourage the migrants. Hundreds now began to leave the island – on hijacked ferries, on rafts and in small boats. While a handful were drowned the great majority reached US waters safely and were picked up.

In the wake of the August riot Castro declared that his government would now officially relax its migration controls. Anyone who wished to leave would be allowed to do so.[59] He hoped his decision would force a change in US policy. Hundreds flocked to the island shores, to embark on boats and rafts. As expected, the United States was seriously alarmed. Fearful of a repetition of the Mariel boatlift of 1980, when more than 100,000 Cuban refugees arrived in Miami, President Clinton decided to suspend the rule, in force since the passage of the Cuban Adjustment Act of 1966, that gave Cubans arriving in American waters the automatic right to asylum.

Clinton had a personal reason for his decision. When governor of Arkansas in 1980, he had suffered unfortunate political repercussions from the Mariel boatlift, comparable to those suffered by President Carter. Some 20,000 Cubans had been deposited at the Fort Chaffee military base in Arkansas, and a riot there in June 1980 had contributed to his failure to be re-elected as governor.[60] In 1994 Clinton was determined to keep the Cuban migrants as far from the United States as possible and the existing use of the Guantánamo base as a refuge for the Haitians provided an exemplary model. The military bases in the US Canal Zone in Panama were later to perform a complementary function.

US coastguards picking up Cuban *balseros* were now under orders from Janet Reno, the US attorney-general, to take them to Guantánamo. A US naval cordon was established around the island and, by the end of September, more than 21,000 Cubans were interned at the makeshift camp at the base – joining the 14,000 Haitians already there.

Soon the numbers were so large that the United States was obliged to make a major and permanent change in its policy towards Cuban migration, as Castro had hoped. The two countries made a deal in September, negotiated on the Cuban side by Ricardo Alarcón, to bring the crisis to an end. Washington agreed to provide 20,000 visas a year for Cubans seeking to migrate to the United States, while the Cuban government promised to try to prevent further illegal emigration. Under the terms of a further US–Cuban migration agreement in May 1995 the *balseros* detained on the high seas who were not eligible for political asylum would be sent back. Thus was the so-called 'wet foot, dry foot' policy established. The US undertook to advise its citizens not to assist any future *balseros*.

To show that he was not being soft on Cuba Clinton announced a number of measures to tighten up the economic embargo, including a ban on the flow of family remittances from the US to Cuba, then estimated at about $500 million dollars a year, as well as an end to travel permits granted to family members and to academic researchers and a stepping-up of the broadcasts of Radio Martí.[61] This was for public consumption in the United States. Apart from increased funding for the radio station the other measures were not put into effect.

The Cuban migrants held in the tented camps in Guantánamo remained until the following year, when they were finally allowed to leave for the United States. Their number had risen to more than 30,000 and some had spent nine months at the camp. The Haitians were not so fortunate; they were returned to Haiti.

The Torricelli and Helms-Burton Acts, 1992 and 1996

The collapse of the Soviet Union in 1991, and the formal ending of the Cold War, might have been expected to lead to a gradual normalisation of relations between Cuba and the United States. This was certainly the assumption of the countries of the European Union. They increased the size of the embassies, elevated their level of contacts and set about the task of promoting economic ties. They recognised that Cuba was no longer the military ally of a nuclear superpower from outside the American continent; that it posed no threat to the United States or to Latin America; and that it no longer had the capacity to send out its soldiers to Africa. This was the European view, but it was not widely shared in Washington. There the old American ambivalence towards Cuba, dating back to the early nineteenth century and reinforced by the events of the twentieth, remained in force. Far from seeking a new relationship with Cuba, American politicians – both Republican and Democratic – stepped up their antagonism.

International Communism might have been defeated, but the US government was faced with a political problem within its own borders. Cuba was no longer a significant issue in foreign affairs, but it remained on the domestic agenda. The weight of the Cuban diaspora living in the United States continued to make itself felt on the electoral arithmetic. Yet while presidents and governments often depended on their votes, both locally and nationally, the influence of Cuban-Americans went far beyond their electoral strength. Their lobbying capacity in Congress was formidable, often influencing legislation through their control of the relevant committees. Important too was their ability to raise campaign finance.

Active in Congress and mobilised in the key states of Florida and New Jersey, Cuban-Americans acquired a vice-like grip on American policy towards Cuba in the post-Soviet decade. A new generation of Cuban-Americans was represented directly in the US Congress – in Florida by Lincoln Díaz-Balart (the nephew of Castro's first wife, Mirta Díaz Balart) and by Ileana Ros-Lehtinen, and in New Jersey by Robert Menéndez. Backed by the fortune of the Bacardi rum family, and by the formidable wealth and lobbying power of Jorge Mas Canosa, the acknowledged leader of the Cuban-Americans in Florida until his death in 1997, these legislators took a tough line against Castro's Cuba. Since it was no longer possible to argue that Cuba posed an overt threat to US security, they concentrated their criticisms on other areas. Research into Castro's socialist economy became a heavily subsidised industry, with many economists and political scientists receiving large grants from the US administration. Much attention was devoted to Cuban-Americans owed compensation for property confiscated on the island some 30 years earlier. Similar campaigns about confiscated assets had been mounted with considerable success in the countries of Eastern Europe.

Mas Canosa's Cuban American National Foundation (CANF), set up in the 1980s, now operated as a political pressure group in Washington. Canosa himself had been born in Cuba in 1939 and had left the island in 1960. He had supported the Bay of Pigs operation and had funded exile activists for more than two decades. In the 1980s he was persuaded of the desirability of establishing a lobbying operation similar to the highly effective American Israel

Public Affairs Committee (AIPAC), which maintained steady pressure on Washington in support of Israel. CANF was set up in AIPAC's image and worked closely with it. 'We had to stop commando raids,' said Mas Canosa, 'and concentrate on influencing public opinion and government.'[62]

The effect of this Cuban-American lobbying, without the participants quite understanding the historical implications, was to resurrect the 'annexationist' dream of the nineteenth century. Themselves now rooted in the United States, many Cuban-Americans had a nostalgic yearning for the Cuba of their memories to be part of America, and, with the collapse of the Soviet Union, they saw their opportunity. They began talking about 'transition' and held regular conferences to discuss how the island would be organised when Castro fell. Miami academics, subsidised by the US government, began for the first time to engage in serious research into the island's economy and society, not for propaganda reasons, but to understand what they would be faced with when, as they expected, the call came to them to run the country. Many Miami residents dusted down the title deeds to their old Cuban properties.

Castro watched these developments with care, explaining to students in 1990 how companies were being set up in the United States 'to determine how property should be returned to the previous owners – the large landowners, the industrialists, the foreign enterprises, and the owners of homes for rent. I imagine this also includes the owners of schools – because here everything once had an owner.'[63]

The Cuban audience were being warned of what might happen to their familiar environment, but Castro also discussed the claims to land, introducing a note of realism into the fantasies of the exiles:

> I do not know how they will manage, since even I, who have been traversing our countryside for more than 30 years and participating in the road and highway construction programmes, can get lost when I go through the province of Havana. It is hard for me to recognise the roads, even the ones that I saw under construction and visited when they were being built . . . In our countryside so many things have happened. Our countryside has been filled with . . . schools, dams, canals, storehouses, workshops, state-owned enterprises and cooperatives . . . I do not think there is anyone alive who knows where his large landed estate once was. It is even possible they will find it under a dam . . . It is impossible for our homeland to turn back.

Yet the hopes of many Cuban-Americans had been aroused by the collapse of communism elsewhere and they looked forward to being the beneficiaries in Cuba of Castro's downfall.[64] Their assertiveness coincided with a new mood in the US government – controlled after 1993 by a Democratic president, Bill Clinton – that perceived itself to be engaged in a crusade to promote democracy in Latin America. This new approach by the US administration was partly a response to the downfall of several long-standing military regimes in the area in the 1980s. The dictatorships that once appeared useful in keeping communism at bay during the Cold War had served their purpose, particularly since they were now discredited at home and abroad by well-publicised revelations about their human rights violations. President Clinton addressed Latin America's democratic deficit with considerable vigour and, as a by-product, this new rhetoric was soon to be directed purposefully against Cuba.

Under pressure from CANF, legislation was brought before Congress that aimed to promote democracy in Cuba by imposing tougher economic sanctions against the island. The Cuban Democracy Act of 1992 (the Torricelli Act) was aimed at frustrating Cuban trade, and was expected to assist in bringing a rapid end to the Castro government. The Cuban Liberty and Democratic Solidarity Act (the Helms-Burton Act) which followed in 1996 was aimed at investment and was originally drafted because of the success of the Cuban recovery and the concern that US business might take second place to European, Canadian and Japanese investors. Its underlying purpose was to scare off foreign investors at a time when Cuba's economic survival depended on its ability to open up to the outside world – to seek markets, investors and managerial expertise in Europe, Canada, Japan and Latin America.

The Cuban government argued that the wording of these new acts, tightening the embargo and defining what kind of democracy should be imposed on the island, resurrected the Platt Amendment of 1902 that gave the United States a pivotal role in Cuban affairs. Ricardo Alarcón pointed out that under the terms of Helms-Burton, 'there would be no Cuban government and no Republic of Cuba. There would be a US council designed by the US President that would look after the Cuban economy.'[65] The Cuban-Americans, however, were well pleased.

The Act of 1992 was sponsored by Robert Torricelli, a Democrat from New Jersey, a state with a large Cuban-American population. The first part of his bill was designed to damage Cuba's trade by tightening up the existing economic sanctions: subsidiaries of US corporations would be prohibited from trading with Cuba, and foreign ships entering Cuban ports would be refused permission to load or unload freight in US ports over a period of six months. The bill's second section dealt with democracy. The US President would be given the power to lift the sanctions only if 'free, fair, and internationally supervised elections' were to take place. The President would also have to be persuaded that the Cuban government had 'given opposition parties time to organise and campaign, allowed full access to the media, shown respect for civil liberties and human rights, and moved towards a market economy'.[66]

These conditions, insulting to Cuban nationalists, were rejected by the government in Havana. The legislation received little support in the rest of the world. Few countries had much interest in the historic quarrel between the United States and Cuba. But the Torricelli bill became the Torricelli Act and its clauses were soon embedded in US foreign policy. Four years later the US Congress, now dominated by Republicans, again turned its attention to Cuba, hoping to discourage investment by tightening sanctions by a further notch.

The protagonists on this occasion were Senator Jesse Helms, a Republican from North Carolina (and the powerful former chairman of the Senate Foreign Relations Committee), and Representative Dan Burton, a Republican congressman from Indiana. Together with the warm support of CANF and Bacardi, they sponsored a fresh anti-Cuba bill in March 1996, the Cuban Liberty and Democratic Solidarity Act, which went far beyond the terms of the Torricelli Act.

One of the controversial elements of the Helms-Burton bill concerned the imposition of democracy. The new legislation reasserted the US right to define the nature of Cuba's democracy and extended the requirements enumerated in the Torricelli Act. Specific clauses declared that neither Fidel nor his brother Raúl would be allowed to participate in any future democratic government in Cuba, and such a government would not be recognised by the United States unless it were to agree to pay compensation to Americans and to Cuban-Americans whose property had been expropriated.

Even more significant and controversial, however, was the provision, embodied in Title III of the bill, concerning property rights. Any individual or corporation 'trafficking in property' that belonged to an American citizen (or to a former Cuban citizen who subsequently became an American) and that had been nationalised by Cuba could be sued in American courts. (For a partial text of the Helms-Burton Act see Appendix C.) This was a direct rejection of one of the first actions of the Cuban Revolution, which had established the Ministry for the Recuperation of Misappropriated Goods in 1959 to sequestrate the properties and companies of Batista and his friends.

The Helms-Burton Act caused immediate concern to companies based in the European Union – by then the principal foreign investors in Cuba – who might already be involved in joint ventures with just such properties, long in the ownership of the Cuban state. The prospect of expensive litigation would have been enough to deter many potential investors. While the United States could ignore the complaints of Havana, it could not close its ears to the hostile clamour that arose from the European Union.

President Clinton was opposed to this fresh legislation and had not intended to sign it into law, but an incident occurred early in 1996 that made him reconsider his opposition. During the 1994 migration crisis Janet Reno, the US attorney-general, had issued an instruction that American citizens were not to provide assistance to the *balseros* who sought to sail from Cuba to Florida. This request was widely ignored and Cuban-Americans in Miami continued to comb the Florida Straits in search of migrants. One Miami-based group, Brothers to the Rescue, possessed six Cessna aircraft that kept a regular look-out. Founded in 1991 by José Basulto it had rescued hundreds of *balseros* over the years.[67] Sometimes their Cessnas crossed into Cuban air space and they would be warned off by Cuban fighter-planes.

The Cubans considered that this breach of the 1994 migration agreement was intolerable and unlawful and *Granma*, the official newspaper, warned in July 1995 that retaliatory action would be taken if Brothers to the Rescue continued to violate Cuban air space: 'Any vessel coming from abroad, which forcefully invades our sovereign waters, could be sunk; and any plane shot down . . . The responsibility for whatever happens will fall, exclusively, on those who encourage, plan, execute, or tolerate, these acts of piracy.'[68]

The Miami pilots ignored the warning and continued their surveillance operations. When they again entered Cuban air space in February 1996 the Cuban air force took action. Two out of three Cessnas were shot down, after several warnings had been issued. Four men were killed. Cuba argued that the shooting-down of the Miami planes was not its responsibility; due warning had been given that these flights were not acceptable.

American opinion was affronted by this drastic action, and the incident caused such commotion that President Clinton felt obliged to sign the Helms-Burton bill into law. This was an historic and fateful step, since the wording of the new Act placed serious limitations on the power of the President, or any future President, to control an important aspect of foreign policy. The Cuban question was taken out of the President's hands, and future relations with the island became dependent on decisions of Congress. Any possibility that Clinton, or some future President, might order the lifting of economic sanctions now evaporated, to the irritation of America's trading partners, notably in the European Union, and of the farmers and manufacturers within the United States who hoped for eventual access to the Cuban market.

The EU took vigorous steps to oppose the legislation, perceiving Helms-Burton as a clear violation of international law and an impediment to trade. A formal complaint was filed against the United States in 1997 at the World Trade Organisation. To appease his European allies, and to mitigate the impact of the Act, Clinton secured an amendment that would allow the President to waive or enforce Title III at six monthly intervals. Clinton did just that, for the first time in July 1996 and thereafter until the end of his presidency. His policy was continued by George W. Bush, who became President in January 2001. Bush had given a pre-election commitment that he would enforce Title III, but realism prevailed when in power. He waived it for the first time in July 2001 and continued to do so. To mitigate criticism from the CANF he called for stricter enforcement of the US trade embargo, though with little effect.

The European Union, meanwhile, in return for the waiving of Title III, agreed to take a tougher public line on human rights in their own deliberations. Drafting a Common Position on Cuba the EU declared that the promotion of democratic reform and respect for human rights in Cuba was now an important European ambition. Future economic aid from the European Union to Cuba would be tied to the pace of political change on the island.[69]

The Helms-Burton legislation made change less likely. Cubans might wish for greater political freedom, and might hope for economic improvement. Some might seek to ditch socialism and take the capitalist road. Yet few were ready to abandon the Revolution at the behest of the United States, or to give up the first genuine attempt in their history to establish an independent republic.

The Cuban government now concentrated its attention on groups within US society who did not wish foreign policy to be controlled by the CANF. They welcomed church groups to the island, made overtures to the farming lobby, and sought the support of new generations of Cuban-Americans who sent money to their relatives and hoped for an amicable rapprochement. In the final years of the twentieth century aspects of this policy began to bear fruit, assisted by the death of Mas Canosa in November 1997. His son, Jorge Jr., proved a less effective lobbyist. Although the Republicans recovered the Presidency in 2001 the Democrats were still powerful in Congress, and US Cuba policy achieved a certain equilibrium. Two unusual events occurred in the last years of the Clinton era that affected US opinion, helping to move it towards a more moderate stand: Pope John Paul visited Havana in 1998, and Elián González, a shipwrecked small boy, was picked up off the coast of Florida in 1999.

Pope John Paul's visit to Havana, 1998

Pope John Paul II flew into Havana's airport on 21 January 1998, the first papal visit to Cuba since Catholicism had been imposed on the country five centuries earlier. The much-travelled Pope had visited Latin America on many occasions, but the Cuban expedition was perceived to have greater significance than these earlier trips. The visit was greeted by the North American media with the expectation that the anti-Communist Polish pontiff would work his destabilising magic on the Cuban population, unleashing 'political currents that will lead at last to Fidel Castro's departure from power'.[70]

The media excitement was dampened when the arrival of the Pope in Havana coincided with the eruption of a sex scandal in Washington, involving President Clinton and Monica Lewinsky, a White House intern. Having flown to Cuba in the hope of reporting a major political upheaval, the journalists and cameramen were obliged to decamp to Washington, to cover what they thought would be a vastly more significant story. The anchormen of the three principal US television networks left Havana immediately they heard the news. Such were the priorities of the Western media. They were to be proved wrong on both counts. The American president did not fall, and neither did his Cuban counterpart.

The Pope's visit was interpreted at the time through US spectacles, with scant regard for the reality of Catholicism on the island and with little understanding of its historical role. A mistaken belief gained currency that Cuba was in some way like Poland, with a large population of frustrated believers deprived for decades of their opportunity to worship by a harsh and avowedly atheist regime. A revival of Cuban Catholicism, encouraged by the Papal visit, might perhaps galvanise opposition to Castro and lead to his overthrow. That was the sub-text of the media interest.

Yet Cuba's situation was very different from that of Poland. Although the revolutionary government had long been indifferent if not hostile to organised religion, the Catholic Church in Cuba over the centuries had never grown deep roots, unlike in some other countries in Latin America. 'It wasn't a church of the people, the workers, the farmers, the poorer sections of the population,' Castro explained to Frei Betto in 1985.[71] More than four million Cubans (out of a population of 11 million) had been baptised, but only 150,000 regularly attended Sunday mass.[72] Cuba, like many of the countries of Latin America and Europe, was becoming an ever less religious society.

The real growth in religious fervour in the 1990s, in Cuba as in Latin America, came from Protestants rather than Catholics. Evangelical sects in Cuba were on the increase. Possibly a million Protestants were active in Cuba in the 1990s with some 900 chapels springing up all over the island, compared with only 650 Catholic churches.[73] Indeed part of the Vatican's enthusiasm for a papal visit to Cuba was the belief that it might help to stem the tide of Protestantism in Latin America. By associating the Catholic Church with Castro, ever popular among the poorest communities in Latin America who were the principal recruits to the evangelical cause, the Vatican hoped to curb the erosion of its own support.

Other contenders were present in Cuba to claim the hearts and minds of the people. The numbers of both Protestant and Catholic believers were rather less than those who practised various forms of Afro-Cuban religion – estimated at over five million. Catholicism had never made significant inroads into the black community, among whom Santeria, Palo Monte and Abakuá were still the most important spiritual manifestations.

Castro's fresh approach to the Church took political shape in the 'special period' of the 1990s. At the fourth Communist Party congress in 1991, after some prolonged (and published) debate, it was agreed that religious believers should be admitted to the Party. Speakers pointed out that several early supporters of the Revolution had been Christians, including Frank País, the leader of the July 26 Movement in Santiago, who had been a Protestant.

Others noted that many revolutionaries were practitioners of Santeria and that an all-inclusive political party should allow members to belong to a wide spectrum of faiths and beliefs. The deliberations at the congress led to a revision of the Constitution in 1992. The Cuban state was declared to be secular rather than atheist.

To pave the way for a papal visit, and to formally make the request, Castro himself met the Pope at the Vatican in November 1996, and the invitation was accepted in principle. Christmas was reinstated as a national holiday (the custom had been introduced into the island a hundred years earlier by the US military government in 1898 but dropped in 1969).

The Pope's visit lasted for five days and he held four open-air masses at different towns in the island, all shown live on national television. Greeted at the airport by Castro and the assembled politburo of the Communist Party, he was told of the Church's poor record in Cuba. Castro recalled his Catholic schooling when he had been taught that 'to be a Protestant, a Jew, a Muslim, Hindu, Buddhist, Animist, or a participant in other religious beliefs, constituted a dreadful sin, worthy of severe and implacable punishment'. He returned to one of his favourite themes: the historical failure of the Catholic Church to embrace the entire population of the island. 'In some of those schools for the wealthy and privileged, among whom I found myself, it occurred to me to ask why there were no black children there. I have never been able to forget the totally non-persuasive responses I received.'[74]

The Pope replied that the Church's presence in the island over five hundred years 'had not ceased to dispense spiritual values', and he set off on a journey through the country. He celebrated mass in Santa Clara, in Camagüey and in Santiago (where Raúl Castro was present in the crowds) before returning for a final ceremony in Havana, attended by Castro and several senior figures. In his sermons the Pope picked up many of his favourite themes: the need to stand against contraception and abortion, the need for the young 'to avoid the emptiness of alcohol, the abuse of sex, drug use, and prostitution', and the need for the state to distance itself from all extremes of fanaticism. With a nod to the prevailing Cuban view he noted bleakly how 'various places are witnessing the resurgence of a certain capitalist neo-liberalism, which subordinates the human person to blind market forces, and conditions the development of people on those forces'.

Such themes had been addressed in other places and before other audiences, but for Cuba the Pope had several specific messages. He drew attention to the phenomenon of migration 'which has torn apart whole families and caused suffering for a large part of the population'. He made suggestions about how the good of the nation might be promoted, so that each individual, 'enjoying freedom of expression, being free to undertake initiatives and make proposals within civil society, and enjoying appropriate freedom of association, will be able to cooperate effectively in the pursuit of the common good'.[75] Much of this fell on stony ground, but by no means all. Catholics and Catholic converts were to play an important role in the growing movement of internal dissidents.

The Pope also sought to recover some of the Church's lost prestige. At a meeting at Havana university he touched on the Church's role in Cuban history, citing the case of Father Felix Varela, precursor of the nineteenth-century independence movement. He described him as 'the foundation stone of Cuban national identity', and suggested, with a degree of historical licence, that there had always been a link between the Church and Cuban patriotism.[76]

Unresolved during the Pope's visit was the attitude of the Church towards the Afro-Cuban beliefs held by a large proportion of the population. Some Afro-Cuban religious leaders complained that the Catholic Church had launched an offensive against them on the eve of the Pope's visit, and had excluded them from an ecumenical meeting the Pope had held with Protestants and Jews. Their offer of 'a drumming rite of welcome' in the cathedral had been rejected.[77] They also noted that the Pope had warned bishops and priests 'against putting Santeria and other Afro-Cuban religions on a par with the Roman Catholic church'. Jaime Ortega, the Cuban cardinal, replied that the Cuban Church had not been critical of the Afro-Cuban religions, but had indicated its dislike of the efforts made 'by the Communist government to promote Afro-Cuban rites as an alternative to Catholicism' – and as a tourist attraction.

At a farewell ceremony the Pope made the obligatory reference to the US embargo that Castro had been waiting for:

> In our day, no nation can live in isolation . . . The Cuban people therefore cannot be denied the contacts with other peoples necessary for economic, social, and cultural development, especially when the imposed solution strikes the population indiscriminately, making it ever more difficult for the weakest to enjoy the bare essentials of decent living, things such as food, health, and education . . . The roots [of this suffering] may be found . . . in limitations to fundamental freedoms, in depersonalisation and the discouragement of individuals, and in oppressive economic measures – unjust and ethically unacceptable – imposed from outside the country.

Castro appeared on television after the Pope's departure to thank the Cuban people for helping to make his 'historic visit a success'. Castro had expected clear benefits and he secured them.[78] He appeared to have enlisted the Pope in his campaign against western capitalism and consumerism, and he had secured a nuanced denunciation of the US economic embargo of the island. He would allow the Church to be more active in Cuban society, but his spokesmen outlined its relatively limited role. Ricardo Alarcón explained to *Time* magazine that although he was in favour of the Church promoting 'certain values of spirituality, of human kindness, and of human solidarity', there would be limits to its temporal activities. It would never hold the hegemonic position that it had once had. 'We cannot go back to the time when one particular religion had the dominant role, because that is a way to discriminate against others. The obligation of the state is to guarantee freedom of religion, and that implies dealing with all of them on an equal footing.'[79] Protestants and the supporters of Santeria would receive the same treatment. No special favours would be granted to the Catholic Church.

Pope John Paul II was a conservative theologian: he opposed the Christian–Marxist dialogue that had been so popular in Latin America; he was no fan of Frei Betto and his friends in the movement of Third World priests; he had excoriated the radical works of Leonardo Boff, the well-known Brazilian theologian; and virtually anathematised the proponents of liberation theology. By no stretch of the imagination could he be described as soft on communism.

Yet he recognised the imaginative grip that the Cuban Revolution still had, not just on Cuba but on the great mass of the people in Latin America. It had been necessary for him to beard the despot in his lair, and by doing so he had secured worldwide publicity for the evangelical message of his Church. He had also secured a number of concrete gains for the Cuban Church, which had recovered its capacity to be a player on the political stage. The Pope's references to Felix Varela became a rallying cry for opposition forces on the island that now began to appear in Catholic guise, some of them looking more to Europe than to Miami.

The case of Elián González, 1999

Elián González was a small boy from the town of Cárdenas, aged five, found bobbing in the water off Florida in November 1999, supporting himself within the ring of a lorry tyre's inner tube. He was a survivor, along with two others, of a small group that had set out from a Cuban beach for the mainland in uncertain weather, in a tiny, unseaworthy boat with an outboard motor. In heavy seas, and almost within sight of the shore, the boat capsized. Elián's mother and eleven others were drowned.[80]

Elián was taken in by his relations in Miami, who offered him a permanent home. His father, who had remained in Cuba, wanted him returned to his family in Cárdenas. The federal government in Washington sided with the father and was soon in bitter conflict with the Cuban community in Florida. The boy became the centre of a political storm for more than six months, that played to the advantage of the Cuban government. The Cuban-Americans lost the battle, and the boy was eventually allowed to return to Cuba, after the intervention of the US Supreme Court.

This was more than a victory for a policy of family reunion. The struggle over Elián's future aroused fresh and public doubts within the United States about the wisdom of the government's policy of isolating Cuba simply to curry favour with the exile communities in Florida and New Jersey. The policy had had no tangible result and, in the wake of Elián's return to Cuba, prominent US business interests, notably farmers and traders seeking commercial possibilities on the island, began to challenge the Administration more forcefully.

Elián's case was also a watershed for the community of Cuban-Americans, with their wistful hopes of returning one day to a Castro-free island. The struggle over the Cuban boy revealed their divisions and illuminated the extent to which a new and more accommodating relationship between the island and the mainland had been developing over the previous decade. Where once there had been extreme hostility between members of divided familes, similar to those experienced by other peoples overtaken by revolution or civil war, the Castro supporters in Cuba and the exiles in Miami were now caught up in a meaningful though complicated relationship. Family visits to Cuba had been made possible since the last years of the Carter administration in the 1970s and had been actively encouraged by Havana in the 1990s. So frequent and regular was the contact that a new terminal was constructed at Havana airport to deal solely with family flights to and from Miami, New York and Los Angeles. A million air tickets were said to have been sold for flights between Miami and Havana in the two decades since 1978.

Cuba was also affected by a phenomenon that swept the entire Caribbean and much of Central and South America – of young men and women seeking by any means possible to gain entry into the United States, attracted by its economic opportunities. Arriving there, and finding work, they would help to fund their families at home by sending back a portion of their earnings. From Mexico and Peru, from Honduras and El Salvador, young *Latinos* poured into the United States. Cuba probably received US$1 billion a year from its diaspora population in the United States, though this was little compensation for the loss of the sugar subsidy and the financial support of the Communist world in 1990.

Elián's parents, by all reports, were exemplary citizens of the Revolution. With no special interest in politics, they were members of their local revolutionary defence committee (CDR) and of the Communist youth movement. Things had worked out well for them. Elián's father, Juan Miguel González, worked as a cashier in the tourist resort of Varadero, with access to the dollar economy; Elisa, his mother, worked there too. The couple had drifted apart, and eventually divorced. Juan Miguel married again, while Elisa became associated with a young man known as Rafa, a less than model citizen. Rafa had been in and out of the army, in and out of prison, and in and out of Miami. With a group of friends and family he set off on his final ill-fated trip to the Florida coast, taking Elisa and Elián with him. Both Elisa and Rafa were drowned.

Elián was taken first to a children's hospital in Miami. He was handed over by the US Immigration Service into the care of Lázaro, his father's uncle. Several generations of the González family had established themselves in Florida since 1959 and Lázaro had arrived in 1984. The Miami family's decision to keep hold of Elián, in spite of his father's requests, were soon to be backed up by the Cuban American National Foundation, which immediately grasped the political possibilities of the case and the chance of mobilising the Cuban-American community in the righteous cause of saving children from Communism. The foundation printed posters with Elián's picture, describing him as a 'child victim' of Castro. It may, perhaps, have imagined initially that Elián's father might have chosen to come to live in Florida with him.

Juan Miguel soon disabused his Miami relations of any such belief and requested the US authorities to return his son to Cuba at once. The US Immigration Service, conscious both of due process and of the political implications of the case, was slow to act. Since this was also the Christmas holiday period, the USIS did not rule that Elián should be returned to his father until 5 January 2000.

The Miami relations, with the aid of the CANF, now attempted to challenge the ruling of the Immigration Service through the courts and requested that the boy be granted political asylum. To persuade him of the delights of life in America they took him, a week after his sixth birthday, to Disney World. An inexperienced Florida judge ruled in January that Elián should remain with his Miami relations until a hearing could be held, in March, to decide whether it would be dangerous for him to return to Cuba. At this stage the US federal government became involved and Janet Reno, the attorney-general, rejected the Florida court's ruling. Reno was herself from Florida and had been a state attorney for Dade County. She knew what she was up against.

The Cuban government, geared up by Castro himself, found itself presented with an enormous propaganda advantage. With his mother dead who could deny that Elián's rightful place was with his father in Cuba? Huge crowds assembled outside the US mission on the Malecón to protest against his detention in Miami. The weeks ticked by while the legal arguments continued. The case became a night-time soap opera for television viewers, both in Cuba and the United States. The cast expanded when Elián's grandmothers were allowed to fly from Havana to New York to press the case for the boy's return. They were sympathetically received by Janet Reno in Washington, but had difficulty in penetrating the family protection surrounding Elián in Miami, though they were eventually allowed to see the boy.

The case absorbed US media attention not just for its intrinsic human interest, but because of its political impact. This was election year. The US vice-president, Al Gore, the Democratic candidate in the presidential elections to be held in November, broke with the government line in March, to curry votes in Florida. He called for Elián to be given permanent US residency. This may not have been to his benefit, since at least one poll suggested that 63 per cent of Miami voters wanted Elián to be sent home. Polls in the US as a whole carried the same message.

Negotiations continued between government lawyers and Elián's Miami family, and for a brief moment a breakthrough seemed imminent after the State Department provided Elián's father with a visa to visit his son. The Cubans thought that Juan Miguel would come home with his son, while the Miami family fondly hoped that he would be persuaded to stay in America. Both sides appeared to be playing for high stakes, although the loyalty of the father to Cuba was never in question. In April a further court decision in Miami ruled that Elián's 'physical presence in this country is at the discretion of the federal government', and that the state court could not 'subvert the decision to return him to his father and his home in Cuba'. Janet Reno tried to broker a personal deal with the Miami family, as did Senator Torricelli, but nothing would break their firm commitment to keep the boy.

Finally, early one April morning, federal agents arrived at the home where Elián was staying and forced the door. Elián, found hidden in a cupboard, was taken out in the presence of an armed agent and a photograph of the incident, opportunely snapped by a local stringer, was soon on the front pages of newspapers across the world. Elián was reunited with his father at an airforce base outside Washington a few hours later, and a happier photograph appeared with the boy held in his father's arms. They were obliged to remain in the United States for a further month, while the legal niceties were attended to, and they finally returned to Havana at the end of June, to be greeted at the airport by Ricardo Alarcón. The entire episode had been an unqualified triumph for the Revolution.

Yet the controversial dawn raid had again divided America. George W. Bush, the Republican candidate in the November election, declared that 'the picture that most of America saw, of the boy being seized by a marshal who had an automatic weapon, is not what America is about'. The US press, with the predictable exception of the *Miami Herald* and the *Wall Street Journal*, had taken the side of Elián's father and had sharply criticised the Miami Cubans who had tried to keep the boy in Florida. David Rieff in the *New York Times* described the Miami community as 'an out-of-control banana republic within the American body politic'.[81]

José Basulto, long an exile leader and founder of Brothers to the Rescue, wrote that he 'couldn't care less what the American public thinks about the Cuban exile community'.[82] It was an understandable reaction from a radical activist, but poor politics. A Gallup poll revealed not just that US opinion had turned against the Miami community, but that 70 per cent of voters now believed in lifting the Cuban embargo.[83] But in Florida itself a different story emerged in November. At two earlier presidential elections, in 1992 and 1996, the majority of Miami Cubans had voted for Clinton, the Democratic candidate. In November 2000 George W. Bush, the Republican, claimed to have won both the state and the presidency, although the result was fiercely contested. Cuba's triumph had been bought at a high price.

Dissent and opposition, 1991–2003

The start of the 'special period' saw the emergence of a new form of opposition to the Revolution. During the 1960s several openly counter-revolutionary groups with US backing took part in terrorist activities, sustaining a form of covert warfare that kept the island on a high state of alert but never got close to achieving its political objective of overthrowing the government. Many opponents in later years abandoned the struggle and chose exile, applying for a US visa and eventually reaching Miami. In the 1990s, the government faced a new phenomenon: citizens who did not care for the Revolution but who remained on the island to try to change things from within. These were often members of the professional middle class, hard hit by the straitened economic conditions of the 'special period' and lacking access to the dollar economy that allowed other citizens – with relatives in Miami or with jobs in the tourist sector – to keep their heads above water.

Although these dissidents, as they came to be called in the international press, were often struggling economically, they also felt themselves constrained by the prevailing lack of intellectual freedom and by the government's unwillingness to accept any significant internal debate about the way forward. Thirty years of something described as 'revolutionary socialism' had come to an end with the collapse of the Soviet Union, and many people sought the right to participate in public discussion about what might come next. The dissidents were not economically powerful, nor were they middle class in an economic sense, but many were intelligent and well educated, possessed of a strong belief that their capacities were under-used within the existing scheme of things. All were aware of the neo-liberal wind of change sweeping through the outside world and interested in what its possible impact might be on Cuba.

One group of economic specialists, unhappy with the speed of reform, published a document critical of the government's economic strategy in 1997. Entitled *La Patria es de Todos* (The Fatherland for All), and written in the wake of the fifth Party congress, the document criticised the Party for dwelling on the past achievements of the Revolution without providing constructive proposals to improve the economic situation in the future. Vladimiro Roca, the group's most prominent member, was not a natural subversive. The son of Blas Roca, one of the founding fathers of the Communist Party, he had trained as a pilot in the airforce and had later worked in a state institution responsible for foreign investment. He had teamed up with three other professionals anxious to promote discussion about other economic strategies – Felix Bonne Carcasses, an engineer; René Gómez Manzano, a lawyer; and Marta Beatriz Roque, an economist.

The group could hardly be described as counter-revolutionary, yet the government had never found it easy to deal with intellectual dissent and it was clearly alarmed by the impact that the group might have on other members of a potentially disgruntled sector of society. Fierce legislation had been enacted years earlier to deal with counter-revolutionary opposition and, since the Revolution still suffered from the US blockade, it was easy to prove that any discussion about the future economic strategy was by definition subversive. The four critics were arrested and put on trial in 1999, charged with inciting sedition and endangering the economy. Bonne, Gómez and Roque were sentenced to four years in prison, but were freed early the following year after petitions for clemency from Canada, Mexico and the Vatican. Roca was not released until May 2002, when he revealed that his opposition was now more political than economic. He declared his belief that the island's political system did not work and would have to be changed. This should be undertaken, he argued, even while Castro was still in power. He had converted to Catholicism while in prison and he told journalists that change would have to come through peaceful and legal means. 'I don't seek confrontation,' he said, 'I seek reconciliation.'

While Roca's group was behind bars, another group had emerged, closely identified with the Catholic Church. The Varela Project, named after Felix Varela, the nineteenth-century advocate of independence, was organised by Osvaldo Payá, who had been associated earlier with a group called the Christian Liberation Movement. The Varela Project was concerned from the start with political rather than economic reform, and it was more activist and less cerebral than Roca's group had been. It set itself the task of collecting signatures for a petition that called for a referendum regarding reform of the country's one-party system. Under the terms of the constitution of 1976 citizens were permitted to propose new legislation if they could garner at least 10,000 voters to support their proposal. Payá's wide-ranging petition also called for an amnesty for political prisoners, for a guarantee that the rights of free expression and free association would be respected, and for greater opportunities to be granted to private businesses. The petition signed off with an appeal for a new electoral law and for fresh elections to be held. 'Changes in every aspect are vitally necessary in Cuba,' Payá told journalists, 'and the Varela Project is a way to achieve these changes peacefully and without exclusions.'[84]

Roca had opposed the Varela Project, and one of his group, Marta Beatriz Roque, had claimed that it was 'unrealistic' to seek to change a constitution that had been designed by the Castro government. On his release from prison, however, perceiving that the Varela Project now had some wind in its sails, Roca declared that he would support it.

Another group of dissidents, known as Todos Unidos (All United) and run by Hector Palacios, also praised the Varela Project for overcoming 'the culture of fear' in Cuba. Palacios's group complained that dozens of its activists collecting signatures had been verbally and physically attacked, as had hundreds of people who had signed the petition. They had suffered from 'detentions, searches, coercion, ill-treatment and humiliation'.

The Project's high point, achieved in May 2002, occurred when Payá delivered the petition, duly signed by 11,000 people, to the National Assembly in Havana, on the eve of a visit to the island by Jimmy Carter. Favourable references to the Project were made by Carter during a live speech on Cuban television, but Castro took steps to crush the initiative. A government-organised referendum was held later in the year, designed to endorse the unalterably 'socialist' character of the existing Cuban constitution. The accumulation of any number of signatures would not now be able to change it.

The most serious difficulty facing the dissidents was the need to keep their activities separate from those organised by the Miami exiles or by the United States 'interests' section' in Havana, and in the end this proved impossible. The US government had promised to support 'civil society' in Cuba, and was soon providing money for the supply of radios capable of tuning in to Radio Martí, and to help fund so-called 'independent libraries'. Possibly to its disadvantage the Varela Project received the public support of the US government, and Vicki Huddleston, the senior US diplomat in Havana, described it to journalists in 2002 as the most important recent activity organised by the Cuban opposition. Her successor, James Cason, was even more publicly active in his support of the dissidents, inviting them into the mission to use its facilities, and travelling around the country to provide encouragement and support.

Early in 2003 the government ordered a further clampdown, and 75 members of the opposition, including Roca, were arrested and accused of collaboration with an enemy power. Payá was left untouched, perhaps because he had received widespread recognition in Europe and was less identified with the activities of the US mission. It was a difficult moment. Castro was pre-occupied by the renewed verbal hostility of the Bush administration, by the downgrading of the United Nations in the run-up to the Iraq war and by the vigour with which Cason was helping to finance and organise the opposition. The government was well informed about what was going on within the opposition, since several secret service agents had infiltrated its organisations, one or two in positions of leadership.

At the same time a fresh wave of aeroplane hijacking to Florida suggested to Castro that the Revolution was again the victim of a destabilisation campaign. In its worst moments, at the time of the US invasion of Iraq in March 2003, the government envisaged that Cuba might also be invaded, should a mass exodus of migrants re-occur. When the US authorities in Florida refused to return the hijackers to Havana the Cubans decided to make an example of the next gang that might fall into their hands. A ferry hijacked in Havana harbour, which ran out of fuel on its way to Florida, was captured by the Cuban coastguards and returned to port. The three ringleaders of the hijack were arrested, tried and sentenced to death.

The executions aroused considerable outside protest, notably in the countries of the European Union where the death penalty had long been illegal. Although this harsh decision may have prevented a serious crisis, it damaged Castro's long-term strategy of dividing the Europeans from the United States. Ever since Helms-Burton many European governments had tried to establish a policy towards Cuba independent of the United States. Now they were forced by their rhetoric on human rights, and even to some extent by the strength of public opinion, unhappy about the death penalty and the prison sentences, to move more closely to the US position.

Castro's familiar tactic was to go on the offensive, leading a protest demonstration to the embassy in Havana of Spain, the old colonial power, perceived as the ringleader of the Europe's hostile critics. The result was further to reinforce his island's defiance against the outside world – and its sense of isolation.

Cuba in the twenty-first century

In January 2001, typically out of step with the rest of the world though technically correct, Cuba celebrated the start of the third Christian millennium – and another anniversary of the Revolution of 1959. Castro, now aged 74, had been in power in Cuba for more than four decades, with his brother Raúl beside him. He had outmanoeuvred, and in most cases outlived, nine American presidents, from Eisenhower to Clinton.[85] A late convert to communism, but a close ally of what was once the Soviet Union, he had worked with six of the Soviet leaders from Khrushchev to Gorbachev.[86] He had also, as a staunch advocate of revolutionary and anti-colonial struggle, been acquainted with all the prominent figures of the Third World.[87] In February 2003 he took tea in Hanoi with 91-year-old General Giap, the Vietnamese soldier who had defeated the French at the battle of Dien Bien Phu in 1954, just a year after the attack on the Moncada barracks.

Castro continued to travel through the continents of the Third World in the new millennium, the only political figure apart from Nelson Mandela that young audiences wished to see and listen to. He continued to speak out against the injustices of capitalism, but downplayed his earlier enthusiasm for Marxism and spoke now in the language of the new movements that arose to combat globalisation and neo-liberalism, soon being enrolled as an honorary member in their ranks. Castro also sustained his opposition to the strains of racism that had once bedevilled Cuban society, telling a UN conference in South Africa in September 2001 that he supported the demand for reparations to be paid to those who had suffered from the slave trade. He called on 'the hegemonic superpower' to pay back 'its special debt to African Americans, to Native Americans living in reservations, and to the tens of millions of Latin American and Caribbean immigrants – as well as others from poor nations, be they mulatto, yellow or black – victims all of vicious discrimination and scorn'.[88]

Castro's search for allies continued wherever he could find them, sometimes in distant continents, sometimes nearer home. He found a soulmate in neighbouring Venezuela, establishing a close friendship with Colonel Hugo Chávez and sending 10,000 Cuban doctors to help out in the shanty towns. A guarantee of a regular supply to Cuba of Venezuelan oil was not the least of the advantages of this relationship. Looking further afield, he travelled in May 2001 to the home of Muslim fundamentalism in Tehran, to tell students at the university of his belief that 'the imperialist king will fall'. He was assured by Ayatollah Ali Khamenei that Iran and Cuba together could 'overcome the United States'.

Castro's government was no longer run in the new millennium by a group of ageing, white-bearded guerrilla fighters from the 1950s. They had been replaced by young graduates from the island's universities and technical schools, often recruited from the provinces. Far from being controlled by veterans of the revolutionary war, Ricardo Alarcón claimed in 2001 that the majority of people in the government and the Communist Party were under forty.[89] Castro had been surrounding himself with young people over many years, watching the emergence of each new generation of university graduates and snapping up the brightest to work at his side.

Enrique Oltuski, an old *fidelista* born in 1930 who worked for decades in the fisheries ministry, said of the efforts made within his ministry to promote the young: 'I am the exception; the rest of our deputy ministers are much younger people, between 30 and 35. We are promoting young people, because the future of the revolution must be in their hands.'

A very particular reason behind the promotion of the young to senior positions in the Revolution, said Oltuski, was to avoid following the Soviet example: 'If they are not in charge, they may stand against it. This is what happened in the socialist camp, where the old guard would not leave their posts and the young ones had to rise up against them. Thus 95 per cent of the positions in the government today are filled with young people.'[90]

Some young people, of course, brought up in the privations of the post-Soviet decade, were not short of post-revolutionary cynicism. Some recalled fondly – with their enthusiasm for American music, art and culture – Cuba's long history of close relations with the United States. Many in Washington who argued that the economic embargo would 'move Cuba toward democracy and a market economy' put their faith in this strata of the population, without perhaps realising the historical implications of such a demand. For a substantial strand in Cuba's nationalist tradition, developed over more than a century and sustained and amplified by Castro's Revolution, has been the ambition to escape from the kind of American tutelage imposed by the Platt Amendment of 1902.[91]

When asked in 1997 about the general attitude of the population towards the Revolution, General José Ramón Fernández, veteran leader of the battles against the invaders at the Bay of Pigs, was realistically phlegmatic:

> I don't mean . . . that there are no discontented people in Cuba, or people who disagree with socialism . . . We have shortages, privations, difficulties. We run risks; there are dangers. There are people who are more consumer-oriented, who would like a more comfortable life, without struggles. There are people who perhaps, consciously or unconsciously, place a shirt, a pair of pants, or a car, above the country's sovereignty or above social justice, and these people are clearly not enthusiastic about the Revolution.[92]

The older generation, meanwhile, contented themselves with their memories of the early years, producing a library of stories recounting the triumphs of the revolutionary war. The middle-aged recalled their wars in Africa (300,000 Cubans had seen service in Angola alone), or maybe their time in Grenada and Nicaragua. Others remembered their long association with the Soviet Union and the obscurer countries of the former Communist world. More than 300,000 Cubans still spoke fluent Russian, and many hundreds spoke Czech, Bulgarian, Polish or German, a reminder of the legions of translators once needed to oil the wheels of Comecon commerce.

Cuba is one of the few countries in the world to have seen off three colonial powers: Spain, the United States and the Soviet Union. All three left a significant imprint on the island and its people, an enduring legacy of buildings, artefacts and children. The Russians were the last to come and the last to leave and, at the start of the twenty-first century – apart from a wealth of discoloured concrete buildings ill-suited to the tropics – they were little more than a memory.

Castro's Revolution put Cuba on the map over a period of 40 years and registered the island as a permanent presence on the world stage. He engendered in the Cuban people an intangible but real sense of pride in their nation. Foreign visitors might gaze glumly at the forlorn and uncared-for appearance of great swathes of Havana, but few could miss the cheerfulness and optimism of its healthy and cleanly dressed population. This was a Revolution that had not ended in fratricidal strife, but had endlessly turned out fresh generations of well-educated citizens, motivated by affection for their ruler and his Revolution, and possessed of a developed sense of patriotism, with pride in their country's long history and the achievements of its people.

Castro bows out, February 2008

The first premonition of Castro's mortality came on October 20, 2004, when the *máximo líder* stumbled badly after a speech made on the parade ground outside the Che Guevara mausoleum in Santa Clara. He fractured an arm and broke a knee, and was for a while confined to a wheel chair. Yet in spite of this setback, he kept up a heavy schedule of television appearances, announcing in March 2005 an end to the 'special period' of austerity that had begun fifteen years earlier at the time of the Soviet collapse. Fresh allies in Latin America, notably Venezuela and Brazil, were now providing Cuba with an economic and political lifeline.

On July 31, 2006, Castro suffered a more serious setback. After emergency intestinal surgery, he formally handed over power on a temporary basis to his brother Raúl, his appointed deputy, and called on half a dozen senior figures to occupy leadership roles. Although he received a handful of foreign visitors, notably Hugo Chávez of Venezuela and Lula de Silva from Brazil, he never fully recovered and was never seen in public again. In 2007, to remind the Cubans that he was still alive and aware of what was going on in Cuba and the wider world, he began to write a regular letter to the newspaper *Granma*.

Finally, on February 19, 2008, at the age of 81, he used one of his columns to announce his resignation, both as president of the Council of State and as commander-in-chief. He had not resigned earlier, he said, because his first obligation 'after so many years of struggle' was to prepare the people for his absence, 'both psychologically and politically.' The tasks of government, he said, referring to his continuing frailty, 'required mobility and the total commitment that I am no longer in a physical condition to offer.'

Raúl Castro, five years younger and Fidel's alter ego since the attack on the Moncada barracks more than half a century earlier, became the new President of Cuba. Change was in the air, though most people expected a long period of transition.

Epilogue

I have returned to Cuba on several occasions in recent years, meeting old friends, interviewing ministers, talking to historians, reviving old memories and absorbing new impressions – and collecting material for this book. Many things have changed over 40 years, rather more have remained the same, for one of the usually forgotten charms of Communist governments is their capacity to stop the clock. Regimes that once wanted to change the world, and promote modernity in all its forms, have often remained resolutely conservative in practice, possibly to the satisfaction of their peoples.

Cuba has stayed much the same as it always was. The island's attraction for today's visitor, apart from the sun and the beach, is not just the final glimpse of a Communist era, but a chance to catch an earlier world of more than half a century ago. I spent a couple of nights at the Havana Libre, the former Hilton hotel built just before the Revolution in the once posh Vedado district west of the old town. In my youth the hotel was awash with revolutionaries from all over Latin America, both serious guerrilla activists and armchair voyeurs. Now it is part of a Spanish chain specialising in tourism. The good-looking black security guards stand by in a relaxed manner in their tailored Italianate tropical suiting, so much part of today's sophisticated scene that you could mistake them for guests. Not a gun in sight. Bookings are done on the computer; rooms unlocked with plastic cards. All that remains of the old days is the Sala Solidaridad meeting-room on the first floor, once home to revolutionary gatherings.

Yet the view north to the Caribbean and the Malecón, Havana's magnificent curved corniche road by the sea, has not changed in 40 years. The gigantic triangular Edificio Focsa, built from the profits of a railway company and once home to innumerable Latin American economists; the vast bulk of the Hotel Nacional, the grey treasure of the Batista era and formerly full of Soviet advisers and their families; the innumerable small colonial-style palazzos of Vedado still in need of a coat of paint; all these buildings remain exactly as they once were, although, with dollars, one can now get grilled lobster at the restaurant at the top of the Focsa, and drink *mojitos* on the incomparable terrace of the Nacional. There are no competitors, no new buildings grace the skyline, not a scrap of investment has been spent on this part of the city, and the tiny parking lots, the small engineering plant and the occasional open-air cafe are all just as they were.

Yet beneath the surface impression that nothing has changed, one stable factor in Cuban life for more than two centuries has been finally removed. The principal girder underpinning Cuba's economy and society has gone. The government made public its decision in the middle of 2002 to abandon the harvesting and production of sugar as the country's principal economic activity. Nearly half the country's mills would close, 71 out of 156; half the acreage formerly devoted to sugarcane would be given over to other crops; and at least one quarter of the sugar workforce of some 400,000 people would be retrained for other jobs.

The writing had been on the wall for some years. The disappearance of the Soviet market, coupled with the collapse of production during the 'special period', led to a dramatic drop in the income from sugar. In 1990, the last year in which sugar had been sold to the Soviet Union under the old arrangement, Cuba received $4.8 billion. In 2002, with sugar sold on the world market, it received less than $0.5 billion. Production had fallen from over 8 million tonnes in 1989 to 3.6 million in 2001.

The tourist industry, which is now the island's chief earner of foreign exchange, had already overtaken sugar in 1995. Sugar struggled on for several years, but the government concluded eventually that Cuban sugar would never secure the special advantage that it had had in the past. The world market had changed out of all recognition. Alternative sources of sugar had been developed, and even alternatives to sugar were now being promoted in the food industry of the West. Cuba was particularly affected by the growth of production in Brazil, vastly extended in the 1970s to produce sugar alcohol as a fuel for motor vehicles during the world energy crisis. When that development was no longer economic Brazil's sugar was diverted to the world market, bringing the price down to a low level that most experts believed would be permanent. The palmy days of sugar scarcity were over.

Cuba had long been sheltered from reality, first in the days of the US sugar quota, more recently through its barter deals with the Soviet Union. In the 1990s it was obliged to take some difficult decisions. I went to see General Ulises Rosales del Toro, the sugar minister, to ask him what had happened. No ordinary figure, Rosales del Toro is one of the most influential men in Castro's government, second only to Raúl Castro in the higher reaches of the army. A veteran of the Sierra Maestra and of the wars in Angola, as well as a participant in Venezuela's guerrilla war in the 1960s, he had also been the senior presiding officer at the trial in 1989 of General Ochoa. Only someone of his rank and seniority would have been able push through such a dramatic historical volte-face, to persuade the sugar workers to accept the changes ahead. Now in his 60s, informally dressed in a guayabera and peering through large spectacles, he has a considerable physical presence. I told him that I had first come to Cuba some 40 years earlier, at the moment when Che Guevara had advocated a dash for industrial development to escape from the tyranny of a single agricultural crop. Did he now feel that he was fulfilling Guevara's ambition?

'Well,' said the general with a twinkle, 'you were here at the exact moment of the last major shift, when we had this fabulous offer from the Soviet Union to buy our sugar at an unprecedented price, far more generous than the sugar quota we had had from the United States.' He went through the figures carefully, explaining what a wonderful deal Cuba had had, producing more and selling it at a higher price. Then, in the 1990s, the figures went all wrong. Production dropped and the price dropped. The arithmetic worked against the sugar industry. Rosales del Toro's job had been to go out to the workers, to explain to them and their families what had happened, and what would happen in the future. He had toured the country, holding thousands of meetings. Everyone would be guaranteed a job, and where possible everyone would remain within the same unit. Some would work at fresh tasks in agriculture, others would be retrained.

I went out the next day to a decommissioned sugar mill at Artemisa, to the west of Havana, one of 13 mills once owned by Julio Lobo, a millionaire sugar magnate who had left the island in 1960 in spite of requests from Guevara that he should stay. No one I met could remember what had happened at the time. They were all too young. The mill stands like some great ruined cathedral, a gigantic construction sheathed in corrugated iron, housing an infinity of grinders and crushers, now lying piled up and disconnected. An elusive fragrance of molasses still lingers in the air. Some 850 workers used to operate this mill and plantation complex, in a village of 3,000. Now it is expected that the workforce will be reduced to 350, while those remaining will receive re-training.

Julio Lobo's old colonial mansion is being used as an adult education centre for the workers, and I talked to some of the teachers. Apart from agricultural courses, including vegetable and fruit production, the students are studying accountancy, computing, veterinary science and languages. I asked a black teacher, who had previously worked as an engineer in the mill, whether he was not a bit sad to see the disappearance of such a significant part of Cuba's history. 'Yes,' he said, 'it's in the blood, and our families grew up here. But we understand that it was necessary.' Looking on the bright side, he pointed out that future work of some kind was guaranteed, their families would continue to live there and they had some opportunities for improvement.

A book of history is not a crystal ball, yet, in the particular circumstances of Cuba, the reader of a survey of 500 years might legitimately expect a postscript that draws attention to certain long-running themes and how these might be extended into the future. People invariably ask what changes will take place when Castro dies, an event that could happen tomorrow or in 20 years' time, and the question usually expects an apocalyptic answer. Chaos on the streets or a velvet revolution? Mass migration or an invasion from Miami? Continuing defiance and a fresh US occupation?

A violent outcome would certainly be consonant with much of Cuba's history, so often dominated by internal rebellion and external intervention. Set against that possibility is Castro's legacy of half a century of social peace, as well as the long tradition of the Cuban people in seeking their own solutions to their problems. Yet the continuing interest of the United States in the island's affairs, long pre-dating the Revolution and going back to the early years of the nineteenth century, will not simply disappear with Castro. Nor will the Cuban desire to be free and independent.

Cuba has been the victim of three empires and has rejected them all. 'We have had Spanish occupation, American occupation, and Soviet occupation,' one revolutionary loyalist told me. 'Now we are all on our own.' Cuba's government no longer justifies its existence on the attempts it once made to construct socialism. It emphasises instead its heroic and long-lasting nationalist struggle against the United States, a campaign that still strikes a sentimental chord in much of Latin America.

Many surprising weapons have been called into service to wage this battle. Museums in the revamped sections of Old Havana ignore the achievements of the island's socialist era and sing the praises of Spanish colonialism. Plantation culture and slavery, only formally ended in 1886, is romanticised rather than excoriated. Former gangster hotels welcome foreign tourists with photographs of the good old days of rampant capitalism, when Argentinian tango stars, Mexican dancers and Brazilian singers rubbed shoulders with the American mafia. Cuba has embraced 'heritage culture' with all the enthusiasm of the postmodernists in the West. After a ten-year flirtation with mass tourism and the increasing use of the American dollar by much of the population, this culture of selective nationalist nostalgia is surely helping to fuel the country's ineluctable drive towards a capitalist future.

Castro is an astute and sophisticated observer of the international scene, and a man familiar with his continent's history, and he knows better than most what the next page will bring. The chief result of the great Mexican Revolution, after decades of revolutionary upheaval dragged large swathes of the population into the modern economy, was to make the country ready for capitalist exploitation. Cuba seems set to follow the same road.

By the bleak standards of Latin America the island has an educated and healthy population, but many Cubans are fed up with pulling themselves up with their bootstraps. Like the gaudy papier-mâché fish, selling at the craft stalls that litter the heritage zones of Old Havana, they have their mouths wide open, gulping thirstily in anticipation of the great draughts of capital that will surely inundate the country as soon as the ancient *máximo líder* dies. This is not an outcome that would have been expected by the revolutionary enthusiasts of yesteryear, yet the resilient and cheerful people of Cuba, isolated for decades, are still capable of producing a few more surprises. The experience of independence gained during the extended 'special period' of the past decade may yet save them from the worst excesses of post-communism in the former Soviet Union and Eastern Europe. Ironically, by surrendering to the inevitable and by reintroducing Cubans to the seductions of capitalism very gradually, Castro may have performed his last great revolutionary service to his country.

Personally I expect little change in the years ahead, or even when Castro dies. Cuba has already been governed for several years by a post-Castro government. Raúl Castro runs the armed forces today, as he has done since 1959. Ricardo Alarcón at the national assembly is the country's political guru, aware of shifts in public opinion as well as a long-serving and expert negotiator with the United States. Carlos Lage is the prime minister and controller of the country's economy. Felipe Pérez Roque is a sure hand at foreign affairs, sustaining Cuba's extraordinary worldwide support. This is a more than competent team that could run the affairs of any country at any time, as one admiring western ambassador explained to me.

Castro himself is now largely absent from the scene. Forty years ago, he was everywhere: on television every night, in the newspapers every day and, if you were lucky, he might turn up at your hotel. Cuba never indulged in a Soviet-style cult of the personality, but almost nothing happened without his say-so, and his enthusiasms became those of the country. Today he has become an emeritus president, an elder statesman, and the machinery of government runs without his hand on the tiller. He remains a figure from all our yesterdays, grey-bearded but eternally youthful like an ageing rock star. He does not run the country, but he presides over a government that is his creation. He has changed his slogan from 'socialism or death', suitable for the violent twentieth century, to 'a better world is possible', appropriate for the more pacifistic revolutionaries of a new era. When he dies, there will be little change in Cuba. While few people have been looking, the change has already taken place.

Appendix A

Letter from John Quincy Adams, US secretary of state, to Hugh Nelson, the American minister in Madrid, 23 April 1823

These islands are natural appendages of the North American continent, and one of them – almost in sight of our shores – from a multitude of considerations has become an object of transcendent importance to the commercial and political interests of our Union. Its commanding position with reference to the Gulf of Mexico and the West Indian seas, its situation midway between our southern coast and the island of San Domingo, its safe and capacious harbour of the Havana, fronting a long line of our shores destitute of the same advantages, the nature of its production and of its wants, furnishing the supplies and needing the returns of a commerce immensely profitable and mutually beneficial give it an importance in the sum of our national interests with which that of no other foreign territory can be compared, and little inferior to that which binds the different members of this Union together.

Such indeed are, between the interests of that island and of this country, the geographical, commercial, moral and political relations formed by nature, gathering in the process of time, and even now verging to maturity, that in looking forward to the probable course of events for the short period of half a century, it is scarcely possible to resist the conviction that the annexation of Cuba to our Federal Republic will be indispensable to the continuance and integrity of the Union itself . . .

There are laws of political as well as of physical gravitation. And if an apple, severed by the tempest from its native tree, cannot choose but to fall to the ground, Cuba, forcibly disjoined from its own unnatural connection with Spain, and incapable of self-support, can gravitate only towards the North American Union, which, by the same law of nature, cannot cast her off from her bosom.

Quoted in Willis Fletcher Johnson, *The History of Cuba*, New York, 1920, vol. 2, pp. 261–2

Appendix B

The Platt Amendment, 1902

The President of the United States is hereby authorised to 'leave the government and control of the island of Cuba to its people' so soon as a government shall have been established in said island under a constitution which, either as a part thereof or in an ordinance appended thereto, shall define the future relations of the United States with Cuba, substantially as follows:

1. That the government of·Cuba shall never enter into treaty or other compact with any foreign power or powers which will impair or tend to impair the independence of Cuba, nor in any manner authorise or permit any foreign power or powers to obtain by colonisation or for military or naval purposes or otherwise, lodgment in or control over any portion of said island.

    (A) That said government shall not assume or contract any public debt, to pay the interest upon which, and to make any reasonable sinking fund provision for the ultimate discharge of which the ordinary revenues of the island, after defraying the current expenses of government, shall be inadequate.

    (B) That the government of Cuba consents that the United States may exercise the right to intervene for the preservation of Cuban independence, the maintenance of a government adequate for the protection of life, property, and individual liberty, and for discharging the obligations with respect to Cuba imposed by the Treaty of Paris on the United States, now to be assumed by the government of Cuba.

    (C) That all acts of the United States in Cuba during its military occupancy thereof are ratified and validated, and all lawful rights acquired thereunder shall be maintained and protected.

    (D) That the government of Cuba will execute, and, as far as necessary, extend, the plans already devised or other plans to be mutually agreed upon, for the sanitation of the cities of the island, to the end that a recurrence of epidemic and infectious diseases may be prevented, thereby assuring protection to the people and commerce of Cuba, as well as to the commerce of the southern ports of the United States and the people residing therein.

(E) That the Isle of Pines shall be omitted from the proposed constitutional boundaries of Cuba, the title thereto being left to future adjustments by treaty.

(F) That to enable the United States to maintain the independence of Cuba, and to protect the people thereof, as well as for its defence, the government of Cuba will sell or lease to the United States lands necessary for coaling or naval stations at certain specified points, to be agreed upon with the President of the United States.

Appendix C

Extracts from The Helms-Burton Act, 1996
(The Cuban Liberty and Democratic Solidarity (Libertad) Act of 1996, PL 104–114)

An Act to seek international sanctions against the Castro government in Cuba, to plan for support of a transition government leading to a democratically elected government in Cuba, and for other purposes.

Be it enacted by the Senate and House of Representatives of the United States of America in Congress assembled,

Title I – Strengthening international sanctions against the Castro government

Title II – Assistance to a free and independent Cuba

Sec. 205. Requirements and factors for determining a transition government.

(A) Requirements. For the purposes of this Act, a transition government in Cuba is a government that

1. has legalized all political activity;
2. has released all political prisoners and allowed for investigations of Cuban prisons by appropriate international human rights organizations;
3. has dissolved the present Department of State Security in the Cuban Ministry of the Interior, including the Committees for the Defense of the Revolution and the Rapid Response Brigades; and
4. has made public commitments to organizing free and fair elections for a new government
   (a) to be held in a timely manner within a period not to exceed 18 months after the transition government assumes power;

(b) with the participation of multiple independent political parties that have full access to the media on an equal basis, including (in the case of radio, television, or other telecommunications media) in terms of allotments of time for such access and the times of day such allotments are given; and

(c) to be conducted under the supervision of internationally recognized observers, such as the Organization of American States, the United Nations, and other election monitors;

5. has ceased any interference with Radio Martí or Television Martí broadcasts;

6. makes public commitments to and is making demonstrable progress in
   (a) establishing an independent judiciary;
   (b) respecting internationally recognized human rights and basic freedoms as set forth in the Universal Declaration of Human Rights, to which Cuba is a signatory nation;
   (c) allowing the establishment of independent trade unions as set forth in conventions 87 and 98 of the International Labor Organization, and allowing the establishment of independent social, economic, and political associations;

7. does not include Fidel Castro or Raúl Castro; and

8. has given adequate assurances that it will allow the speedy and efficient distribution of assistance to the Cuban people.

(B) Additional Factors. In addition to the requirements in subsection (A), in determining whether a transition government in Cuba is in power, the President shall take into account the extent to which that government

1. is demonstrably in transition from a communist totalitarian dictatorship to representative democracy;

2. has made public commitments to, and is making demonstrable progress in—
   (a) effectively guaranteeing the rights of free speech and freedom of the press, including granting permits to privately owned media and telecommunications companies to operate in Cuba;
   (b) permitting the reinstatement of citizenship to Cuban-born persons returning to Cuba;
   (c) assuring the right to private property; and
   (d) taking appropriate steps to return to United States citizens (and entities which are 50 percent or more beneficially owned by United States citizens) property taken by the Cuban Government from such citizens and entities on or after January 1, 1959, or to provide equitable compensation to such citizens and entities for such property;

3. has extradited or otherwise rendered to the United States all persons sought by the United States Department of Justice for crimes committed in the United States; and

4. has permitted the deployment throughout Cuba of independent and unfettered international human rights monitors.

Sec. 206. Requirements for determining a democratically elected government

For purposes of this Act, a democratically elected government in Cuba, in addition to meeting the requirements of section 205(a), is a government which

1. results from free and fair elections
   (a) conducted under the supervision of internationally recognized observers; and
   (b) in which
       (i) opposition parties were permitted ample time to organize and campaign for such elections; and
       (ii) all candidates were permitted full access to the media;
2. is showing respect for the basic civil liberties and human rights of the citizens of Cuba;
3. is substantially moving toward a market-oriented economic system based on the right to own and enjoy property;
4. is committed to making constitutional changes that would ensure regular free and fair elections and the full enjoyment of basic civil liberties and human rights by the citizens of Cuba;
5. has made demonstrable progress in establishing an independent judiciary; and
6. has made demonstrable progress in returning to United States citizens (and entities which are 50 percent or more beneficially owned by United States citizens) property taken by the Cuban Government from such citizens and entities on or after January 1, 1959, or providing full compensation for such property in accordance with international law standards and practice.

Title III – Protection of property rights of United States nationals

Sec. 301. Findings

The Congress makes the following findings:

1. Individuals enjoy a fundamental right to own and enjoy property which is enshrined in the United States Constitution.
2. The wrongful confiscation or taking of property belonging to United States nationals by the Cuban Government, and the subsequent exploitation of this property at the expense of the rightful owner, undermines the comity of nations, the free flow of commerce, and economic development.
3. Since Fidel Castro seized power in Cuba in 1959
   (a) he has trampled on the fundamental rights of the Cuban people; and
   (b) through his personal despotism, he has confiscated the property of

(i)   millions of his own citizens;

(ii) thousands of United States nationals; and

(iii) thousands more Cubans who claimed asylum in the United States as refugees because of persecution and later became naturalized citizens of the United States.

4. It is in the interest of the Cuban people that the Cuban Government respect equally the property rights of Cuban nationals and nationals of other countries.

5. The Cuban Government is offering foreign investors the opportunity to purchase an equity interest in, manage, or enter into joint ventures using property and assets some of which were confiscated from United States nationals.

6. This 'trafficking' in confiscated property provides badly needed financial benefit, including hard currency, oil, and productive investment and expertise, to the current Cuban Government and thus undermines the foreign policy of the United States

(a) to bring democratic institutions to Cuba through the pressure of a general economic embargo at a time when the Castro regime has proven to be vulnerable to international economic pressure; and

(b) to protect the claims of United States nationals who had property wrongfully confiscated by the Cuban Government.

7. The United States Department of State has notified other governments that the transfer to third parties of properties confiscated by the Cuban Government 'would complicate any attempt to return them to their original owners'.

8. The international judicial system, as currently structured, lacks fully effective remedies for the wrongful confiscation of property and for unjust enrichment from the use of wrongfully confiscated property by governments and private entities at the expense of the rightful owners of the property.

9. International law recognizes that a nation has the ability to provide for rules of law with respect to conduct outside its territory that has or is intended to have substantial effect within its territory.

10. The United States Government has an obligation to its citizens to provide protection against wrongful confiscations by foreign nations and their citizens, including the provision of private remedies.

11. To deter trafficking in wrongfully confiscated property, United States nationals who were the victims of these confiscations should be endowed with a judicial remedy in the courts of the United States that would deny traffickers any profits from economically exploiting Castro's wrongful seizures.

Notes

Introduction

1. See Luis Martínez-Fernández, 'Life in a "Male City": Native and Foreign Elite Women in Nineteenth Century Havana,' *Cuban Studies*, vol. 25, 1995.
2. Elsewhere in the Caribbean, slavery was ended rather earlier, between 1834 and 1848. It ended in the United States in 1863, and in Brazil in 1888.
3. Louis Pérez, *Winds of Change: Hurricanes and the Transformation of Nineteenth-century Cuba*, University Press of Florida, 2000, p. 17.
4. A visitor to Cuba from Jamaica in 1795 (presumably a Protestant) explained how 'many of the largest and best sugar estates in the island of Cuba belong to the different ecclesiastical orders, who are the most rapacious of planters. Under the mask of discouraging a vicious intercourse with the sexes, some of them religiously resolved to purchase only male negroes ... Deprived of connections resulting from one of the chief laws of nature, and driven to desperation, the unhappy negroes, not unlike the first Romans, have been known to fly to neighbouring estates, seize on the women, and carry them off to the mountains.' R. C. Dallas, *The History of the Maroons*, London, 1803, p. 60.
5. Spain, France, Portugal, Britain, the United States, Russia and even Germany has a footnote in Cuban history. In August 1942 German pirates – submarines – attacked and sank two Cuban freighters, an event that encouraged President Batista to allow the United States to establish military bases in Pinar del Rio, for the training of US and British airforce personnel. Ernest Hemingway spent much of the war looking for the German submarines off what later became the tourist resort of Cayo Coco, and wrote about his experiences in his novel *Islands in the Stream*.

Chapter 1

1. The island that embraces today's Haiti and the Dominican Republic was called Hispaniola by the Spaniards.
2. Quoted in Jaime Suchlicki, *Cuba from Columbus to Castro and Beyond*, London, 1997, p. 8.
3. Bartolomé de las Casas provides a long description of the population of Cuba, as well as the flora and fauna, in his *Historia de las Indias*, vol. 3, Biblioteca Ayacucho, Caracas, 1986, pp.81–101.
4. Roland Ely, *La Economía Cubana entre los dos Isabeles, 1492–1832*, Havana, 1960, p. 21.
5. Quoted in Willis Fletcher Johnson, *The History of Cuba*, vol. 1, New York, 1920, p. 28.

6. Johnson, *History of Cuba*, vol. 1, p. 59.

7. Bartolomé de las Casas, *A Short Account of the Destruction of the Indies*, London, 1992, p. 28.

8. Las Casas, *A Short Account*, p. 29.

9. Irving Rouse, *The Tainos: The Rise and Decline of the People who Greeted Columbus*, New Haven and London, 1992, p. 157.

10. Ely, *La Economía Cubana*, p. 17. Ely calculated that 84,000 ounces of gold would have been worth about $1,500,000 in the 1960s.

11. Quoted in Ramiro Guerra y Sánchez, *Sugar and Society in the Caribbean: An Economic History of Cuban Agriculture*, New Haven, 1964, p. 32.

12. Girolami Benzoni was an Italian traveller from Milan who came to the Americas between 1541 and 1556 and wrote an account of what he had seen at Cubagua, a Spanish settlement on the coast of Venezuela. He did not witness any Indian slaves being transferred specifically to Cuba, but described the fate of those who ended up in Santo Domingo. Girolamo Benzoni, *History of the New World, shewing his travels in America from 1541 to 1556*, London, 1857.

13. 'More than 7,000 children died of hunger, after their parents had been shipped off to the mines, and I saw many other horrors also. It was later decided to hunt down the natives who had fled into the mountains, and the subsequent hunting parties were responsible for carnage beyond belief. Thus it was that the whole of the island was devastated and depopulated, and it now affords, as we discovered on a recent visit, a moving and heart-rending spectacle, transformed, as it has been, into one vast, barren wasteland.' Las Casas, *A Short Account*, p. 30.

14. Bernal Diaz del Castillo, *The Conquest of New Spain*, London, 1963 p. 26. 'It was said that better lands had never been discovered in the world; and when the pottery idols with so many different shapes were seen, it was said that they belonged to the Gentiles, and others

said that they were the work of the Jews whom Titus and Vespasian had turned out of Jerusalem and sent to sea in certain ships which had carried them to this land.'

15. Suchlicki, *Cuba from Columbus to Castro*, p. 28.

16. Fernando Ortíz, *Cuban Counterpoint, Tobacco and Sugar*, Durham, N. C., 1995, p. 99.

17. Bartolomé de Las Casas, *Historia de Indias*, Mexico, 1951, vol. III, p. 103.

18. Rodrigo Rangel, the secretary of Hernando de Soto who led an expedition from Havana to Florida in 1539, explained how the conquistadores were always accompanied by 'Irish greyhounds and very bold, savage dogs.' The reader should understand, he wrote, 'that *aperrear* (to throw to the dogs) is to have the dogs eat him, or kill him, tearing the Indians in pieces.' See E. G. Bourne, ed., *Narrative of the career of Hernando de Soto*, New York, 1904, vol. II., p. 60. Colonel Henry Bouquet, engaged in combat against North American Indians in 1763, wrote that 'I wish we could make use of the Spanish method, to hunt them with English dogs, supported by Rangers and some light horse, who would, I think, effectually extirpate or remove that vermin.' Later, the British heard news of how the Spanish in Cuba had sent 36 dogs and 12 handlers to expel the Mosquito Indians from the coastal zone of Nicaragua, and in 1795, the Spanish authorities sent dogs and doghandlers from Cuba to Jamaica to help crush a Maroon rebellion.

19. Las Casas, *A Short Account*, p. 30.

20. Irene Wright, *Cuba*, New York, 1910.

21. Rouse, *The Tainos*, p. 161.

22. Grover Flint, *Marching with Gómez: a war correspondent's field note-book kept during four months with the Cuban army*, London, 1898, p. 28.

23. Stewart Culin, 'The Indians of Cuba,' *Bulletin of the Free Museum of Science and Art*, Philadelphia, vol. III, no.4, May 1902.

24. Antonio Núñez Jiménez, *Geografía de Cuba*, 2nd edn, Havana, 1960 (1st edn, 1954) p. 652.

25. According to Robin Moore, this movement had its roots in the literary works of Ramón de Palma (1812–1860), Cristóbal Napolés Fajardo, known as 'El Cucalambé' (*c.* 1829–1862), and José Fornaris (1827–1890). See Robin D Moore, *Nationalising Blackness, Afrocubanismo and Artistic revolution in Havana, 1920–1940*, Pittsburgh, 1997, p. 127.

26. Quoted in Moore, *Nationalising Blackness*, p. 128.

27. Moore, *Nationalising Blackness*, pp. 129-30.

28. Levi Marrero, *Cuba: Economía y Sociedad*, Madrid, 1978, vol. I, p. 211.

29. Hubert Aimes, *A History of Slavery in Cuba, 1511–1868*, New York, 1907, p. 8.

30. Bishop Sarmiento y Castilla reported that 744 slaves had arrived in 1544, but the figure appears to refer to both 'blacks and foreign Indians'. Eduardo Torres Cuevas and Oscar Loyola Vega, *Historia de Cuba, 1492–1898*, Havana, 2001, p. 60.

31. Aimes, *History of Slavery*, p. 11.

32. Marrero, *Cuba: Economía y Sociedad*, vol. I, p. 220.

33. Jorge and Isabel Castellanos, *Cultura Afrocubana: el Negro en Cuba, 1492–1844*, Miami, 1988, vol. I, p. 20–25.

34. Marrero, *Cuba: Economía y Sociedad*, vol. I, p. 211.

35. Marrero, *Cuba: Economía y Sociedad*, vol. I, p. 219.

36. Marrero, *Cuba: Economía y Sociedad*, vol. I, p. 221.

37. Irene Wright, 'Rescates with special reference to Cuba, 1599–1610', *Hispanic American Historical Review*, vol. III, no. 3, August 1920, p. 358.

38. Luis Martínez-Fernández, *Torn Between Empires: Economy, Society, and Patterns of Political Thought in the Hispanic Caribbean, 1840–1878*, Athens, Ga., 1994, p. 11.

39. Henry Kamen, *Spain's Road to Empire,*

the Making of a World Power, 1492–1763*, London, 2002, p. 121.

40. Kenneth Andrews, *Trade, Plunder and Settlement: Maritime Enterprise and the Genesis of the British Empire, 1480–1630*, Cambridge, 1984, p. 118.

41. Irene Wright, *Historia Documentada de San Cristóbal de la Habana*, Havana, 1927.

42. Marrero, *Cuba: Economía y Sociedad*, vol. I, p. 271.

43. Quoted in Kamen, *Spain's Road to Empire*, p. 249.

44. Portugal was joined with Spain after the death of Philip's nephew, the Portuguese king Sebastião, killed at the battle of Alcázarquivir in Morocco in 1578.

45. Guerra, *Sugar and Society in the Caribbean*, p. 35.

46. Hudson Strode, *The Pageant of Cuba*, London, 1935, p. 66.

47. Kenneth Andrews, *The Spanish Caribbean: Trade and Plunder, 1530–1630*, New York, 1958, p. 245.

48. Kenneth Andrews, *Elizabethan Privateering: English privateering during the Spanish War, 1585–1603*, Cambridge, 1964, p. 120.

49. Quoted in Andrews, *Elizabethan Privateering*, p. 37.

50. Kenneth Andrews (ed.), *English Privateering Voyages to the West Indies, 1588–1598*, Cambridge, 1959, p. 30.

51. Irene Wright, *The Early History of Cuba, 1492–1586*, New York, 1916, pp. 370–71.

52. Wright, *The Early History of Cuba*, p. 369.

53. Andrews, *Trade, Plunder and Settlement*, p. 243. 'Time and again they were defeated by wind and weather, distance and disease, the intractable forces of nature, and the inevitable limits of their own resources, technology and skills. The naval power at their disposal was small; the army available was scarcely adequate for the capture of a major seaport, let alone its tenure as a base in the heart of enemy territory; expertise in the mounting and handling of large-scale amphibious operations took many decades to mature, as some disastrous

expeditions of the next century were to show; men had still to work out the strategy and tactics of oceanic warfare and tended to underestimate the difficulties of a blockade, for example, or the seizure of an Atlantic island or a West Indian base.'

54. Andrews, *Trade, Plunder and Settlement*, p. 248.

55. Petrus Blok, *History of the Peoples of the Netherlands*, New York, 1900, vol. IV, p. 37.

56. Rafael Fermoselle, *The Evolution of the Cuban Military, 1492–1986*, Miami, 1987, p. 23. and see also, Saturnino Ulibarri, *Piratas y Corsarios de Cuba*, Havana, 1931.

57. Irene Wright, 'The Dutch and Cuba, 1609–1643', *Hispanic American Historical Review*, vol. IV. no. 4, November 1921.

58. Johnson, *The History of Cuba*, vol. I, p. 295.

59. Captain Myngs (1625–1666) had been the captain of the *Elizabeth* and later, in 1655, of the *Marston Moor*, with which he sailed out to the West Indies, remaining there for several years.

60. Olga Portuondo, *Santiago de Cuba: desde su fundación hasta la guerra de los diez días*, Santiago, 1996.

61. Quoted in Strode, *The Pageant of Cuba*, 1935, p. 69. Morgan (*c.* 1635–1688), subsequently sailed to Panama and seized the well-fortified port of Porto Bello, agreeing to leave only after payment of a large ransom. He attacked Maracaibo in 1669 and returned to Panama in 1670, capturing the Chagres castle and sailing up the Chagres river, finally capturing Panama City in January 1671.

62. Kamen, *Spain's Road to Empire*, p. 85.

63. Johnson, *The History of Cuba*, vol. I, p. 225.

64. Quoted in Joan Casanovas, *Bread, or Bullets: Urban Labour and Spanish Colonialism in Cuba, 1850–1898*, Pittsburgh, 1998, p. 22.

65. Aimes, *History of Slavery*, p. 21.

Chapter 2

1. The Americans arrived on 6 June 1898, when a hundred US marines landed at Guantánamo to establish Camp McCalla on the shores of the bay. The US commander, General William Shafter, had been reading up on Admiral Vernon's expedition of 1741 as he sailed over to Cuba. Frank Freidel, *The Splendid Little War*, New York, 1958, pp. 56 and 77.

2. *The Vernon Papers*, Navy Records Society, London, 1858.

3. A thinly veiled fictional account of this expedition can be found in the novel *Roderick Random*, by Tobias Smollett.

4. Olga Portuondo, 'La Consolidación de la Sociedad Criolla (1700–1765)', *Historia de Cuba*, vol. I, *La Colonia*, Havana, 1994, pp. 205–7.

5. Edward Vernon, *Original Papers relating to the Expedition to the Island of Cuba*, London, 1744, p. 44. Vernon had excellent, first-hand information about the road from Guantánamo to Santiago supplied to him by John Drake, an English sailor who had been living in Cuba for many years as a fisherman and cowhand.

6. Cojímar was to be Ernest Hemingway's favourite fishing port.

7. Rafael Fermoselle, *The Evolution of the Cuban Military, 1492–1986*, Miami, 1987, p. 13. Over 650 British soldiers were wounded, and several thousand were later to die of disease, yellow fever as usual taking its toll. The Spanish and Cuban losses amounted to 380 killed, and 1,500 wounded.

8. Louis Pérez, *Cuba, Between Reform and Revolution*, Oxford, 1995, p. 66.

9. Alexander von Humboldt, *The Island of Cuba, a political essay*, Princeton, 2001.

10. Louis Pérez, *Cuba and the United States: Ties of Singular Intimacy*, Athens, Ga, 1997, p. 9.

11. Gustave d'Hespel d'Harponville, *La Reine des Antilles*, Paris, 1850.

12. So unsettling was the entrance of these newcomers into Cuba that Madrid gave

orders in 1807 for all foreigners to be expelled from the island, a decree reiterated two years later after riots between French settlers and Cubans in Havana in March 1809. The Havana authorities found the decrees impossible to enforce. Many refugees simply disobeyed the order, others swiftly arranged their naturalisation papers. Duvon Cubitt, 'Immigration in Cuba', *Hispanic American Historical Review,* vol. XXII, May 1942, pp. 280–88, citing José Antonio Portuondo, *Proceso de la Cultura Cubana,* Havana, 1938, an appendix called 'La inmigración francesa'.

13. Roland Ely, *La Economía Cubana entre los dos Isabeles, 1492–1832,* Havana, 1960, p. 80.

14. Ramiro Guerra, *Sugar and Society in the Caribbean: An Economic History of Cuban Agriculture,* New Haven, 1964, p. 49.

15. In 1827, out of a total Cuban population of 704,487, the whites numbered only 311,051. The black total was 393,436, made up of 286,942 slaves and 106,494 'free coloureds'. Philip Howard, *Changing History: Afro-Cuban Cabildos and Societies of Color in the Nineteenth Century,* Baton Rouge, La., 1998, pp. 82–3. Howard claims that by the time of the census of 1841, the whites were outnumbered not just by the black slaves, but by the 'free coloureds' as well. The figures do not seem to bear this out.

16. Pérez, *Cuba and the United States,* p. 12.

17. Robert Paquette, *Sugar is Made with Blood: the Conspiracy of La Escalera and the Conflict between Empires over Slavery in Cuba,* Middletown, Conn., 1988, p. 125.

18. Levi Marrero, *Cuba: Economía y Sociedad,* Madrid, 1978, vol. III, p. 23. Slaves brought into Cuba by Portuguese slavers in the late sixteenth century came from ports along the entire length of the west African shore, from Senegal to Angola. A census recorded in 1608 at the copper town of El Cobre, outside Santiago, noted the various ethnic origins of the slaves held at the mine:

Angolas (the majority), Congas, Enchicos, Minas, Mohongos, Biohos, Brans, Banones, Manicongos, Nalúes, Carabalíes, Terranovas, and Criollos. Many of these slaves and their offspring retained their specific ethnic identity for more than two centuries.

19. Paquette, *Sugar is Made with Blood,* p. 37.

20. Paquette, *Sugar is Made with Blood,* p. 37.

21. Willis Fletcher Johnson, *The History of Cuba,* New York, 1920, vol. I, pp. 230–31.

22. Ramiro Guerra Sánchez (ed.), *A History of the Cuban Nation,* Havana, 1958, vol. III, pp. 118–122.

23. The conspirators were Román de la Luz Silveira, a prominent landowner, and Joaquín Infante, a lawyer from Bayamo. Both were enrolled in masonic lodges, and had embraced the latest radical ideas from Europe. The military leader was General Luís Francisco Bassave y Cárdenas.

24. *Historia de Cuba, La Colonia,* Havana, 1994, p. 337.

25. Etienne-Michel Masse, *L'isle de Cuba et La Havane,* Paris, 1825, p. 249.

26. Paquette, *Sugar is Made with Blood,* p. 123.

27. Howard, *Changing History,* pp. 76–7.

28. Paquette, *Sugar is Made with Blood,* p. 76.

29. Similar misunderstandings occurred in the British colonies in the Caribbean, where many slaves were led to believe that the successful campaign against the slave trade meant the abolition of slavery itself.

30. The evidence was published subsequently by the authorities. Howard, *Changing History,* p. 75.

31. Howard, *Changing History,* p. 76.

32. Elias Entralgo, *La liberación étnica cubana,* Havana, 1953, quoted in Howard, *Changing History,* pp. 74–5.

33. Other members of this internationalist conspiracy included a former president of Colombia (José Fernández la Madrid) and a future president of Ecuador (Vicente Rocafuerte), as well as a

Peruvian writer (Manuel Lorenzo Vidaurre) and an Argentine adventurer (José Antonio Miralla).

34. *Historia de Cuba, vol. 1, La Colonia,* Havana, 1994, p. 339.

35. General Manrique, the leader of the invasion force, died just as he was about to sail to Cuba.

36. Quoted in Hugh Thomas, *Cuba or the Pursuit of Freedom,* London, 1971, pp. 103–5.

37. Quoted in Tom Chaffin, *Fatal Glory: Narciso López and the First Clandestine US War against Cuba,* Charlottesville, Va, 1996, p. 33. The minister was José María Calatrava.

38. Quoted in Duvon Corbitt, 'Immigration in Cuba', *Hispanic American Historical Review,* vol. XXII, May 1942, p. 284.

39. Arango's plan was proposed on 14 January 1792, barely five months after the rebellion in Saint-Domingue. See Francisco de Arango y Parreño, *Obras,* Havana, 1888, vol. I. pp. 97–100, quoted in Corbitt, 'Immigration in Cuba', p. 282.

40. Quoted in Corbitt, 'Immigration in Cuba', p. 284.

41. Corbitt, 'Immigration in Cuba', p. 286. The government's newly created development agency, the *Consulado Real de Agricultura y Comercio,* looked favourably on Arango's plan, reporting in 1796 that 'the first precaution to be taken is without doubt the promotion with prudence and discernment of white colonisation in the rural districts . . .'

42. Corbitt, 'Immigration in Cuba', p. 288.

43. Earlier attempts at settlement in the bay had failed, although the harbour was once popular with smugglers; a small fort, the Castilla Nuestra Señora de los Angeles, was built there in the 1740s to curb their activities and to guard against the incursions of the British.

44. Laird Bergad, *The Cuban Slave Market, 1790–1880,* Cambridge, 1995, p. 106. The campaign for white immigration subsidised by the state lost much of its

impetus after the death of Ramírez in 1821, and complaints were made years later at Cienfuegos that blacks were outstripping the whites. 'Instead of an increase in the white population,' a report of 1859 noted with regret, 'that of the Negroes has grown in the district . . .' White immigration continued, but now more the result of a natural flow than because of official encouragement. The *Junta de Población Blanca* was dissolved in 1842. As the inevitable end of slavery drew near, the demand was less for white farmers than for white labourers. When these were not forthcoming on the scale needed, the plantation owners were forced to look further afield – to China.

45. Other contributors were José de la Luz Caballero; Domingo del Monte, an educational innovator; and José María Heredia, an exiled poet.

46. Quoted in Guerra, *A History of the Cuban Nation,* p. 183.

47. Quoted in Louis Pérez, *On Becoming Cuban: Identity, Nationality, and Culture,* New York, 1999, p. 90.

48. Quoted in Franklin W. Knight, *Slave Society in Cuba during the Nineteenth Century,* Madison, 1970, p. 99.

49. Quoted in Paquette, *Sugar is Made with Blood,* p. 105.

50. Antonio Elorza, *La Guerra de Cuba 1895–1898,* Madrid, 1998, p. 59. See also Eduardo Torres Cuevas, *José Antonio Saco: acerca de la esclavitud y su historia,* Havana, 1982, and José Opatrny, 'José Antonio Saco's path toward the idea of Cubanidad', *Cuban Studies,* 24, 1994.

51. José Antonio Saco, *Parallels between Cuba and some English Colonies,* Havana, 1837.

52. Quoted in Pérez, *Cuba and the United States,* p. 109.

53. Spanish Florida had been a constant irritation to the United States, a haven for fugitive slaves from the Southern states as well as a source of endless trouble from its population of Seminole Indians. US forces under General Andrew Jackson had struck out against

the Indians in 1818, crossing the border into Florida and capturing two Spanish forts. John Adams requested the Spaniards to control their territory or sell it. The Spaniards agreed to abandon Florida in exchange for a US agreement to give up their claims to Texas, then still part of New Spain (Mexico). The US treaty with Spain was signed in 1819.

54. Quoted in Willis Fletcher Johnson, *The History of Cuba*, New York, 1920, vol. 2, pp. 261–2.

55. Bergad, *The Cuban Slave Market*, p. 38.

56. Paquette, *Sugar is Made with Blood*, p. 135.

57. Paquette, *Sugar is Made with Blood*, p. 135, and Thomas, *Cuba*, 2nd edition, p. 124.

58. David Eltis, 'The Nineteenth Century Transatlantic Slave Trade,' *Hispanic American Historical Review*, February 1987.

59. The slaves hoped to sail on to Africa, but others on board had different ideas and the ship eventually arrived off Long Island. Detained by the US coast guards and put on trial, the slaves were eventually freed in 1841.

60. Hugh Thomas, *The Slave Trade: The History of the Atlantic Slave Trade 1440–1870*, London, 1997, p. 774.

61. David Murray, *Odious Commerce: Britain, Spain, and the Abolition of the Cuban Slave Trade*, Cambridge, 1980, p. 122.

62. Murray, *Odious Commerce*, p. 125.

63. Thomas, *The Slave Trade*, p. 665.

64. Bergad, *The Cuban Slave Market*, pp. 65–6.

65. Howard, *Changing History*, p. 86.

66. Thomas, *The Slave Trade*, p. 746.

67. Paquette, *Sugar is Made with Blood*, p. 133.

68. Paquette, *Sugar is Made with Blood*, p. 141. The captain-general was Pedro Téllez de Girón, the Prince of Angola.

69. Rodolfo Sarracino, *Los que volvieron a África*, Havana, 1988, pp. 99–100.

70. Paquette, *Sugar is Made with Blood*, pp. 163–4.

71. Turnbull returned to Cuba from the Bahamas in 1842 with several British blacks, hoping to liberate some Bahamians who he believed to have been held as slaves. Landing near Gibara, on the north coast of the island, he was detained and accused of seeking to organise a rebellion. Many Spaniards demanded his execution, but he was deported and warned never to return. Thomas, *The Slave Trade*, p. 668.

72. Paquette, *Sugar is Made with Blood*, p. 159.

73. Paquette, *Sugar is Made with Blood*, p. 164.

74. Paquette, *Sugar is Made with Blood*, p. 167.

75. Paquette, *Sugar is Made with Blood*, p. 168.

76. Quoted in Paquette, *Sugar is Made with Blood*, p. 177.

77. Paquette, *Sugar is Made with Blood*, p. 167.

78. Ramón Gonzalez was one of the more sadistic operatives of the ladder. He 'ordered his victims to be taken to a room which had been white-washed, and whose sides were smeared with blood and small pieces of flesh, from the wretches who had preceded them . . . There stood a bloody ladder, where the accused were tied, with their heads downward, and whether slave or free, if they would not avow what the fiscal officer insinuated, were whipped to death . . . They were scourged with leather straps, having at the end a small destructive button, made of fine wire . . . Their deaths were made to appear, by certificates from physicians, as having been caused by diarrhoea.' Quoted in Paquette, *Sugar is Made with Blood*, p. 220.

79. Paquette, *Sugar is Made with Blood*, p. 178.

80. Quoted in Paquette, *Sugar is Made with Blood*, p. 236. O'Donnell's ancestors had come to Spain from Donegal.

81. Paquette, *Sugar is Made with Blood*, pp. 219–20.

82. Quoted in Paquette, *Sugar is Made with Blood*, p. 220.

83. Quoted in Paquette, *Sugar is Made with Blood*, p. 227.

84. Quoted in Paquette, *Sugar is Made with Blood*, p. 232.

85. Chaffin, *Fatal Glory*, Charlottesville, Va., 1996, p. 33.

86. J. G. F. Wurdemann, *Notes from Cuba*, Boston, 1844.

87. Quoted in Paquette, *Sugar is Made with Blood*, p. 228.

88. Quoted in Paquette, *Sugar is Made with Blood*, p. 231.

89. Pérez, *Cuba and the United States*, p. 13.

90. Anthony Trollope, *The West Indies and the Spanish Main*, London, 1862.

91. Quoted in Pérez, *Cuba and the United States*, p. 20.

92. Quoted in Pérez, *Cuba and the United States*, p. 25.

93. Luis Martínez-Fernández, *Torn Between Empires*, Athens, Ga., 1994, p. 2.

94. Quoted in Pérez, *Cuba and the United States*, p. 44.

95. After López's death, his widow, Dolores Frías y Jacott, from whom he had long been separated, married José Antonio Saco, who had been opposed to López's expeditions.

96. Quoted in Chaffin, *Fatal Glory*, p. 216.

97. Joan Casanovas, *Bread or Bullets: Urban Labour and Spanish Colonialism in Cuba, 1850–1898*, Pittsburgh, 1998, pp. 72–3.

98. Quoted in Casanovas, *Bread or Bullets*, p. 79.

99. Javier Rodríguez Piña, *Guerra de Castas: la venta de indios mayas a Cuba, 1846–1861*, Mexico City, 1990.

100. Howard Blutstein, *Area Handbook for Cuba*, Washington, 1971, p. 80, and Knight, *Slave Society*, p. 119.

101. Lord Elgin, a former governor of Jamaica sent to China as a British 'special plenipotentiary' in 1857, described how the city of Swatow was dominated by the agents of the two great opium-houses, Dent and Jardine, who also did 'a considerable business in the coolie-trade – which consists in kidnapping wretched coolies, putting them on board ships where all the horrors of the slave-trade are reproduced, and sending them on specious promises to such places as Cuba.' Frances Wood, *No Dogs and Not Many Chinese*, London, 2000, p. 85.

102. Blutstein, *Area Handbook for Cuba*, p. 80.

103. Chinese immigration was prohibited by the US administration in Cuba in 1902, but thousands continued to arrive illegally whenever the price of sugar was high, notably during the sugar boom during and after the First World War.

104. Juan Jiménez Pastrana, *Los Chinos en la lucha por la liberación Cubana, 1847–1930*, Havana, 1963, pp. 71–5, quoted in Thomas, *Cuba*, p. 256.

Chapter 3

1. On 2 May 1866, Colonel Mariano Ignacio Prado had successfully defended the Peruvian port of Callao against the Spanish fleet, after a short war sparked by Peru's ill-treatment of a group of Basque immigrants.

2. Fernando Ortiz's introduction to James O'Kelly's *La Tierra del Mambí*, Havana, 1930, quoted in Antonio Elorza, *La Guerra del Cuba, 1895–1898*, Madrid, 1998, p. 477.

3. Luis Aguilar, 'Cuba, c.1860–c.1930' in Leslie Bethel (ed.), *Cuba: A Short History*, Cambridge, 1993.

4. Laird Bergad, *Cuban Rural Society in the Nineteenth Century*, Princeton, 1990, p. 187.

5. Joan Casanovas, *Bread or Bullets: Urban Labour and Spanish Colonialism in Cuba, 1850–1898*, Pittsburgh, 1998, pp. 97–106.

6. Antonio Gallenga, *The Pearl of the Antilles*, London, 1873, p. 20.

7. Spain was eventually obliged to find extra troops to send to Cuba, despatching a quarter of a million soldiers between 1868 and 1880. In May 1878, after ten years of war, Spain

revealed that 100,000 of its soldiers had been killed, and the final figure may well have been more. At least 50,000 were killed on the Cuban side.

8. Raymond Carr, *Spain, 1808–1975*, 2nd edition, Oxford, 1982, p. 308.

9. Gallenga, *The Pearl of the Antilles*, p. 41.

10. Gallenga, *The Pearl of the Antilles*, p. 17.

11. Gallenga, *The Pearl of the Antilles*, p. 17.

12. Casanovas, *Bread or Bullets*, p. 106.

13. Oscar Zanetti and Alejandro García, *Sugar and Railroads: A Cuban History, 1837–1959*, Chapel Hill, N. C., 1998, p. 131.

14. Justo Zaragosa, *Las insurrecciones en Cuba*, Madrid, 1872, vol. 2, p. 374.

15. Gallenga, *The Pearl of the Antilles*, pp. 164–5.

16. Hugh Thomas, *Cuba, or the Pursuit of Freedom*, London, 1971, p. 265. The issue of race in the Ten Years War is well addressed in Ada Ferrer, *Insurgent Cuba, Race, Nation, and Revolution, 1868–1898*, Chapel Hill, N. C., 1999.

17. Carr, *Spain*, p. 336.

18. King Alfonso was to die ten years later, in November 1885, and was replaced by his pregnant Habsburg wife, María Cristina, who ruled as the regent of Spain from 1885 until 1902, presiding over the great Spanish disaster of 1898, when Cuba, Puerto Rico and the Philippines were lost to the United States. Her son, Alfonso XIII, was to reign until his overthrow after the elections of 1931, which closed another era in the chequered history of the Spanish monarchy.

19. The Pact of Zanjón has traditionally been regarded by Cuba as a national humiliation, and El Zanjón has effectively been rubbed off the map. It lies to the south of Carretera Central, between Sibanicú and San Agustín del Brazo. I am grateful to Hal Klepak for providing me with this geographic detail.

20. Ronald Segal, *Black Diaspora*, London, 1999, p. 225.

21. Aline Helg, *Our Rightful Share, The Afro-Cuban Struggle for Equality, 1886–1912*, Chapel Hill, N. C., 1995, p. 50.

22. The old Partido Reformista of the early 1860s had re-formed itself as the Partido Liberal y Autonomista.

23. Quoted in Thomas, *Cuba*, p. 301.

24. A useful compilation of some of Martí's writings can be found in a collection edited by Philip Foner: *Inside the Monster: Writings on the United States and American Imperialism by José Martí*, New York, 1975.

25. See further, Richard Gott, 'Karl Krause and the Ideological Origins of the Cuban Revolution', Institute of Latin American Studies, London, *Occasional Papers*, No. 28, 2002.

26. Peter Turton, *José Martí: Architect of Cuba's Freedom*, London, 1986, p. 77.

27. Quoted in Turton, *Martí*, p. 12.

28. Turton, *Martí*, devotes an entire chapter to a discussion of the impact of the Haymarket affair on Martí, pp. 115–44.

29. Letter to Ricardo Rodríguez Otero of May 1886, quoted in Turton, *Martí*, p. 17.

30. Thomas, *Cuba*, p. 300.

31. Martí had hoped to start the rebellion a year earlier, but the demands of the sugar industry came first. Planters favourable to his plans remained anxious to get one more harvest in before hostilities began, and asked for the war to be postponed until 1895.

32. Randolph Churchill, ed., *Winston Churchill, Companion*, vol. 1, 1874–1895, London, 1967, pp. 617–18.

33. Zanetti and García, *Sugar and Railroads*, pp. 235–55.

34. Deborah Schnookal, ed., *José Martí Reader: Writings on the Americas*, New York, 1999, p. 222.

35. See José Cepeda Adán, *Sagasta, el político de las horas difíciles*, Madrid, 1995.

36. See Javier Tusell, *Antonio Maura, una biografía política*, Madrid, 1994.

37. See José Luis Comellas, *Cánovas del Castillo*, Barcelona, 1997. See also Melchor Fernández Almagro, *Cánovas: su vida, su política*, Madrid, 1951.

38. Quoted in Thomas, *Cuba*, p. 320.

39. Martin Gilbert, *Churchill: A Life*,

London, 1993, p. 36, and Thomas, *Cuba*, 2nd edition, p. 185. Churchill, then a young officer and journalist-on-the-make, had been sent by British military intelligence to investigate the effectiveness of a bullet that the Spanish army was using in their new issue of German Mauser rifles. He briefly accompanied the Spanish forces in the region between Sancti Spíritus and Camagüey in November 1895.

40. Grover Flint, *Marching with Gómez: a war correspondent's field note-book kept during four months with the Cuban army*, London, 1898, p. 25. See also Rosalie Schwarz, *Lawless Liberators, Political Banditry and Cuban Independence*, Durham, 1989.

41. Edwin Atkins, *Sixty Years in Cuba*, Cambridge, Mass., 1926, quoted in Thomas, *Cuba*, p. 323.

42. Thomas, *Cuba*, 2nd edition, p. 190, and see further Luis de Arminán Pérez, *Weyler, el Gran Capitán*, Madrid, 1946.

43. Hugh Brogan, *The Penguin History of the USA*, London, 2001, p. 342.

44. Thomas, *Cuba*, p. 328.

45. *Historia de Cuba*, vol. II, 'Las luchas por la independencia nacional, 1868–1898', Havana, 1996, p. 489.

46 Thomas, *Cuba*, 2nd edition, p. 191.

47. Flint, *Marching with Gómez*, p. 28. See also Joseph Wisan, *The Cuban Crisis as reflected in the New York Press (1895–1898)*, New York, 1965.

48. *Historia de Cuba*, vol. II, 'Las luchas por la independencia nacional, 1868–1898', Havana, 1996, p. 502.

49. 'Las luchas por la independencia nacional', p. 503.

50. Helg, *Our Rightful Share*, p. 76.

51. The new ruler in the Philippines was General Polavieja, an old Cuba hand of the Weyler school, who had once raised the racist flag against Maceo. His first decisive act, on arrival in Manila in December 1896, was to order the execution of the leading Filipino nationalist, José Rizal, sometimes considered as the José Martí of the Philippines. Rizal had been held in prison, after a brief sojourn in London's Camden Town, and Polavieja thought that his death would curb the zeal of the rebels supporting the independence movement. Maybe he regretted the fact that he had once ordered Maceo's exile rather than his execution. Killing Rizal was an error, since his death inflamed the rebellion, and the Spanish military situation in the Philippines became as desperate as it had been in Cuba. Polavieja demanded reinforcements, but was informed in April 1897 that all available soldiers had been sent to Cuba. He resigned in protest, to be succeeded by General Fernando Primo de Rivera, who came in the knowledge that no extra troops would be forthcoming and that he would have to negotiate with the rebels, now led by Emilio Aguinaldo. A truce agreement was signed at Biacabató in December 1897 and an amnesty was granted. Aguinaldo went into exile in Hong Kong, accompanied by the governor's nephew, Miguel Primo de Rivera, later to be the leader of the Spanish Falange.

52. Thomas, *Cuba*, 2nd edition, p. 209.

53. The Americans had taken Emilio Aguinaldo with them to Manila, hoping that he would cooperate with their invasion, but he soon renewed his rebel campaign in Luzón. Refused entrance into Manila, he set up an independent Visayan republic at Malolos, which continued to resist after the Philippines were ceded to the United States under the terms of the treaty of Paris of December 1898. The Americans brought in reinforcements, bringing their forces up to 60,000, and gradually swept up the rebels, who lost heart after Aguinaldo's capture in March 1901.

54. Theodore Roosevelt, *The Rough Riders*, London, 1899, p. 6.

55. Hermann Hagedorn, *Leonard Wood: A Biography*, New York, 1931, vol. I, p. 147.

56. Hearst was the author of a famous exchange with his correspondent (and war artist) Frederic Remington. In

February 1897 Remington had cabled Hearst from the Hotel Inglaterra in Havana with a message that all foreign reporters will recall having sent at one time or another: 'Everything is quiet . . . There will be no war. I wish to return.' Hearst's reply was prompt and brief. 'Please remain. You furnish the pictures and I'll furnish the war.'

57. Irene Wright, *Cuba*, New York, 1910, p. 502.

58. Thomas, *Cuba*, 2nd edition, pp. 1039–40. See Hyman G. Rickover, 'How the Battleship Maine was Destroyed', Dept. of the Navy, Naval History Division, Washington, 1976.

59. John Black Atkins, *The War in Cuba: The Experiences of an Englishman with the United States Army*, London, 1899, p. 9.

60. Quoted in Thomas, *Cuba*, 2nd edition, p. 218.

61. Richard Harding Davis, *The Cuban and Porto Rican Campaigns*, New York, 1899.

62. Hermann Hagedorn, *Leonard Wood: A Biography*, New York, 1931, vol. 1, p. 160.

63. Black Atkins, *The War in Cuba*, p. 98.

64. Thomas, *Cuba*, 2nd edition, p. 238.

65. *New York Times*, 7 May, 1900, quoted in Louis Pérez, *On Becoming Cuban: Identity, Nationality, and Culture*, New York, 1999, p. 96.

66. Thomas, *Cuba*, 2nd edition, p. 246.

67. Quoted in Pérez, *On Becoming Cuban*, p. 101.

68. Rafael Martínez Ortiz, *Cuba: los primeros años de independencia*, Paris, 1929, pp. 76–7.

69. Rafael Fermoselle, *Política y Color en Cuba: la guerrita de 1912*, Montevideo, 1974, p. 29.

70. Quoted in Thomas, *Cuba*, p. 445.

71. Thomas, *Cuba*, 2nd edition, p. 259.

72. Quoted in Helg, *Our Rightful Share*, p. 95.

73. Quoted in Thomas, *Cuba*, p. 431. See also Charles Gauld, *The Last Titan: Percival Farquhar, American entrepreneur in Latin America*, Stanford, C alif., 1964.

74. Root's immediate concerns in 1899 were with the three territories acquired in the Spanish–American war. Apart from his plan to hand Cuba over to the Cubans, he drafted a democratic charter for the Philippines, and settled the details of the tariff arrangements with Puerto Rico. Later, in 1905, he was appointed by President Roosevelt to run the State Department. A Republican Senator from 1909 to 1915, he was awarded the Nobel Peace Prize in 1911 and devoted the rest of his life to the promotion of international arbitration. He was the first president of the Carnegie Endowment for International Peace. He died in 1937. See Philip C. Jessup, *Elihu Root*, vol. 1, *1845–1909*; vol. 11, *1905–1937*, New York, 1938; and Richard W Leopold, *Elihu Root and the Conservative Tradition*, Boston, 1954.

75. Jessup, *Elihu Root*, vol. 1.

76. Louis Pérez, *Cuba: Between Reform and Revolution*, Oxford, 1995, p. 182.

77. Pérez, *Cuba: Between Reform and Revolution*, p. 182.

78. A letter from Wood to Root in March 1901, quoted in Pérez, *Cuba: Betwen Reform and Revolution*, p. 183.

79. *New York Times*, 7 August 1899, quoted in Fermoselle, *Política y Color en Cuba*, p. 30.

80. Quoted in Thomas, *Cuba*, p. 448.

81. Thomas, *Cuba*, 2nd edition, p. 260.

82. Thomas, *Cuba*, 2nd ediiton, p. 262.

83. Quoted in Thomas, *Cuba*, 2nd edition, p. 262–3.

84. Technically, the Platt Amendment was an amendment to an Army Appropriations Bill designed to finance the continuing military occupation of Cuba.

85. Quoted in James Hitchman, *Leonard Wood and Cuban Independence, 1898–1902*, The Hague, 1971, pp. 90–91.

Chapter 4

1. Luis Aguilar, 'Cuba, c.1860–c.1930' in Leslie Bethel (ed.), *Cuba: A Short History*, Cambridge, 1993, p. 40.

2. Louis Pérez, *On Becoming Cuban: Identity, Nationality, and Culture*, New York, 1999, p. 6.

3. Louis Pérez, *Cuba: Between Reform and Revolution*, Oxford, 1995, p. 197. A further 15 per cent was owned by resident Spaniards.

4. Irene Wright, *Cuba*, New York, 1910, p. 502.

5. Wright, *Cuba*, pp. 152–3.

6. H. A. Ellsworth, *180 Landings of the US Marines, 1800–1934*, 2 vols, Washington, 1934.

7. Hugh Thomas, *Cuba, or the Pursuit of Freedom*, 2nd edition, London, 2001, p. 283.

8. Thomas, *Cuba*, 2nd edition, p. 276.

9. Quoted in Aline Helg, *Our Rightful Share: The Afro-Cuban Struggle for Equality, 1886–1912*, Chapel Hill, N. C., 1995, p. 162.

10. Pérez, *On Becoming Cuban*, p. 46.

11. Quoted in Thomas, *Cuba*, 2nd edition, p. 280.

12. David Lockmiller, *Magoon in Cuba: A History of the Second Intervention, 1906–1909*, Chapel Hill, N. C., 1938.

13. One hundred years later, Cuba remains obsessed by the thought that the United States might arrive once again to re-organise the island's electoral system.

14. Approximately 800,000 Spanish immigrants arrived between 1902 and 1931, at an average rate of 25,000 a year. Jordi Maluquer de Motes, *Nación e immigración: los españoles en Cuba*, Oriedo, 1992, p. 112.

15. Thomas, *Cuba*, 2nd edition, p. 295.

16. Figures from the census of 1899, organised by the US War Department, quoted in Pérez, *Reform and Revolution*, p. 200. The figures exclude women and children under 15 and appear to underestimate the size of the black population.

17. Pérez, *Reform and Revolution*, p. 202.

18. Landowners continued the nineteenth-century tradition. Laureano Falla Gutiérrez, the largest sugar baron in the country, gathered a group of landowners together in 1912 to found the *Asociación de Hacendados para el Fomento de la Inmigración Europea*, the association to promote European immigration, with the aim of maintaining Cuba's whites-only immigration policy. The *Asociación* dropped the word 'Europea' in 1917, but retained the emphasis on whites.

19. Rafael Serra, *Para blancos y negros*, Havana, 1907, quoted in Helg, *Our Rightful Share*, p. 117.

20. Quoted in Pérez, *On Becoming Cuban*, p. 323. Arturo Schomburg was originally from Puerto Rico.

21. George Clark Musgrave, *Under Three Flags in Cuba: A Personal Account of the Cuban Insurrection and Spanish-American War*, Boston, 1899, pp. 162–3; quoted in Helg, *Our Rightful Share*, p. 78.

22. Helg, *Our Rightful Share*, p. 150. Fidel Castro was also to adopt the horse as his symbol.

23. Quoted in Helg, *Our Rightful Share*, p. 172.

24. Quoted in Helg, *Our Rightful Share*, pp. 190–91.

25. Jorge Dominguez, *Cuba: Order and Revolution*, Cambridge, Mass., 1978, pp. 48–9. One result of the US intervention, and the reactivation of the base at Guantánamo, was a fresh treaty, of December 1912, that reaffirmed US rights over the base in return for an annual rent of $2,000.

26. Rafael Fermoselle, *Política y Color en Cuba: la guerrita de 1912*, Montevideo, 1974, p. 167.

27. Helg, *Our Rightful Share*, pp. 298–9.

28. Louis Pérez, *Lords of the Mountain: Social Banditry and Peasant Protest in Cuba, 1878–1918*, Pittsburgh, 1989.

29. Helg, *Our Rightful Share*, pp. 196–8.

30. Helg, *Our Rightful Share*, p. 211.

31. Helg, *Our Rightful Share*, p. 222.

32. Louis Pérez, *Intervention, Revolution, and Politics in Cuba, 1913–1921*, Pittsburgh, 1978, p. 3.

33. *Historia de Cuba, La Neocolonia, organización y crisis, desde 1899 hasta 1940*, Havana, 1998, p. 106.

34. Teresa Casuso, *Cuba and Castro*, New York, 1961, pp. 9–10.

35. *Historia de Cuba, La Neocolonia*, p. 115.
36. *Historia de Cuba, La Neocolonia*, p. 112.
37. Ruby Hart Phillips, *Cuban Sideshow*, Havana, 1935, p. 259.
38. Quoted in Thomas, *Cuba*, p. 548.
39. Thomas, *Cuba*, p. 587.
40. Thomas, *Cuba*, p. 584.
41. David Lockmiller, *Enoch H. Crowder, Soldier, Lawyer, and Statesman, 1859–1932*, St Louis, 1955, p. 244.
42. Thomas, *Cuba*, p. 593.
43. Throwing dissidents into the sea from the Morro castle was a Cuban tradition followed by the Argentine military in the 1970s, who dropped them from aeroplanes.
44. Thomas, *Cuba*, p. 577.
45. José Tabares del Real, 'Proceso revolucionario: ascenso y reflujo (1930–1935)', chapter 7 of *Historia de Cuba, La Neocolonia*, the third volume of the History of Cuba published by the Instituto de Historia de Cuba.
46. Thomas, *Cuba*, p. 594. Thomas refers to C. Gonzalez Peraza, *Machado, Crímenes y horrores de un regimen*, Havana, 1933, pp. 115–50, for the details of ABC's programme, which is also summarised in Tabares del Real, 'Proceso revolucionario'.
47. Tabares del Real, 'Proceso revolucionario', p. 238. The exact figure for 1929 was $198,661,078, and that for 1932 was $41,862,427.
48. Quoted in Thomas, *Cuba*, p. 620.
49. The US occupation of Haiti did not end until August 1934.
50. Charles Thomson, 'The Cuban Revolution: Fall of Machado,' *Foreign Policy Reports*, 11, no. 21, 18 December 1935, p. 254.
51. Quoted in Thomas, *Cuba*, p. 628.
52. *Problems of the New Cuba*, Foreign Policy Association, New York, 1935, p. 183; and see also Samuel Farber, *Revolution and Reaction in Cuba, 1933–1960: A Political Sociology from Machado to Castro*, Middletown, Conn., 1976, p. 39.
53. Hart Phillips, *Cuban Sideshow*, p. 112.
54. Tabares del Real, 'Proceso revolucionario', p. 303.

55. Quoted in Hart Phillips, *Cuban Sideshow*, p. 115.
56. Quoted in Thomas, *Cuba*, pp. 640–41.
57. *Problems of the New Cuba*, p. 33.
58. Hart Phillips, *Cuban Sideshow*, p. 115.
59. Frei Betto, *Fidel and Religion*, Sydney, 1986, p. 83.
60. *Problems of the New Cuba*.
61. Pérez, *On Becoming Cuban*, p. 297.
62. Tabares del Real, 'Proceso revolucionario', p. 332. See also José Tabares del Real, *Guiteras*, Havana, 1973.
63. *World News and Views*, No. 60, 1938, quoted in Thomas, *Cuba*, p. 711.
64. Thomas, *Cuba*, 2nd edition, pp. 448–9.
65. Pérez, *Cuba: Between Reform and Revolution*, pp. 282–3.
66. The Communist Party was renamed the Partido Socialista Popular in 1944.
67. Julia Sweig, *Inside the Cuban Revolution: Fidel Castro and the Urban Underground*, Cambridge, Mass., 2002, p. 5.

Chapter 5

1. Tad Szulc, *Fidel: A Critical Portrait*, London, 1987, p. 159.
2. Castro and Mirta Díaz were divorced in 1954. Many members of the Díaz Balart family left Cuba after the Revolution, and Mirta's nephew, Lincoln Díaz-Balart, became a prominent anti-Castro Republican congressman in the United States.
3. Fidel Castro, *History Will Absolve Me* (the Moncada trial defence speech, 16 October 1953), London, 1968.
4. Under Castro's fifth 'revolutionary law' it was proposed that 'special courts with full powers would gain access to all records of all corporations registered or operating in the country, in order to investigate concealed funds of illegal origin, and to request that foreign governments extradite persons and attach holdings rightfully belonging to the Cuban people.' Castro, *History Will Absolve Me*.
5. A comprehensive account of Castro's time in prison, with details of his

reading, is in Robert Quirk, *Fidel Castro*, New York, 1993, pp. 60–82.

6. Grau San Martín remained in Cuba after 1959, and died in 1969.

7. Quoted in Quirk, *Fidel Castro*, p. 85.

8. Jon Lee Anderson, *Che Guevara: A Revolutionary Life*, London, 1997, pp. 170–75. Guevara had first heard news of the Cuban revolutionary movement in Guatemala a year earlier, where he had made friends with Antonio 'Ñico' López, a survivor of Moncada who had been exiled there. López was later killed during the *Granma* landing in 1956.

9. Quoted in Quirk, *Fidel Castro*, p. 141.

10. The first of Herbert Matthews's three reports appeared in the *New York Times* on 24 February 1957, and he subsequently wrote a book about his early contacts with Castro: *The Cuban Story*, New York, 1961.

11. Julia Sweig, *Inside the Cuban Revolution: Fidel Castro and the Urban Underground*, Cambridge, Mass., 2002, p. 13.

12. In the 1990s Julia Sweig, an American researcher, was given unprecedented access to the archives of the Cuban Revolution, including documents referring to the activities of the urban underground in the 1950s. According to Sweig's account, 'The Cuban documents demonstrate that until the last six to eight months of the two-year insurrection, the lion's share of decisions regarding tactics; strategy; resource allocation; political ties with other opposition groups, Cuban exiles, and clandestine adversaries; and relations with the United States (in Havana and Washington) were made by lesser known individuals from the urban underground.' They were not made by Guevara and the Castro brothers in the Sierra. Sweig, *Inside the Cuban Revolution*, p. 9.

13. Sweig, *Inside the Cuban Revolution*, p. 14.

14. Sweig, *Inside the Cuban Revolution*, p. 20, and Hugh Thomas, *Cuba, or the Pursuit of Freedom*, London, 1971, p. 950.

15. A good account of the attack on the

16. Sweig, *Inside the Cuban Revolution*, p. 29.

17. Sweig, *Inside the Cuba Revolution*, p. 120.

18. Szulc, *Fidel*, p. 348.

19. Szulc, *Fidel*, pp. 345–6.

20. Sweig, *Inside the Cuban Revolution*, p. 12.

21. Sweig, *Inside the Cuban Revolution*, p. 159.

22. Szulc, *Fidel*, p. 349.

23. Sweig, *Inside the Cuban Revolution*, p. 150.

24. Szulc, *Fidel*, p. 353.

25. The average annual income in Cuba at the time of the Revolution was $374 dollars, while Venezuela's, at $857, was more than double.

26. Marifeli Pérez-Stable, *The Cuban Revolution: Origins, Course and Legacy*, Oxford, 1993; p. 5.

27. Jorge Ibarra, *Prologue to Revolution: Cuba, 1898–1958*, London, 1998. See also, Louis Pérez, *Cuba and the US: Ties of Singular Intimacy*, Atlanta, 1990.

28. Thomas Bogenschild, 'Dr Castro's Princeton Visit, April 1959', Program in Latin American Studies, Princeton, 1998. See http://www.princeton.edu/plasweb/publications/Essays/Castro.htm

29. To Santeria believers, doves are symbols of Obatalá, the Son of God, a god who shapes the human body and rules the mind, the thoughts and the dreams of everyone. The doves perched on Castro's shoulder were perceived by believers as a sign that he had been chosen by the Santería gods to guide and protect his people.

30. Carlo Feltrinelli, *Senior Service*, London, 2001, p. 184.

31. Philip Bonsal, *Cuba, Castro, and the United States*, Pittsburgh, 1971.

32. Quoted in Quirk, *Fidel Castro*, p. 224.

33. Quoted in Quirk, *Fidel Castro*, p. 225.

34. Carlos Franqui, *Family Portrait with Fidel*, London, 1980.

35. Quirk, *Fidel Castro*, p. 229.

36. The compensation offered initially came in the form of 20-year-bonds bearing an annual interest rate of 4.5 per cent.

37. Quoted in Thomas, *Cuba*, pp. 1217–18.

38. *Making History: Interviews with four generals of Cuba's revolutionary armed forces*, New York, 1999, pp. 127–30.

39. According to Carlos Franqui, 'there was no discussion within the July 26 Movement on the issue of the situation of blacks in Cuba. There was a purely formal condemnation of racial discrimination, but no more.' Quoted by Carlos Moore, *Castro, the Blacks and Africa*, Berkeley, 1988, p. 7.

40. Castro speech, 22 March 1959. All Castro speeches quoted in this book are taken from the Castro Speech Data Base prepared by the University of Texas, using the English translations provided by the US Foreign Broadcast Information Service, located at http://lanic.utexas.edu/la/cb/cuba/castro.html

41. Teresa Casuso, *Cuba and Castro*, New York, 1961, p. 241.

42. Ronald Segal, *Black Diaspora*, London, 1999, p. 235.

43. Franqui, *Family Portrait with Fidel*, p. 25.

44. Louis Pérez, *Lords of the Mountain: Social Banditry and Peasant Protest in Cuba, 1878–1918*, Pittsburgh, 1989; and Aline Helg, *Our Rightful Share: The Afro-Cuban Struggle for Equality, 1886–1912*, Chapel Hill, N. C., p. 150.

45. Quoted in Antoni Kapcia, Cuba, Island of Dreams, Oxford and New York, 2000, p. 200.

46. Jean-Paul Sartre, *Sartre on Cuba*, New York, 1961, p. 14.

47. Leo Huberman and Paul Sweezy, *Cuba: Anatomy of a Revolution*, New York, 1960, p. 77.

48. C. Wright Mills, *Castro's Cuba*, London, 1960, p. 184.

49. Claude Julien wrote one of the first histories of the Revolution, *La Révolution Cubaine*, Paris, 1961.

50. Robert Scheer and Maurice Zeitlin, *Cuba: An American Tragedy*, New York, 1964.

51. E. Van Gosse, *Where the Boys Are: Cuba, the Cold War, and the Making of the New Left*, London, 1993.

52. A US report in 1961 on the Fair Play for Cuba Committee, published after hearings before the Senate Fact-Finding Subcommittee on Un-American Activities in California, gives a flavour of the official atmosphere at the time: 'This organization was formed in April 1960, obviously for the purpose of spreading propaganda for the Castro revolution and its Communist affiliates. Units of the organization are active on many university campuses throughout the United States, although in California they seem to have been sporadic in character, springing into activity to participate in a march or demonstration with other organizations, then dropping out of notice again until the next opportunity presents itself ... There is a scattering of do-gooders who decorate the fringe of this Communist front and echo the Party line contention that the Castro revolution was actually caused by American Imperialism, the exploitation of the Cuban people by American big business. This line is a typical piece of clever Communist manipulation that is calculated to make us look like the villain, and the "democratic people's government" appear as the hero in the international drama.'

53. Eisenhower claimed in his memoirs to have been interested in Latin America for 'nearly half a century', having served in the Panana Canal Zone for three years in the 1920s. He had even once thought of making his career in Argentina, 'a place which, I understood, resembled our own West in the 1870s'. As President, he used his brother Milton as his special envoy to the continent, whose book, *The Wine is Bitter*, gave an informed and realistic account of the growing hostility to the United States.

54. Dwight Eisenhower, *The White House Years: Waging Peace, 1956–1961*, London, 1966, p. 519.

55. Eisenhower, *Waging Peace*, p. 521.

56. Szulc, *Fidel*, p. 384.
57. Eisenhower, *Waging Peace*, p. 522.
58. Eisenhower press conference, 28 October 1959.
59. Richard Nixon, *Six Crises*, New York, 1962, p. 379.
60. Quoted in José Luis Llovio-Menéndez, *Insider: My Hidden Life as a Revolutionary in Cuba*, New York, 1988, p. 17.
61. Thomas, *Cuba*, p. 1217.
62. US NSC meeting, 14 January 1960, quoted in Piero Gleijeses, *Conflicting Missions: Havana, Washington, and Africa, 1959–1976*, Chapel Hill, N. C., 2002, pp. 14–15. Livingstone Merchant, under-secretary at the State Department, defined the US programme in this way at a meeting of the NSC in January 1960, and made clear that the policy had first been formulated in June 1959.
63. Quoted in Gleijeses, *Conflicting Missions*, pp. 14–15.
64. Quoted in Gleijeses, *Conflicting Missions*, pp. 14–15.
65. Thomas, *Cuba*, p. 731.
66. Strobe Talbott, ed., *Khrushchev Remembers*, Boston, 1970, p. 488.
67. Anderson, *Che Guevara*, pp. 414–5.
68. Anderson, *Che Guevara*, pp. 425–34.
69. Anderson, *Che Guevara*, pp. 441–3.
70. Anderson, *Che Guevara*, p. 443.
71. Edward Boorstein, 'The Economic Transformation of Cuba, a First-Hand Account', *Monthly Review Press*, New York, 1968, p. 27.
72. Account by Gray, Eisenhower's special assistant for security affairs, quoted in Gleijeses, *Conflicting Missions*, p. 15.
73. Quirk, *Fidel Castro*, pp. 316–18.
74. Quirk, *Fidel Castro*, p. 289.
75. Boorstein, 'The Economic Transformation of Cuba, p. 28.
76. Quoted in Quirk, *Fidel Castro*, p. 322.
77. All Cuban-owned banks were nationalised in October. Only the Canadians escaped the net. The Bank of Nova Scotia and the Royal Bank of Canada were closed in December after 'special mutually acceptable compensatory arrangements' had been made.

78. Castro speech, 2 September 1960.
79. Dudley Seers, ed., *Cuba: The Economic and Social Revolution*, Chapel Hill, N. C., 1964, pp. 46 and 395.
80. Quoted in Seers, *Cuba: The Economic and Social Revolution*, p. 47.
81. Edward Boorstein, 'The Economic Transformation of Cuba', p. 41.
82. See Claus Brudenius, *Revolutionary Cuba: The Challenge of Economic Growth with Equity*, Boulder, Col., 1984.
83. Seers, *Cuba: The Economic and Social Revolution*, p. 49.
84. Carmelo Mesa-Lago, ed., *Revolutionary Change in Cuba*, Pittsburgh, 1971, p. 386.

Chapter 6

1. 'On March 17, 1960 . . . I ordered the Central Intelligence Agency to begin to organise the training of Cuban exiles, principally in Guatemala, against a possible future day when they might return to their homeland. More specific planning was not possible because the Cubans living in exile had made no move to select from among their numbers a leader who we could recognise as the head of a government-in-exile.' Dwight Eisenhower, *The White House Years: Waging Peace 1956–1961*, London, 1966, p. 533.
2. According to the account by Peter Wyden, 'the "Guatemalan model" was on everyone's mind, especially Bissell's. In one week the CIA had overthrown the Guatemalan government. A force of 150 exiles, firing hardly a shot, and a handful of World War II P-47 fighters, flown by American pilots hired by the agency, were the overt weapons. CIA deception was the real one. The agency had used the same base it would activate for the Bay of Pigs: a two-storey barracks of the largely abandoned US Navy air base at Opa-Locka, in suburban Miami. Both of the agency's senior field operators, the elegant Tracy

Barnes and the unconventional E. Howard Hunt, would occupy pivotal posts in the Cuban operation. Together they had recruited a propaganda chief for the Guatemala venture: the man who was to do the same job in Cuba, David Atlee Phillips.' Peter Wyden, *Bay of Pigs: The Untold Story*, London, 1979, p. 20.

3. Karl Meyer and Tad Szulc, *The Cuban Invasion*, New York, 1962, pp. 66–7.

4. *Making History: Interviews with Four Generals of Cuba's Revolutionary Armed Forces*, New York, 1999, p. III. See also the official Cuban account of the Bay of Pigs in Juan Carlos Rodríguez, ed., *The Bay of Pigs and the CIA*, Melbourne, 1999, p. 68.

5. The real nature of the US strategy was much debated in the wake of the Bay of Pigs fiasco. Was the CIA hoping that the invasion would provoke a general uprising? Or did they believe that the establishment of a Cuban beach-head would force President Kennedy to sanction American military action in support of the provisional government? In practice there was no conflict between the two schemes; they tried one, then the other. Both led to disaster.

6. This was a well-prepared speech, and Armando Hart and Blas Roca told Tad Szulc years later that Castro had planned to make it on May Day. Understandably, the date had been brought forward. Tad Szulc, *Fidel: a Critical Portrait*, London, 1987, p. 443.

7. By happenstance, the mill had played a role in the Ten Year War of the nineteenth century, seized by the independence forces in February 1869 and recaptured by the Volunteers, the forerunners of the invaders of 1961. This coincidence was verified on the ground by Laird Bergad, who mentions it in his book *Cuban Rural Society in the Nineteenth Century: The Social and Economic History of Monoculture in Matanzas*, Princeton, 1990, p. 184.

8. *Making History*, p. 110.

9. Ernest R. May and Philip D. Zelikow, eds, *The Kennedy Tapes: Inside the Whitehouse during the Cuban Missile Crisis*, Cambridge, Mass., 1997, p. 26.

10. Szulc, *Fidel*, p. 465.

11. May and Zelikow, *The Kennedy Tapes*.

12. May and Zelikow, *The Kennedy Tapes*, p. ix. 'Throughout the crisis, American decision-making was centred in the White House, and during much of that time, a tape-recorder was running. Except for President Kennedy and possibly his brother Robert, no one taking part in the discussions knew this. As records of frank deliberation in a time of crisis, these tapes have no parallel at any other time or place in history.'

13. May and Zelikow, *The Kennedy Tapes*, p. 657.

14. May and Zelikow, *The Kennedy Tapes*, p. 54.

15. May and Zelikow, *The Kennedy Tapes*, p. 101.

16. The decision was taken at an OAS foreign ministers' meeting at Punta del Este in Uruguay in January. Only Cuba and Mexico opposed the OAS motion; Argentina, Bolivia, Brazil, Chile and Ecuador abstained. The Venezuelan foreign minister resigned.

17. Accused of 'sectarianism', Escalante's crime was to have packed the new party with old Communist apparatchiks, at the expense of figures from the July 26 Movement and the student Directorate.

18. James G. Blight and David A. Welch, *On the Brink: Americans and Soviets re-examine the Cuban Missile Crisis*, New York, 1989, p. 238.

19. Castro interviewed by Tad Szulc, January 28–29, 1984, in Szulc, *Fidel*, p. 471.

20. Szulc, *Fidel*, p. 472.

21. Jon Lee Anderson, *Che Guevara: A Revolutionary Life*, London, 1997, p. 525.

22. Tomás Diez Acosta, *October 1962: The 'Missile' Crisis as seen from Cuba*, New York, 2002, p. 101. In writing his account, Diez Acosta had access to the records of the central committee of the

Cuban Communist Party, housed in the Institute of Cuban History in Havana.

23. In March 1962 the two principal revolutionary movements, the July 26 Movement and the Revolutionary Directorate, had been amalgamated with the Communist PSP to form the Integrated Revolutionary Organisations. A year later, in 1963, the ORI was transformed into the United Party of the Cuban Socialist Revolution (PURS), and in October 1965 the PURS was renamed as the Communist Party of Cuba.

24. Diez Acosta, *October 1962*, p. 102.

25. Diez Acosta, *October 1962*, p. 102, and James G. Blight, Bruce J. Allyn and David A. Welch, *Cuba on the Brink: Castro, the Missile Crisis, and the Soviet Collapse*, New York, 1993, pp. 198–9.

26. During the crisis itself the United States requested the governments of Guinea and Senegal to refuse landing rights to Soviet planes. Sékou Touré, although a Cuban ally, agreed to do so on the grounds that he was a firm opponent of foreign military bases.

27. Diez Acosta, *October 1962*, p. 103.

28. Anderson, *Che Guevara*, pp. 527–8.

29. Diez Acosta, *October 1962*, p. 103.

30. Diez Acosta, *October 1962*, pp. 121–2, quoting the minutes of a Cuban Communist Party meeting on 25 January 1968.

31. Diez Acosta, *October 1962*, p. 103.

32. Diez Acosta, *October 1962*, p. 104.

33. Anderson, *Che Guevara*, p. 528.

34. May and Zelikow, *The Kennedy Tapes*, p. 711.

35. Diez Acosta, *October 1962*, p. 110.

36. Anatoli I. Gribkov, William Y. Smith and Alfred Friendly Jr., *Operation Anadyr: US and Soviet Generals recount the Cuban Missile Crisis*, Chicago, 1994, pp. 23–4.

37. Diez Acosta, *October 1962*, p. 113.

38. Diez Acosta, *October 1962*, p. 114.

39. Diez Acosta, *October 1962*, p. 114.

40. Ernest May and Zelikow, *The Kennedy Tapes*, p. 711.

41. Anderson, *Che Guevara*, p. 529.

42. The exercise involved a naval landing on the island of Vieques, off Puerto Rico, designed to overthrow an invented tyrant called Ortsac – Castro spelt backwards.

43. May and Zelikow, *The Kennedy Tapes*, p. 55.

44. May and Zelikow, *The Kennedy Tapes*, p. 59.

45. May and Zelikow, *The Kennedy Tapes*, p. 67.

46. Diez Acosta, *October 1962*, p. 159.

47. The full text of the Kennedy speech is in May and Zelikow, *The Kennedy Tapes*, pp. 276–81.

48. The full text of Castro's speech is in Diez Acosta, *October 1962*, pp. 224–55.

49. Robert Quirk, *Fidel Castro*, New York, 1993, p. 434.

50. May and Zelikow, *The Kennedy Tapes*, p. 77.

51. Mikoyan received news on arrival that his wife had died, and his son Sergo, who usually worked as his private secretary, was obliged to return to Moscow while Mikoyan remained in Havana.

52. Diez Acosta, *October 1962*, pp. 199–200.

53. James Blight and Philip Brenner, *Sad and Luminous Days: Cuba's Struggle with the Superpowers after the Missile Crisis*, New York, 2002, pp. 275–6.

54. Castro's 'secret' speech of 26 January 1968, quoted in Blight and Brenner, *Sad and Luminous Days*, p. 66.

55. Quirk, *Fidel Castro*, p. 460.

56. Quirk, *Fidel Castro*, p. 473.

57. Quirk, *Fidel Castro*, p. 477.

58. Quirk, *Fidel Castro*, p. 475.

59. Quirk, *Fidel Castro*, p. 474.

60. Richard Fagen, Richard Brody and Thomas O'Leary, *Cubans in Exile: Disaffection and the Revolution*, Palo Alto, Calif., 1968, p. 63.

61. Fagen et al., *Cubans in Exile*, and Louis Pérez, *Cuba and the United States: Ties of Singular Intimacy*, Oxford, 1988, p. 245. Different writers have slightly different figures. According to José Luis Llovio-Menéndez, the first mass exodus in 1959, of nearly 75,000, consisted of

wealthy Cubans or those connected to the Batista regime, or both. Between 1960 and 1962 a larger group, of about 190,000, left the island, consisting of members of the professional classes, technical specialists and craftsmen. Llovio-Menéndez, *Insider: My Hidden Life as a Revolutionary in Cuba*, New York, 1988, p. 88.

62. Philip Bonsal, *Cuba, Castro, and the United States*, Pittsburgh, 1971, p. 164.

63. Yvonne Conde, *Operation Pedro Pan*, London, 1999.

64. Alistair Hennessy and George Lambie, eds, *The Fractured Blockade: West European–Cuban Relations during the Revolution*, London, 1993, p. 3.

65. Wayne Smith, *The Closest of Enemies*, London, 1987, p. 90.

66. Smith, *The Closest of Enemies*, p. 91.

67. Quirk, *Fidel Castro*, p. 683.

68. Robert M. Levine, *Secret Missions to Cuba*, New York, 2001, p. 68.

69. Of the one million Cuban migrants to the United States, more than half congregated in southern Florida, chiefly in Dade County. Some 80,000 settled in New Jersey, 60,000 in California, 20,000 in Illinois and 15,000 in Texas. Louis Pérez, *Cuba and the United States: Ties of Singular Intimacy*, Athens, Ga., (2nd edition), 1997, p. 253.

70. Dudley Seers, *Cuba: The Economic and Social Revolution*, Chapel Hill, N. C., 1964, p. 32.

71. Pérez, *Cuba and the United States*, p. 255.

72. Talk to the Nuestro Tiempo society, Havana, 29 January 1959, in Ernesto Che Guevara, *Obras, 1957–1967*, Havana, 1970, pp. 21–2.

73. Fidel Castro, Second Declaration of Havana, 4 February 1962.

74. Alberto Bayo, *Mi aporte a la revolución cubana*, Havana, 1960.

75. Anderson, *Che Guevara*, pp. 534–5 and 560.

76. Richard Gott, *Guerrilla Movements in Latin America*, London, 1971, pp. 93–165.

77. Anderson, *Che Guevara*, pp. 537–55, 573–9 and 587–94.

78. The best account is in Anderson, *Che Guevara*.

79. 'Estimates of such numbers vary widely and sometimes wildly', writes Timothy Wickham-Crowley in *Guerrillas and Revolution in Latin America: A Comparative Study of Insurgents and Regimes since 1956*, Princeton, 1992, pp. 85–90.

80. Régis Debray, *Revolution in the Revolution?*, London, 1967.

81. Quoted in Piero Gleijeses, *Conflicting Missions: Havana, Washington, and Africa, 1959–1976*, Chapel Hill, N. C., 2002, p. 98.

82. The former Belgian Congo became the Congo on independence in 1960, changed its name to Zaire in October 1971 and reverted to the Democratic Republic of Congo in May 1997. Here it is referred to as the Congo throughout, while (to avoid confusion) the neighbouring state, the former French colony known as the Republic of Congo, is described as Congo-Brazzaville.

83. Lieutenant Rafael Noracen, interviewed by Gleijeses, *Conflicting Missions*, p. 89.

84. Gleijeses, *Conflicting Missions*, p. 105.

85. Gleijeses, *Conflicting Missions*, p. 199.

86. Carlos Moore, *Castro, the Blacks, and Africa*, Berkeley, 1988, p. 95.

87. Gleijeses, *Conflicting Missions*, p. 31.

88. By 1978 some 11,000 Cuban civilians were working in sub-Saharan Africa, according to calculations made by US researchers. Some 8,500 of them were in Angola. In the early 1990s, Cuban civilians were working in 21 African countries in public health, education and sports training. They were also providing technical expertise in sugar production, fishing, animal genetics and in the construction industry. Thousands of young Africans were also brought to study in Cuba. There were 22,000 foreign students studying in Cuba in June 1992, from 101 countries. Three-quarters of them – about 17,000 – came from Africa. Francine Marshall, 'Cuba's Relations with Africa: The End of an Era', in Donna Rich Kaplowitz, ed., *Cuba's Ties to a Changing World*, London, 1993.

89. Gleijeses, *Conflicting Missions*, p. 51.

90. In an interview in February 1961, Castro said that 'the unspeakably appalling assassination of the courageous Lumumba' was 'the result of a mixture of imperialism, colonialism and savagery, brought about by mercenaries and puppets of imperialism, and financial monopolist companies who seek to place the peoples of the world under their domination . . . It is an act of savagery. It will provoke an uprising in all Africa.' Prensa Latina, quoting an interview with Castro in *Combate*, 14 February 1961.

91. Gleijeses, *Conflicting Missions*, p. 83.

92. Che Guevara, *The African Dream: The Diaries of the Revolutionary War in the Congo*, London, 2000, p. 7.

93. Che Guevara, *The African Deam*, p. 216.

94. Gleijeses, *Conflicting Missions*, p. 98.

95. Robert Carl Cohen, *Black Crusader: A Biography of Robert Franklin Williams*, Seacaucus, N.J., 1972. Williams claimed that Guevara was sympathetic to his black nationalist position, but this has never been substantiated by other evidence. More probably, Guevara took an intelligent interest in a subject about which he must have been somewhat under-informed.

96. Subsequently, in 1968, Williams became the first chief of state of the Republic of New Africa, a US separatist group that advocated the creation of a black country to be made up of the five southern states of the US. Ruth Reitan, *The Rise and Decline of an Alliance: Cuba and African-American Leaders in the 1960s*, East Lansing, Mich., 1999, p. 53.

97. Reitan, *The Rise and Decline of an Alliance*, p. 40.

98. The language was sufficiently convincing to lead many people to believe that the charges were true, and Williams in Peking had some difficulty in proving that they were forgeries. Moore, *Castro, the Blacks, and Africa*, p. 266.

99. *Time* magazine, 12 May 1967. Further Carmichael quotes from Maurice Halperin, *The Taming of Fidel Castro*, Berkeley, 1981, p. 259. See also Stokely Carmichael and Ekweme Michael Thelwell, *Ready for Revolution: The Life and Times of Stokely Carmichael*, New York, 2003.

100. Quoted in Moore, *Castro, the Blacks, and Africa*, p. 260.

101. Gleijeses, *Conflicting Missions*, pp. 193–4.

102. Quoted in Moore, *Castro, the Blacks, and Africa*, p. 261.

103. Martin Kenner and James Petras, eds, *Fidel Castro Speaks*, London, 1969, p. 213.

104. Reitan, *The Rise and Decline of an Alliance*, p. 65.

105. Moore, *Castro, the Blacks, and Africa*, pp. 161–2.

106. Moore, *Castro, the Blacks, and Africa*, p. 302. Carlos Moore himself deserves a small footnote as an interpreter of black Cuba and critic of the Revolution's attitude towards the black population. Born in Cuba in 1942, of immigrant parents from Jamaica and Barbados, he left the island in 1963 and subsequently studied and worked in France and Africa – in Egypt, Nigeria and Senegal – before settling in the French West Indies.

107. Alice Walker, 'Secrets of the New Cuba,' *Ms* magazine, September 1977, quoted in Quirk, *Fidel Castro*, p. 774.

108. The best account of the life and death of Che Guevara is Anderson's *Che Guevara*.

109. John Gerassi, ed., *Venceremos: The Speeches and Writings of Che Guevara*, New York, 1968, pp. 413–24.

110. One victim of the change of policy was Francisco Caamaño, leader of a revolt in the Dominican Republic in 1965, who established himself in Cuba in November 1967 with the intention of launching a guerrilla war in his own country. The Cubans kept him on a tight rein for several years, but were eventually obliged to let him go. He landed with a small band in the Dominican Republic in

February 1973, and was captured and killed almost immediately. Gleijeses, *Conflicting Missions*, p. 221.

Chapter 7

1. José Luis Llovio-Menéndez, *Insider: My Hidden Life as a Revolutionary*, New York, London, 1988, pp. 217–18.
2. Llovio-Menéndez, *Insider*, p. 218.
3. Castro speech, 23 August 1968.
4. Quoted in Llovio-Menéndez, *Insider*, p. 239. For a wry account of the atmosphere in Cuba in 1970 see Alma Guillermoprieto, *Dancing with Cuba*, New York, 2004.
5. Robert Quirk, *Fidel Castro*, New York, 1993, p. 754. The sugar economy was also affected by the weather. Severe drought in successive years affected both the sugar and the coffee crops, commodities that were in short supply on the home market.
6. George Lambie, 'Western Europe and Cuba in the 1970s: The Boom Years', in Alistair Hennessy and George Lambie, eds, *The Fractured Blockade: West European–Cuban Relations during the Revolution*, London, 1993. The world sugar price in 1970 was 3.68 US cents a pound. In 1974, it went up to 29.66 cents a pound (and to 56.60 cents in November), while in 1977 it had dropped back to 8 cents a pound. Japan and Spain were Cuba's largest and most reliable Western partners in the 1970s. The Cubans made a major error in 1975 by refusing a Japanese offer to purchase one million tons of sugar a year until 1980 at a fixed price of 17 cents a pound. The Cubans offered 19 cents, but the Japanese got the deal from Australia at 17 cents. When the price dropped from 25 cents to 8 cents, the Cubans were mortified.
7. Gerry Hagelberg and Tony Hannah, 'Cuba's International Sugar Trade', in Hennessy and Lambie, *The Fractured Blockade*.
8. Quirk, *Fidel Castro*, p. 682.

9. Quirk, *Fidel Castro*, p. 717.
10. Pérez was finally replaced early in 1985, on the eve of a significant change of direction – the 'rectification' campaign of April 1986.
11. Andrew Zimbalist, 'Perspectives on Cuban Development and Prospects for the 1990s', in Hennessy and Lambie, *Fractured Blockade*.
12. These figures are from Andrew Zimbalist and Claes Brundenius, *The Cuban Economy: Measurement and Analysis of Socialist Performance*, Baltimore and London, 1989.
13. Quoted in Marifeli Pérez-Stable, *The Cuban Revolution: Origins, Course, and Legacy*, Oxford, 1993.
14. Some have claimed that the attack on Padilla, written by 'Leopoldo Avila', was actually the work of Raúl Castro himself. Llovio-Menéndez, *Insider*, p. 264.
15. Quoted in Quirk, *Fidel Castro*, p. 672. Castro's speech was on 1 May.
16. Heberto Padilla, *Heroes are Grazing in my Garden*, New York, 1984.
17. Llovio-Menéndez, *Insider*, p. 270. In spite of his private comments, Castro was happy to welcome Allende on a state visit to Cuba in December 1972.
18. Llovio-Menéndez, *Insider*, p. 272.
19. Piero Gleijeses, *Conflicting Missions: Havana, Washington, and Africa, 1959–1976*, Chapel Hill, N. C., 2002, p. 244.
20. It amounted to $6,000 a year in 1961, increased to $10,000 a month in 1974, with a one-off payment of $300,000 in January 1975. Gleijeses, *Conflicting Missions*, pp. 279–83.
21. Gleijeses, *Conflicting Missions*, p. 247.
22. Gleijeses, *Conflicting Missions*, p. 293. Roberto and Savimbi each received $200,000 a month.
23. Gleijeses, *Conflicting Missions*, pp. 258–9.
24. Gleijeses, *Conflicting Missions*, p. 260.
25. Gleijeses, *Conflicting Missions*, pp. 270–71.
26. Gleijeses, *Conflicting Missions*, p. 303.
27. Gabriel García Márquez, 'Operation Carlota: the Cuban mission to Angola',

New Left Review, Nos 101–2, February–April 1977. Operation Carlota was one of the more ambitious operations mounted by Castro, and a full account of it was written up subsequently by Garcia Márquez, after a full briefing from Castro himself and other Cuban participants.

28. Gleijeses, *Conflicting Missions*, p. 319.
29. Gleijeses, *Conflicting Missions*, p. 345.
30. Herbert Matthews, 'Forward with Fidel Castro, Anywhere', *New York Times*, 4 March 1976, quoted in Gleijeses, *Conflicting Missions*, p. 391.
31. Quoted in Gleijeses, *Conflicting Missions*, p. 346.
32. *New York Times*, 21 February 1966.
33. Robert Levine, *Secret Missions to Cuba, Fidel Castro, Bernardo Benes, and Cuban Miami*, New York, 2001, p. 91.
34. Interview by Simon Malley in *Afrique-Asie*, May 1977.
35. Quirk, *Fidel Castro*, p. 763. President Salim Ali Rubayyi of South Yemen was executed the following year, in June 1978. See Fred Halliday, *Revolution and Foreign Policy, the case of South Yemen, 1967–1987*, Cambridge, 1989.
36. Quoted in Quirk, *Fidel Castro*, p. 766.
37. *Afrique-Asie*, May 1977. Africa was of great importance, Castro told Simon Malley, because 'imperialist domination is not as strong there as it is in Latin America'.
38. Wayne Smith, *The Closest of Enemies, a personal and diplomatic account of US-Cuban relations since 1957*, London, 1987, p. 132.
39. Mengistu was forced into exile in May 1991 and took refuge with Robert Mugabe in Zimbabwe. His downfall was the result of internal factors as much as the loss of Soviet support. The Ethiopian military were affected by the military successes of the Eritrean and Tigrayan guerrillas, as well as by the cost of the continuing separatist war, and they took action to remove him. Eritrea swiftly unshackled itself from Ethiopia in 1993, and became an independent state. See Francine Marshall, 'Cuba's relations with Africa: The End of an Era', in Donna Rich Kaplowitz, ed., *Cuba's Ties to a Changing World*, London, 1993.

40. Ann Louise Bardach, *Cuba Confidential: Love and Vengeance in Miami and Havana*, New York, 2002, pp. 186–9.
41. Quirk, *Fidel Castro*, p. 731.
42. Several US senators and congressmen flew in to inspect developments on the island, including Senator George McGovern, the Democrat candidate defeated by Nixon in 1972, who came in May 1975 with a large entourage of journalists and businessmen.
43. Quirk, *Fidel Castro*, p. 741.
44. Smith, *The Closest of Enemies*, London, 1987, p. 105.
45. Department of State Bulletin, US State Department, Washington vol. LXXVII, December 1977.
46. Smith, *The Closest of Enemies*, pp. 122–3.
47. Smith, *The Closest of Enemies*, p. 128.
48. Cyrus Vance, *Hard Choices*, New York, 1983, p. 71.
49. Quirk, *Fidel Castro*, p. 772.
50. Quirk, *Fidel Castro*, p. 742.
51. Other prime ministers and presidents who visited Havana between 1972 and 1976 included Salvador Allende of Chile (December 1972); Houari Boumedienne of Algeria (April 1974); Julius Nyerere of Tanzania (September 1974); François Mitterrand, leader of the French socialists (October 1974); Yasser Arafat from Palestine (November 1974); Forbes Burnham of Guyana (April 1975); Eric Williams of Trinidad and Tobago (June 1975); Michael Manley of Jamaica (July 1975); Marien Ngouabi of Congo-Brazzaville (September 1975); Omar Torrijos of Panama (January 1976); Agostinho Neto of Angola (July 1976); Kaysonme Phomvihane of Laos (September 1976); Luis Cabral of Guinea-Bissau (October 1976).
52. Benes also claimed to have played football with Raúl Castro at the university of Havana. The details of Bernardo Benes's visits to Cuba are to be found in Robert Levine, *Secret Missions*

to Cuba, Fidel Castro, Bernardo Benes, and Cuban Miami, New York, 2001.

53. Levine, Secret Missions to Cuba, p. 118.
54. Smith, The Closest of Enemies, p. 163.
55. Levine, Secret Missions to Cuba, p. 130.
56. Levine, Secret Missions to Cuba, p. 129.
57. Smith, The Closest of Enemies, p. 198.
58. Smith, The Closest of Enemies, p. 198.
59. Quoted in Llovio-Menéndez, Insider, p. 383.
60. Pérez-Stable, The Cuban Revolution, p. 150.
61. Quirk, Fidel Castro, p. 809.
62. Rafael Fermoselle, The Evolution of the Cuban Military, 1492–1986, Miami, 1987, p. 6.
63. Sebastian Balfour, Castro, London, 1995, p. 137.
64. Sandino's guerrilla war was fought with the slogan Patria libre o morir, Fatherland or Death. When the Americans withdrew from Nicaragua in 1933 Sandino came down from the hills but was promptly assassinated on the orders of Anastasio Somoza, the US-appointed commander of the National Guard. Somoza himself was assassinated in 1956 and replaced by his son, also Anastasio.
65. Jorge Castaneda, Utopia Unarmed: The Latin American Left after the Cold War, New York, 1993, pp. 51–89.
66. One account describes Castro at a meeting in Havana with five groups from El Salvador, placing an M-16 rifle on the table and obliging those present to place their hands on it, as a symbol of unity. Thus was born the Farabundo Martí National Liberation Front that launched a guerrilla war in El Salvador in January 1981, at the very moment that Ronald Reagan was inaugurated as US President. Raymond Bonner, Weakness and Deceit, US Policy and El Salvador, London, 1985, p. 96. Something similar occurred with the squabbling groups that founded the Sandinista Front for National Liberation earlier in the 1970s.
67. Castro speech in Holguín, 26 July 1979.
68. Smith, The Closest of Enemies, p. 181.
69. Making History: Interviews with Four

Generals of Cuba's Revolutionary Armed Forces, New York, 1999, pp. 33–4.
70. Grenada had become independent from Britain in February 1974, under the leadership of Eric Gairy, a long-standing labour organiser since the 1950s and leader of the Grenada People's Party (later the Grenada United Labour Party, GULP). The New Jewel Movement (Joint Endeavour for Welfare, Education and Liberation) was led by Maurice Bishop and Unison Whiteman and had emerged in 1973, the year before independence, in opposition to Gairy.
71. Quoted in Tony Thorndike, Grenada: Politics, Economics and Society, London, 1985.
72. Michael Manley went on several state visits to Cuba, in 1975, 1978 and 1980, and Castro visited Jamaica in 1977.
73. Ronald Reagan speech, 23 March 1983, announcing the Strategic Defence Initiative ('Star Wars'), which made reference to the airport.
74. Granma, 20 October 1983. Bishop's opponents deplored 'the deep personal friendship between Fidel and Bishop which has caused the Cuban leadership to take a personal and not a class approach to the developments in Grenada'.

Chapter 8

1. Yuri Pavlov, Soviet–Cuban Alliance, 1959–1991, Boston, 1994, p. 61.
2. Andrew Zimbalist, 'Perspectives on Cuban development and prospects for the 1990s', in Alistair Hennessy and George Lambie, eds, Fractured Blockade: West European–Cuban Relations during the Revolution, London, 1993.
3. Sebastian Balfour, Castro, London, 1995, p. 146. There was a subsequent speech on the anniversary of Playa Girón, on 19 April 1986.
4. Balfour, Castro, p. 148.
5. Zimbalist, 'Perspectives on Cuban Development'.

6. Quoted in Sergio Roca, 'Reflections on Economic Policy: Cuba's Food Programme,' in Jorge Pérez-López, ed., *Cuba at a Crossroads: Politics and Economics after the Fourth Party Congress*, Gainesville, Fla., 1994, p. 96.

7. Economist Intelligence Unit, Country Report: Cuba, no. 4, 1986.

8. Castro speech of 26 July 1989, given in Camagüey on the Moncada anniversary: 'We have to warn the imperialists not to create so many illusions with reference to our revolution, or to the idea that our revolution will not be able to resist a debate within the socialist community. If we were to wake up tomorrow, or any other day, to the news that there had been a large-scale civil war in the USSR, and even if we were to wake up and learn that the USSR had disintegrated – something that we hope never happens – even under those circumstances Cuba and the Cuban Revolution would continue to struggle and to resist.'

9. Castro speech of September 1986, at the summit of non-aligned countries held in Harare, Zimbabwe.

10. Castro speech of 5 December 1988, in David Deutschmann, ed., *Changing the History of Africa*, Melbourne, 1989, p. 109.

11. Victoria Brittain, *Death of Dignity: Angola's Civil War*, London, 1998, p. 36.

12. Castro speech of 9 July 1989, in *Vindicación de Cuba*, Havana, 1989, p. 395.

13. Castro speech of 9 July 1989, in *Vindicación de Cuba*, p. 394.

14. Brittain, *Death of Dignity*, p. 36.

15. Brittain, *Death of Dignity*, p. 36.

16. Speech by Nelson Mandela of 26 July 1991, at the Moncada anniversary celebrations in Matanzas. Mandela's visit to Miami is recalled in Ann Louise Bardach, *Cuba Confidential: Love and Vengeance in Miami and Havana*, New York, 2002, pp. 105–6.

17. The details are in Chester Crocker, *High Noon in Southern Africa: Making Peace in a Rough Neighbourhood*, New York, 1992.

18. Hennessy and Lambie, *Fractured Blockade*, p. 323.

19. The details of this episode are well told in Andrés Oppenheimer, *Castro's Final Hour: The Secret Story Behind the Coming Downfall of Communist Cuba*, New York, 1992, pp. 17–129.

20. Oppenheimer, *Castro's Final Hour*, p. 29.

21. Bardach, *Cuba Confidential*, pp. 273–7. Vesco had escaped to Cuba in 1982 and was arrested there in May 1995, on charges of being 'an agent for foreign special services', and given a 22-year jail sentence.

22. *Time*, 10 July 1989, quoted in Max Azicri, *Cuba Today and Tomorrow: Reinventing Socialism*, Gainesville, Fla., 2000, pp. 98–9.

23. Rafael del Pino, *Proa a la libertad*, Mexico City, 1990. Del Pino was himself an interesting figure. A loyal officer since the early years of the Revolution, he had trained as a Mig pilot in the Soviet Union and had several years service in Angola. He indicated that he was a supporter of Gorbachev's reforms, and made a number of allegations concerning corruption in Cuba. One of the victims of his claims was Luís Orlando Dominguez, the secretary-general of the Cuban Young Communists, who was charged on charges of corruption and imprisoned.

24. Oppenheimer, *Castro's Final Hour*, p. 127. Ann Louise Bardach interviewed Castro in 1994, and asked him directly about the Ochoa trial. 'There is a great difference between Ochoa and Tony de la Guardia,' he said. 'There is no comparison between their crimes. I mean in personality, and in historical merits, there is no comparison. Tony de la Guardia was the organiser, an irresponsible individual who risked his country's security, and Ochoa, because he knew everything going on, and let himself be carried away by crazy ideas about converting drug money into a

resource for the country. He sent an aide to meet with Escóbar. Can you imagine what it meant for a captain in the Cuban army to be making that contact in Colombia? The case of Ochoa was very moving . . . It was hard for all of us, but it was an unavoidable decision.' Bardach, *Cuba Confidential*, p. 270.

25. Ileana de la Guardia, *Le Nom de mon Père*, Paris, 2001, and Jorge Masetti, *El Furór y el Delirio, itinerario de un hijo de la revolución cubana*, Barcelona, 1999. Patricio de la Guardia was eventually released from prison in March 2002 after pressure from President Vicente Fox of Mexico.

26. *Making History: Interviews with Four Generals of Cuba's Revolutionary Armed Forces*, New York, 1999, p. 74.

27. *Making History*, p. 107.

28. Azicri, *Cuba Today and Tomorrow*, p. 99.

29. Luís Suárez Sálazar, *Cuba: aislamiento o reinserción en un mundo en cambio*, Havana, 1997.

30. Quoted in Carmelo Mesa-Lago, *Cuba after the Cold War*, Pittsburgh, 1993, p. 10.

31. Ana Julia Jatar-Hausman, *The Cuban Way: Capitalism, Communism and Confrontation*, West Hartford, Conn., 1999, pp. 46–8.

32. Hugh Thomas, *Cuba, or the Pursuit of Freedom*, 2nd edition, London, 2001, p. 1038.

33. Marifeli Pérez-Stable, *The Cuban Revolution*, Oxford, 1993, p. 213.

34. Castro speech of 28 January 1990.

35. *Granma*, 29 August 1990.

36. Quoted in Sergio Roca, 'Reflections on Economic Policy: Cuba's Food Programme', p. 96.

37. Jatar-Hausman, *The Cuban Way*, p. 48.

38. Jatar-Hausman, *The Cuban Way*, p. 50.

39. Jatar-Hausman, *The Cuban Way*, p. 49.

40. Henry Wallich, *Monetary Problems of an Export Economy*, Harvard, Mass., 1950.

41. Jatar-Hausman, *The Cuban Way*, p. 97.

42. Castro speech of December 1993.

43. Jatar-Hausman, *The Cuban Way*, p. 73.

44. Decree-Law 191 of September 1994.

45. Other important items on the government's list of reforms were measures to tackle the monetary imbalance. These included an increase in taxation and social security contributions, as well as the lifting of price controls and the reduction of subsidies to state industries.

46. Gail Reed, *Island in the Storm: The Cuban Communist Party's Fourth Congress*, Melbourne, 1992, p. 20.

47. Municipal elections were held in December 1992 that allowed the leadership to secure a snapshot of its popularity. The customary 97.7 per cent of eligible voters participated in the elections, but the government had commissioned a private exit poll whose results were leaked (and turned up in Madrid's conservative newspaper *ABC*). According to the poll (not the official result), 30.5 per cent – 2.4 million people – voted no to the slate of candidates (by crossing out their ballots), while a further 2.1 per cent abstained (leaving blank ballots). The poll was given considerable publicity outside Cuba to indicate the regime's lack of support. Yet it could also be read to suggest that over 65 per cent of the country was prepared to participate in local elections, and to vote positively for the official slate. The government must have been reasonably content with the result, considering the difficulties that everyone had been living through. *ABC Madrid*, 17 January 1993, quoted in *Cuba in Transition*, vol. 4, ASCE, Miami, 1994, p. 189.

48. Jatar-Hausman, *The Cuban Way*, p. 83.

49. Solon Barraclough, 'Protecting social achievements during economic crisis in Cuba', in Dharam Gai, ed., *Social Development and Public Policy: A Study of Some Successful Experiences*, London, 2000.

50. General Nestor López Cuba, interviewed in 1997, in *Making History*.

51. Azicri, *Cuba Today and Tomorrow*, pp. 162–4.

52. General Nestor López Cuba in *Making History*, New York, p. 43.

53. Quoted in Carmelo Mesa-Lago, ed., *Cuba after the Cold War*, p. 263.

54. *Miami Herald*, 21 February 1998, quoted in Azicri, *Cuba Today and Tomorrow*, p. 161.

55. Oppenheimer, *Castro's Final Hour*, Jean-François Fogel and Bertrand Rosenthal, *Fin de Siècle à la Havane, les secrets du pouvoir cubain*, Paris, 1993.

56. *Time*, 26 January 1998.

57. Jorge Domínguez explained the government's staying power by examining the evidence of a government opinion-poll, taken early in 1990, when people had begun to see trouble ahead, and seemed on the surface to show considerable dissatisfaction. Only one fifth of respondents thought the food supply was good, and only one tenth were impressed with the quality of transport. Domínguez read this evidence of discontent as a sign that the poll was credible, and concluded that it would be reasonable to believe its other findings, namely 'that three-quarters of respondents thought health services were good and that four-fifths believed the same about their schools'. For most people, it seemed, the advantages of the system outweighed the disadvantages. See Jorge Domínguez, 'The Secrets of Castro's Staying Power', *Foreign Affairs*, Spring 1993.

58. According to one account some 50,000 Haitians and Cubans were interned at Guantánamo by the end of the year. Some 7,000 Cubans were flown to new camps in the Panama Canal Zone, where the conditions were so bad that one camp was burnt down. These Cubans did not complain at the time about the conditions, fearing that they would be sent back to Cuba. Robert Levine, *Secret Missions to Cuba: Fidel Castro, Bernardo Benes, and Cuban Miami*, New York, 2001, p. 243.

59. Louis Pérez, *Cuba: Between Reform and Revolution*, Oxford, 1995, p. 400.

60. Morris Morley and Chris McGillion, *Unfinished Business, America and Cuba after the Cold War*, Cambridge, 2002, pp. 72 and 212.

61. Radio Martí had been authorised by the US Congress in September 1983 to transmit 'news, commentary and other information about events in Cuba and elsewhere to promote the cause of freedom in Cuba'. It received a US government subsidy of $12 million and first went on air in 1985. It was scheduled to be followed by TV Martí, which received US government funding in 1988.

62. Morley and McGillion, *Unfinished Business*, p. 12. Mas Canosa's career is well described by Ann Louise Bardach in a chapter, 'The Man Who Would Be King', in her book *Cuba Confidential*, pp. 126–50.

63. Castro speech of 29 December 1990 to the Federation of University Students in Havana.

64. Susan Kaufman Purcell and David Rothkopf, eds, *Cuba: The Contours of Change*, Boulder, Col., 2000, p. 84.

65. Quoted in Roy Joaquín, *Cuba, the United States, and the Helms-Burton Doctrine: International Reactions*, Gainesville, Fla., 2000.

66. Purcell and Rothkopf, *Cuba: The Contours of Change*, p. 84.

67. Bardach, *Cuba Confidential*, p. 133.

68. *Granma*, 26 July 1995.

69. Morley and McGillion, *Unfinished Business*, pp. 124–5.

70. Jim Hoagland in the *Washington Post*, 22 January 1998.

71. Frei Betto, *Fidel and Religion: Conversations with Frei Betto*, translated by Mary Todd, Melbourne, 1990, p. 147.

72. *Newsweek*, 'The battle for Cuba's soul', 19 January 1998.

73. Figures from a Havana professor quoted in Azicri, *Cuba Today and Tomorrow*, p. 370.

74. Quoted in Azicri, *Cuba Today and Tomorrow*, p. 260.

75. Quoted in Azicri, *Cuba Today and Tomorrow*, p. 262.

76. Felix Varela was a progressive philosophy professor at the University of Havana in the early years of the nineteenth century, the first to give lectures in Spanish rather than Latin. He formed part of the political delegation sent to the Cortes in Madrid in the 1820s, during the three-year liberal interlude from 1820 to 1823. An early supporter of Latin American independence, he was a radical educational reformer and a vocal abolitionist, recommending immediate freedom for the slaves, with compensation for their owners. When the conspiracy known as the *Soles y Rayos de Bolívar* was uncovered in 1823, Father Varela and other liberals fled abroad.

77. Quoted in Azicri, *Cuba Today and Tomorrow*, p. 262.

78. One immediate result was a decision by Guatemala and the Dominican Republic to renew diplomatic relations.

79. Quoted in Azicri, *Cuba Today and Tomorrow*, p. 268.

80. The story of Elián is told at great length in Bardach, *Cuba Confidential*.

81. Quoted in Bardach, *Cuba Confidential*, p. 100.

82. Quoted in Bardach, *Cuba Confidential*, p. 100.

83. Bardach, *Cuba Confidential*, p. 289.

84. Reuters report from Havana, Friday 10 May 2002.

85. The US Presidents in Castro's era were Eisenhower, Kennedy, Johnson, Nixon, Ford, Carter, Reagan, Bush, Clinton, and Bush Jr.

86. The leaders of the Soviet Union during the Castro era were Khrushchev, Kosygin, Brezhnev, Andropov, Chernenko, Gorbachev, and Yeltsin.

87. Among the figures that Castro outlasted were Tito and Nasser, Ben Bella and Houari Boumedienne, Kwame Nkrumah and Julius Nyerere, Sékou Touré and Samora Machel, Amilcar Cabral and Agostinho Neto, Nelson Mandela and Gadafy, Mugabe and Mengistu.

88. Fidel Castro speeech in Durban, 1 September 2001.

89. Interview with Ricardo Alarcón, published in *El Nacional*, Caracas, 12 July 2001.

90. Enrique Oltuski, *Vida Clandestina: My Life in the Cuban Revolution*, New York, 2002, p. 288.

91. Purcell and Rothkopf, *Cuba: The Contours of Change*, p. 100.

92. Interview in 1997, in *Making History*, p. 103.

Guide to further reading

The outside world was first woken up to the intrinsic interest of Cuban history and society at the start of the nineteenth century by Alexander von Humboldt, the German traveller, scientist and writer. The most recent edition of his book, *The Island of Cuba: A Political Essay*, is published by Markus Wiener, Princeton, 2001.

American historians took a serious interest in the island after the US invasion in 1898, and some of their early work still has value: almost everything written or edited by Irene Wright is particularly useful: *Cuba*, New York, 1910; *The Early History of Cuba, 1492–1586*, New York, 1916; 'Rescates with special reference to Cuba, 1599–1610', *Hispanic American Historical Review*, vol. III, no. 3, August 1920; 'The Dutch and Cuba, 1609–1643,' *Hispanic American Historical Review*, vol. IV, no. 4, November 1921; *Spanish Documents concerning English Voyages to the Caribbean, 1527–1568*, London, 1929.

In addition, there is Willis Fletcher Johnson, *The History of Cuba*, New York, 1920; Charles Chapman, *A History of the Cuban Republic*, New York, 1927; and the English translation of Ramiro Guerra Sánchez ed., *A History of the Cuban Nation*, Havana, 1958.

A brilliant and irreplaceable general history, covering 1762 to 1970, is Hugh Thomas, *Cuba, or the Pursuit of Freedom*, 1st edition, London, 1971, 2nd edition, London, 2001.

Special mention must be made of the innumerable works of Louis Pérez, indefatigable researcher into almost every aspect of Cuban society: *Intervention, Revolution, and Politics in Cuba, 1913–1921*, Pittsburgh, 1978; *Lords of the Mountain: Social Banditry and Peasant Protest in Cuba, 1878–1918*, Pittsburgh, 1989; *Cuba and the US: Ties of Singular Intimacy*, Atlanta, 1990; *The War of 1898: The United States and Cuba in History and Historiography*, Chapel Hill, N. C., 1998; *Cuba: Between Reform and Revolution*, Oxford, 1995; *Cuba and the United States*, Athens, Ga., 1997; *Winds of Change: Hurricanes and the Transformation of Nineteenth-century Cuba*, Gainesville, Fla., 2000; *On Becoming Cuban, Identity, Nationality, and Culture*, New York, 1999.

Indispensable for readers of Spanish is Levi Marrero, *Cuba: Economía y Sociedad*, 15 vols, Madrid, 1978. Also useful, if you look behind the Marxist–Leninist façade, is the *Historia de Cuba*, a collective work by the Cuban Instituto de Historia in Havana: vol. I, *La Colonia, evolución socio-económica y formación nacional*, Havana, 1994; vol. II, *Las Luchas por la independencia nacional y las transformaciones estructurales*, Havana, 1996; and vol. III, *La Neocolonia, organización y crisis, desde 1899 hasta 1940*, Havana, 1998.

Castro and the Revolution have provided material for entire libraries. The most useful biographies of Castro are: Tad Szulc, *Fidel: A Critical Portrait*, London, 1987; Sebastian Balfour, *Castro*, London, 1995; Robert Quirk, *Fidel Castro*, New York, 1993; Peter Bourne, *Castro: A Biography of Fidel Castro*, London, 1986; Volker Skierka, *Fidel Castro: A Biography*, Oxford, 2004; Leycester Coltman, *The Real Fidel Castro*, New Haven and London, 2003.

Innumerable biographies of Che Guevara have now been published, of which the best is Jon Lee Anderson, *Che Guevara: A Revolutionary Life*, London, 1997; the most voluminous is Paco Ignacio Taibo, *Guevara, Also Known As Che*, New York, 1997; the most caustic is Jorge Castañeda, *Compañero, The Life and Death of Che Guevara*, New York, 1998; also useful is Henry Ryan, *The Fall of Che Guevara: A Story of Soldiers, Spies, and Diplomats*, Oxford, 1998.

Full reference to books used in the writing of this book are included in the footnotes, but the following – published in the past 20 years – proved exceptionally illuminating:

Azicri, Max, *Cuba Today and Tomorrow: Reinventing Socialism*, Gainsville, Fla, 2000

Casanovas, John, *Bread, or Bullets: Urban Labour and Spanish Colonialism in Cuba, 1850–1898*, Pittsburgh, 1998

Chaffin, Tom, *Fatal Glory: Narciso López and the First Clandestine US War against Cuba*, Charlottesville, Va, 1996

Ferrer, Ada, *Insurgent Cuba, Race, Nation, and Revolution, 1868–1898*, Chapel Hill, N. C., 1999

Gleijeses, Piero, *Conflisting Missions: Havana, Washington, and Africa, 1959–1976*, Chapel Hill, N. C., 2002

Helg, Aline, *Our Rightful Share: The Afro-Cuban Struggle for Equality, 1886–1912*, Chapel Hill, N. C., 2002

Howard, Philip, *Changing History, Afro-Cuban Cabildos and Societies of Color in the Nineteenth Century*, Baton Rouge, La, 1998

Ibarra, Jorge, *Prologue to Revolution: Cuba, 1898–1958*, London, 1998

Jatar-Hausman, Ana Julia, *The Cuban Way: Capitalism, Communism and Confrontation*, West Hartford, Conn., 1999

Kapcia, Antoni, *Cuba: Island of Dreams,* Oxford, 2000

Kutzinski, Vera, *Sugar's Secrets: Race and the Erotics of Cuban Nationalism,* Virginia, 1993.

Moore, Robin D., *Nationalising Blackness, Afrocubanismo and Artistic Revolution in Havana, 1920–1940*, Pittsburgh, 1997

Morley, Morris, and Christ McGillion, *Unfinished Business: America and Cuba after the Cold War, 1989–2001*, Cambridge, 2002

Pérez-Stable, Marifeli, *The Cuban Revolution: Origins, Course and Legacy*, Oxford, 1993

Schwarz, Rosalie, *Lawless Liberators: Political Banditry and Cuban Independence*, Durham, 1989

Scott, Rebecca J., *Slave Emancipation in Cuba: The Transition to Free Labour, 1860–1899*, Princeton, 1985

Sweig, Julia E., *Inside the Cuban Revolution: Fidel Castro and the Urban Underground*, Cambridge, Mass., 2002.

Photograph credits

Index